OASIS

CDS 90

OASIS ⬡TDK 14/1/92
IEC1/TYPE I NORMAL POSITION

BY NOEL
90

⬡TDK
SF
IEC II/TYPE II
HIGH POSITION
SUPER FIDELITY CASSETTE HIGH RESOLUTION

SUPER PRECISION RIGID CASSETTE MECHANISM

ROCKFIELD MONITOR MIX

06
90

A: REF MAYBE OUTTAKES

LARRY VOX

Live Forever

Live Forever

The Rise, Fall and Resurrection of Oasis

John Robb

Harper
North

HarperNorth
Windmill Green
24 Mount Street
Manchester M2 3NX

A division of
HarperCollins*Publishers*
1 London Bridge Street
London SE1 9GF

www.harpercollins.co.uk

HarperCollins*Publishers*
Macken House, 39/40 Mayor Street Upper
Dublin 1, D01 C9W8, Ireland

First published by HarperCollins*Publishers* 2025

1 3 5 7 9 10 8 6 4 2

© John Robb 2025

Endpapers by Brian Cannon, Microdot Creative

Every effort has been made to trace the copyright holders for quotes from historic publications. Any inadvertent omissions will be swiftly corrected.

John Robb asserts the moral right to be identified as the author of this work

A catalogue record of this book is available from the British Library

[HB] ISBN 978-0-00-875136-4
[TPB] ISBN 978-0-00-876096-0

Printed and bound in the UK using 100%
renewable electricity at CPI Group (UK) Ltd

MIX
Paper | Supporting
responsible forestry
FSC
www.fsc.org FSC™ C007454

This book contains FSC™ certified paper and other controlled
sources to ensure responsible forest management.

For more information visit: www.harpercollins.co.uk/green

'I was the last one to make it from my crowd and from my generation.' **Noel**

'I'm made up of all sorts me. I'm not just an angry little lunatic. People say it's not work being in a band but it is but it's also the best fucking job in the world.' **Liam**

CONTENTS

Contents

Unless otherwise noted, all interviews are the author's own.

INTRODUCTION

The ballad of Noel and Liam.
The ballad of Liam and Noel.

In the same way that 'John, Paul, George and Ringo' sum up the sixties, the brothers' very names evoke the nineties.

In that decade, Noel and Liam Gallagher were the most famous people in the country. Their attitude, style, hair, banter and rivalry captured the era, and their music soundtracked the pre-Internet end of the century. Their relationship and their sibling rivalry was the very core of the band that fascinated fans and the press for years.

There is much said about Oasis and it's all weaponised. They celebrated rock 'n' roll in all its shades, from the sublime to the ridiculous, from the poetic to the profane, and from noise and confusion to its fire and soul. Every great band is a combination of thrilling contradictions. Oasis had both a swagger and a melancholy, juggernaut anthems and sensitive B-sides. They had a wilful Mancunian disdain of art while being art-rock on their own terms. There was a method to their madness and a pop culture perfection to their bricolage of ideas. They delivered 11/10 riot anthems or

1

acoustic soul-searching songs which were often on both sides of the same single. There was an introverted sensitivity often lurking below the noise and a poetic twist in lyrics that were often derided by Noel himself for being meaningless.

At their heart were the two iconic brothers who were different sides to the same coin . . . Noel and Liam, yin and yang, Cain and Abel, Morrissey and Marr, Lennon and McCartney, Brown and Squire . . .

Liam and Noel.

Noel and Liam.

Noel wrote the classic songs, and Liam sang them with one of the great rock 'n' roll voices with its mixture of sweetness and rasping intensity. Somehow in their music they found a perfect harmony in their sibling rivalry that also came with a mutual respect as Noel Gallagher explained to Ann Scanlon in 1995: 'Liam is young, he's brash. I see a lot of things in him that I'd like to be. I think if you could cross the two of us, we'd be a really fuckin' good person.'[1]

They were also a band. Lads with names like Bonehead, Guigsy and Tony McCarroll grafting a rock-solid unit of their own in the council estates of south Manchester before the Gallaghers took over and the magic happened. They ended up being the last great British rock 'n' roll band in the high-decibel British canon that started with the Beatles and ended in Paris in 2009 when Oasis imploded.

They were the end of the sixties dream when rock 'n' roll dared to go over the top. They were the last band from the pre-internet age when music still mattered, before it became the noise in the background.

They were at the heart of their own northern working-class revolution. The last gang in town with a close-knit extended family of talented mates: sound guy Mark Coyle; art designer Brian Cannon; photographer Michael Spencer Jones; DJ and road crew Phil Smith; the curveball of energy label boss Alan McGee; older brother Paul, plus many others who coalesced around their charismatic core.

Oasis helped to define the nineties when, as the UK's biggest band, they swaggered from the Manchester council estates and put the rock and the roll back into the euphoric rush of that post-acid house, post-ecstasy decade before it all inevitably crashed and burned.

Unlike most modern bands, Oasis were working-class art. Nothing was handed to them on a plate. There were no stylists or helpers or bank of Mum and Dad. There was no visionary team of supporters, no Tony Wilson, no Malcolm and Vivienne, no future in England's dreaming – just a kid with an acoustic guitar sat in a council estate bedroom dreaming of escape with a vision, and his wild younger brother who was convinced he was a star, and was right.

How far out of the musical loop and how defiantly brilliant they seemed to be as they stood their ground and waited for the adulation; just like Liam's stock-still stage presence and his dead-eyed stare into the abyss of the crowd with their impenetrable wall of sound, they were just waiting for the reaction.

They didn't have to try . . . they just knew.

I first met Noel Gallagher at late eighties gigs in Manchester. He was a youthful music head who was already sussed and super smart. Later on, he would become the Inspiral Carpets' roadie and I would see him in the twilight hours in the city-centre warren of parties, band spaces, rehearsal rooms and offices.

In that post-Madchester lull, the rich seam of bands inspired by the famous Sex Pistols gigs in 1976 – from Buzzcocks to Joy Division, New Order to the Smiths, Happy Mondays to the Stone Roses and then on to the Haçienda and acid house – had seemingly run out.

The production line had been faultless but the music biz were now busy creating London-based scenes, from shoegaze to Britpop, to grab the narrative back.

'They had the stage set for Blur and Britpop,' Noel Gallagher once told me, 'and then we turned up and they never forgave us.'

Let's take a trip to the bleak post-Madchester period and watch the astonishing certainty of a band who somehow combined the claustrophobic 'fuck you' psychodrama of the Sex Pistols with the Beatles art pop adventure into their own Sex Beatles vision. They added the 'crowd is the star' aesthetic of acid house with a teenage crash course in greatest hits compilations. They then went from zero to hero in an astonishing 18-month period. They became the legends they always knew they were and caught everyone out with a combination of talent, charisma and madness.

This book grows up with the band underneath the council skies of the Anglo-Irish community of sixties and seventies Manchester, it hangs around in the damp rehearsal rooms of the eighties local band scene, it runs around the venues as the band spend a couple of years on the fringes, and then it enjoys the supersonic ride to the toppermost of the poppermost, with deep dives into the albums. It looks at the unique dynamic between the two brothers perfectly described by a pre-fame 18-year-old Pete Doherty in 1997: 'I subscribe to the Umberto Eco view that Noel Gallagher's a poet and Liam's a town crier.'

Let's thrill to Alan McGee's instinctive signing of the band after they famously gatecrashed a gig in Glasgow. Let's join them on that surge of hits and the battle of Britpop with Blur that underlined the fault lines in British culture. Let's get high to the supernova heights of their second album, when within two years they were the biggest band in the world, and then let's enjoy the bonkers madness of when they were Being Here Now at the top of the helter-skelter. Let's feel the inevitable comedown after the record-breaking Knebworth shows. Let's follow them as they reconvene into a different band for four quite different and underrated albums. Let's deep-dive into the music and immerse ourselves in the great songs and the way they changed their sound far more artfully than anyone is prepared to admit.

It's a remarkable story and the only people who never looked surprised were the Gallaghers themselves . . .

1

ROCKFIELD

As the plate of pasta flew across the room Liam finally exploded.

Prodded and provoked, he had been in a genial mood until a guest at the ad hoc gathering at Rockfield Studios in South Wales pushed their luck. The party had initially been laid back, but as the drink flowed and the music got louder, it had got more and more out of control.

It was Saturday, 13 May 1995, and I was there with an excellent up-and-coming post-punk band from Derby called Cable, who I had been producing at Monnow Valley Studios half a mile down the road.

We had heard that Oasis were recording nearby and that there had been all kinds of exploits with air rifles and scooters in their downtime but that they had recorded several tracks for their second album, *(What's the Story) Morning Glory?*, and the sessions were going well.

The first time Cable met Oasis was in 1994 when they supported them on the first Oasis UK tour, and the second meeting on that long lost night in the quiet Welsh countryside has become one of the legendary rock 'n' roll yarns; it started as a chance encounter and an invite back to the studio and ended up with an inter-band brawl and then an explosive argument between Noel and Liam.

Up the road at Monnow Valley, the Cable album was finished, and we had gone to the village of Rockfield to celebrate in the Green Dragon Inn. Booking the only taxi in the village to return, we climbed in, squeezing in with a couple of women who were in very high spirits. In the gloom of the taxi's interior I noticed a figure slumped over the front seat. There was a lot of shouting and laughing as the minibus bounced along the country roads back to the studios.

Just out of town it bumped around a corner and the figure at the front turned round and from under his fringe grinned, 'Fucking hell, it's John Robb . . . what are you doing here?'

It was Liam Gallagher and he invited us to up to Rockfield to hang out. He was returning from the pub after taking a break while Noel was working on the track 'Champagne Supernova' with producer Owen Morris in an epic, fast-moving session.

When we arrived at the studio, Liam got the drinks out while I made a cup of tea. There were some tunes getting played and the women from the taxi were getting crazier and dancing and shouting. For some peace, Cable drummer Neil Cooper went for a jam with Noel in the studio and a couple of us sat in Guigsy's room for a bit, where the bass player was cheerfully getting stoned. Meanwhile Liam was the generous host handing out the drinks to his guests while being affable and hilarious and the congenial rock 'n' roll party host. But a few drinks in and Cable were starting to get a bit, er, giddy.

At about one in the morning, Liam popped out to get a cassette of the newly recorded songs. It would be the first time anyone had heard them outside the tight small circle of the band and producer. He stuck the tape into the stereo in the front room and 'Hello' burst out of the speakers, cranked up to full blast.

It sounded great – full of explosive life – and surged like the best of glam rock/Sex Pistols/punk rock and every other British street music cranked up to the max. Liam's vocals really caught the 100 per cent confident rush of the times as it poured into the room like liquid noise. The song captured the thrill of youth and the swagger of turning up at life's party uninvited and owning it. This was sheer, unapologetic rock 'n' roll at its best. The song sounded monstrous – like all the good times rolled into one with that world-beating cool that British youth are always so good at.

As 'Hello' surged out of the speakers, Liam was nodding his head and singing along and I was glowing with the power of the music.

As the song crackled to a halt, Liam was beaming – of course he was, when your band gets it right in the studio it's one of the best feelings in the world. He then modestly asked Cable what they thought of it. There was none of the tabloid arrogance about him, just a genuine buzzing enthusiasm.

It was at this point that Cable's young guitar player, Darius Hinks, who had been swigging whisky from a bottle he had been given by the singer, decided to tell Liam that it sounded like the Beatles. It wasn't meant as a compliment. The drink was talking louder than the normally timid Darius who hadn't noticed that the track was more glam anthem than the Beatles.

The room briefly fell silent, and everyone looked up.

Luckily, Liam laughed it off – he just wanted a good time – but Darius, now poisoned with the demon whisky he was slurping, pushed his point and his luck and kept going on about the Beatles.

Liam put on the next track, 'Roll With It', and as the song ended Darius staggered across the room and told Liam that this next track was also shit and started prodding him in the chest to make his point. Oddly, Liam still didn't seem to care and was quite charming, putting up with the slurred observations, and put on another track which was possibly an unmixed version of the freshly recorded 'Champagne Supernova'.

The new song was filling the room with its elixir of sound and was anthemic. Being the only sober person in the room, I told Darius to cool it, and for a few minutes, it calmed down. Cable drummer Neil Cooper had popped in just in time to see Darius jokingly mount Liam from behind. Liam, with a totally straight face, said, 'You better get rid of your mate.'

A minute later a plate of pasta flew across the room thrown by a delirious looking Darius. The tray crashed on the floor and the pasta flew through the air in slow motion, resulting in something between handbags and a scuffle between Liam and Bonehead and the Cable guitar player. Somehow, I managed to defuse this, being put in the odd position of having to play dad on a school trip gone wrong, before trying to gather the band together to get them back to Monnow Valley before it was too late. Someone then decided there was going to be a kangaroo court trial of the offending pasta thrower, that was to take place outside in the courtyard. I decided that this was not going to happen and shoved Cable down the drive, which took 10 long minutes and then what seemed like forever to get the drunken band back to Monnow Valley walking along the dark country lanes. Meanwhile, back up the drive at Rockfield, things were escalating. Noel and the new drummer Alan White popped out of the studio and asked where the guests had gone before telling the remaining people that they had to leave. Angry about his brother's attempts to break up the party, Liam exploded and minutes later tried to kick the door of Noel's room in; the elder brother then grabbed a cricket bat and there was a proper fight before Noel locked himself in his room, climbed out the back window and got Alan to drive him back to London. Meanwhile, Liam trashed the communal area.

Back at Monnow Valley the next morning a hungover Cable emerged to be told about all the chaos at Rockfield and how they were going to be charged for it! There were stories of cricket bats, fighting and a lot of trashed fixtures and fittings, with every light switch smashed, a door off its hinges, the main table in the living area trashed, a smashed TV and drinks machine, and a room full of bits of cold pasta crunched into the carpet. Guigsy then did a good job cleaning up, and the band had paid for all the damages and bought flowers for all the women who worked at the studio. On hearing the news, Kingsley Ward, the legendary studio boss, just laughed. After all, this was a studio that Lemmy-era Hawkwind, Iggy Pop and Black Sabbath had all used, with all manner of high jinks and madness being part and parcel of its legendary story.

Back in London Noel took some time out. He may have mulled on the volatile nature of the band. He may have wondered if it was worth the hassle, but these would have been, at the most, fleeting thoughts. A week or so later, the band were back in Rockfield.

'Liam and Noel hugged each other and we carried on with the work,' producer Owen Morris told *Sound on Sound*. 'After all, they'd been breaking up regularly, so to them it was just another argument. There was no way they weren't going to come back and finish the record.'[1]

A few weeks later I bumped into Liam at Glastonbury and he was laughing about the whole incident: 'That was a proper laugh that night. Rocking!'

Later that year, in October, Cable supported Ash at the Astoria. At the aftershow Liam and Bonehead spotted the band's other guitar player Pete Dorrington and came up to him. Recalls Dorrington: 'I'm thinking, "Fuck, they're still sore after Darius threw pasta all over their kitchen and told them they were shit and now they're gonna kick my head in." So I said, "I'm alright lads, how are you?" Liam: "It is you innit?" Me: "What do you mean?" Liam: "What was cheeky 'n' that and knackered our tea and caused me and my brother to have a scrap." Me: ". . . er yeh, sorry about that . . ." Liam: "Fuck it. It were a top laugh. We nearly split up that night. Our Noel says I was out of order for hittin' your mate, so we had a fight."'[2]

As the years rolled by Liam continued to laugh it off. 'The whole studio got smashed to pieces, everything just got blitzed to bits. It was probably me not giving a fuck, and him trying to write fucking "Bohemian Rhapsody", and me going, "Bollocks, let's have it".'[3]

While Noel remembered, 'I ended up having a proper fight with Liam with a cricket bat. It might have been the biggest fight we ever had.'

In 2011 the cricket bat was sold at auction, with a letter of authenticity, and the bust-up has become threaded into rock 'n' roll history. As the engineer on the album, Nick Brine, remembers, 'It's funny because when they do the tours of the studio, it's like "This is Freddie Mercury's piano where he wrote 'Bohemian Rhapsody' and over there is where the battle of 1995 took place!"'

This snapshot of the band and their inner explosive nature is the overriding image of Oasis for many. Yet it's a 2D tabloid tip-of-the-iceberg deflection from a much-loved band who created the soundtrack of a generation.

For every punch thrown there was also a remarkable creative symbiosis between the brothers, with Liam's innate understanding of how to sing Noel's songs key to a much-loved complex alchemy of personalities whose attitude, energy, style, honesty and wit made them the key British band of the nineties.

The destructive element of Oasis is a small part of the story, but the constructive side is where the fascination lies. Like everyone else, they were a thousand different people on a hundred different days but who could also somehow articulate this in life and song, as we will discover.

2

THE NORTH WILL RISE AGAIN . . . AND AGAIN . . . AND AGAIN

In the nineteenth century British Prime Minister Benjamin Disraeli said, 'What Manchester does today, the world does tomorrow.' He was talking about the then modern industrial city but he could also have been talking about the pop culture city of the future . . .

The revolutionary Manchester of Peterloo and people's orchestras, Cottonopolis and suffragettes, always seethed with music and noise. It always had a revolution at its soul.

Manchester was the world's first industrial city; it inevitably became the world's first post-industrial city; and then, sparked by the famous two 1976 Sex Pistols gigs, it became the world's first post-punk city, with a rebirth driven by bands like Buzzcocks, Joy Division and New Order and their Haçienda, then the Smiths, the

Stone Roses and the Happy Mondays – a production line that set the standard for British alternative music culture.

The seventies Manchester the Gallaghers grew up in was not the current megalopolis with its towering skyline and its well-earned reputation as one of the world's music culture capitals. Back then it was a post-industrial city with boarded-up warehouses and derelict wastelands.

Music sparked the change: from the bands and local TV face and label boss Anthony Wilson's visionary zeal at his Factory Records label to Mike Pickering's DJ skills and band-booking policy at the Haçienda; from Linder, Malcolm Garrett and Peter Saville's artwork to the comedians that sprang from its piss-taking soul like Steve Coogan, Craig Cash and Caroline Aherne; from L.S. Lowry to Alan Turing; from splitting the atom to the world's first computer; from the stubborn underground idealists of Peterloo to the musical mavericks driving the city's prevalent 'fuck you' dislocated genius.

Stepping into these cellarfuls of noise and these high-decibel land-scapes, Noel Gallagher was, perhaps, the then youngest and the last of the punk generation to make it. Oasis were the last roll of that genera-tional dice before becoming the biggest UK band in the nineties and their eventual huge success dwarfs the city itself. As Mick Rossi from Manchester's original punk band Slaughter and the Dogs explains, 'No other band has captured the Mancunian swagger and spirit more than Oasis has and to see them play live, WOW! Unapologetic, defiant and sexy; Quite simply, Oasis are one of the all time greats.'

Old enough to just about remember the Sex Pistols and young enough to be a teenage fan of the Smiths and the Stone Roses, Noel Gallagher was typical of the Irish Blood, English Heart of the city and one of the pop culture obsessed daydreamers armed with guitars and visionary ideas. He was typical of the music and clothes-obsessed youth who hung around the record and guitar shops and the clubs and gigs beneath the iron grey sky. The north-ern youth striding through the drizzle with their heads full of tunes and Adidas on their feet, talking perfect hair and keks and jackets, soundtracked with the best record collections.

On the outside looking in, Oasis came from the sprawling suburbs and council estates that stretched south of the city and it was in this backdrop that they somehow found the magic combination . . .

About 4 miles south of Manchester city centre is Burnage with its council estate where the Gallaghers grew up. It's a tight-knit community that runs along Kingsway – one of the main artery roads leading straight into the promised land of the city centre. Under the council skies 16,000 people live in the thirties-built brick semi-detached housing laid out in the avenues and octagons that are so typical of British estates.[1]

Wedged between the more affluent suburb of Withington, the rougher-round-the-edges Levenshulme, and the more well-heeled Heaton Chapel, Didsbury and Heaton Mersey to the south and east, Burnage is working-class Manchester with its defiant 'like it or lump it' attitude, sharp sense of humour and genuine warmth tied together by family, community, football and music.

Over the years a drip-drip of creative people have been born and bred there. Amongst them Frances Hodgson Burnett, the author of *Little Lord Fauntleroy*, actors David Threlfall and Max Beesley and, in the pop culture years, musicians like Eddie Mooney – the lead singer of seventies pop band the Fortunes.

It was in this sprawl of south Manchester's council estates and back-to-back terraces that Oasis would eventually come together. Growing up in the strongly Irish south Manchester sprawl where a tight-knit community was centred around the churches, pubs, social clubs and Irish sports, mixing a culture of communion and confirmation, community and tradition.

Extended families of cousins and aunts formed a support network for matriarchs and sometimes errant fathers. It was a world both uniquely Irish and uniquely Mancunian.

The close-knit Irish diaspora was built around clubs like the Carousel where both the Gallaghers' and future Oasis drummer Tony McCarroll's parents would go. There would be chance meetings at Irish football and boxing clubs or in local parks where teenagers let off steam running around in loose gangs swapping punches, girls, soft drugs, music and clothes, and playing endless footy.

Waves of Irish immigration had changed and remoulded Manchester over generations, turning the industrial powerhouse into a cultural hybrid. The Irish love of words, music, good times, storytelling and parties made them born to rock 'n' roll. Many legendary Manchester musicians came out of this melting point. The cast includes Johnny Marr, who would learn guitar from another Anglo-Irish musician: Billy Duffy of the Cult. Morrissey was of Irish stock, as was the Smiths' late bassist Andy Rourke. Gary 'Mani' Mounfield's family had emigrated to England from Athy, where his and Johnny Marr's mothers had grown up on the same boreen. Then there was John Maher and Steve Garvey from Buzzcocks, various key members of the Fall, and the Ryder brothers from the Happy Mondays. And it went back through the decades to Peter Noone from Herman's Hermits.

Future Oasis members Tony McCarroll and Paul 'Guigsy' McGuigan were also part of the close-knit Irish community growing up in Levenshulme, as was future guitarist Paul 'Bonehead' Arthurs, born in Longsight to Irish parents. He once commented, 'It's an Irish thing. There isn't some magic fog sitting over the North West, but there is a lot of Celtic blood in the area.'[2]

Iconic local comedians like the late Caroline Aherne and Steve Coogan also had Irish roots, and even Mick Hucknall's maternal grandfather was Irish.

Margaret Sweeney was typical of the post-war Irish influx. Born in County Mayo's biggest town, Bellina, in 1943, and christened in nearby Charlestown, she was one of 11 growing up in the poverty of rural Ireland. Her father was a remote figure who suddenly disappeared, leaving her mother to put Peggy (as she was known) and some of her sisters into a convent for safekeeping. Just after Christmas 1962, after a couple of jobs as a childminder, the 18-year-old joined the drift across the Irish Sea, along with seven of her siblings.

In January 1964, in this new world of the big city, she found work at Manchester's Central Station, and in the network of extended families, Irish clubs and socials she found a community. It was in the Astoria on Plymouth Grove that she met Tommy Gallagher.[3]

One of six brothers and sisters, Tommy Gallagher was born in Duleeth in County Meath, just north of Dublin, and made his move to Manchester at 17. Within a year, in 1965, Peggy and Tommy had married at the Holy Name Church on Oxford Road. The newlyweds set up home at 33 Montgomery Road in the inner city area of Longsight, 3 miles south of the city centre, before moving to the now demolished 2 Sandycroft Street, just off the winding and bustling high street. Finding their feet in the big city, Peggy now worked as a dinner lady and then at the McVitie's biscuit factory. Meanwhile, Tommy worked in construction, building up his own small business.

The first of their three children, Paul Anthony Gallagher, named after Pope Paul VI, was born on 11 January 1966 when the Beatles classic 'Day Tripper'/'We Can Work It Out' was beginning its six-week stint at the top of the charts. A year later, Noel Thomas David Gallagher was born on 29 May 1967 – the same week as the Beatles classic and decade defining *Sgt. Pepper's Lonely Hearts Club Band* album was released – a sign sent from the rock 'n' roll gods!

In 1972, with their house due to be demolished, the family moved from Longsight to nearby Burnage and two weeks later on 21 September, just as Slade's 'Mama Weer All Crazee Now' was somewhat aptly starting to enjoy its raucous third week at number one, William John Paul Gallagher was born – his middle names being perhaps a somewhat fortuitous nod to his future.

His birth was the day the most famous sibling rivalry of them all started, or as Noel once joked to the *Guardian*, 'I liked my mum until she gave birth to Liam.'[4]

The youngest of the family by a few years, William, or as he soon became better known in the Irish version of the name, Liam, was the centre of attention, which he revelled in – a perfect crash course for future adventures.

Now living in Ashburn Avenue – a relatively quiet cul-de-sac in the middle of the council estate in nearby Burnage – meant a switch in primary schools to St. Bernard's Primary.

'He [Liam] was seven years younger, which is quite a gap then. I used to have to make his tea and look after him because I was the oldest brother. My mam used to make us take him out with us, which was awkward when you were 14 and he was seven! My mates liked him though because he was cocky. And he loved hanging out with the big boys. . . . He was demanding! Christ! It was cheaper to take a bird out than take him out,' remembers Paul.

Noel was squeezed in the middle and was sometimes the most introverted and quietest. 'He was quite happy to be alone looking out the window daydreaming,' recalls Paul.

Noel was living in a dreamland that he would actually turn into a reality a few years later. While Paul initially found it hard to mix with other kids, Noel would be a storyteller with a shrewd smartness and edge. Settling into Burnage they began to hang out with other kids in the area, getting up to the normal high jinks of a seventies childhood: messing about on bikes, footy in the park, play fights, gang banter and general low-level scrapes. Burnage was less of a war zone council estate than some in the city and there was a strong sense of community with lots of other kids to hang out with and an extended family of Irish aunties creating a safety net, as Noel remembers.

'I was born in nearby Longsight in 1967. Our house was on a cobbled alleyway of proper grim two-up, two-down outside toilet, working-class, northern houses and got knocked down to build an Asda and a new job centre, which was a sign of those times, so we moved to Burnage in the southernmost part of Manchester, just before you get to Stockport.

'My mam still lives in the same council house with the same friends and the same neighbours on either side of her. She's got five sisters living nearby so she wasn't going to move, even when the money started to come through but I paid off the mortgage and all that.

'I then said what else do you want because I've got all this money and she said, "I want a new gate because that gate squeaks in the night and it keeps me awake," so I got her a new gate with a gold number on it.

And that was all she wanted!'

Every summer the boys would go back to their mother's birthplace of Charlestown in Ireland for their holidays. A long high-street bus-stop town of a thousand people, it's only 20 km from Foxford, where Bonehead's family were from. For those brief few weeks they felt wild and free back in their homeland, with trips to the seaside in Enniscrone or the holy shrine at Knock and the weight of the city and the negative aspects of home life and an errant father lifted from their shoulders.

Noel ponders his roots: 'We went to church every Sunday with my mother and I kind of envy people who have religion to guide them through life, but I have my own path. I remember we used to go to Ireland for our six-week summer school holidays and spend it with me mam in East Meath at our gran's.

'It was a bit of a culture shock but we grew to love it. We had never seen fields and proper countryside with stacks of hay before because we were from the city.

'There was nothing on the telly in Ireland but I clearly remember one pivotal moment in 1977 when everyone surrounded the radio because of the news that Elvis had died. In those days southern Ireland was a backwater and it seemed amazing that Elvis had penetrated that far and that the recital of the bible passage on the radio had been interrupted by the news of his death. All my aunties, who were in their late 20s/early 30s at the time, broke down and started crying and I thought, "Wow, Elvis is dead." It was hard to believe that it had happened.'

Home life was difficult. From the start, the marriage hadn't felt right. Tommy had a quick temper and would disappear for long stretches of time, ostensibly for work, but also his drinking and gambling was overtaking his family life and spiralled into violent outbursts at home when he returned, often in a dark mood. It was an upbringing that inevitably scarred all three brothers and their strong and saint-like mother in different ways.

Both Liam and Noel have spoken of the fractious and volatile nature of family life which was created by their father who drank heavily and beat his older sons and Peggy. Being the youngest meant that Liam was spared the beatings but the surrounding atmosphere would create its own scars. It was an unhappy childhood and both Paul and Noel developed stammers from the emotional and physical stress of their father's abuse, which were resolved with weekly sessions of speech therapy.

At this stage the two older brothers were at the local St. Robert's Primary School in Longsight – Paul in 1971 and Noel the year after. In the cruel world of the school playground Paul was bullied for his stammer, but his younger brother, with his charm and lesser pronounced speech impediment, swerved the playground banter. They both also cultivated a razor-sharp wit as a defence mechanism with a stand-up's timing and a deflecting shield of quips and banter.

In the late seventies, the two older brothers left primary school and went to St. Mark's RC High School, an all-boys Catholic comprehensive on Parrs Wood Road in East Didsbury. Peggy was a dinner lady at the school and Noel would slip in every day for his dinner and slip out again, skiving.

Across the road from the school was where Bob Dylan made his very first live appearance in the UK on 14 May 1964 at the old ABC Studios a year after the Beatles had recorded an appearance on ABC Television's *Big Night Out* on 1 September 1963 and where an early version of *The Avengers* called 'The Police Surgeon', starring Ian Hendry and Patrick Macnee, was filmed.

Pop culture was so near . . . and yet so far away.

Peggy did her best to shield her sons from their father and thankfully being Irish there was an extended family of sisters on Peggy's side to provide emotional, physical and spiritual support, as Liam told the *Sunday Times* in 2019:

'Any good that comes out of me is all from Peggy and all her sisters and brothers – they were a good, close bunch of people. I never missed my father because my mother was both a mother and a father figure. She was there with the cuddles, she was also there with the whack. I'm generalising dads there because normal dads give cuddles as well. But if I needed bringing down a peg or two, she could do that, as well as elevate me.'[5]

You can feel the traumatic upbringing played out in their music a few years later with Noel's claustrophobic sounding yet anthemic early anthems with lyrics of escape that never felt sorry for themselves, or the contemplative soulful songs that displayed a level of tenderness from the songwriter. From an early age, music was the escape, and Noel would become more reclusive, retreating from the tension into creativity or, as ever, wittily and succinctly describing his father in 2016's *Supersonic* documentary as beating the talent into him.

Not that Noel ever saw his background as anything but normal for the time, as he told Gay Byrne on RTÉ's *The Meaning of Life*: 'I just think he was a bit of a rubbish husband. But I've got to say, all my friends who are my age, all their families are split up. So it's kind of par for the course. The seventies was a tough time in Manchester, not only for working class people, but for Irish people with the Troubles. There wasn't a lot of work and there wasn't a lot of money. It kind of makes you what you are.'[6]

You could hear it in the barely concealed anger in Liam's voice, making it one of the greatest voices in rock 'n' roll. His sweet choir-boy range and innate musicality was scarred by the emotional angst of a tempestuous youth soundtracking the internal anger, but finding beauty despite the pain. Meanwhile, Noel's voice often had a melancholy to it, a yearning for escape, and both brothers soundtracked universal emotions sparked by their painful family life.

A few years later, like his hero John Lennon, Liam found a way to use his youthful turmoil as a creative whole, turning his brother's songs into emotional rollercoasters. The words could mean anything but they sounded like they meant everything. His caustic voice turned Noel's often introspective melancholy into thrilling psychodramas, but he could also hint at the sensitivity that the brilliant songwriter intended just below the surface.

Liam may not have written the majority of the songs but his voice and interpretation of Noel's lyrics was something else. It demanded attention while also connecting with listeners on a profound primal level.

This is what made Oasis sound and feel different from their contemporaries. The bands who made up the so-called Britpop scene were great examples of British art pop delivering constructs of arch pop art with knowing nods and nuanced frames of reference which, of course, is another form of pop perfection. In comparison, Oasis were an emotional flame thrower – in the words of Johnny Rotten 'they mean it maaan'. You could feel the volcanic rage and the Pandora's box of emotions in their huge sound. While they never really talked about it or wallowed in it, they internalised their angst and anger, and they couldn't help it infusing their music with a dramatic energy that even coloured their good-time songs – the rasping raw power of that vocal was going to have a good time whatever the consequences.

Fuck everything!

Which is the true heart of the primal scream of great rock music.

Growing up, they were infused with the twin godheads of Manchester culture . . . football and rock 'n' roll, and all three brothers were Manchester City fans. It was one of the rare moments when their father handed something to them that they embraced. He had decided to support what Sir Alex Ferguson would later call the 'noisy neighbours'. It was some kind of perverse reaction to his Irish Catholic workmates, who all supported Manchester United and its heritage of Irish connections – and to this day all three brothers are true blues.

In their youth the club were enjoying a boom time after winning the league in 1968 and the FA Cup a year later. In 1970 they completed a rare double, winning the European Cup Winners' Cup and the League Cup, and four years later they lost the League Cup final to Wolves before winning the 1976 League Cup final beating Newcastle United 2–1 at Wembley. In that decade, Maine Road was a riotous place of celebration as the club became arguably the dominant side in the city following their rivals' slump after winning the 1968 European Cup before relegation in 1974. Like any club, the terrace chanting and singing and the surging sense of community and noise is a powerful sound and would feed into the creative psyche.

By 1987, though, City had been relegated back to the old Second Division. Oddly their fans seemed to enjoy this period and celebrated their dogged support for a lost cause through the thin years. Noel and Paul decided to go to every away game of the 1987/88 season, visiting the broken towns and cities of the lower league in a precursor to touring with a rock 'n' roll band a few years later. Sometimes, it would be a laugh, and sometimes they would get jumped by the home fans despite not being hardcore hooligans and regular, if spirited, fans.

Being part of the Irish community, the young Noel and Paul were railroaded into sports from their homeland. Noel became a pretty handy Gaelic football player for local Manchester side CLG Oisin. With Paul, he had been forced to play the game until his father fell out with the club and started his own, called St. Bernard's, before the brothers returned to CLG Oisin where Paul was the goalkeeper and Noel played up to under-18s level, even scoring at Dublin's Croke Park – the Mecca of the sport – in 1983.

Despite the tension of their home life, when Paul and Noel were old enough they were expected to work with their father who now had a concreting business with a mate, called Holmcrete. Of course, they rarely got paid properly by him, but they turned up anyway, keeping the peace.

Tommy Gallagher would also take his young sons DJing with him, getting them to carry his records and gear to big Irish clubs like the New Ardri in Hulme or the 32 Club in Ardwick, as Noel recalls:

'There's no musicians in my family on either side as far as I know, so I guess it's something to do with being Irish. The Irish are either writers, drinkers, singers or musicians. My dad, before he left, was a DJ and he had a big record collection in the house with hundreds of those *Top of the Pops* albums. He was a country and western fan and used to DJ that and a bit of soul and Stevie Wonder and the Beatles, Bee Gees and Irish folk music in social clubs. It was all seeping in. He would do weddings, pubs and the Irish social clubs and we'd help him carry his gear. He was always playing records so that's where the music thing came from. Plus, added to the fact that you're Irish, and the Irish social clubs always had bands on, and there was always singing.

'It was an escape, of course, but my childhood was no more miserable than anybody else's. When people say, "You play it down" I can genuinely say that everyone that I hung out with were in the same circumstances. Dads then were either errant fathers or gamblers. They were tough times in the seventies and kids bore the brunt of their parent's frustration and that was just the way it was. Mine was pretty grim, but it was not more grim than the other lads I hung out with in Levenshulme.'

Even the 10-year-old Liam would be press ganged into working with his part-time DJ dad, as he remembered to Ann Scanlon: 'I would help him make tapes of Irish music and pop hits when I'd rather have been watching TV. I used to set his gear up; I was like his roadie at the age of 10. All I remember is being given a Coke and a packet of crisps and being as bored as fuck.'[7]

Paul has his own recollections of this time: 'We used to carry his records around like his roadies and we would get 10 pence for pool and a bottle of Coke. Playing pool taught us to win. If you lose, you're fucked, yeah? So you've got to, like, hustle for five hours, to win at all costs. . . . He would DJ at all the Irish clubs and he was quite big on that scene. His DJ name was Tommy DJ or Tommy Disco. It was embarrassing. He would record songs off the radio to play and sometimes he left the radio DJ's voice on and not notice and play it live.

'The music in the family didn't come from him though. If you want to go down the Irish route, my mother's family were the musical ones, the O'Briens, the Gallaghers didn't have any music apart from him doing a disco. He had shit like Demis Roussos and Engelbert Humperdinck, middle of the road, kind of nothing, or a lot of Irish stuff that you've never heard of.'

There was an acoustic guitar lying around the house that one day Noel picked up.

'It was leant against the inside of the backdoor and I could never understand why it was there. According to my mum, my dad had gone out one Saturday afternoon to buy her a present for her birthday and he came back with a guitar. I think he had always fancied himself as a country and western singer but he could never play it.

'By then I used to get kept in a lot because I had been glue-sniffing and shoplifting and there was nothing to do, so I picked it up and that is how I started. It was my escape from everything and I'd take the guitar upstairs. The only thing I could do at first was play one string along to Joy Division bass lines or the Sex Pistols for hours! And my mam would go, "Will you stop it!" I loved music and I loved *Top of the Pops* and as soon as I started playing I instinctively started to write songs and I knew my talent lay in putting songs together.'

Music was a place to escape into, a place to communicate, with a language beyond language that could articulate everything and soundtrack the daydreams – and he was determined to master it. 'I wasn't practising with the grand idea of one day being in a band or anything like that,' Noel says. 'I was just fascinated by the music and playing along to these songs. And it whiled away the hours and even to this day I can just pick up the guitar at home and two hours will go just like that.'

It also gave him a world to disappear into. Slipping up to the bedroom he would spend hours hunched over the guitar, learning the chord shapes until his fingers ached, working out songs from his increasing pile of cassettes and records bought or borrowed from local second-hand record shop Sifters, creating a safe space of sound and escape.

He soon realised that not only was he dyslexic like John Lennon, he was a wrong-way-round kid and only music could save him, he told Ann Scanlon:

'Somebody was playing a joke when they made me. You know: "Let's make this guy a writer and a guitar player, but let's make him write with his left hand but play with his right, let's have him born

THE NORTH WILL RISE AGAIN . . .

in May and give him a Christmas name; and let's make him a dodgy schizophrenic, two-faced Gemini." Cheers!'

Other kids thought he was a 'music weirdo', but he was not lost. He was now found. A semi-reclusive music nut, Noel was going to have to look further afield for like-minded souls.

'Then, as I got into smoking weed, there was an older brother of a mate of mine on our estate who said, "Hey man I heard you got a guitar." He obviously never had one but he could play and he said, "Can I come round and see it?" He came round and tuned it all up and I had to learn to play it all over again! He then showed me the chords to "The House of the Rising Sun" and that was it. I was off!'

Paul remembers, 'Our dad had a guitar, and he didn't play very well. Then I got a guitar because it was compulsory in Catholic schools to take an instrument. So you had a choice of a guitar or a fucking trombone. Liam had a violin because he just wanted to be different, and of course he never learned it. The violin cost more than the guitar and my mam was broke because it was like five quid a week for a year. For a silly violin . . . '

Without the patience to put in the hours to learn how to play, Liam ditched music and followed his wild early teenage nature to become a hooligan, which earned him far more respect than the few years of violin lessons ever would on the streets of Burnage.

'Noel was happy to be alone playing his guitar but then he got quite good so then he gets popular and he just wanted to be alone, so that backfired!' laughs Paul.

After so many tumultuous years, the brothers finally found relief when Peggy acquired legal separation from her husband in 1976, but it wasn't until 1984, after waiting on the council list for a home for three years, that she was finally given one. In a midnight flit while Tommy was out running around the clubs she took her three sons to their new home on Cranwell Drive on the other side of Burnage.

Speaking to the *Daily Telegraph*, Liam said, 'One night, while he was out, my mam got her brothers round, got all our gear in a truck, left him a mattress, and we went off to our new house.'[8]

Peggy and her three sons had finally escaped and she divorced Tommy two years later. 'I left him a knife and a fork and a spoon,' was her verdict on the split. 'And I think I left him too much.'

Liam told Craig McLean: 'I was about seven when my mam left my dad. He was out all the time, fighting, beating my mam up, beating Noel and Paul up.'[9]

In their new home they started again with nothing but they were free. They hardly had any furniture or even carpets but the dark cloud had been lifted from their lives and the remarkable Peggy raised her three wilful sons alone as a single mother, bringing in what she could as a dinner lady. Now squeezed into their much smaller new home, Paul being the oldest got his own room, while Noel and Liam shared the other bedroom, squashed together for years at home as a precursor to 16 years in a band on the road.

It was in this shared bedroom where Noel's younger brother, coming home drunk after his first night out as a teenager, soaked Noel's precious stereo with piss after not being able to find the bedroom light.

Defying the combined hopelessness of eighties Britain, far away from the loadsamoney Thatcher elite and the emotional scars of a violent father, they would, like most teenagers, drift around in and out of trouble, as Noel explained to Gay Byrne:

'Me and my brothers. We're not bad lads. We come from quite a large council estate in south Manchester, and we were all lads. My dad was always working away, and we never really saw him as a father figure. So we were kind of out there in the Wild West where there was all sorts going on, crime and drugs. I'm just glad I got through the other side and found something in music that took me in a different direction.'[10]

It was all teenage kicks, as Noel told Ann Scanlon: 'That's what kids did in the early eighties. You wagged school, burgled houses and glue-sniffed. No one was into smoking pot and there was no ecstasy or hard drugs like there are now. It was just glue-sniffing, smoking cigarettes, drinking cider and listening to the Sex Pistols. Between the ages of 13 and 17, I was completely out of fuckin' control. I didn't give a shit. But I crammed everything into those four years, and at 17 I suddenly thought: "What the fuck am I doing?"'[11]

Another Burnage local was Paul Bardsley, who would go on to play music with Noel and have his own band Molly Half Head who landed a big record deal just before Oasis.

'The Gallaghers literally lived round the back of my house, so of course I knew them. I still remember the time when Noel got caught robbing a frozen chicken from the Co-op and it was the talk of the street!'

Bardsley's memories of Burnage are of a typical British council estate with its high jinks, kick-offs, gangs and laughs.

'It was greener than other estates but it was still a pretty rum area. There were gangs of lads and girls running around doing mad stuff like playing football with a hedgehog and fighting and soft drugs. It could get a little crazy but it was also an exciting place to live and there was always stuff going on. A lot of people would play football at the community centre and the parks. When the punk thing was going on, a lot of the guys round there seemed to be Teds and in Levenshulme there were a lot of scooter boys who would come into the area when the fair was on and there would be fights with different areas and different tribes.'

Bardsley and Noel even had a sort of fight.

'It was in the park when I was about 10 and he was 11. The fight was set up by another kid who said that Noel had been saying things about a mutual friend of ours and he tried to make Noel fight this guy which didn't happen, so we were stirred up to have this punch-up instead, even though we were mates. There were some older glue-sniffers there who were sort of the spectators. Before the fight, I remember Noel doing a sort of Teddy Boy dance in front of his girlfriend. We both had people in our corners advising us what to do, like cornermen in boxing! My person said just smack him on the nose when he's not looking! It ended up being more of a scuffle of course and it was quickly forgotten and I'd see him around and we stayed friends. Noel was always a great story-teller and he had a gift of the gab, but somehow he always kept his cards close to his chest.'

Despite being several years younger, Liam would insist on being with his older brothers, which, as any older brother knows, can be hard work. The youngest Gallagher was the centre of attention, cajoling, piss-taking and joining in as they tried to play footy in the park.

He was outgoing and with a wilful streak of explosive temperament and a real live-wire. By the time he had started at St. Mark's secondary school he was locked into the kind of itinerant lifestyle that could only result in personal disaster for most people, but with a unique focus and an innate smartness that would see him on the trajectory to being iconic. His unfettered wildness and lack of filter are impossible for most people to deal with but a true asset for eventually fronting a band.

Born to be the centre of attention, he had to have the best clothes, the loudest jokes, the coolest friends and be the cock of the class. He was surrounded by girls who were always knocking on his front door to walk him to school, cooing at his looks and fired by his wild, carefree attitude and his excessive grooming, as Paul Bardsley recalls: 'I remember a friend's sister saying to someone that Liam was going to break some hearts when he was older.'

Liam was the spotlight kid and already a rock star way before he was into music, which he thought was for weirdos. He spent his youth getting kicked in and out of school with Peggy endlessly going in to see the headmaster, trying to explain his behaviour was the result of his father.

The buzz of reputation has its ups in terms of your fists earning you respect, but it also has a downside in that word travels and there is always someone who wants to knock you off your perch. Three kids from the rival St. Thomas Aquinas school came down to sort him out and in the ensuing scrap hit him on the head with a hammer. There was blood everywhere but of course Liam didn't back down and, enraged, he somehow put the three assailants on the floor. The unprecedented violence shocked the school, with his legion of female admirers in tears and his myth enshrined with the lads that saw him suspended for three weeks before Peggy managed to talk the authorities into allowing him back into the school.

For Liam, the hammer incident 'knocked the music into him.'

'I wake up in hospital, I've got a load of stitches in my head. But after that, I believe, I started hearing music man,' he told American broadcaster Howard Stern in 2017. 'Noel was always into it. I was more into playing football in the park, being a little dickhead, letting people's tyres down, knocking on doors running away, and just being a little shit. I thought music was for weirdos, man. Then in the weeks after, I think it was Madonna's "Like a Virgin", I heard it and thought, "That's a fucking tune that, man." It's like when people wake up from comas and speak Japanese. So whoever it was, thank you, man.'[12]

Born in 1967, Noel Gallagher was perhaps the last of the pop culture kids who grew up with glam and were just about old enough to feel punk, and teenage enough to live the Manchester post-punk scene in real time.

'As shit and as laden with poverty and unemployment as childhood was, how lucky were we to have *Top of the Pops* and glam in the seventies,' he recalls. 'Then I remember the Sex Pistols being this controversial thing and a kid on the estate had their album [*Never Mind the Bollocks*] with swearing on it! When you are a kid you don't particularly understand what it all means, you just go,

"Wow! he sang 'fuck' on a record!" but the album was more than that and its attitude and sound changed everything. It was an absolute left turn. There is no argument. It cannot be bettered. For me it's the most influential record of all time. It changed lives. It made people start bands or end up running the music biz.

'The first record that I was given when I was really young was "The Show Must Go On" by Leo Sayer, but the first proper single that I bought for myself was the Sex Pistols' "Anarchy in the UK" and then the Damned's "I Just Can't Be Happy Today" and then the *Never Mind the Bollocks* album, and the first record I bought the day it actually came out was "Start" by the Jam. Yes! I am that cool!'

The Sex Pistols influence 'can never be overstated: everything about the band was perfect – from the wild psychodrama of the vocals to the enormous wall of sound of Steve Jones' guitars. Despite the intensity and the beautiful madness, the Sex Pistols were also a thrilling pop band, sending the album to number one, delivering a whole explosive series of question marks and ideas.

Beyond the 'fuck you' attitude the Sex Pistols were a pop art experience, as Noel explains.

'It's one perfect statement,' Noel continues. 'No second album. It sounds like it was made yesterday. Everything that surrounds the Pistols album from the artwork to the music was perfect. Punk was all over by 1977. It was such a short period, the same as the next great cultural thing, acid house, yet who would have thought after those few people who saw the Sex Pistols at the Free Trade Hall in Manchester in 1976 that their album could still be considered, to my mind, the greatest album of all time. It's the year zero for every single thing that was any good, from bands to cool clothes.'

In the noise and confusion that the Sex Pistols created there were now plenty of other bands making their own great racket.

'I was also a big fan of the Damned. I loved them because I loved punk and I was checking it all out. The Damned would be the first gig I went to when they played Manchester Apollo just down the road from me in 1980, when I was 13.'

The Damned had been one of the original big three of punk along with the Pistols and the Clash. Their wild vaudeville take on punk saw them sniffed at by the punk inner circle, but they more than made up for it with their incendiary rock 'n' roll.

Now with the gig bug, Noel also went to see Adam and the Ants at the same venue on their Kings of the Wild Frontier tour in 1981 when the band were at the height of their commercial success with their swaggering and technicolour slice of piratical rock 'n' roll pop perfection.

The whole avalanche of bands coming out of punk saw a revival in the core ideas of British pop art's instant karma culture and auto destruct pop art. At the same time there was also the precise immersion in classic sixties British pop of the Jam, who cranked that golden decade into a punk 1977 now. Perhaps it was their music having a familiarity to it, or their short, sharp songs with brilliant lyrics that were like picture postcards from a working-class reality, or their mod-style sharp suits and intense passion with a wired intensity that struck a chord with many council estate youths, helping to make them the biggest band to come out of the punk generation.

'I first saw the Jam on the *The Old Grey Whistle Test* doing "Going Underground". Paul Weller with his Rickenbacker and you know how he is, intense as fuck, and I thought, "Wow!" He was 19 at the time. It was the noise and the clothes that were really cool. The intellectual side and what he was talking about went over my head then but he was amazing.'

If the Sex Pistols or Joy Division had been great bands surrounded by cultural visionaries who helped create the vision, then Oasis or the Jam were bands dreamt up by their driving force in a teenage wasteland. Bands who somehow constructed their own vision with no helping hands. It's no coincidence they were both also two of the key bands in the glorious UK lineage – bands who made a great sonic pop/noise racket but also had the style and the cultural impact that went beyond *Top of the Pops* and into the hearts of the people. All self-constructed from the scraps of ideas that had filtered down to them, they made sense of this with their own instinctive artfulness that really connected emotionally with people – it's a rare alchemy and the finest of balances.

Paul Weller's homespun take on British culture with his neat mod aesthetic and angular lines and poet laureate Ford Cortina, magic in the so-called mundane worldview, sounded closer to the everyday world of the Burnage council estates where punk was now turning up in unlikely shapes.

Noel recalls: 'I was just too young to be involved in punk, but I recall when I was 10 walking down Burnage Lane with my mum when I saw this punk with white hair and a big black exclamation mark on his head.[13] I later found out that he was a mate of the Stockholm Monsters, a band from Burnage before Oasis.

'I was like, "Wow what the fuck is that! He's got a what!" Bands didn't come from round our way and they must have been the first. They even had a bit of an indie hit with a song called "Fairy Tales", and I eventually got into that and then Joy Division because they were on the same label, which was Factory Records, and then from that, I got into New Order and then the Smiths.'

Fronted by Tony Wilson, Factory Records saw this local culture powerhouse, who was a familiar face from local TV news with his trendy long hair, denim shirts and a beguiling smirk, become the key driver in the city. He had entered the scene with his own influential local music TV programme called *So It Goes*, which ran from 1976 to 1977. The show was key in the rapid development of post-punk music and culture in the North West and saw the Sex Pistols making their first ever TV appearance in September 1976.

Determined to make something happen in his home city and region, Wilson half-jokingly forbade any of the bands or the emerging local media to move to London and instead make something out of Manchester, stemming the culture flow that in the previous generations had seen a brain drain from the northern city.

Somehow, his vision worked and enough of the post-punk movers and shakers stayed in the city to change the narrative. With Alan Erasmus, he then set up Factory Records and eventually released Joy Division, and their vision fell into place.

Music was moving quickly in 1981 and for a 14-year-old like Noel Gallagher it was all mixed signals and scraps of information from an exotic yet attainable nearby world, as his older brother remembers:

'Noel was a punk. He had skinny jeans with zips and shit on them. Then he had a donkey jacket with a confederate flag on the back like a rocker. He was very young and a bit of a confused punk/Teddy boy mix. He had a mate, and they used to play the Pistols album from start to finish over and over again, like 15,000 times.'

For Paul it was the mod end of the scene that saw him nicknamed 'Bod the Mod' as he went the whole hog with a brown suit, fish-tail parka and Jam shoes.

'The Jam were it for me. They dressed like mods but they were punk and exciting. I was really into Buzzcocks as well. Also a lot of two-tone: the Specials, the Selecter, the Beat who were one of the best bands ever. Not so much Madness who were too poppy.'

Mixing the social realism of punk and its amphetamine logic, mod and two-tone were the sweet spot for many, combining the nitro-glycerine of punk rock with sixties art pop and creating one of the many youth tribes.

'Burnage is quite vast. It goes down to West Point, which is where Bonehead was from, and then all the way to Didsbury. In the late seventies it was like the film *The Warriors*. I remember, there was big fights on Cringle Fields. It was a free-for-all in a big field. You got punks, Teddy boys, all the Perry Boys from Levenshulme fighting the rockers, the mods,' explains Paul.

The fast moving pop culture was a shopping list of possibilities for Noel.

'I would read Weller interviews and he would go on about the Beatles. I'd heard "She Loves You" on the radio, but Weller would go on about this other type of Beatles who had done "Strawberry Fields Forever". He would also talk about the Small Faces, the kinks and the Who. Down the road from our house was a second-hand record shop called Sifters. I started going there and I would just buy the records with all the hits on them and that's where I started getting into the sixties stuff and guitar music took over.'

Paul was also a regular visitor: 'Me and my mod mates would get off the bus from St. Mark's, and go to Sifters and switch the tags on the records. So we could get them for 50p instead of, like, two quid! And it was already much cheaper there than the city centre shops!'

It was the greatest hits collections that were the key to Noel's future musical adventures. The hits were often the group's music stripped down to its perfect essence of verse/chorus and middle eight – a distillation of pop at its most perfect and providing a template for disciplined songwriting where every note counts and the hooks are celebrated. What better education for a potential young songwriter than a pile of greatest hits albums?

Opened in 1977, Sifters is still run by Pete Howard, who, since being mentioned in the 1994 Oasis 'Shakermaker' single, has become an unlikely legend in the Oasis story. In the late seventies, bored of his town hall job, he had initially set the shop up on Mauldeth Road in West Didsbury built around his record collection, before moving to its current home on Fog Lane in Burnage in 1983 where it became a key space for local teenagers.

To this day, the shop is little changed with its racks of second-hand albums and walls covered in posters of classic bands like the Beatles, U2, Stones, Jimi Hendrix, Joy Division – a pictorial guide to many of the key parts of Noel's musical lexicon. Fittingly, the only poster that has joined the slightly faded wall of greats is of Oasis themselves.

Also added to the music mix for Noel were contemporary bands like U2 and other mid-eighties groups: 'I guess it's an Irish thing but U2 was a big deal plus the fact they played guitars with the anthemic quality of their songs. I remember going to see them on the Zoo TV tour with all the TVs and it was like the greatest show on earth.'

In 1983 there was a new band in town, who combined pop classic with post-punk: the Smiths. The band's television debut was an inspirational moment that cut through the mundane flicker of mainstream. As the hypnotic melody of 'This Charming Man' snaked around the mesmerising chiming guitar, the singer, Morrissey, flailed around waving a bouquet of flowers provocatively; it was a powerful visual impact and a stick to beat pop's often mundane parade with the singer making a fabulous spectacle of himself.

'Noel brought the Smiths in and I brought the Jam in and the Roses were kind of intertwined,' says Paul Gallagher, 'but I think at about 14 or 15, we had kind of drifted apart and had different friends. We didn't swap records in my family because one minute they're there and next minute they're not!

'I had to put stickers on my records with "Bod" on them, so if you rip that off, you're ripping the label and therefore I know you've damaged the fucking sleeve! I had to work hard to earn the money to buy them! If you want nice stuff, you've got to earn it. It would be like, "Have you seen that pinky, kind of Paisley shirt? No?" Fucking next minute, Liam's bouncing through the door with a shirt 20 sizes too big for him. "All right, get that off. Where's my records gone?" And they would come back scratched and that kind of shit.'

The Smiths would become the key band in Noel's teenage years, and their mixture of northern cool, poetic defiance and brilliant musicianship with every member at the top of their game was crucial. The fact that they were from Manchester was also an inspiration as he sat in his bedroom playing their records over and over and reaching for his guitar and trying to figure those melodies out.

He would buy every Smiths single the day it came out, and there were a lot of singles released rapid-fire every few months – a tip that Johnny Marr would later pass on. He finally got to see them play on 19 July 1986 at the Greater Manchester Exhibition Centre for the Festival of the Tenth Summer, which Tony Wilson had put on to celebrate the anniversary of punk arriving in the city.

Now swapping his acoustic for an electric guitar with a small amp, he blasted out riffs and chord sequences in the cramped house until being told to turn it down, which for a brief few minutes he did before turning it up again – just like every guitar player in the world there was no such volume level as 9 when there was a 10 on the amp!

Several years younger than his brothers, Liam was, ironically, perhaps the purest punk spirit despite initially having no interest in bands and often looking at guitar music as 'weirdo'.

Initially he was not involved in these new drifting musical adventures. Half a decade is a big age gap that feels like an eternity in a teenage world and his early teenage obsessions were football and being teenage cool.

A massive Manchester City fan like his brother, and a regular at their then Maine Road ground in Moss Side, Liam said he didn't get into music until he was 18. 'I know there's a lot of people that get into it when they're two and that, but I was into football until I was like 18. So I was a latecomer,' he said.

Yet while sharing the cramped bedroom with his brother he had no choice but to eavesdrop Noel's musical journey, and while Noel was diving into punk, post-punk and the classics, his younger brother had a brief adventure in breakdancing, perhaps more to do with its street cool than anything.

Hip-hop culture first made a serious impression in the UK in 1982 and had become a new voice and style played out by breakdance crews across the UK laying down pieces of lino in the street and, in a blur of Sergio Tacchini and Fila tracksuits, Puma trainers, sovereign rings and rope chains, throwing a complex series of dance shapes. Local lads were having a go and Liam was one of them, working his moves outside Kwik Save in Burnage. He was also running around with his teenage peers getting into all kinds of mischief and school was not going to be his salvation, as he explained to Ann Scanlon:

'I went to fuckin' school and I got some dick telling me what I was gonna do. "You're gonna do this, you're gonna do that, and you're gonna be in prison soon," and, at the time, I thought: "You're a teacher, maybe you're right," and yet I'm the only one that ended up with anything out of 600 fuckin' people.'

Having honed his rudimentary guitar skills, Noel would wander around Burnage with his guitar looking for people to play with, reconnecting with Paul Bardsley who was also becoming a music-obsessed youth and a fan of Frankie Goes To Hollywood, the Jam and Magazine.

'I was in and out of loose local bands from about 14 years old,' remembers Bardsley. 'I was looking for an environment to be comfortable in making music, and that would eventually become my band Molly Half Head. Before that we would just mess around with different people and one of them was Noel. I remember him coming round and sitting there trying to figure out the chords to Paul Weller's "My Ever Changing Moods" with me. I also remember doing some music at Noel's, and Liam was outside the room. We even had this sort of band thing, which was pretty brief and called Fantasy Chicken and the Amateurs who never played any gigs. We'd get stoned at another pal's place and Noel would bring his guitar round and he'd play it and I would sing with my Kevin Rowland from the Dexys type of voice. I remember Noel doing a sort of rockabilly tune and singing random stuff like "Da Dong Da Dong Da Dong Da Dong" and meowing down the mic along to the guitar, and him being pissed off because it just reminded me of a fucking cat walking down an alleyway! I guess we must have had some sort of ambition to do something because we even got into a proper rehearsal space called the Greenhouse on Brighton Road in Stockport and we even made a rough demo in 1988. We did some covers as well, like a version of that tune, "Is Vic There?"'

The band was never a serious concern and they drifted apart, with Paul Bardsley and Neil Daly ending up in Molly Half Head who appeared on the scene at the same time as Oasis and released a couple of albums, 1993's *Sulk* and 1995's *Dunce* that erred towards the Magazine/Fall end of Manchester art/pop, but with a nod to the big indie pop of their noisy neighbours back in Burnage.

Interestingly, Paul Bardsley's vocals have the same kind of reso-nating sneer that would typify Liam Gallagher's voice in Oasis, especially on their 1993 mini hit, 'Barny'.

Maybe it was a Burnage thing?

'After Fantasy Chicken had fizzled out, I would occasionally bump into Noel,' says Bardsley. 'I'd also always ask about him when I saw his auntie [14] who worked where I worked as a hospital porter for a while at the Christie hospital in Manchester. I was still inter-ested in trying to do some music with him even though I had my own band by then and he was working for the Inspiral Carpets.'

Oscar Wilde once said, 'Work is the curse of the drinking classes', and in the collapsed job market of the Thatcher years there was plenty of time to drink in between doing whatever you could find in a succession of jobs that were more often factory floor than Factory Records . . .

Drifting, grafting, hustling and skiving with no job for life secu-rity, in the mid-eighties job certainty was over. UK cities were full of low-paid cash-in-hand odd jobs and long stretches on the dole that helped bankroll creativity.

Paul Gallagher: 'I worked at a butcher's which was actually all right, I got 25 quid a week and a bag of meat at the weekend. I would keep 15 quid for myself, give my mum a tenner and the bag of meat to feed my brothers. Happy days because there was no jobs in Manchester, in '82 nothing. I worked everywhere, butcher, baker, curry maker . . . which I actually did on Stockport Road making curry sauce. I was even briefly a door-to-door salesman selling these patchwork fucking hippie handbags and there was no chance of selling them in 1983 Manchester!'

After leaving the school he had hardly ever been to, Noel was drifting. He worked on an ad hoc basis with Paul and with his father, which wasn't a great experience and their relationship continued to be tempestuous. It must have been awkward but they put up with it as they drove across the north of England laying concrete floors in hard manual graft that Noel would sensibly swerve at any given opportunity.

'Because we were always arguing, we'd still be working at nine o'clock every night,' says Noel. 'We still saw him after our parents had split up. He only lived 200 yards up the road and my mom didn't say, "You can't see him." So we worked a bit with him after leaving school and his concrete laying business but we grew up and then did our own thing.'

Noel was also a sign manufacturer and a fish tank builder. He also used to work at the Jabberwocky in Fallowfield as a dishwasher on Saturday nights.

Finally free from school in 1988, Liam had found a job working with fences on nearby Parrs Wood Road. The jump into the real world was oddly not one he was initially keen to make. Despite his rowdy few years at school it had been like a mini empire for him to lord over. Suddenly the school heart-throb and hardest kid was thrust into an unforgiving big world that might not be so easy to conquer – just like Ace Face in *Quadrophenia*, who defied the world as the king of the mods but was spotted as a bellhop on his weekdays.'

Liam, though, was not going to end up in that rut.

It was just a matter of time and he was going to be a star, he told himself and any work mate who crossed his path. Drifting through odd jobs had initially brought him down to earth with a bump but not enough to dent his self-belief in his true destiny in his eventual iconic status.

The fence job was never going to last long and he quit after being asked to clean the bogs. His mate then got him a job working with illuminated signs but that didn't last long either. He was then a builder's mate before working at Parfitts the printers. When he was given the most menial of tasks he told the foreman that he was going to be rich and famous and a big star one day. His workmates laughed but Liam knew it was a matter of time. He dreamt of escape from the humdrum town like a latter-day Billy Liar but with one crucial difference: he made it happen.

All the brothers also did some car cleaning and valet work with a local legend called Paul 'Bigun' Ashbee who had blagged a driving job for footballers like Manchester United's Brian McClair, who remembers them:

'They were working for this lad from round their way who had this car cleaning business called Formula One. They were all big City fans but Alex Ferguson said they were allowed to come to The Cliff training ground to clean the cars as long as the gaffer's car got cleaned first. I remember Noel had a penchant for Penguin biscuits with his coffee and Paul gave me a really early demo of the band. Years later Liam told me how he would nick all the small change out of our cars!'

Noel's first proper job was for a firm subcontracted to British Gas, as fellow worker Mike Joyce recalls: 'Norwest Holst was the company. I knew some dudes who worked with him and remembered him being a nice guy who didn't do much work!'

He hadn't been at his new job that long when a heavy cap from a steel gas pipe injured his right foot meaning time off to recover. On his return, physical work was not on, so he ended up in the company's storehouse near the Haçienda, signing out bits of equipment. Noel would joke that the anonymous looking storehouse was called 'The Hit Hut' and that the walls were painted gold because not only was this less physically demanding, it also gave him lots of free time to fill in playing his guitar which he had brought into work. He sat there working on songs including early versions of the classic 'Live Forever', which he would eventually present to the band at the Boardwalk rehearsal room just up the road.

Paul Gallagher recalls: 'He was put in the toolshed. Best place for him, to be fair. We all used to work but in different parts of the site. I'd be actually fucking doing some graft. Liam will be on the stop and go signs in Stockport, backing the traffic up on a Friday night and Noel in the shed not doing very much.'

Next door to Burnage is Levenshulme which, in the eighties, had the largest community of Manchester Irish, resulting in its occasional nickname of County Levenshulme. It was here that the future Oasis drummer, Tony McCarroll, the oldest of three brothers, was born on 4 June 1971 to Anthony McCarroll, a native of County Tyrone, and Bridie O'Donnell, a native of County Offaly.

He grew up in a typical two-up, two-down terrace on Wetherall Street in a musical family with instruments everywhere and the record player always cranked up. They were at the heart of the Irish community, with the local construction business his father built up for his close-knit family creating a happy childhood.

It was the pounding sound of a live drummer in a passing Boys Brigade band that captivated Tony to the possibilities of percussion and he nagged his parents into buying him a cheap drum kit to play on. He became obsessed with the drums and either played or daydreamed about playing them for hours when at St. Mary's primary school near Errwood Park.

'I didn't even know that you could go to the music shop for drums or skins and when I put the bass skin through I used to sellotape it up,' says Tony. 'I had no notion of ever being in a band. I just liked the sound. At the time I had aspirations of becoming a footballer more than anything else.'

The Irish in Manchester would always talk of moving 'back west' and returning to the homeland, yet so few do, so it was a shock to the eight-year-old lad that his parents decided to move back home to what seemed like the middle of nowhere in County Offaly. For two years he had a rural lifestyle thrust upon him that he would grow to love after the culture shock of moving out of the big city. In the evenings, he pounded out the rhythms on his beloved drum kit, now stored in a caravan at the bottom of the garden, while learning to speak Gaelic at the local school.

In 1981, though, his parents moved back to Manchester. On their night of arrival, the Moss Side riots went off in the city, creating a unique welcome home before they settled back into the Irish diaspora.

'Round our way it was all second generation Irish with Irish pubs and community and lots of Irish country music and show bands,' he says. 'It was its own world and I didn't even know at the time that there was a bigger Mancunian kind of a feel because that was all I knew.

'My parents would go to the Carousel Club and they were actually friends of the Gallaghers' parents. Bonehead's mum and dad were in that world as well. The club was a big deal then with massive rooms and a big PA system and it was where the big Irish bands like the Wolftones or the big show bands would come through. The Irish scene influenced all of us and we all grew up with the sentiment and melody of the songs and the swing of Irish country became part of my drumming.'

It was never just music though; sport was part of the fabric and Tony McCarroll met future Oasis bassist Paul McGuigan at the Northern Rebels football club, where they would play every week.

'We had nothing else to do but play football,' recalls Tony. 'From 10 o'clock in the morning when you were kicked out the house until 10 o'clock at night we would play football in the parks or clubs, that was it. Nothing else. I supported Manchester United and we tried to be hooligans, calling ourselves the Sweet and Tender Hooligans after the Smiths song of course. We decided to go get these jackets made with the name of the gang on the back to let people know who we were and how we were going to take over the area. I think we had been watching too many mafia films!'

In this teenage wasteland of playing drums, footy in the park and mates, Tony was finding his own soundtrack and all the paths led to the Smiths, who were connecting all the dots across the city with their melodies and melancholy and the way they were rock 'n' roll but with a very northern filter. Football and music is everything in the city and Manchester now had the new coolest band in the UK in the Smiths. The band's already iconic guitar player had had trials at Manchester City and now played guitar with a George Best cool so he chimed with the local lads. Morrissey may have been something else with his dark and funny lyrics and many nods to the surrounding city, but the guitar player was hip and cool and looked like he knew about football and wore street gear that was rock 'n' rolled up a bit. For Tony, the soundtrack blended well with his roots:

'The Smiths and then, a few years later, the Stone Roses blended into the Irish music in a really beautiful way,' he says. 'I wasn't listening to much music from down south at the time, that came afterwards. The Smiths were the tightest band and it was the rhythm section of Andy [Rourke] and Mike [Joyce] that I listened to. Then I noticed that they had a brilliant guitarist in Johnny Marr, and then afterwards, I started to realise the presence of

Morrissey and his lyrics making me wonder what it actually all meant. What was he saying? It was brilliant and beautiful. It was poetic, and everything about it was great.'

His new mate from the football, Guigsy, had taken an even deeper dive into music. Living on Barlow Road in Levenshulme a hundred yards away, Guigsy, with his roots as an Ulster Protestant, was at a different school – Burnage High School – which he had entered in 1982 with another local music head, Chris Hutton.

School was all high jinks and kick-offs and the usual testosterone-driven flurries until one tragic day when Burnage High found itself with an unwanted reputation and headlines with the murder of Ahmed Iqbal Ullah, on Wednesday, 17 September 1986. It sent shockwaves through the school and the community.

Football was always the first love for the youth. It was a definer, and it demanded its own loyalties that dominated the discourse. Its own pervading culture was now celebrated by a new generation of fans who had moved away from the cliché of the 'superyob' seventies hooligans of Docs and scarves on wrists to a more linear casual look that would filter into the band scene as the decade played out. Wedge haircuts, Adidas trainers and a myriad of competing labels and styles were now central to the teenage terrace awaydays style. Football, clothes and music were central to everything.

For Chris Hutton, it was his passion for Manchester United and the bands like Joy Division that gave him hope and helped him get through school and its seemingly pointless grind to a job market where there were no jobs. Guigsy himself was a smart yet indefinable presence and was also a purveyor of entertaining tales and merry myth-making with stories about his father knowing George Best back in his Ulster youth and of boxer Barry McGuigan not only sharing a name but being a distant relative. Whether true or not it made for an entertaining diversion on long grey school days, just as Noel Gallagher, another master of shaggy dog stories, was finding out over at his school.

There were other faces in the school crowd, like Tony French, who had an artistic side that would one day play out in the early Oasis artwork.

'It was strange growing up in Levenshulme because there wasn't many girls around,' says French. 'It was very lad-heavy and a lot of gangs. You had the Dolans, who were Tony McCarroll's cousins who had a boxing gym and were big characters. Richard Dolan was an amazing footballer, and he got scouted by Man United and when they knocked on his door he opened and shouted, "I'm a City fan!" and closed the door on them! I grew up in Levenshulme and Guigsy grew up on the street behind me. I knew him from nursery school onwards. I met Tony McCarroll in the park when I was about 15, playing football on the bowling green. Everyone would just converge on Cringle Fields, other local parks, or go up to Burnage and play football, so we got to know each other through playing football in the park.'

It was in these parks that Tony McCarroll got to know Noel and brother Paul who was the more outgoing of the two. Sometimes their younger brother turned up as well and despite being the youngest showed no fear and had an hilarious attitude that made him instantly likeable. Liam, or Will as he was known at the time, already had a certain swagger and unique vibe about him despite his youthful years and had his own fearless reputation – unblinking in a kick-off. In the future all these attributes would help create a perfect frontman for a band staring down huge crowds and owning the room.

The endless footy games, smoking, girls and getting pissed was interspersed with Noel and their various mates sitting in the park or falling out of trees while glue-sniffing. Sometimes the more exotic cannabis would make an appearance and, as the nights drew in, the magic mushrooms sometimes popped up. It was the kind of scene played out across most parks in the North West, creating the bedrock to the curiously psychedelic twist that many of the region's bands have.

With odd jobs paying for his first drum kit, and spending time sitting in the local Greenbank park before moving on to Errwood Park for kickabouts, laughs, cider and weed, Tony McCarroll was just another kid getting stoned in Thatcher's Britain where the high times were out of reach and good times at street level were lower budget.

'We were young and we didn't know quite what we were up to,' he says. 'Somebody else in the park could influence us, saying try a bit of this. On a typical Friday night, we were doing what other kids do and we were experimenting. We did anything that would take you away from reality for a little while.'

Music was now entering their world and Guigsy would pop up the road and watch Tony McCarroll play drums at his home and they bonded over a love of the new Manchester scene of ground-breaking bands.

'The first person I met from the band was Guigsy when we were eight or nine years of age,' remembers Tony. 'I met him playing football and I don't remember talking music at that point, but by our early teens, Guigsy was right on his music. When we went back to his house after a game of football he'd have a collection of records and tapes with all these Manchester bands on them like Joy Division and other bands from out of town like the Jam. It was all there. Even when Guigsy was really young he was well on top of the scene. I don't know where he got it from but he was a smart lad and well-read and he opened my eyes to a lot of things.'

Tony French was also getting drawn into the musical spell.

'Music started creeping in with Guigsy who I was knocking around with and we got into the Smiths,' recalls French. 'The Who were massive for us, and so was smoking weed. It was basically sitting in bedrooms getting stoned or going out and playing football. Guigsy was a big pot head and it made him more withdrawn. He was also always stylish but so was I. I had the coats with all the pockets in them and army-style coats. Bomber jackets with the zips on the sleeves, which Liam always used to ask about.'

In an area riven with its own gangs, loyalties and identities were split along football and neighbourhood lines and then subdivided into shifting territories. Gangs came and went, demarcated by football and background. In this flux of gangs, areas like Burnage and Levenshulme each had their own reputation, like the West Point Boys named after an unclaimed area on the fringes of Burnage.

After a kick-off in Burnage, Chris Hutton had crossed the divide and was hanging with The West Point Boys and it was here that he met up with Paul Arthurs who even then, back in the long lost days of youth, was often spotted with keyboards or a guitar, underlining his reputation as a bit of a muso – an unusual pastime in the area where playing guitar was strictly for 'weirdos'.

They were all likely lads immersed in mid-eighties Manchester and making sense of their world in their own ways. Music was sometimes a soundtrack and style, with gigs to see and records to get lost in, and football was everything, and now in their mid teens there were Levenshulme boozers like the Horseshoe, the Midway, the Church Inn and the Little Vic.

It was just a matter of someone joining all these dots together.

3

MANCHESTER VIBES

In the mid-eighties, Noel Gallagher began to explore the burgeoning music scene on his own doorstep.

Usefully, he was within walking distance of two key new venues – the Internationals, which both opened in 1985 at the same time as the Boardwalk, which had opened in the city centre.

The International 1 and 2 would both be key venues for touring bands. The new owners included Gareth Evans who eventually managed the Stone Roses, turning the Carousel Club into the International 2 and the nearby Oceans 11 into the smaller International 1 where the Stone Roses would soon rehearse, taking full advantage of the big stage and club PA.

This spate of new venues was going to have an impact on the scene and if the Haçienda grabbed all the column inches these venues were equally important in bringing all manner of music into the city while creating a live space for local bands.

The bands were booked by the legendary Roger Eagle – whose huge impact on the Manchester music scene often goes undocumented. He was the DJ at the Twisted Wheel in the sixties, with his exquisite taste in black music paving the way for what would be termed Northern Soul by a visiting London music writer called Dave Godin.

After a decade in Liverpool where he booked the city's first punk club, Eric's, Eagle was back in Manchester at the Internationals booking the bands. It was here that he would often be seen at the bar at the back of the venue with his Hawaiian shirt, gruffly acknowledging passers-by. The small bar was also where a youthful Noel Gallagher would lurk, soaking up this thrilling new world as part of a small community of gig-goers who seemed to go to everything.

'I went to International instead of going to town and to discos and all that shit. I was obsessed with music and I was hooked and I would go all the time on my own because none of my mates went.'

Just beginning to appear on the scene in 1985 onwards with a fervent local following were the Stone Roses, who were slowly crafting their songs and gradually ditching their leather trouser and Paisley shirt homage to the early Creation Records style into a more modish pre-Madchester look. The Happy Mondays' off-kilter Northern Soul and funkadelic laced grooves had an added freeform 'mad fucker' poetry and a bug-eyed dancer, while the Inspiral Carpets were paying homage to psychedelia with their bubble light show and Farfisa-driven sonic trips. Noel caught this next wave of local mid- to late- eighties bands.

'The Inspirals did a great cover of the Velvet's "What Goes On",' he says. 'I saw them with the Waltones and Ed Barton who was singing a song about his dog dying! I would go and see Yargo all the time who were fucking brilliant. "The Word" music column had started in the *Manchester Evening News* writing about local bands and I was always in local guitar shop Johnny Roadhouse looking for guitars. I saw the Chameleons in September 1986. It was the launch of their *Strange Times* album, which was a big record for me. It came out around the same time as the Smiths' *The Queen is Dead*, which blew my mind, and the Smiths were the first band that made a difference to me.'

The local scene was punching well above its weight, as Noel could see: 'I realised that all the cool bands were now from Manchester. It's funny with iconic British bands [they] all make way for each other. The Pistols made way for the Jam, then the day the Jam split up is the day the Smiths arrived, then the day the Smiths split up is the day the Stone Roses got big, and the day the Roses faded then we would come along. I put the Jam up there with the Beatles but the Smiths were the game-changer for me. I was right into the Jam, but Morrissey and Johnny are from my home town and that made a big difference.

'It's really funny with Morrissey because he's obviously got a bril-liant take on the mundanity of life and romance and love and hate and yet like most Mancunians if you start to get pretentious there's enough people to call you out. Even though it came across vastly different, Morrissey was never pretentious. It was real as fuck. It was just him being him. On paper the guy is into poetry and Oscar Wilde, but he could see the light and shade of everything.

'It wasn't just Morrissey though, that was more of a southern thing. The words, when you read them, were fucking amazing but it never inspired me to be like him. For me, it was always, hang on a minute, who's the dark horse in the corner? The guy on the left with the Brian Jones hair, the sunglasses and the big red guitar – that's who I wanted to be . . . Johnny Marr – he's fucking cool as fuck. Also the chemistry of the whole band was absolutely stagger-ing and that's the part of the magic. Also, they were Irish Catholics and Johnny was a football kid and he supported Manchester City, and he loved the Stones. They were now on *Top of the Pops* and they were, without a doubt, the greatest band in Britain at that time. You would hear them on the radio on *Roundtable* and they would talk about the releases and they would destroy every other single in the charts. Morrissey was the poet and he was into things that I didn't really understand, but when I heard the words of songs like "Rusholme Ruffians" and "The Headmaster Ritual" I thought, I've been to those kind of schools and that fair that he's singing about used to come to Cringle Fields near Burnage and it went all the way round Manchester and you would think, "Wow! He's talking about things I know" and it would encapsulate my life.

'I saw the Smiths at the Haçienda and at the Free Trade Hall. I then saw them at Gmex at the Festival of the Tenth Summer gig.[1] I then started to realise that Manchester had a thing that no other city had, not even London. Manchester had all these really unique groups like the Smiths, Section 25, Yargo, Chameleons and ACR. All the other groups were completely different and the city was only 6 miles wide. You could not get any more unique than the Happy Mondays who were really out there like a big gang of desperados. I spoke to Shaun and Bez at the time but you wouldn't go round to their house for fear that you'd never get out!

'They don't have this kind of scene in Ipswich or in Leeds. I think the difference between Manchester and Liverpool is that scousers just want to be the biggest band in Liverpool and that's quite commendable really. In Manchester, it was different. Johnny Marr was always the ambitious one in the Smiths. He wanted to play Wembley Stadium and have the biggest guitar collection in the world, whereas Morrissey was going to take on the vivisectionists and all that carry on. I was allied more to the Johnny Marr school of what it meant to be a rock star. My musical Mount Rushmore would be Johnny Marr, Paul Weller, any of the Roses, and Steve Jones in there as well.'

Manchester also had the world's coolest club . . . the Haçienda and one night in 1988 Noel had an E epiphany.

'Then I discovered the Haçienda and what that meant and how its story went back to punk and I was thinking, "Wow! This is a fucking great city to be right in the middle of . . ."'

Opened in 1982, the Haçienda was a unique club envisioned by New Order's brilliantly visionary manager, Rob Gretton, and his partner in Factory Records, Tony Wilson, and mainly funded by New Order. A clean break from the sticky carpet clubs of the times, it was a revolutionary new space and came with brilliantly artful pretensions mixed with hedonistic adventures.

No other club was named after a situationist slogan[2] and no other club came with a Ben Kelly purpose-designed stark industrial decor creating an arty playground. With a then ambitious capacity of 1,600, it was initially often empty, yet open nearly every night with a daring music policy of a cutting-edge game-changer. If Joy Division had sounded like the future, the Haçienda turned their sound and vision into bricks and mortar, and it just needed everyone to catch up.

And it was in Manchester, not in London, that this state-of-the-art New York-style super club was built, soaking up the New York vibes and bringing them all back home as a totally unexpected addition to the then decayed city centre; it sparked a regeneration riot that continues to this day.

Driven by Mike Pickering, who booked the music and became a DJ by default in 1987, when he launched and DJd the club's 'Nude' night on Fridays with Martin Prendergast. Soon to be joined by Graeme Park, it became one of the first British clubs to play house. They sparked a cultural revolution fired by the new drug in town, ecstasy, which helped turn the club's fortunes around, and the Haçienda was now packed and the centre of British youth culture. This sparked another new Ibiza night, 'Hot', hosted by Mike Pickering and Jon Dasilva in July 1988.

The new dance music totally suited the club's famously booming sound system, and the pounding kick drum and itchy rhymes filled every corner of the old yacht warehouse as the bug-eyed youth went crazy in a sea of glorious humanity.

'With the Haçienda it seemed natural for Manchester to be the centre of the universe,' explains Noel, 'and Mike Pickering was the key to the club creating the playground for everyone to play in. Nowadays everything is a business but in those days that place was pissing away money because the art and good times came first. You always knew when they were up against it because New Order would play two nights to pay the tax bill.'

The atmosphere in the club was unique and to this day *The Haçienda Classics* album – a box set of almost 50 tracks that soundtracked the legendary dancefloor – remains one of Noel Gallagher's favourites, with classics from K-Klass, Farley Jackmaster Funk, plus deep cuts like 'Don't Scandalize Mine' by Sugar Bear as well as brilliant local tunes like A Guy Called Gerald's classic 'Voodoo Ray' and 808 State's 'Pacific State'.[3]

By the late eighties the club was unique with a sweat-shod of northern youth dancing euphorically to the pulsating music in the glow of ecstasy. All in a building whose architecture and style made it stand out like a steel and chrome palace of good times in the crumbling post-industrial wasteland at the then edge of the city centre.

Something unique was happening in Manchester in that the seemingly opposing forces of indie guitar music and the DJ culture of acid house somehow combined, and it was with open minds and open hearts that the youth embraced both forms and remoulded them into their own version, pick 'n' mixing from both. New Order, the Happy Mondays and 808 State synthesised these styles into new wholes; the Stone Roses' psychedelic guitar rushes somehow slotted neatly into the tripped-out yet danceable vibe and even Oasis, whose music is often looked on as guitar trad, would be steeped in the communal vibe of rave culture – the fundamental idea that the audience is the star in that glorious getting lost in the communal rush of ecstasy and flailing bodies on the dancefloor.

Acid house had now erupted all over the UK and was the biggest sea change since punk. It would turn everything upside down and affect the music, style, fashion, culture and ultimately Manchester's city skyline. It also turbocharged the local scene with new music, new drugs and a new style that saw the Haçienda turning from an often empty space into party central as part of an ecosystem of wild scenes in other spaces like the Kitchen in Hulme that continued the 24-hour party people vibe. Like many contemporaries it took a chemical nudge for Noel Gallagher to see the light.

'I remember there was all the scaremongering at the time that if you took an E you would have a great night and die in the morning. I remember thinking, "Fucking hell, I'm not sure about that!" I went to the Haçienda on my own because the guys that I grew up with were not into music or drugs and were more into football. Ecstasy hadn't hit Burnage at that time so I bought some speed, the good ol' honest punk drug, and I just remember standing there thinking this music that they are playing is monotonous mechanical music and it was doing my head in. I didn't know what was going on and everyone was going mad. Then these people from Warrington started talking to me, and they said, "Are you on one?" and I said, "I don't know about that. I've read all about that stuff and I'm not sure", and they said, "No it's fucking great!" The next week I met them again and I had my first E and the same music was getting played and it was like listening to music for the first time!

'It was like, wow! It was literally incredible that now on E it sounded mind-blowing. Then for the next two years it was like time stood still and everybody was having it.'

The Haçienda, though, was not everything.

Noel continues: 'That first night on E, I went to the Kitchen with the people from Warrington. I would never have dreamed of going anywhere near Moss Side and Hulme, where it was, at three o'clock in the morning back then, and now it seemed like the most natural thing in the world to be walking around thinking, "What could possibly go wrong?"[4]

'It was only a 10-minute walk from the Hac and it was a brilliant place. I tell people about it now, and they don't believe me when I describe it. It sounds like it's some gritty northern drama but it was real.'

Now knocked down, the old Hulme was a confusion of deck flats and the notorious bullrings – four huge blocks of concrete flats built in the late sixties that had already decayed into rat runs and were full of students and squatters and genuinely damaged people who had drifted there.

Just on the edge of the city centre it was an ideal space for creative bedlam. The Kitchen was set up by the late Jamie Nicholson, who lived in Charles Barry Crescent. When he noticed that the flat next door had become unoccupied in 1986, he got a pickaxe and smashed his way through the dividing wall to create a unique space that would be part studio and part rehearsal room for local bands. Inevitably this also became a party space, and the rest of the flat was now sledgehammered, removing walls and even floors to create a squat club with the Jam MCs DJing for a packed nocturnal bedlam of ravers and 24-hour party people. Parties and raves lasted over the weekend, with the booming sound system bouncing off the walls of the surrounding flats and the thumping bass drum motif of acid house pumping like it was the heartbeat of Hulme's amphitheatre of chaos and creativity.

The whole area was full of shebeens,[5] blues parties and travellers' bonfires with smoke and music rising to the night sky and the constant boom of the sound system shuddering the decayed madness of Hulme. It was like Mad Max on ecstasy and the Kitchen became the space where the ravers would congregate after the Haçienda closed at two in the morning. They would turn up with their eyes on stilts, peaking on E, walking and half dancing along the road, or arriving in cars that were parked in the empty parking lots in the semi-derelict psychic playground of Hulme.

'I would go to the Kitchen and it always ended up as one of those "the sun is coming up" type scenes,' says Noel. 'I'd be stood next to this guy all night in the pitch black in the club passing him a spliff and the sun comes up and it would be Mani from the Stone Roses and I was like "Wow! Fucking hell!" He had just come back from recording a demo of "Made of Stone" at Suite 16 Studios and was saying it's like Led Zeppelin and I was saying, "I fucking love Led Zeppelin" and here he was right fucking there at an illegal house party at seven o'clock in the morning.[6] This guy who was widely regarded now in Manchester as being in the biggest new band in the city and who I'd seen play and thought were brilliant and here he is dressing like me and hanging out in the same places as me, and this gave me so much faith in them because if it wasn't for the Stone Roses I don't know what I would have done.

'Later on we used to play the Roses album from the Haçienda to the Kitchen in a car. I remember we would always pull up in the car park in Hulme and the same part of the album would be on and then we got out of the car and went raving.'

There were other ports of call like Justin Robertson's Most Excellent nights with its glam Balearic mix-up or Solstice 91 that sprung up in 1991, with Noel a regular at the club and Liam getting in free as well. It was DJ'd by the late and great Manchester DJ Dave Booth who, despite never having his name in the lights, was arguably the most influential of all the local DJs on the band scene, playing a mixture of dance records and trippy classics that blew your mind like the Beatles' 'Tomorrow Never Knows', Hendrix, the Doors or Love. Dave would turn the young crowd on to these decades of psychedelia whether it was guitar, rave or freak scene, mixing the new dance music with the trippy classics. All this would be followed by all-nighters at someone's bedsit where the eclectic record collections came to life, from the Beatles to the Bee Gees who Noel discovered at future Oasis road crew and DJ Phil Smith's flat in late-night sessions.

Noel Gallagher was one of those people who seemed to be everywhere, another face in the crowd and an engaging presence with a deep and encyclopaedic knowledge of pop culture.

'I say to people that I've lived such a great life and a big part of that was being in Manchester before 1988 with the Smiths and then early Roses and then being in the middle of that E thing with the Haçienda and then being the roadie of one of the main bands on the scene, and then being in Oasis. It's like I've literally been at the centre or part of youth culture since 1986 from all different angles and seen it all.

'I used to say to people that acid house boiled down to two years in total when it was utterly fucking inspiring. The Haçienda was the centre of the universe and the music was amazing. Acid house changed everything. It was a big influence with the communal thing. When I wrote songs I didn't write about "you" or "me", I wrote about "us". Sadly, when the nineties kicked in, it was like people were bored of this and decided to go back to violence and intimidation and it ended on New Year's Eve 1989/90. As the clocks struck 12 someone got glassed and things changed. Then all the bad drugs and the guns came into the city and it was never the same again.'

Despite the scene ending he never lost his love for the music.

'When that *Haçienda Classics* album came out in 2006 I took it home, and it nearly brought a tear to my eye! It took me right back to that space. When I have a few people around like Mike Pickering I put it on and it's so evocative of that time in that nightclub and those songs, and that soundtrack brings me back to my youth.'

It took a special and legendary gig from a fast rising local band to coalesce everything. When the Stone Roses walked on stage as special guests for James at Manchester's International 2 on 30 May 1988 they suddenly looked, felt and sounded like the future and the packed audience just knew it.[7]

At the back of the room, a 15-year-old Liam Gallagher was gobsmacked by Ian Brown's presence, and it turned his life upside down as he watched the rock 'n' roll John the Baptist to his rock 'n' roll Jesus.

Up on the balcony, his brother Noel was celebrating his 21st birthday and chatting to someone who was taping the gig. He arranged to get a copy sent to him in a conversation that would change his life when the bootlegger turned out to be Graham Lambert from the Inspiral Carpets.

All around the room, different versions of this story were being played out.

'Me, Noel and Liam all went to the gig but with different mates and in different parts of the venue,' recalls Paul Gallagher. 'I remember having been up on a balcony. I didn't know where the rest of them were but that gig changed everything.'

The Stone Roses were that kind of band. That night they started their fast track to the top with their own take on sparkling guitar pop filled with a punk attitude and drenched with lysergic head-twisting melodies. They had the vibes and an added huge dose of innate Mancunian cool from an already iconic singer who walked the walk and talked the talk and knew it. With a series of one-off shows and a couple of releases, the Stone Roses were starting to find young ears to listen to their crystalline perfection.

They were the right band in the right place at the right time.

In June 1987, the Smiths had split after the music media had jumped the gun by publishing a rumour overheard at a Manchester party about tension in the camp. This left a void at the top of the guitar band tree in the UK. Pre-ecstasy for the masses, the Happy Mondays were not making sense to anyone apart from Tony Wilson's evangelism and a small coterie of wild-eyed believers. The Inspiral Carpets were building up a small following with their psychedelic garage rock and the Stone Roses had a good local following but were unknown outside the city.

The band had been around since 1984 and had been trying to find their way. There had been a leather keks, rockier earlier version which had now morphed into a Jackson Pollock modish look with perfect bowl cuts as they started to resonate with upcoming youth in the city.

Noel Gallagher had stumbled over them and was one of the earliest fans of their new phase.

'The first time I saw the Stone Roses was at the International 1 in 1987,' he remembers. 'I didn't have any idea of who they were then. It was one of those nights put on by Gareth Evans, their manager. He would go around town and come up to you in the street and give you free tickets if he thought you looked like a Stone Roses fan. I wonder what jacket I was wearing that day!

'It was the Lord Mayor's parade and he came up to me and gave me the tickets and said, "Have you got any friends?" I said I had loads of them in Levenshulme, and he said bring them all. That night I was round our way with nothing to do so I went down to the gig which wasn't too far away. I was on my own because nobody else wanted to come.

'The Roses were then in their so-called goth/early scally period. Ian had a harlequin shirt on and slicked-back hair and looked like Dracula and he had a walking stick as a prop. They still had their long-haired bass player [Pete Garner] and Andy Couzens on the second guitar.[8] They were never a goth band though – fucking good is what they were!'

Out of sync with the times and unsupported by the Manchester music inner circle, the Stone Roses were outsiders left to their own devices and an innate self-belief. This gave them the space to hone their sound down from their rockier roots to the sublime genius guitar melodies that they would become famous for.

Their early following had faded away and the next generation like the young Noel Gallagher stepped in.

'It was one of their early gigs and it was virtually empty and Ian was doing this thing where he was singing in the middle of the dancefloor. He would go into the audience and front people out and I thought, "That's mad as fuck."'

News of the Roses was spreading by word of mouth.

In 1987 their second single 'Sally Cinnamon' had been released by FM Revolver and I had written a full-page feature for them in *Sounds*. The single then had a nine-week run in the indie charts and they were playing a few small shows around the UK and had now signed to the bigger Silvertone label. Outside Manchester they remained a best kept secret but the anti-Clause 28 International 2 gig with James was a turning point for them and, indirectly, for the Gallagher brothers.

'It was just at the point where the Roses were starting to break through. They were our band,' remembers Noel. 'They were like us. They sang in our accents. They wore the same clothes. They went to the same clubs and the same shops. Ian Brown and John Squire's interviews were lean answers and they were straight to the fucking point. Whether the Roses believed it or not they made me believe it and they made millions of other people believe it.

'I mean I loved Joy Division but I can't be like them, but the minute I saw the Stone Roses that was it. I fucking loved that group and everything that they stood for. I loved Mani when he joined because he's a proper toerag from North Manchester and he's a fucking brilliant bass player and that made me feel I could do it as well.'

That famous night saw Noel Gallagher celebrate his 21st in the club where his parents had met almost 25 years previously. He had gone on his own, of course, leaving 15-year-old Liam to go with his own mates. From opposite ends of the room they both felt the tension as the Roses delayed their stage time as long as they could, pushing the headliners into a tighter time slot. When Ian Brown finally walked on stage, cool as fuck, he was ringing a bell: ringing out the old, ringing in the new.

With the Roses on peak form, the gig itself was life changing for both brothers in quite different ways. Liam was transfixed by Ian Brown's cool while Noel spotted a bootlegger.

'I see a guy on the balcony, and he's got a little tape recorder with red lights on, and he's obviously taping the gig. So I went up to him because I wanted to have more of their music. At this point, the Stone Roses had released "Sally Cinnamon", which I had bought at their gig at the International the year before and I wasn't aware of their earlier 1985 single. So I went up to this guy and said, "What you are doing there?", and he said, "I'm taping it" and because I didn't know him from Adam I said, "If I give you my address will you send me a copy," and he said, "Yeah of course." That tape changed my life and I've still actually got it. So we got talking and he said what other bands are you into and I said, "I like the Waltones,[9] Happy Mondays, the Inspiral Carpets and I'm going to see them on Friday," and he said, "I'm the guitar player in the Inspiral Carpets!" I went, "Oh wow!" and we chatted away about music and guitars and we kept in contact through this Stone Roses tape and then a few days later I went to the Inspirals gig.'[10]

Like Noel, the Inspiral Carpets' guitar player Graham Lambert was another one of those faces from every gig and he often came armed with his tape recorder.

'I was stood there with my little tape player and he [Noel] asked, "What are you doing?" and obviously you don't want a voice on the tape so I quickly said I'm recording this gig. Then when I moved the tape recorder away a bit we chatted. He said, "Are you going to the Inspirals on Friday?" I said, "Well, I'll be there because I'm the guitarist!" I then said, "Come down in the afternoon and help us, watch us set our gear up," which he did. And then he just started kinda roadying for us from there.'

The Stone Roses' gestation had been arduous, but when they arrived, they hit the target perfectly for Noel.

'When they played it was a real "fuck me these are brilliant" moment,' he remembers. 'Ian Brown walked on stage totally cool and ringing a great big bell and their songs were brilliant. I always say this about the Stone Roses, bless them! The look that they were famed for – they were the last people to look like that in Manchester apart from Mani. When they did get the look though, Ian Brown looked the coolest of them all.

'I saw the Roses a lot of times and on a good day they were the best band in the world. They had the songs though, like "I Wanna Be Adored" and once you hear that bass coming in, it's game over, and they also had the presence of Ian Brown. Some people used to slag him off for not being able to sing but it never seemed to matter.

'They were our band. Without the Stone Roses there would be no Oasis. 'Liam was at that gig at the International 2 as well and it made him join Bonehead's group which I joined later, which became Oasis, and we sounded like the Roses when we started.' I also went to Spike Island in 1990 but not Blackpool in 1989 – I was at a rave down south that night.[11]

Manchester was about to have another moment . . .

'Of course the Stone Roses would come from Manchester, where else could they be from?' explains Noel. 'Where else could the Smiths and Joy Division be from? Where else could Ian Curtis be from? Where else could Factory Records be from? Where else could the Haçienda be?

'It was so fucking natural that all the bands, all the fashion, all the great writers and all the great people come out of the city. All around the world people ask what is it about Manchester? And I say I just don't know.'

In another part of the venue a 16-year-old Liam Gallagher was having another kind of epiphany. Borrowing £15 from his mother he went to the gig separately from his older brothers and he was transfixed by the Stone Roses and their charismatic singer. Within minutes of seeing Ian Brown's swagger, demeanour and empowering confidence, and the band's perfect music and clothes equation, he saw the future.

It was his first transcendental guitar band moment. It had always been swirling around from his brother's record collection and guitar playing back home but its potent, mesmerising and messi-anic power suddenly made sense to him.

The Stone Roses were turning yet another teenager on to the possibilities of guitar music proper, as he explained to the *NME*:

'That was my favourite gig of all time, killed me dead, changed me fuckin' life. . . . I remember our kid having "Sally Cinnamon", but it was "I Wanna Be Adored" that first got me . . . I must have been about 15 or 16 when I finally heard the record properly. It had a real fucking summery feel and a real lightness to it. I was going through all this family shit at home and all that, and I just needed a bit of uplifting like having a B12 shot or something.'[12]

The Stone Roses frontman inspired Liam to be a singer. Ian Brown was totemic and a new generation were picking up his and the band's baton. The game-changers had changed the game.

Within weeks Noel would be on the road with the Inspiral Carpets and Liam knew his destiny. He just had to convince the rest of the world, starting with his mother, as he explained in the *As It Was* documentary in 2019.

'I told my mum I was going to be a singer and she said: "You can't sing!" I then said: "I'm going to be famous", to which she replied: "You want to bloody hurry up and be famous then."'

4

WHEN IT RAINS . . .

The Stone Roses truly had been the resurrection.

They didn't play much but when they did there were more true believers, and by the time they played the Haçienda in February 1989, just after finishing recording their debut album, it was truly happening. When the debut album came out on 2 May it caught a perfect wave, although it wasn't a wam-bam straight in at number one and, like all the best albums, it was a slow-burn, word-of-mouth affair.

For the music heads looking for a band to fill the Smiths space with a nod to rave, a sound like liquid ecstasy and dressed loose fit, here they were, and the band became the soundtrack to that wonderful year.

And 1989 was a riot and the Roses were the cool rulers. They were untouchable.

From 1989's Blackpool Empress Ballroom to 1990's Spike Island, every gig was a stepping stone for the baggy pied pipers. Jiving alongside them were the Happy Mondays who had been the first to somehow synthesise the street clobber with a warped rock 'n' roll and a nod to the dancefloor. Their frontman Shaun Ryder's vagabond poetry and leering vocals sounded like a mad-head conversation amplified through a wonk groove. They soundtracked the druggy weird trip of that period perfectly.

The Madchester vibes were now in the area and as 1988 morphed into 1989, the styles, music and life got baggier.

Everything that year was a signpost. There were albums like the Stone Roses' debut that grew and grew. New Order's *Technique* with its sophisticated future pop owned the dancefloor but still retained that addictive melancholy. The Happy Mondays' second album *Bummed* was a leering, druggy masterpiece full of weird and warped characters that sounded like people you already knew. There were also great singles like the Inspiral Carpets' 'Joe', the Mondays' 'Wrote for Luck' – a song that made you feel stoned simply by listening to it – and the Stone Roses' glorious 'Made of Stone', a perfect slice of shimmering guitar brilliance that led up to the band playing the most legendary of gigs at the Empress Ballroom in Blackpool in July, the moment when the whole scene went overground. Then there was the classic Manchester takeover of *Top of the Pops* on 30 November when the Roses and the Mondays shared dressing rooms, spliffs and attitude and brought the new northern sound to the nation.

Around town there was an atmosphere. Some Manchester pubs had gone feral, like the Midland in West Didsbury where it was easier to buy Es from behind the bar than pints. Crazy scenes would erupt out of the ether with mad all-nighters in bedsits, endless raves in Hulme, sound systems in old clubs, new club nights setting their controls for the heart of the sun, and the twin godheads of house and guitars mixing and merging.

Getting dressed up was always the quintessential core of the heart and soul of British pop culture and Manchester had its own style. The Happy Mondays may have been the first to wear the flares – famously buying them from Phil Saxe's stall in town. This had morphed into a baggier, looser fit to move and dance, with long-sleeved baggy T-shirts (with designs on the front, back and sometimes sleeves), Joe Bloggs, Reni[1] bucket hats, Kickers shoes or Adidas shell-toes, half-buttoned shirts, and kagouls for style and the omnipresent weather.

What had once been the twin local godheads of Joy Division and the Smiths was now the Roses and the Mondays. What had once been Ian Curtis's dark lyrics and death disco futurism or the Smiths' sardonic take on life with Johnny Marr's casual cool was now a street walking parka with a fistful of napalm.

This new sound and vision filtered into the south Manchester pubs. Sex and drugs and acid house! The soundtrack, style and stimulants were changing, and everybody was now getting stoned to the new sounds and new styles.

It was a potent mix. Back in 1990, inspired by all the excitement going on around them, a bunch of second-generation Irish lads as fearless as any and bitten by the music bug, sat around one night in the pub and decided to have a go.

There are plenty of people from the old days before all the madness who remember Bonehead. 'He was very musical. He can play anything,' they relate, while also talking about his legendary bonhomie and sense of humour.

Paul Arthurs, AKA Bonehead, was born 23 June 1965, the day before local heroes the Hollies hit number one with 'I'm Alive', which, with its huge yearning chorus, captured the aching hope of the sixties and the northern beat boom and was, perhaps, the last great hit from that era.

A few years later, he would be the oldest member of Oasis – a good six years senior to Tony McCarroll and even a couple of years older than Noel. His parents had moved from Mayo to Manchester. A smart lad, he attended St. Peter's Roman Catholic Grammar School in Prestwich and was a music obsessive. Already, in 1984, he had played keyboards in a band called Pleasure and Pain with his brother, Martin, on guitar and they were one of the earliest bands to rehearse at the Boardwalk.[2] It was also at the same time that he met his future wife, Kate. The younger Bonehead had a full head of hair but had already picked up his famous nickname on account of his cropped hair in a time of longer post-Beatle haircuts in his school days.

A fellow Anglo-Irish Manc Mike Joyce (not the Smiths drummer) remembers, 'I was good pals with Martin and I thought it would be him who would make it out of all of them because he was a quiet lad and he could really play.'

In 1985, after Pleasure and Pain split, he spent six months cycling and hopping trains around Europe with a mate and had returned to the UK to on/off dole and plastering jobs.

In the early nineties, and now a building contractor, Bonehead hadn't given up the band dream. Looking for potential band members he tried to corral mates into loose bands in the pubs he frequented such as the Packhorse on Stockport Road in Levenshulme. A proper boozer with banter, brawls and bitter, it was frequented by Guigsy and Chris Hutton and sometimes Noel Gallagher back from roadying on another Inspiral Carpets tour.

After a couple of years out of music, Bonehead was now inspired by the Stone Roses.

'I used to go to loads of gigs. The Haçienda had a local band night in the eighties. The Stone Roses were always influential to forming a band. We used to go and see them at the International which was owned by their manager Gareth, so they played there a lot. We actually tried to nick Reni when we didn't have a drummer in the eighties but he didn't want to know!'[3]

With their drinking residency at the Packhorse under threat with newly installed bouncers on the door, the motley crew moved to a new pub – the Milestone in Burnage – and set up there, gradually changing its culture to a more youthful zest.

The pub was full of this new noise and new attitude. Good tunes, good mates, good times. Chris Hutton would be singing along with New Order on the jukebox, someone had some spliff and Manchester vibes were in the area.

It was a logical step to have a go and form your own band. Anyone who had the bottle was inspired and you didn't need anyone's permission to create . . .

5

...AND SHINES

Coined by Factory Records' video directors Philip Shotton and Keith Jobling, the phrase 'Madchester' caught the mood of the city in 1990.[1] It was certainly in the area with the Stone Roses' Spike Island gig and their 'One Love' single, while the Happy Mondays were in their pop prime with 'Lazyitis' and 'Kinky Afro'. There was also a clutch of new bands on Factory like Northside and, perhaps, the greatest band of that period who somehow never made it, World of Twist.

Fronted by the charismatic Tony Ogden, World of Twist's stage shows were pure pop brilliance with the 'rock 'n' roll' spinning wheel, keyboard player MC Shells' outfits and the wacky slide show. They sounded fully formed and managed to twist (ha!) indie, with the talcum powder stomp of Northern Soul and a lysergic psychedelic pop and sounded like the next logical step after Madchester.

Of course, Noel Gallagher was a fan of their pulsating romp through the bric-a-brac of pop culture and so was his younger brother who was blown away by the launch gig for the band's debut *Quality Street* album at Manchester Ritz on 23 December 1990.

'World of Twist were a top band,' Liam later said of them. 'I remember going to see them at the Ritz. When we used to rehearse at the Boardwalk in Oasis, Tony [Ogden] used to come into our room, close the door and slide around the wall like in a spy movie as if we wouldn't notice him, and I would carry on singing. He would pick something up and I would think, "Why don't you walk past us and get what you wanted?" Top man. Top band. What a dude.'

In 1990 Madchester was in every area of the city including the local pub where a band formed around a few drinks, as Tony French remembers.

'We were in the Milestone and Bonehead had a conversation about forming a band. Chris Hutton said, "I'll be the singer" because he was a massive Ian Curtis fan and also into the Roses. Bonehead said he had a drum machine and he could programme it and because he was concentrating on playing guitar he asked if I would switch it on and off.'

Fresh back from a six-month stint running around Europe, Bonehead was looking for a new adventure and music was his life-blood. He liked playing things but didn't want to sing or write lyrics.

The initial idea aired, they decided to have a go. Overhearing the conversation, Guigsy took his chance and asked if he could be in the band as well, which was a bold move considering he could not play anything, so Bonehead resolved to teach him the bass.

A few days later they went to Johnny Roadhouse – the legendary guitar shop on Oxford Road in Manchester – to buy a bass.

Now they had a band. Sort of.

On arriving at Bonehead's to put the band together, Chris Hutton was ushered into a flat that looked like a bohemian treasure trove of musician lore filtered through a Mancunian street lens. There were instruments everywhere – all of which Bonehead could play – and souvenirs of recent travels created the perfect backdrop for band plans.

Bonehead got out his drum machine on which he knew how to programme varying versions of the iconic drum pattern on New Order's 'Blue Monday' and in the following weeks he taught Guigsy the basics of bass. They then rehearsed for a month in Guigsy's front room after being offered the space by his generous mother, shifting their musical equipment from house to house in Bonehead's Bonemobile that would become core to the story.

Those first months saw them write songs built around the guitar player's much superior musical skills, with the bass chugging along on the root note in the background and Chris Hutton's lyrics co-written with the bassist.

They then set up a proper rehearsal space in Chris Hutton's garage, creating a proverbial den and party central, which they called Club 061, after their initial band name, 061 – the then Manchester phone code until Guigsy pointed out that there must be a better name to work under. It wasn't long before Chris Hutton came up with another name for the band, the Rain, inspired by the famously damp local weather.

In the garage they honed the clutch of songs down in the fug of smoke now that there was a debut gig on the horizon.

'I was on the drum machine,' recalls Tony French, 'which was quite funny, because basically Bonehead pre-programmed it and all I had to do was press start and stop. Then after we had been rehearsing a few months we were ready in our heads to start doing a few gigs around the place.'

During rehearsals on 27 May the Stone Roses played their iconic Spike Island gig and they all had tickets and to mark the occasion they famously redecorated the Bonemobile.

'The night before Spike Island me, Guigsy and Bonehead painted the Stone Roses' Jackson Pollock-style artwork on the side of the

Bonemobile,' recalls Tony, 'and when we parked up at Spike Island there ended up being a photo of us all in front of the van which was all over the music press. It was an amazing day apart from the wind, the food and the sound! Ian Brown totally had it on stage. He was a god to a lot of people in Manchester. Everyone could see it like Liam did after the International.'

Post Spike Island and back down to earth, the new band needed a new rehearsal space as Club 061 had now been served a noise notice. Bonehead's brother Martin stepped in, letting them rehearse at his flat which was vacant after he had moved to Los Angeles to fix desks in recording studios. Martin would soon return for their debut gig at the Withington Bridge Club at a party for Chris Hutton's partner Jorja. The gig came complete with the band's first artwork – a Tony French designed poster that still had the band name 061 on it because no one had mentioned to him the name change! With an art background Tony was an asset to the band beyond switching the drum machine on and off and would go on to design the fledgling band's T-shirt and also artwork for the early Oasis.

First gigs are a mixture of excitement and nerves even for Bonehead who, even though he had played before in his other band, stood with his back to the audience with Guigsy trying to disappear into a corner. Aided and abetted by a few pints, Tony French tried to control the drum machine while Chris Hutton stepped up to the plate and threw himself around the stage for the three songs with his arms in the air in a version of mesmeric Ian Curtis's trance dance – the opposite approach to the 'stillism' that Liam Gallagher would bring to the mic a couple of years later.

With the first show out of the way in front of friends and family, the fledgling band played a clutch of other gigs, some half remembered and some long forgotten, all leading to their first gig proper, their big homecoming show in their madcap local, the Milestone. Now the word was out and everyone they had ever drunk with was in the pub to see what the band was all about, as Tony French describes.

'By 7pm on the Saturday night it was, I swear to God, busy as fuck. I've never seen a pub so packed to the rafters and I had to concentrate. Bonehead, Guigsy and Chris were squashed up by the hearth near the bar and I have the drum machine on a little table. Ridiculous!'

The gig went well. The raucous crowd embracing the band and their new cover of the Troggs' classic 'Wild Thing', which the singer had upgraded with weed-referencing lyrics that the 24-hour party people in the sweat-shod room obviously embraced.

'At a stretch we had about six songs and all I had to do was press stop at the end of each song,' recalls Tony, 'but I kept missing it and the drum machine would keep playing and Bonehead would yell, "Tony switch the fucking drum machine off!"'

'I guess I wasn't cut out to operate a drum machine, so after that gig, my fourth, I got fired! Guigsy said to me, "Learn the drums" but I'm not a drummer bashing around on the skins. That's not my thing and I was much happier doing the artwork for the band.'

The drum machine was only a stop gap. The band knew they needed a human drummer and looking around they realised that there was a drummer right in front of them . . . Tony McCarroll.

'Guigsy was the only one who knew Tony apart from me,' remembers Tony French, 'so he got in touch with him because he knew he played the drums in Irish bands in Levenshulme. They asked him along to the gig at the Milestone so my drum machine days were already numbered!'

The young drummer went to the gig and the rough and ready band making its noise in the tightly packed pub was exciting enough to make him want to join.

'They asked me to join and it was without a doubt that I said, "yes",' recalls McCarroll, 'and I jumped on board with them after seeing them play. Bonehead had already given Guigsy a crash course in bass and they sounded pretty good. Bonehead really could play, and they played a couple of covers and they had about seven of their own songs that Bonehead and Huts had written. Bonehead was the most impressive member of the band. He was already very musical and he could get a tune out of a radiator. There's nothing he couldn't play or get a version of some kind of tune out of. I think at some point he must have got some kind of schooling, some kind of musical education, whereas the rest of us didn't. We just picked up our instruments. I have been trying to play the drums since two or three years of age, and I'm still not there!'

The gig at the Milestone had also seen the band make another connection. The late Andy Rourke, the brilliant bass player from the Smiths, was then living in Burnage and a few years before the famous Oasis connection with Johnny Marr was made, the Rain had hooked up with a Smith.

They had spotted the affable Andy in the Milestone a couple of times and decided to approach him. Piling into the Bonemobile they went round to his house where the nervous young band knocked on the door and fumbled an introduction to the iconic bassist who had been so much part of their teenage soundtrack.

Andy Rourke was a beautiful soul and instead of blanking out the young band, he came to check out their packed gig at the Milestone. Post-gig he joined the band in the pub lock-in, still smiling at the show, and there was even talk of recording a demo with him.

With nowhere to rehearse again it was the support band from the Milestone and school mates, Reluctance, who suggested they room share rehearsal space in Stockport. A week later they moved into their first proper rehearsal space where they honed their songs down aided by their new rock-solid powerhouse drummer whose metronomic thud was now the key.

'We rehearsed for the next eight months,' says Tony McCarroll. 'It was a very simple approach. There was a lot of jamming . . . One really evident thing was the rhythm section. It was a solid, simple, punch in your face and I credit Bonehead for that and for the wall of sound that would become Oasis.' Mark Stagg worked at the rehearsal rooms, 'Rain were regulars at Noise rehearsal studios in Stockport, which was owned by John Breakell of Spirit fame. They were regulars there twice a week, Wed and Fri if I recall, 8pm–11pm, but always used to arrive at least an hour late with plenty of beer, and were a devil to get out at closing time! I'd knock on and tell them we were closing but they'd just open more beer. They always had that swagger I guess, a bit intimidating, but were always friendly with me and often just gave me a can to placate me. Nevertheless, when I'd arrive about 6pm I'd always look at the bookings and if I saw "Rain" I'd be like, oh bollocks!'

The band wrote a clutch of songs like 'Rooftop Rave' with lyrics from Guigsy and his sister Mary about the 1990 Strangeways Riot. The prison riot at the notorious Strangeways in Manchester resulted in the place getting trashed and all the drugs stolen from the hospital wing and then consumed by about 30 prisoners who sat on the roof for weeks. It created folk heroes out of rioters like ringleader Paul Taylor, from Birkenhead, who was serving a three-year sentence for theft, deception and assault and was often seen on the roof with his guitar. Along with other inmates they were now seen as almost Robin Hood like characters defying the law. After all-nighters, ravers would congregate outside the crumbling jail and shout encouragement to the prisoners as they danced on the precarious roof, defying the authorities with their own version of *Madchester Rave On*.[2]

At that time most of the songs were written by Bonehead and Chris Hutton, driven by Bonehead turning up his guitar to 10. Tony McCarroll was enjoying playing with this larger-than-life character.

'Bonehead was very smart and a real character,' remembers Tony. 'He was so funny, absolutely comical. What a guy. When we toured in Oasis, Bonehead and I shared hotel rooms throughout it all and it was always the best room to be in. He introduced me to things like red wine. He's quite cultured really! Until the red wine, or any kind of alcohol, kicked in and then he got louder and louder, and then he would be lying on the floor because he was one of those drunks whose legs would collapse!'

The summer's rehearsing had made a big difference. The tight and powerful young drummer had pulled it all together and the band were starting to sound pretty good and ready for their next gig that September in nearby Didsbury.

Now with a full line-up they took another trip to Johnny Roadhouse to get fully kitted up with drums, proper leads for the guitars and a ferocious new distortion unit that would crank Bonehead's guitar up towards the sound that would become his trademark.

They had yet another new rehearsal room that Guigsy had found at Raffles Hotel on Anson Road, round the corner from the International 2. The hotel came complete with a members' bar where the drinks were sort of free . . . and they jumped over the bar to help themselves. There were often mates coming to the rehearsals, including a much younger, cool-looking youth from Burnage who Tony French remembers.

'I met Liam before Noel when he came along to watch them rehearse in the basement of Raffles Hotel because Guigsy was going out with the woman who managed it. There were free drinks from the bar, and you could sleep in the rooms. We were all hanging out there for months.'

They now had just over a month to get ready for the next gig on 5 September at the Times Square pub in the well-heeled Didsbury village in south Manchester. They hyped up the gig by word of mouth and by selling 100 newly Tony French designed T-shirts emblazoned with the 'listen to the Rain' logo on it to create local buzz about the band. This was another step up for the fledgling group and in the audience was a friend of the band, Mike Joyce.

'I remember being on Chorlton Green one summer evening outside the pub with Bonehead who had been back from Europe for a few months and had got this band together,' recalls Mike. 'They were playing one of their first gigs in Didsbury, so we went down. I remember his brother Martin was more nervous than him and he wasn't even playing!'

The gig went well and now with the added power of a drummer and a full eight-song set. This included songs like 'All of You', 'Blues of Youth', 'Kinetic' and 'Black', and a rumoured cover of Joy Division's driving bass-driven 'No Love Lost' which would have made sense as a nod to the band's darker take on the Mancunian music legacy – a mix between Joy Division and the current baggy utopia – a kind of Perry Boy Division. The gig was a big jump forwards and the packed venue reciprocated.

Now with Martin taking over as manager of his brother's band, they grabbed some local press and another gig at Times Square on 31 October, which was again packed but marred by handbags in the crowd adding a bit of extra tension in the room.

Also in the audience that night was a young Liam Gallagher who had come to check the band out again, intensely watching the live band experience, looking at each member and then the singer.

Soaking it in.

A few weeks later Liam turned up at Raffles once more and watched the band rehearse, hanging out or huddling in a corner with Bonehead and Guigsy before splitting without saying much to Chris Hutton. Just another local face hanging out at rehearsals which were always social occasions with mates coming down, skinning up, drinking cans and messing about, while the band joined in or kicked a few songs around.

That autumn Martin, who repaired and fitted studio equipment, came up managerial trumps, blagging a free demo session at the Manchester city centre Out of the Blue Studios on Blossom Street in Ancoats. The studio was one of a small handful of key recording facilities in the city and built around a partnership between Nick Garside and Adam Lesser who had drummed in Cath Carroll's band, the Gay Animals. The studio was the core of the Madchester scene, and also bands like the Fall, 808 State and the Inspiral Carpets had recorded there.

The first time in a studio is never easy – the process exposes any new band's flaws and stifles performance. The recording engineer that day was David Scott who would also work with the band again later when they had morphed into Oasis. The session is documented in Chris Hutton's book *Don't Look Back in Anger*, and remembered very clearly by Scott, though the band themselves have no recollection of it. The demo has never surfaced, but Scott recalls:

'The studio asked me to do a production job as well as engineer the session,' says David. 'It was, as far as I know their first session and they were learning. It was difficult to know what the songs were like because the singer was inexperienced. As the producer you have to exploit what the strengths are. What came across was the simplicity of the drums and the bass and Bonehead's distinctive, really solid rhythm guitar which had this kind of stomping direct, fuck you attitude to it, which I think eventually contributed to the sound of Oasis.

'Bonehead was really buzzing about the way they were starting to sound in the studio and was up for ideas like "try this on the guitar" or a suggestion for an intro. I pointed out to Bonehead that the band needed a singer that suited them more because there was something in what they were doing musically, some potential.'

When the band needed some extra guitars a phone call was made to a mate of the band's from Burnage who appeared half an hour later.

David continues: 'This is quite interesting; Bonehead said that his mate was coming down to bring some guitars, and Noel Gallagher showed up with some extra guitars for them to use. Noel was one of those characters that once you meet him you remember him. He was working for the Inspirals at the time and he's quite a distinctive personality. He sat there for over an hour and commented on the tracks. He was very respectful while saying a few things and he thought it sounded great.'

David Scott did what he could and they demoed three tracks: 'Kinetic', 'All of You', 'Blues of Youth' and an unfinished version of 'Rooftop Rave', when they ran out of recording time and had to ditch the song so they could mix the other three tracks.

The first port of call with the demo was Tony Wilson – the maverick boss of Factory Records and champion of most things Manchester.

Bonehead knew which road he lived on in Withington, which was just on the other side of Fog Lane Park from Burnage. Guigsy also somehow knew what car Tony drove, so putting two and two together they drove round to his house and nervously knocked on the door and were surprised when Tony answered. Cold calling is always worth a try when your options are slim, but it doesn't always pay instant dividends. Tony Wilson told them to get the tape to Phil Saxe, his A&R [scout] at Factory Records, before closing the door.

Of course, it was a long shot and as much as they loved Factory's key bands they were not a fit for the label even if the mercurial boss had listened to the cassette. It was still early days, and they had a growing local following. Their Xmas 1990 show was at another venue in Didsbury called Squires, where they were again supported by their former rehearsal room buddies, Reluctance, and the gig cemented their burgeoning south Manchester local reputation.

Now it was time to get into the city centre. Just after Christmas Bonehead had driven into town and to the Boardwalk on Little Peter Street. The 400-capacity venue was the key touring and up-and-coming band venue in town. Getting a good support or even a headline show on one of those local band nights was a big jump at getting a band connected into the city's music scene.

Armed with the demo he walked in and spoke to Sue Langford from the Boardwalk, and he landed a gig at the venue a couple of weeks later on the Sunday 6 January local band night with long lost bands, Too Many Hands and Cut the Ice.

They didn't get the headline slot but the gig went well enough and they had a foot in the ever-busy city centre band world. Their Levenshulme crew created an atmosphere and were again joined by Liam and his mates. Also at the gig that night probably having a drink after rehearsing downstairs in the Boardwalk rehearsal rooms were Shaun Ryder joined by Andy Rourke supporting his local south Manchester band. Three weeks later the Charlatans made their debut at the club and sold it out – the next wave of Manchester bands was starting to come through and the Rain needed to up their game.

Needing a manager, they asked the former Smith if there was anything he could do, and he said he was willing to help. Calling the band round to his house for a meeting he said he had spoken to the late Mike Hinc who was the Smiths' gig agent and he was interested in having a listen. Andy said he was really keen to record a new demo of the band in his home studio. Thrilled, the band elected to record a song called 'Black', a darker piece, with music from Bonehead and lyrics from Guigsy reflecting on his melancholic side.

The demo was recorded in 1991 on DAT (Digital Audio Tape) but with drum loops and samples because they could not fit Tony's drum kit into the cellar of Andy's small house. During the session there was loose talk of extending the band's line-up to add some firepower to the sound. Apparently, Chris Hutton had suggested getting Noel Gallagher in on lead guitar. The band had a listen to the 1989 demos of his solo songs and didn't feel there was a fit and nixed the idea.

The new demo finished, it was sent to Mike Hinc who was impressed but suggested the band change their name to avoid confusion with the upcoming Liverpool band Rain who were emerging out of the La's and Real People scene at the time. They also managed to get played on Manchester's KFM Radio station[3] and get a plug for the next band show – again at the Boardwalk on 15 April. The April gig went well and the band were at the top of their game with new songs and hints at a more jangly guitar style nodding at the Roses. This combined with Tony McCarroll's punky Stephen Morris-style rolls, adding to the band's sound with an armoury of powerful and tight drumming.

Yet again, Liam Gallagher had shown up at the gig, and post-show there was a different vibe as he spoke to the band's bass and guitar players. Something was going on.

In the next couple of weeks Bonehead and Guigsy fudged the issue and avoided conversation with their singer. Something didn't feel right.

6

WE ARE THE ROAD CREW

Meanwhile Noel Gallagher had got himself on the road. After that momentous Stone Roses gig, he went to the Inspiral Carpets gig a week later and started helping out unpaid while still holding down his day job in town.

Graham Lambert remembers: 'Noel worked for the Kennedys Civil Engineering at the store handing out nuts and bolts. They had a boneyard where [Manchester arts centre] HOME is now. We used to go and see him after we had been rehearsing at the Boardwalk. One day a JCB dropped a section of gas mains pipe and broke his foot, so he had time off work, and would come with us to gigs on crutches.'

The broken foot meant downtime to hone his guitar playing and songwriting and at some point in late 1988 he recorded his first demo tape. The eight tracks were recorded on Peacock Grove in Gorton, Manchester with a mystery person called Pete who had advertised in the *Manchester Evening News* for people to record/ work with.

'He had a little 4-track and we wrote these songs together,' recalls Noel. 'I remember playing the demo tape to people and the over-riding reaction was a look of surprise: "Fucking hell, is this what you do?"'[1]

The 'Noel's Tunes' recordings may be under lock and key now, but the following year he re-recorded some of the songs for his second solo demo, and the surviving recordings give a rare insight into his earliest music making.

The songs are driven by a brisk acoustic guitar with an occasional electric on top picking out the melodies and sometimes a keyboard playing the bass lines. There is already a degree of lyrical and musi-cal sophistication that marked him out as a singer-songwriter of some promise with a wit and sensitivity which to a certain extent he continued throughout Oasis in his parallel B-sides to the band's anthemic A-sides.

It was also the start of his demo-making process that contin-ued for each Oasis album – carefully preparing songs for future recording. 'What's It Got To Do With You?' is a brisk acoustic guitar-driven song of yearning for escape that asks if there is 'another world'; 'I Didn't Think So' laments a lost relationship with a Johnny Marr strum; and 'England' gives a nod to the Jam and even Billy Bragg in perhaps the most political Noel ever got in his songwriting; while 'Gotta Have Fun' sounds like an acoustic take on the Jam.

'No Cause for Alarm' is a feistier number with layers of guitar freak-outs, while 'BAj', which Noel once claimed was the first song he had ever written when he was 13, is a neatly cynical song about rock stars wearing badges for a cause – hence the title. While 'I Am the Man' reflects the songwriter's sometimes more introspective side and 'Womb to Tomb' was a song of defiance until the grind of life kicks in.

In July the Inspiral Carpets released a new EP *Keep the Circle Around* on Playtime Records before vocalist Stephen Holt announced he was leaving. He played his last gig with the band on

15 December at the Cricketers in London with Jesus Jones supporting, before moving on to his own band the Rainkings. The band
now needed a new singer and Graham Lambert called their some-
time roadie.

'At the time, he was the scally kid with the broken leg from
Burnage that used to hang out with us and help with the gear,'
recalls Clint Boon, the Inspirals' keyboard player. 'We had not
really heard him sing apart from the demo of his own songs, but he
was a friend and a fan and he was one of the first people who said
he wanted to audition.'

A few weeks earlier Graham had mentioned the aspiring musi-
cian to another local band, Intastella, who were looking for a guitar
player as band member Martin Mittler remembers: 'When Craig
Gannon left to join the Smiths, Graham said, "Try out our roadie.
He's really good. He can play all our songs", but we thought
Inspirals tunes are not that hard to play so Noel missed out there!'

Intriguingly, also in that flux of pre-fame musicians a pre-Char-
latans Tim Burgess had been mentioned for the vacant role but
never auditioned. Noel recalls: 'Graham rang and said, "You know
the tunes do you want to audition?" I thought, "Wow! Fucking hell
I can be the singer!" I had never sung live before but they thought
I knew the songs and obviously I must have looked the part!'

Just before Christmas on the night of the Lockerbie bombing on
21 December 1988, Noel set off from Burnage to Guide Bridge
Mill, Ashton-Under-Lyne to audition, taking three different buses
on the epic trip to the edge of Greater Manchester.[2]

'I went down to their rehearsal room at the Mill. It was fucking
miles away. It was on a real dark winter's night and I'd never been
that far out of town in my fucking life 'he jokes,' I met Graham at
the bus stop and went to the room. They were talking to me like I
was a professional audition expert. They said, "What do you want
to do?" I said, "I haven't got a fucking clue!" I only asked him for a
copy of the Roses tape and now I'm here! I was winging it. They

assumed I was a musician but all I am is a glorified glue-sniffing pothead from Manchester! The first song we did was "Gimme Shelter" by the Rolling Stones, so I shouted my fucking head off then I did a few of their tunes.'

The small room in the old mill then bounced to Inspirals' songs 'Keep the Circle Around', 'Butterfly', 'Garage Full of Flowers', 'Whiskey' and 'Love Can Never Lose Its Own' – and maybe 'Seeds of Doubt' and 'Commercial Rain'.

Noel continues: 'I remember it was quite alright but they didn't say yes immediately, which is always a bad sign, although I didn't know that then. They obviously thought he's obsessed with music and a good lad who doesn't wear a Megadeth T-shirt but he's not the singer, but let's keep him on the road with us. Which is what they did and I looked after their equipment for years. Me, Graham and Clint really got on and it was a great chance to suss out how to be in a band. I was around managers, agents, record company people, journalists, and I would just sit there and just take it all in.'

It was Tom Hingley from perennial support band Too Much Texas – who had one good single played by John Peel – who passed the audition. He was not only classically trained but could also do the punkier singing and he made it his own with his voice being on all the hits. Meanwhile Noel, who ironically for a roadie couldn't drive, was now on the pay roll.

'Graham asked me to be his guitar roadie proper and I was like fuck yeah! I had to learn on the hoof. I remember changing strings on the guitar and Graham said, "You don't half put them on fucking weird!" I was like, "Aaargh, I hope it stays in tune!" I just winged it at first. I hadn't told them this because I just wanted to do it. All Manchester roadies were the same. They were just people's mates!'

Also on the crew was Mark Coyle who had graduated to the Inspirals from his own local band Wild Strawberries.

Noel again: 'On the first night of the tour I met their monitor engineer Mark Coyle and we shared a room.[3] Years later he would end up co-producing Oasis. Every gig we set the gear up and before the band did their soundcheck he would get on the drum kit and I would play Graham's guitar. One day he said, "Those are fucking great chords, you should write a song round them" and that was where that original thing came from. He also helped come up with the drum intro for "Live Forever".'

Noel was always more than a roadie. More like a sixth member of the band he had his own take on their look with an upgrade on Clint Boon's iconic bowl cut and Paisley patterned shirts that reflected the band's home-spun garage psychedelia. Every Manchester band at the time had the 'cool mate' like the Happy Mondays with Bez, who Shaun Ryder had brought into the band at the second gig to dance in front of him so he didn't have to be the frontman. The Stone Roses had Cressa who danced on stage and changed the effects pedals. He also brought the bottle-green flared cords into the band's wardrobe and helped change their image into the classic style.

'Noel was always more than a roadie really,' explains Graham Lambert, 'and we would bounce ideas off him because he always had an opinion. Like, even at the audition when he told us he didn't like the words on "Whiskey". When we'd write a new song we would play the cassette in the office to get an unofficial seal of approval and if he liked it that was a plus. Also, he knew people in town. He would be playing us a white label of the Roses or the Mondays before it came out and if he liked our new song then he'd tell other people. He could also play every instrument really well and nearly stepped in on drums for a tour once when our drummer Craig [Gill] couldn't make it.'

An astute organiser and business-minded musician, Clint Boon was a good mentor. He had set the Inspiral Carpets up with Graham Lambert and they were actually making it work on their own terms. They may not have had the cool of the Mondays or the Roses, but their trump card was their knack of writing brilliant pop singles and they were very much part of the scene, as Mancunian music head John Brice, who tried to sign them when he was working in A&R for CBS/Epic, recalls:

'"Madchester" was all kicking off and there was word about a band from Oldham called the Inspiral Carpets. Just the name made me like them, it made you think of sixties psychedelia like Strawberry Alarm Clock or the Chocolate Watchband. The first London venue I saw them at was tiny, sweating and jumping. They had a big swirling organ sound and an outrageously tight drummer who I was told was only 15. They also had rousing choruses and the band name flashing up from a projector and it was the perfect mix of sixties and what was going on now.

'They had a manager called Anthony and a roadie called Noel, but he was much more than a roadie. He was the guy that kept it all ticking. I'd pop up into their management office in Manchester and Noel was always there on the phone. They were knocking out EPs which all went straight to number one in the independent charts and the venues were growing in size, the merch was already going insane with the "cool as fuck" cow T-shirts, which was a masterstroke in marketing because they didn't even need the band name on them. I saw Noel go out one night and confront the T-shirt bootleggers. I don't know what he said but they packed up and got off and that took some front.'

Liam Walsh worked for Inspiral Carpets on the T-shirts.

'I printed the first "cool as fuck" T-shirts for Clint and went on tour with the band as their merchandise person, where they famously made more money from their T-shirts.

'Noel worked for the Inspirals at the same time as a roadie, and we had a brilliant time touring worldwide.

'I ended up working at the Boardwalk, where Rain/Oasis rehearsed downstairs. I saw the band regularly, as most bands would come to the bar and watch whoever was playing at the venue upstairs.'

In September Noel recorded a new demo of songs with Mark Coyle, now his key musical collaborator. They worked on acid house side projects and ambient film scores that were never released, filtering the ideas through Coyley's psychedelic mind and deep understanding of rock culture from reading every book out there.

'Coyley was really encouraging,' explains Noel. 'He would say, "You're pretty good man" but I had no ambitions to be in a group. I thought I'd arrived being a roadie. I remember going to see a careers officer when I was leaving school and saying I wanted to be in the music business and him saying no! And I would say that's all I'm interested in. He was trying to get me a job in a guitar shop and even that would have done me, it's all I'm good at!'

The new Noel demos had one new song, 'But What If', which rushes along with brisk acoustics and poetic vocal lines that mix a sardonic humour with a melancholic twist. Maybe re-recorded from the previous demo, 'No Cause for Alarm' was now called 'Hey You'. 'What's It Got To Do With You?' and 'Gotta Have Fun' retain a Johnny Marr sense of melody; the latter is a song of self-affirmation about trying to have fun despite the odds and underlines an already sophisticated songwriter using exotic chords like Em7, or Dsus2. 'I Didn't Think So' is now called 'What's Been Happenin'' and details a chance meeting between old lovers before ending on an exquisite acoustic guitar solo.

With a proper job in music Noel was earning enough to move out of Burnage and into the city centre, to India House on Whitworth Street, with his partner Louise Jones (with whom he was in a relationship for six years). Louise was part of the inner core of the fledgling new Manchester with her engaging personality, and was a well-known face from her job at the desk of New Mount Street before working for local promoter Simon Moran's SJM in their earliest days.

Now at the centre of the local scene of bands, roadies, labels, managers and creatives, Noel would be everywhere in the city. He would have happily spent all his life as the star roadie.

'Manchester was great because there was a community and a lot of creative people in the city,' he says. 'Everything that dropped out of the sky came to Manchester. When I worked with the Inspirals I thought this is my bit in the music thing, I get to travel the world, set up guitar amps and take loads of fucking drugs. That will do me!

'I would be sitting in Buenos Aires and the Carpets would be doing a festival with Paul Simon and the Cult – what a bill! I would be sitting with Billy Duffy and I was just a roadie and we were all out of it and I was thinking, "This is the life! It doesn't get any better than this! I get paid 300 quid a week to travel the world to lug stuff in and out of venues. It's a mind-blowing job." Little did I know what was coming!'

'Everyone was working very hard and Noel was part of a small entourage we went around with,' remembers Tom Hingley. 'He was young, very bright and very funny, and even if I was from down south and we came from different places we got on. There was a lot about him. I would speak to him a lot when I used to give him a lift home. He was a face on the scene, but the one thing about him that was different from the other iconic scene people at the time like Cressa was that Noel had a massive musical talent and that led him to do Oasis.'

7

FROM RAIN TO OASIS

There often comes a time in a band when the blurred line between mates making a noise and having to make sacrifices causes all manner of pain. Whatever the pros and cons of the decision to dump Chris Hutton and replace him with Liam Gallagher, the band felt like some kind of change was needed if they were going to proceed.

Tony McCarroll explains: 'Bonehead already had that Oasis wall of sound with his guitar, and Chris was doing the Ian Curtis swinging the microphone up in the air thing and basically everyone else didn't get what he was trying to do. So, when the opportunity came up with Liam the band jumped at it. This was tough for us. I totally respect Chris Hutton but there was something not quite right. We needed something else if we were going to try and make it.'

Every band goes through these fluctuations as they stumble towards their 'classic' line-up and it's often not a deliberate slight on the members that don't get to the finishing line.

In the past couple of months Liam Gallagher had spotted a vehicle for his ambition. He was younger and newer to rock 'n' roll than the others, but since the Roses gig in May 1988 it had been nagging at him.

'Liam wanted to be a singer since being hit over the head with a hammer outside school and then seeing the Stone Roses,' comments Tony French. 'It made him see his future.'

Local face Paul 'Bigun' Ashbee was also manoeuvring.

'"Bigun" was pretty important to the band then,' recalls Tony McCarroll. 'He was the one that spotted a lot of things that were going on, like that we needed a different singer. He said, "Look, I know a singer, this guy who sits in his bedroom but he looks the part and he works for me as a valet." So he pushed Liam into the band.'

Liam had been going on to 'Bigun' about how he was a singer and he was going to be a star so when 'Bigun' heard that the band were looking for a singer he pushed Liam at them. As Ashbee told the *Manchester Evening News*. 'When it came to music Liam was a shy and unassuming lad. He needed someone to put the belief in. I gave him the passion to audition for Bonehead's band.'[1]

Liam agrees: 'I kind of just knew I could do it. I went to see the Rain in Didsbury; it left me buzzing. I knew Guigsy and Bonehead. They lived up the road. I mean, the music wasn't any good, but they asked me to audition. . . . So I went and had a little singsong. . . . In the back of my head that day I knew that if I could get in there, I could go back to our kid, who'd been writing a shit load of songs, and see if he could join as well and then we'd be a top band.'[2]

Just like Noel a couple of years before, Liam set off for an audition.

'Calling it an audition makes it sound more big time than it was,' remembers Tony McCarroll. 'Everyone agreed that we needed a new singer and we needed to see what Liam was all about. He had been to see us play and we knew he had the looks, the presence, the clothes, the haircut and the trainers, so we arranged for him to go to my flat on Ryton Avenue in Gorton for an audition.

There was nothing in there apart from a pair of bongos from the Inspiral Carpets and a one-string bass.

'Liam turned up with "Bigun" who had been pushing for him to join and was quieter than usual. Normally, he was full of insults and humour, but he seemed nervous. Understandably.

'Me and Bonehead started jamming and "Bigun" literally pushed Liam into the room because, believe it or not, Liam had taken a bit of persuasion to come and do the audition. Jumping on to the mic for him wasn't easy and he needed some reassurance.

'He must have been stood there thinking what are these all about? I think he wanted to be in a band and this was the only band that he knew so he put up with it. Bonehead played the one-string guitar and I played the bongos because my drums were in the rehearsal room. The audition was chaotic, but we ended up with Liam, who was born to be a frontman.

'He looked the part of course. Brown cords ripped at the knee, a denim shirt, desert boots and smart hair. We used to say he was the walking wardrobe. You could hang anything on him and he looked good in it. He had a total presence and was a real character and we were going, "He's fucking brilliant!" A friend of mine worked with him at Holmes pies in Levenshulme and Liam would say, "I'll be out of here soon. I'm going to be a rock star," and everyone laughed but he knew it. There's no denying that since he had seen that Stone Roses gig at the International that Ian Brown was an early influence. People would sometimes shout "Ian Brown" at him walking down the street and he didn't like that. 'Liam looked the part but the aggravation he caused!' smiles Tony McCarroll, adding 'But that's rock 'n' roll and it worked for the band.'

A few days later, Guigsy and Bonehead called Chris Hutton from a telephone box and broke the bad news. It was especially awkward as they were all mates, but the band had to come first even if it broke these ties.

Tony French recalls the uneasy period soon after: 'I was actually in Guigsy's bedroom getting stoned when Chris called round shortly after, trying to start the band again after the call and when he knocked on, his mother told Chris that Guigsy wasn't in.'

Chris Hutton was out of the band he had helped to form and had been replaced with Liam Gallagher. While the Rain would not have become the Oasis juggernaut without the Gallaghers, the early line-up were moving in an interesting direction and they had a niche that could have worked in a cult kind of way: a council estate take on Joy Division dealing in a dark side you could dance to.

Over the next few weeks the band changed its singer and also its name. As ever there are a few different versions of the story of when and where the new name came from. Noel remembers that Liam had taken it from a tour poster on his shared bedroom wall of a 28 April 1991 Inspiral Carpets gig at Swindon Oasis Leisure Centre.

'Originally the band he joined were called the Rain and I was like, that's the shittest name for a band ever plus there's already another band called Rain,' remembers Noel. 'I had this poster on my wall at home of the Inspiral Carpets tour dates and he took it from there. Later on I said to Liam don't fucking take that, not from the Oasis centre when you can use a name like the Underground Market where they sell really cool trainers. He wouldn't have it and said Oasis sounds miles better. In my own head we're the Underground Market but in his we're a leisure centre in Swindon.

'So it became Oasis. Funnily enough in the scene of that period of time that we would be famed for everybody had one name for their bands – Blur, Pulp, Suede . . . but we didn't know this then.'

That spring of 1991 the new line-up started to rehearse for a debut gig at the Boardwalk coming up in August. Raffles had been a laugh, with access to the bar and hotel rooms, but the lads had overstayed their welcome. Paul Gallagher stepped in and got them a new rehearsal room at the Grove in Longsight, as Mike Joyce explains: 'Paul Gallagher, who we called Bod, used to DJ there and had asked the manager Liam Dennehy about using the space at the back.'

Just round the corner from the Carousel Club, the Grove at the time was an Irish bar with a 400-capacity venue where people would get married or where showbands and singers like Brendan Shine[3] would play. It was also where many of the local Irish community would have a drink and inevitably the Gallaghers, Bonehead and Tony McCarroll would hang out.

'I used to manage the Grove Club in Longsight and Bod was a regular,' Dennehy explained to Kyle Dale. 'All the lads used to come in and one day Bod said any chance the band could use the cabaret stage to rehearse because it's got a mixing desk and a PA. So, for about a month they would come in on a Tuesday night when no one was in and set up and give us a tenner to cover the cost. I would serve them a couple of bottles of beer and they would rehearse.'

'When I started going out drinking as I got older, Paul [Gallagher] would be on the Irish scene and I knew him from there,' remembers Tony McCarroll. 'He had connections to the Grove. It wasn't too far to get our gear down there and set up. When the barman had gone we would grab some lagers and smoke certain substances! It was mayhem from the word go and we were a band that had the chaos.'

For the few weeks that the new line-up rehearsed there the new singer was gung-ho with his new band, working up a few new tunes with Bonehead that saw the band move to a more pronounced Stone Roses style. It was beginning to fall into place until one of the staff noticed the scent of marijuana hanging in the air. He reported it to the venue owner who was surprised to learn that the band was rehearsing in his club and asked them to leave.

'I was going to give them their debut gig on a Sunday night,' remembers Dennehy, 'but the owner of the gaff, Michael Costello, came down and said that the Gallaghers have made a right mess so get rid of them. I think it was because Bod grated on him as he was noisier than Noel and Liam put together. I said I'm putting a gig on with them. They're not going to get anywhere but I'll give them a go, but he said tell them to practise somewhere else. A few months later Bod comes in and he gives me the first demo and some badges as a thanks for letting them practise and said, "They are going to be the biggest band in the world." I just laughed but they are laughing now. Somebody saw something in them but it wasn't me.'[4]

Homeless again the band needed a new rehearsal space, and finally made the move to the city centre when Bonehead found a room at the Red House rehearsal rooms in Ancoats where many local bands practised. This was a step up as proper bands rehearsed in city centre rehearsal rooms. The Red House might have been dingy but it hummed with the noisy throbbing heartbeat of Manchester's premier culture.

'When we started in town it was a case of whoever was last out had to sit in the back of Bonehead's pickup,' remembers Tony McCarroll. 'It was probably not legal swerving around at 10 o'clock at night on the back waving at people.'

Sometimes Liam mentioned it would be good to bring his brother into the band in some role, maybe as a manager, but Noel was away a lot on tour with the Inspiral Carpets. It was now only a matter of weeks before their debut gig with their new singer at the Boardwalk on 18 August 1991. This time it wasn't a local bands night but supporting a proper touring band who had a bit of a buzz about them, a band from Birmingham called Sweet Jesus.

8

TAKE ME

It was Thursday 16 May 1991 and the Inspiral Carpets were playing Munich Theatre Fabric. After the soundcheck Noel phoned home.

'I make my weekly call home. I say to my mam, "I'm in Munich" and she goes, "Where?" I said, "In Germany" and then I ask what's Liam up to and she says, "Oh he's in a band . . . "

'And I say, "What!? He's the singer in a band!?? What band? Who?" It was literally like the last thing I expected to hear. The most shocking thing she said was that he was in a band with Paul McGuigan. I said, "What? Guigsy? He's constantly stoned and he hasn't got a clue what he's playing!" I then said this is something I've got to fucking see when I get back from the tour.

'I didn't even know Liam was into music. He had no records. Nothing. So it was a complete "what!" When we used to share a bedroom I would be sitting around playing guitar all night and never once had he seemed interested!

'His mates would all be going out doing mad shit and I would be staying in smoking draw and playing guitar and they would be like, you fucking weirdo playing guitar!

'The thing with Liam is that he always looked the part. Always. Even to this day he takes that long to make a move because he's got to be utterly convinced it's the right move so that he doesn't look a cunt. So I was thinking if he's in this band, they've got to have something because he would not make a cunt out of himself.'

After the phone call Noel returned to the venue bemused and intrigued, mentioning Liam and his new band to the Inspirals with his mind ticking it over . . .

A couple of months later, the debut gig of the newly christened Oasis was upon them. In fact they were so newly christened that they were still called the Rain on some of the advertising. It was four months since their last gig at the same venue and much had changed.

The headline band, Sweet Jesus, were a buzz band at the time, and hardworking local band the Catchmen were second on the bill with Oasis opening. Signed to Rough Trade, Sweet Jesus's shoegaze-tinged indie psych was getting a buzz. Roy Priest, the band's guitarist, remembers the gig.

'We got a review from Ian McGregor which was not that bad although there was no mention of the support band. I remember seeing Clint Boon at the gig, no doubt he was with Noel, but I wouldn't have recognised him then. Our drummer, Paul, chatted to Tony McCarroll about sharing kits. I vaguely remember Liam but have no recollection of their soundcheck or set.'

Sweet Jesus singer Ben Bentley smiles. 'I don't remember Liam doing any of the swaggering around he'd soon become known for. There was no "let's fuckin' have it" yet. He was like a big puppy backstage, bounding around, dead charming and enthusiastic, asking questions about music and about getting on. Musically they seemed a bit unsure and unsteady. A bit baggy, a bit beat group. Except minus the beat.

'Liam looked great, though. Those big doe eyes were always going to bring the world to its knees. If only they had the tunes – which, of course, they very soon would have.'

Oasis's first gig was, as expected, a band trying to find its way with a new singer. They shuffled on to the stage a touch nervous and played three songs, 'Alice', 'Take Me' and 'Reminisce', with 'Alice' getting played twice after they had fluffed it. In front of them adding to the nerves was Noel and the Inspiral Carpets, and some other faces from the local music scene in among the 40 or 50 people checking them out.

Noel recalls: 'I was back in Manchester and they've got this gig so I go and see them with the Inspiral Carpets who had come to see "Noel's brother's band".

'Liam gets on stage and it's like, "Wow!" He's a fucking singer and the lights were on him and even if it's the Boardwalk on a Tuesday to about 11 people, there's still sound coming out of the speakers and it's like, "Fucking hell! That's my brother on stage!" I thought, "Fucking hell, they are really good." They did "Take Me", which Liam and Bonehead had written, which was actually pretty good and which they steadfastly for the next 20 years refused to record. I went to see them backstage afterwards and said, "That was really fucking good." They asked me to be their manager and I said, "I'm not a manager – get a proper manager. I'm not being a fucking manager so that's that." But I was thinking maybe I could join and bring my songs in . . . '

Noel may have ostensibly been there to check his younger brother's band, but with an armoury of songs and the clock ticking away maybe this was the opportunity. Being a roadie for the Oldham band was a cosy number, but as he watched Oasis play their debut gig that night all manner of ideas must have been running through his head. Even if he wasn't going to say it too loud there was something about Liam that worked and the band made a good noise. Maybe it was time to make a move, as Alison Bell, who ran the PR company Red Alert and who went to the gig with Noel and Louise Jones, remembers.

'We went to a lot of gigs together and one day Noel said, "Oh, do you want to come and see Liam, he's in a band." So we popped round the corner from India House where we all lived to the Boardwalk. When they came on stage the first thing we thought was that Liam has got real stage presence. That was evident even then.'

That night, somewhere on the way home on Little Peter Street or Whitworth Street, Oasis proper was born. Walking back to India house, Noel confided in Alison, as she recalls: 'The tunes were a bit messy and everything but they obviously had something, and when the three of us left the gig Noel said, "What do you think?" and I said, "Liam has got great stage presence but the songwriting could be improved." And Noel said, "I've been writing loads of songs, and I think I might join the band and give them my songs and take it from there."

'I said, "Why not? Good idea . . . " because I knew that Noel could play loads of instruments, but I didn't realise he had written many songs although I think Louise had told me that he was song-writing on the side.'

Noel pondered his future. Here was a rough and ready-made vehicle for his songs and his brother definitely looked the part. But maybe at 24, he thought, he was already too old to start going through the process of getting a band together – the painstaking hiring and firing, and seeking out the right players. Far better to find a ready-made band, especially one with an inbuilt good, tight and raw sound giving your songs a genuine edge – like David Bowie had done when he brought Mick Ronson and the Rats down from Hull to add the rock and the roll to Ziggy back in the early seventies.

That night in the Boardwalk Noel saw a future. The band certainly made a good noise but they just needed the songs.

He was still pondering when he bumped into Alison again.

'A few weeks after the gig he said to me, "What do you think of the name Oasis?" I said that sounds good but there's a girl's clothes shop called Oasis. It also makes me think of duos with keyboards, rather than the guitar band, but I said it is a really good name for a band.'

And yet he didn't join straight away. Noel was like a cat, calculating the best option. He had a vision, contacts and songs which the band needed, even if it meant them giving up a measure of their control. What happened that autumn was by osmosis.

With Noel hovering around, not quite decided what course of action he was going to take, the rest of the band went to record their first demo proper as Oasis at Out of the Blue Studios in the autumn of 1991. In the session they recorded three Liam/Bonehead songs, 'Alice', 'Reminisce'[1] and 'Take Me', that are a rare glimpse into the pre-Noel Oasis.

The songs have a surprising complexity for a new band, with almost baroque arpeggios and guitar lines from Bonehead and a rock-solid rhythm section far more together than most bands at this stage. Liam hasn't quite nailed his classic voice yet and sounds closer to the Ian Brown school and there are moments when the whole band has a shade of the sixties psyche pop of the Inspiral Carpets to them. 'Alice', also known as 'She Always Comes Up Smiling', has a Manc shuffle beat and a chiming acoustic guitar with the garage flowers shuffle of the Inspirals. 'Reminisce' has a long intro and is more of the same style, while the standout track is 'Take Me' which has a Manc psyche rush.

'We were doing the demo as a four-piece before Noel had properly joined,' Tony McCarroll points out, adding, 'He was in the background obviously as Liam's brother but he was away a lot with the Inspiral Carpets. We had been rehearsing and we decided to do some demos. Bonehead's brother Martin had been doing some work at Out of the Blue Studios in Manchester city centre and he said if you plaster the studio they will give you a day or two recording for free. That was gold to us. Bonehead was a plasterer, so he turns up with his famous spirit level that hasn't got a bubble in it and we got to "work", well not quite "we" as Liam was a typical frontman. He didn't even make cups of tea and he sat there annoying everybody!'

While they were rehearsing in the Red House they got a visit from Noel, as the then roadie remembers:

'After the Boardwalk gig Liam had said come and jam with us and I said I can't be arsed. They used to rehearse every Sunday at the Red House. It was a real shithole where all the band's gear was in one lock-up and if somebody's amp got nicked then a band would just nick somebody else's amp because, in Manchester, two wrongs do make a fucking right!'

'Then one Sunday Liam knocked on when they were passing my flat, and said, "Come on for fuck's sake!" So I went down and played along to the four songs that they had. I set my gear up and I'm bashing away in there sat on my amp before anything starts. They then start playing their tunes and I start playing along and it suddenly dawned on me that they were all stood up apart from the drummer and I was sat down. Bonehead says, "Have you not got a guitar strap?" I then realised that I had never played guitar stood up! I had always played in the soundchecks sat on the drum riser and it really freaked me out getting a guitar strap on and standing up!'

Bonehead remembers things slightly differently: 'Noel was touring with the Inspiral Carpets, and he had got wind we were in a band. He said to Liam, "Can I come down to rehearsal and have a bit of a jam with you?" We were like, "Yeah, not a problem. Send him down."'[2]

That day Graham Lambert had returned roadie favours for Noel. 'I remember giving Noel a lift to the Red House with his gear. It was just by our office at New Mount Street north of the city centre.

It was a total dump – really damp and run down and not the sort of place you would want to leave your gear.'

Little by little Noel was gradually joining, cajoled by his brother.

'Then in the next weeks, Liam said, "You've got the fucking tunes, let's do them." Then we did this instrumental of "Columbia" and that's when the light came on. Not long after that, in January, they had a gig at the Boardwalk, and they were like, "Are you doing it or what?"'

Tony McCarroll recalls the process: 'He gradually came on board and it just developed. He then said, "I've got a few songs, shall we have a jam through them?" We then put our heads down and it worked. I don't know exactly what he was thinking, but he had an arsenal of songs and there were a lot of gems and he just perfectly fitted in.'

Liam knew. 'I'd been sharing a room with him for God knows how many years so I'd heard what he was writing. I knew how good he was, how good we could be. And we were. It happened. It began.'[3]

There was no big decision. No big moment. Just a gradual process, as Bonehead points out: 'Noel's got a heap of attitude, but he didn't walk in like "I've got these songs so I'm taking control . . ." We spent a couple of weeks jamming. It was more a case of, "Is it OK if I join your band?" "Well – yeah." It was a bunch of mates making a racket.'[4]

Noel laughs. 'I don't know what Bonehead was thinking. I think our Liam had bigged me up properly like I was the roadie from the Inspiral Carpets and I had an "in". I remember them having songs which they had played at the gig and I then started playing the songs that me and Coyley had been messing around with. The moment they all joined in I thought this is going to be fucking brilliant.

'I then took the Paul McCartney role of the saying, "Play it like this." They were sat there going you got to join the band! This is fucking brilliant! I said in a tongue-in-cheek way years ago that I came in and said I was taking over, and it wasn't quite like that.

'I had so many other bits of chords that were already there, so if anybody was going to write one song a week I was going to write five a day and they were all better than their songs. It was like let's do another one, which was even better than the last one, and at that point people stopped saying, "Well I've got a tune . . ."'

Later in autumn 1991 the band went to the 8-track studio at the Cutting Rooms in the Abraham Moss centre in Crumpsall, Manchester and recorded their second demo – only this time it was as a full five-piece. The result was a sonic jump forward towards the band's more classic sound, with this session being the bridge between the early Rain/Oasis hybrid and the more fully fledged Noel vision of the band.

It's fascinating to hear the development in the sound in the few weeks since their last demo. 'Colour My Life' has slowed the pace down and is a move away from the kick and rush of much indie towards the classic slower tempo of Oasis. The lead guitar has genuine hooks while the vocal is more measured and less baggy. It's the same with 'See the Sun', where there is more attitude to the vocal and hookier guitar lines. The new version of Bonehead and Liam's 'Take Me' is given an extra flavour by the great lead line that vamps up the guitar from the previous demo.

The demo was sent to venues and local media. A few weeks later, on 22 October, *Uptown* magazine gave them their first interview written by Steve Cowell and conducted with Noel, Guigsy and Liam. For the first time Noel was named as one of the guitarists and it was accompanied by their first ever full line-up photoshoot by Steve Manford a few days later behind Noel's India House flat on Whitworth Street.

The perceptive piece pointed out 'Oasis will succeed. They've got what it takes. They have arrogance that is genuine rather than cosmetic. I'll just suggest that Oasis are going to be the next big thing to happen in Manchester music . . . ' With Liam quoted as saying: 'It's happening right now for us. There's gonna be a new movement that's got little to do with music but lots to do with attitude, maybe a kind of punk revival. Let's face it, the press have mocked Manchester music to death. They jump on the bandwagon but don't have the intelligence to know when to jump off.'

Decades later Steve Cowell remembered. 'I was the first person in the world to interview Oasis back in 1991 for *Uptown* magazine. We met in Monroes Hotel on London Road near Noel's.

'Guigsy, Noel and Liam showed up. Liam had just been to sign on the dole. Noel was fine and Liam . . . well Liam is just Liam. He had belief in himself and the band. He told me they were going to be the next biggest thing to hit the Manchester music scene. I guess he was right!!!!! Nobody, and I mean nobody, cared about Oasis back in 1991.'[5]

The demo was also reviewed in the Christmas 1991 issue of Manchester listings magazine *City Life* by music editor Chris Sharratt who gave it a fair review. 'Take Me' was described as, ' . . . urgent and weird, sort of Inspirals on psychedelics.' 'Colour My Life' was described as '[going] for the dramatic build-up here, first acoustic guitar, then pattering drums and bass, then vocals. A bit nasally in places, sort of like Dermo from Northside but with a cold. In fact, the whole song is in that Northside vein. Interesting, but I'm not too excited.'

The demo was getting around, as Paul Ashbee told the *Manchester Evening News*. 'We were washing cars at Manchester United one day and I heard Liam chatting to David Beckham. They were arguing about music, Liam was telling Becks that the music he had in his car was crap. He tried to hand him a tape of Oasis's music saying, "We're going to be the biggest band in the world." I was laughing but I knew he was right.'[6]

9

NEW MOUNT STREET

In early 1991 the Inspiral Carpets had moved to their new office at 23 New Mount Street, which at the time was the epicentre of the village Manchester pop powerhouse.

The echoing corridors of the former the Co-operative Printing Society building resounded to most of Manchester's key players like James, the Charlatans, Mark E Smith's Cog Sinister label, Johnny Jay... artists, DJs, designers, and Liam Walsh's T-shirt company that made the Inspiral Carpets' classic 'cool as fuck' T-shirt. It was also home to the likes of Sunset Radio and music PR Red Alert. The receptionist was Noel Gallagher's then partner Louise Jones, about whom he would go on to write songs like 'Live Forever' and 'Slide Away'.

New Mount Street was where Noel connected with the new generation Manchester music scene and everyone was only too happy to help out, as Red Alert's Alison Bell remembers:

'It was Clint Boon who originally introduced me to him as their roadie. It soon became obvious that Noel's role was clearly more than the roadie. He would also be working in their office when they weren't on the road and doing all sorts of jobs. He was also the best musician in their band and crew.

'Noel wasn't someone who wanted everyone to know him when he walked into a room. He had a really dry sense of humour and was very easy to get along with. He was also quietly single minded. We were neighbours in India House in the city centre in 1990. Noel and Lousie had a one-bedroom flat. I remember one wall was just full of cassettes. I used to go around and see them and often we would walk to work together. The Haçienda was nearby and we treated it like a local pub and would pop in for an hour or two.

'The first time I met Liam he had come across a load of Gore-Tex jackets that he was selling. I bought one for 20 quid which was a bargain, and Liam and Bonehead then helped us move office as well.'

Liam would sometimes join Noel on Inspirals jobs. Clint Boon remembers a younger, quieter Liam sat in the dressing rooms observing band life: 'Liam would sometimes work with his brother claiming he did "all the humping as Noel never had a sweat on him!"'

Liam also lived at India House, 'My flat was the biggest, so we had parties, and Noel and Louise attended some of them. We spent a lot of time in the Haçienda.

'Manchester was buzzing during this period. It felt like everyone we knew was involved in music or the creative industries. We lived a five-minute walk from the Haçienda so it was our local. I was out at least five nights a week, working at the Haçienda, clubbing or at gigs. I do remember that Noel was not a dancer.'

The heart and soul of the new scene, 23 New Mount Street was the sort of place that if you went in at two in the morning, Noel would be in there pottering around – ostensibly looking after the Inspirals' T-shirts or answering fan mail with amusingly sarcastic letters signed by 'the insider' and, when asked, adding his current listening to the letters as 'mostly old stuff and acid house with

Santana, KLF, Blur, Roses, Mondays, Beatles, Doors, Guns N' Roses, Stones, U2 and the La's.'

Steve Harrison who managed the Charlatans – the first big breakout band after the Roses and the Mondays – remembers the youthful roadie:

'I became aware of Noel because he was always hanging around and a cheeky chappy. He was a good networker and always inquisitive and very easy to talk to. I didn't particularly connect him with playing in bands because I always had him down as working with the Inspiral Carpets. I remember when Mark Collins was put forward as a guitarist for the Charlatans the link came through Alison Bell. There was also a notional hint from someone that Noel was interested but nothing more.'

Liverpool DJ Greg Wilson had also moved there in spring 1990 and soon after, the future Oasis sleeve designer Brian Cannon would join him in the next-door office, setting up as Microdot, having moved back up north because of the Haçienda and the burgeoning new Manchester scene.[1]

At the time Greg Wilson was managing Manchester premier rap crew the Ruthless Rap Assassins[2] mixing their Public Enemy sociopolitical poetic raps with psychedelic samples and daisy age beats, with Brian Cannon designing the sleeves – as on their 1990 'Just Mellow' single that combined the designer's distinctive design aesthetic with an Ian Tilton photo that was distorted into a colourful and powerful image. It was a striking artwork that was an early harbinger of Cannon's distinctive style collage of pop culture ideas and references that would be a staple through many of his sleeves for Oasis.

He also designed the new Red Alert logo for Alison, as she remembers: 'I think I drove him mad, because I knew exactly what I wanted, but through that I then introduced him to Noel.'

Born in 1966 and growing up in Wigan, a former mill town and mining community on the western edge of Greater Manchester,

Brian Cannon, like Oasis, would have to make his own journey to create the art he wanted.

Greg Wilson had met him when he moved to Wigan in 1984, DJing at the rival club to the legendary Wigan Casino. 'I saw a "Planet Rock" graffiti mural sprayed on the side of a building and I asked some local lads who did this, which led to Brian turning up at my door,' says Greg. 'He was playing cat and mouse with the local press and when he got blamed for an inferior graffiti piece he got in touch with them to point out that it had absolutely nothing to do with him.'

As an 11-year-old in 1977, Brian had become a fan of punk rock after seeing Buzzcocks on *Top of the Pops*. Digging deeper into the punk rock aesthetic, he was further fascinated by the record sleeves and the explosion in pop art that went with that fervent period when many brilliant designs became very much part of the punk experience.

To the consternation of his art teachers and his post-school art foundation course, Brian was obsessed with becoming a sleeve designer. He had his own singular vision and despite the obstacles of the time, like the huge cost of early computers, he was determined. Again, it was the DIY aesthetic of punk that showed him the way.

'I'd be in little print shop at the bottom of Library Street in Wigan all day,' he says, 'with a scalpel and a tin of glue, putting these things together in the shop – and that's how it all started.'[3]

Our paths first crossed in 1989 when he sent me a book, *Going Nowhere: The Art and Design of the Punk and New Wave Movements*, that he had written while still at Leeds University doing a BA (Hons) degree in graphic design. The book looked at the brilliant punk graphics and I reviewed it for *Sounds* music paper.

For Brian, the Sex Pistols' *Never Mind the Bollocks* cover remains the greatest piece of artwork of all time because it said everything that needed to be said in a striking visual way. He also loved the artwork of Central Station Design for their brilliant dayglo Happy Mondays stuff, as well as Hipgnosis and post-punk designers Peter Saville and Malcolm Garrett.

In return, Malcolm Garrett rated Brian's own work.

'It stands as a masterclass in building a consistent visual narrative while allowing each release to tell its own story, helping define the visual identity of the band. He crafted a cohesive design language that spanned both landmark albums *Definitely Maybe* and *(What's the Story) Morning Glory?* and their accompanying singles. What's particularly striking is how Cannon's work eschewed the typical Britpop aesthetic of the era and took a very different approach to visualising music. Instead, Cannon drew inspiration from more traditional rock photography and album art and consistently lent Oasis a timeless visual authority.'

Graduating in 1988 Brian had moved down to London, linking up with Greg Wilson again to try their hand in the big city. This would result in Brian's first foray into record sleeve design when he designed the front cover photo for Greg's partner, the singer Tracey Carmen, and he also designed a couple of sleeves for Kym Mazelle. Despite this, the epicentre and axis of the British music scene was now shifting back north.

Brian: 'I went back up north because the Haçienda from 1987 to 1989 was like the Garden of Eden where rock 'n' roll and dance-fused. I was into the Roses and the Mondays big time and I was pilled out my head in the Haçienda on a Friday night. It was all going off every week and I decided to stay.'

Now in the creative hive of New Mount Street, Brian Cannon's room was a blur of scalpels, paper, photos and ideas as he worked on his next projects, which included an upcoming new band from his own home town who were then called Verve.

It had been a chance meeting back home in Wigan a couple of years before in 1989 that sowed the seeds that would change his life and spark a game-changing new northern art. He was at an ex-girlfriend's party and met the then 17-year-old future Verve singer Richard Ashcroft who was fascinated that this wild-eyed Wigan local had designed a bunch of record sleeves for the Ruthless Rap Assassins and Kiss AMC.

'When I first met Richard at that party in 1989 I was a football hooligan-style nutter who hated students and he was still at college and didn't have a band,' recalls Brian. 'I then saw him a few months later at the Stone Roses at Alexandra Palace and I didn't see him again for two years until I bumped into him at a petrol station.'

Back in Wigan, and after being at another all-night party, Brian was at the 24-hour garage looking for some milk for a cuppa. He spotted the same gangly guy he had met a couple of years previously getting out of a car. Richard Ashcroft told him he was now in a band called Verve and that they had just been signed and if he wanted the job designing their sleeves then he had it.

Virgin, who had signed the Verve to their in-house Hut label in 1992, were not so sure and asked him to come to London for a meeting. It was already seen as a gamble to sign the band, who had taken the northern psychedelia of the Roses into a transcendental new space with one foot in the north and one in the new London shoegaze scene, while transcending both. Richard Ashcroft had a Jaggeresque charisma and a voice to match and the band spiralled off on psychedelic tangents that floated away from the music's core and back again with a brilliant intensity.

Arriving in London, the young sleeve designer's charismatic bluster bowled the label over and he was given free rein. The artwork for the band's debut 'All in the Mind' single matched the tripped-out music with the band surreally sat in Mesnes Park in Wigan on furniture brought from Richard's flat and given an infra-red tint in Michael Spencer Jones's photo. It was the debut of a new, very northern artfulness that would continue with the Wigan band and eventually Oasis.

'The Verve was my band, and not just the designs,' says Brian. 'I was totally immersed in that band. On their Gravity Grave tour in October 1992 nobody in their entourage was over 25 so I drove the tour bus and I've seen them over a hundred times, which has got to be a world record! And I designed everything that band ever released . . . '

Back up north Brian Cannon was dreaming up sleeve concepts that were creating an astonishing hybrid of post-punk aesthetic, a big dose of mid-seventies Hipgnosis and a localised twist using locations in and around the North West that would help to define the Verve and, in the future, Oasis, with sleeves creating hyper-reality dreamscapes. Photographed impeccably by Michael Spencer Jones, it was the beginning of a team that years later Paul Weller, when speaking to Noel Gallagher, would describe perfectly as 'the Lennon/McCartney of sleeve art'.

Born and raised in Sheffield, Michael Spencer Jones had developed a fascination with photography after leaving school. Influenced by the iconic imagery of photographers like Alfred Stieglitz, Edward Steichen, Paul Outerbridge and Angus McBean, he took night classes in painting and scientific photography in a duality of disciplines that became the foundation of his technically inventive style.

In the mid-eighties he studied photography and film at Bournemouth and Poole College of Art while assisting advertising photographer Stak in his Mayfair studio, where he learned about detail and the abstract before deciding to move to Manchester after getting a distinction at art college.

Arriving in town in 1990 he was commissioned by local magazine *Uptown* to shoot the Stone Roses' seminal Spike Island gig and soon teamed up with Brian Cannon where they created a visual revolution bringing both their crucial skills and vision into play. Along with Noel's own sleeve ideas they were core to the iconic artwork that would perfectly match the music in the early years.

10

UNDER THE BOARDWALK

After months of prevaricating Noel finally threw his lot in with the band in late 1991 and things were now moving quickly. Tony Wilson had once said that Manchester didn't do rock, but Oasis were building something that would prove him wrong while adding a Mancunian cool filter.

Not so much never mind the bollocks . . . this was the bollocks. The pop/noise of claustrophobia and confusion was coming together in the rehearsal room with a wall of sound constructed around Liam, who stood stock-still in the eye of the hurricane singing with his increasing levels of rasping intensity, combining a choirboy tone with a hooligan rabble-rouse in a Stoned Rose style.

No other band anywhere else in the UK in 1992 sounded this defiant and loud. The indie scene was dominated by the shoegaze discourse, with Ride hitting the top 10 with their Creation released debut *Going Blank Again*, a youthful and soaring album of dynamics, noise and harmonies, which the label's biggest hit so far. Curve were the big hopefuls with their chiselled proto shoegaze while the

Charlatans' second album, *Between 10th and 11th*, had not had the impact of the first despite great singles like 'Weirdo'. Meanwhile, hardy perennials like the Cure had their first number one album with *Wish*, while the biggest noise in music was Nirvana, whose own transatlantic take on the Sex Beatles melody maelstrom was fast-tracking them to being the biggest band in the world.

The first Oasis gig as a five-piece band was at the Boardwalk on an inauspicious Wednesday night on 15 January 1992. 'We did a gig within weeks of me joining,' explains Noel. 'We already had songs and then there was "Columbia", so that's six songs – so that's half an hour set – now we're a band. We are Oasis. It's time to play.'

On stage early, the band played to about 30 people including members of the Inspiral Carpets like the band's late drummer Craig Gill:

'A friend of mine lived next to Noel in India House. He said he must have joined a band as he was leaving the flat every night with his guitar. Noel had kept this quiet from us, but when quizzed, he came clean and told us that he had joined his brother's band who had taken their name from an Inspiral Carpets tour poster. We found out Oasis had a gig booked at the Boardwalk and we couldn't miss the chance of finally seeing Noel on stage performing for the first time.'

Meanwhile Noel Gallagher bumped into Steve Harrison.

'He said, "I've made a decision and joined our kid's band," remembers Steve, 'and when he mentioned Liam it would always be "our kid" and he didn't mention the rest of the lads.'

At the Boardwalk Mark Coyle recorded the gig from the desk for an early demo capturing them very much in their formative stages. It was the debut of set opener 'Columbia', the then instrumental with its big guitars playing that descending ominous riff, making a virtue of its piledriving simplicity and driven by an almost Happy Mondays swing on the drums. Still in the set, 'Take Me' was the sole survivor from the pre-Noel period with its nods to the Stone

Roses and Liam's youthful vocal halfway between baggy Manc and his trademark rasping intensity. Spotlighting another side to the band was the introspective 'Life in Vain', which is an interesting twist being an acoustic song in the middle of the set. 'Arkayla', also titled 'I Will Show You', is driven by a melodic guitar riff that is a nod to Johnny Marr which connects to the propulsive drumming. The punkier 'Better Let You Know' is a cover of house track 'Feel the Groove' by Cartouche which nods to Noel's nights out at the Haçienda and sees the guitars cranked in a nagging repetitive riff, ending with a great speaker to speaker delay on the vocals that adds an early psychedelic edge to their punky blues aggro.[1]

Noel's debut gig was a work in progress with hints of flourishes of what was to come. During the next year they would hone down their sound while discarding songs in their new rehearsal space downstairs in the Boardwalk.

On the other side of the city centre from New Mount Street, next door to where Joy Division had filmed the video for 'Love Will Tear Us Apart', the Boardwalk was a real hub. Opened in 1985 on Little Peter Street around the corner from the Haçienda, it was an ambitious project in the pre-gentrification city centre. A derelict former inner-city school built in the nineteenth century, it had been converted into a medium-sized club with multiple floors and, crucially, rehearsal spaces in the basement.

By the early nineties, the Boardwalk was thriving as a key venue on the UK touring circuit, with club nights. Over the years bands like the Happy Mondays and A Certain Ratio had rehearsed there and in 1991 the Inspiral Carpets were sharing the big upstairs room with the Railway Children. Any band worth its salt was waiting to get into one of the rehearsal rooms plus you got in free to the venue. And for Noel Gallagher, living in India House on Whitworth Street, it was only a 10-minute walk.

One day when he was loading the Inspiral Carpets backline into the upstairs room, he made enquiries about room availability to

Sue Langford, who famously managed the Boardwalk rooms for years, and got a rehearsal space.[2]

The new room was a much better set-up than Red House, and although still a windowless cellar space it was quickly brightened up by painting the room white with a small Union Jack on the wall as a tribute to the pop art take on the flag. Next to it a couple of classic Beatles posters would be added, including the psychedelic April 1967 photoshoot by American photographer Richard Avedon that had each of the Fab Four as a psychedelic guru; plus the poster of the band on the steps of Brian Epstein's London flat on the day of the launch party for *Sgt. Pepper's Lonely Hearts Club Band* that had been gifted to Noel by Manc face and A&R, John Brice.

Their new room-mates, Sister Lovers, were fronted by one of the faces on the local scene: Debbie Turner. 'I knew Noel from going to gigs in the eighties when he was working for the Inspirals. He just stood out because he had that bowl haircut and as much as everyone now says they had that haircut there was probably about four lads in Manchester with it. I met Liam independently of Noel. I didn't know they were brothers.

'Me and my friend Lorraine had come back from hitching around Europe and were in a pub in 1990 and Liam came in with his mates and straight away, me and Lorraine were like, "Wow, he looks cool in an Ian Brown sort of way with the haircut and nice clobber." Back then I think every single one of me and my friends fancied Ian Brown – that's not front page news is it? I think everybody in Manchester did.

'So, Lorraine was like, "Oh, he's nice" and you remember those men that used to go around pubs selling red roses? We got this red rose for a quid, and I just went up to Liam and I went, "This is from my mate over there behind the bar". And he was like, "Alright, nice one."

'I had a boyfriend at the time, Nigel, who used to have the shop, Oi Polloi in Affleck's Palace selling trainers and casual gear and because I was with Nigel, I had some cool trainers on which were like a little basketball boot, and Liam spotted them, asking, "Where'd you get your trainers from?" I told him all about Nigel's shop and the lengths Nigel went to find these rare old-school Adidas trainers and it sort of carried on from there!'[3]

The style-obsessed kid was oozing a Mancunian cool.

'At the time he had a haircut where it came sort of forward but then cut over the ear like in a bob almost,' continues Debbie. 'He thought we had said his hair looked like Betty Boo but we had said "You look like a young Paul Weller" and he's like, "Oh, that's all right!"

'He asked where we lived and we said Burnage and he said they could give us a lift back. I was a bit apprehensive because I was thinking maybe they were just joy riders! But they came back to our house and in the hallway we had that life-size cutout of Alan McGee that had been in Eastern Bloc record shop in town. Liam was like, "Who the fuck is that!" Which is now hilarious because that's the guy that one day is gonna make you famous!

'Nigel was there, so him and Liam were talking trainers while me and Lorraine were putting records on and from then on we became friends.

'When we moved in 1991 Liam would come round to our new flat on Old Lansdowne Road in West Didsbury. Me and Lorraine had done a sound recording course at Spirit Studios in town and we had bought a 4-track recorder, so we were always in the bedroom writing and recording songs and Liam would come round and listen. Then, in 1991, his band was now rehearsing in the Boardwalk, and he said, "Why don't you share the practice room with us?"

'So, me and Lorraine with Tony Ogden helping out on drums moved in. We didn't even have a mic stand. We just used to get a broom handle and stick a mic on and put it in a milk crate!'[4]

In these rudimentary settings the two fledging bands would rehearse. 'There was something about Liam,' says Debbie. 'He was really up and positive and vibey and, you know, mad for it! There was no idea then that he was going to be famous but he had that bravado. Because you've got to remember that all that Madchester stuff had gone and people thought that they were just another bunch of lads wearing the coats on stage and being Manc'd up to fuck.'

The Boardwalk was a great set-up and a base for the band and their mates who hung out watching them blast through the new songs that Noel Gallagher was bringing in every week. Despite the erratic payment of the rent, which was mostly subsidised by Noel, the venue and rehearsal rooms loom large in the band's early legend and helped to shape them. The Inspiral Carpets' guitarist Graham Lambert recalls his roadie moving in.

'We had an upstairs room in the Boardwalk and Oasis were rehearsing downstairs with "the Sergeant Pepper room" written over the frame of the door. I don't ever remember going in there because it's a bit funny going in another band's rehearsal room, but I know they used to rehearse our "Two Worlds Collide" because Noel liked the song.'

In the room next door to the fledgling Oasis, my band (the Membranes) would sometimes rehearse and no matter what time you went in there Oasis seemed to be endlessly honing down the riff from 'I Am the Walrus' or with a lone guitar chugging away. This was not a band of chancers or a middle-class hobby band but a one-shot chance of escape from a life of dead-end jobs.

Harry Stafford of the Inca Babies was another band that rehearsed next door. 'I remember them playing "Digsy's Dinner" a lot and thinking, "Actually that's a really great tune." So they were probably gathering material for the album a year before. They rowed quite a lot as well but they kept it together to make a great first album.'

Their Pistolian cover of 'I Am the Walrus' was their first fusion of their twin godheads, the Sex Pistols and the Beatles, into the Sex

Beatles combination. Originally released as a double A-side with 'Hello, Goodbye' back in 1967, Lennon's sneering snarky anthem, full of warped humour and caustic wind-ups, was a perfect piece of grinding psychedelia that matched the mindset of the Manchester council estate kids who were immersed in second-hand records and stoner culture. Stripped away of the effects, Oasis piled their wall of sound on to the song and stretched it out into a relentless never-ending apocalyptic ooze, with Liam going Lennon-plus on the vocals.

In their endless rehearsing, the band would hone each song to perfection while enjoying the running battle of football banter with Man United v Man City graffiti on the doors.

It was in the Boardwalk that Noel gradually implemented his vision. Initially he had brought three songs down when he joined. 'Must be the Music' and 'See the Sun' didn't gel with the band, but 'I Better Let You Know' did. With the vehicle in place, Noel's creativity accelerated.

'I then started to think of being a songwriter seriously,' he remembers. 'I was writing songs for Oasis while still working with the Inspirals but I was now more into writing songs and recording songs in the rehearsal room. I was starting to think in terms of this could actually go somewhere.'

Noel would spend hours round at Bonehead's house in West Didsbury, guitar to guitar, honing everything down or showing the band the new songs on his acoustic in the Boardwalk. Often they would jam and often record the sessions with the sonics looked after by another member of their ever-expanding music gang, and arguably the sixth member of Oasis, Mark Coyle.

'Mark Coyle is my best mate,' says Noel. 'He's a sound engineer and he knows what he's talking about. He said we needed a better drum kit and he tuned it up. He had a portable recording studio at his house which he brought down to the Boardwalk. It was now like a little family of all six of us. Me and Liam couldn't make it ourselves and we were relying on the rest of the band so we used to push them to rehearse all the time. If you weren't going to the football then five days a week Monday to Friday we would rehearse, no argument. Guigsy, Bonehead and Tony all had jobs, but me and Liam, to coin his phrase, "we're living it."

'Even though we hadn't done anything we knew this was it. The drug was the music. When you are young and you have no kids, music is everything. If you're not playing music then you're talking about music. If you're not talking about music, then you're thinking about music, and if you're not reading about music, then you're writing it. They were great days, brilliant days.'

Often their mates like Tony French would join them in the room, creating a party vibe and an audience to play to.

'I got to know Liam and Noel when the band rehearsed at the Boardwalk,' says Tony. 'I was in there most nights for a couple of years while they were putting the album together. Basically, after work, I would pick up my mate and the weed, and then we would drive into town and get there for about seven. Tony and Guigsy were working and Liam was some sort of valet driving cars. We would sit in there and listen to the music, smoke weed and Noel would work hard on the songs. By then he was very much in charge. Bonehead was a seasoned guitarist and he had come to terms with the fact he might never make it so he was happy to go along with it.

'Noel was one of those people you would listen to. He could be quite broody but that was because he was thinking all the time. He was the boss but he knew what he was doing and he was confident in where he was going, especially in the music industry. He was so focused but he was easy to get on with. Liam's humour was out there like the Goons and really surreal.

'It seemed like every night Noel would turn up with a new song and Liam would sing them straight away after Noel had handed him the words and melody. It was unbelievable how Liam would get it right in two attempts, and of course, he added to it as well, with his sort of simmering anger and frustration. It was very punk.'

Of course, every band is driven by many motives, from the buzz of making that beautiful sound to the gang mentality, but there was something else about Oasis. They had the sheer willpower to prove themselves through music and to escape as much as the glory of standing on the shoulder(s) of the musical giants they adored. Filling in the emotional void and reaching for the sky, it was that drive to succeed and prove themselves pushed them on and you can hear it in the music, from its wall-of-sound rage or its melancholic twists. Its anger had an energy and an emotional rush all entwined in the huge melodies that millions would eventually connect with, as Tony McCarroll notes.

'That's what made it special. It was not overdone. It was pure, absolutely pure. We thought we should be more complicated musically but it just didn't happen. It was just what we were. The best bands are people who have grown up together while playing together. It's a perfect thing. You know how to fill each other's gaps. You can read where the others are going. You can hear where they're going.'

11

FAC YOU!

Much has been made of the Beatles connections with Oasis, but interestingly their first out of town gig on 19 April 1992 was an unlikely 225-mile jaunt from Manchester to the other side of London to Dartford – the birthplace of the Rolling Stones.

In the unlikely surroundings of Dartford Polytechnic Students Union they played with the Oldham-based band the Ya Yas, who were managed by the Stone Roses' former manager Gareth Evans and who Noel knew from when they had supported the Inspiral Carpets.[1]

It might have been early days and a long drive but that didn't dent the band's attitude and Liam objected to the 'nondescript student band', The World Jones Made, headlining; the local band backed down and the bill was flipped, with Oasis going on last.

The long drive home that night got them back for the following day's gig in Middleton,[2] North Manchester at the Hippodrome where they were supporting Peter Hook's then New Order side project, Revenge, which reflected the bassist's more leathery SM side with a sort of industrial take on the Pet Shop Boys. It was an odd bill and yet another connection from Noel's little black book of contacts built up running around town with the Inspiral Carpets.

Both gigs were a long way from the current heartbeat of the music scene. That same week Suede were acclaimed as the 'best new band in Britain' on the front cover of the *Melody Maker* – the first of many front covers for the band who that year dominated the music press discourse that was gung-ho about androgynous bands from the capital city and its surrounding satellite towns.

The Revenge gig was being filmed by Factory Records' new A&R Phil Saxe, who had just started working for the label. Already a key face on the scene, his stall in the Underground Market in mid-eighties Manchester had sold all the flares to the Happy Mondays that had sparked a style war before he went on to manage the band.

Now that Phil Saxe had seen the band could this be an opportunity for Oasis to sign to the iconic Manchester label?

Factory Records had been a game-changer. Any label that had signed Joy Division and the Happy Mondays was always going to have a place in the musical narrative. They also had an undercard of other great bands, from the Stockholm Monsters and Section 25 to early James and early Orchestral Manoeuvres in the Dark.

Under Tony Wilson, the label had a very strong aesthetic with its random artful A&R policy, and its Peter Saville sleeve designs. Factory had a real sense of itself that placed Manchester and the north in the middle of its musical and visual identity, which in turn played with the city's industrial heritage while inspiring creatives to stay in the city to make this happen. Much of modern Manchester can be traced back to Factory.

'I had already seen Noel around because he worked for the Inspirals but we were just on nodding terms,' remembers Phil Saxe. 'I knew Liam more for some reason. I would bump into him and we used to chat quite a bit. Because I was into clothes and used to have the stall, I noticed a good dress sense and Liam looked better than anybody else in Oasis. I was at Factory by then and Liam used to tell me about his band, and, he was, how can I put it? Confident . . .

'I always remember he used to have a belt that had Elvis on it and would say, "We're going to be bigger than Elvis." A lot of people used to think he was a big-headed bugger and ignore him but I never did. I always remember after the gig in Middleton Liam saying to me, "Come on Phil, when are you going to sign us up? We're better than the Wendys," who I had just signed to Factory.'

Noel arranged to go in and play the demo. He recalls: 'We only ever went to one label when we started and that was Factory. They came to see us rehearsing at the Boardwalk and we then arranged a meeting with them at their new office on Charles Street in the city centre and played the demo to Phil Saxe.

'It was the really early stuff but "Columbia" was on it. Phil had said we were "too baggy" but said he was going to send Tony [Wilson] down to see us play a gig because we were playing the next week. To this day I'm not sure if anyone ever turned up. At that time though I don't think we were ready. We didn't have "Live Forever" or "Slide Away" or "Rock 'n' roll Star".'

Factory was in a state of flux according to Phil Saxe: 'Factory had its early era – the Joy Division period which a lot of people think was the golden age. Then it was New Order, Happy Mondays. I was nothing to do with the first bit of it but when Mike Pickering left Factory, Rob Gretton said to Tony you ought to use Phil to do the A&R, he just brought you Northside. So that's how I ended up being the head of A&R, which in reality was only me. Tony gave me sort of a carte blanche to try to change what was going on. I know people might look at all the early bands with great fondness and how cool they were, but they weren't making any money and there were a few artistic cul-de-sacs.

'Tony wanted to change things but wouldn't because he never sacked anybody. So he gave me the power to do that, but what Tony didn't tell me was that the label was just about to go bust. So the bands I signed like the Adventure Babies and the Wendys didn't have the money to do it, which was a shame.

'Oasis wasn't really Tony's thing although I think he would have ended up getting into it, in the same way as the Mondays weren't Tony's thing but they ended up being. It was my thing because I always had that affinity for the sort of Manchester scally type of band. One of the things I was trying to do at the time was put together an album that was going to be two tracks each on it by new bands and Oasis were going to be one of them, and one of the other bands was Pulp, which didn't happen. It's not like Factory ever turned Oasis down. It's just that Factory couldn't really sign them, but let's be honest about it, the worst thing in the world for Oasis then would have been to sign to Factory because it wasn't a commercial label. It had a reputation that far exceeded its capabilities.'

A few months later on 23 November 1992 Factory went bust, closing down in front of the media. Oasis had a lucky escape, as Phil Saxe explains:

'Brushing it off Noel knew it was still early days. Very few bands get a deal at this stage of the game. A tiny handful of gigs and no discernible local following does not often a record deal make. Noel's vision of how good the band were was based on how good they were going to be and he knew he had the talent to pull it off.'

12

A CELLARFUL OF NOISE

Away from the numbers and back in the Boardwalk it felt good to crank those amps louder and louder. That year the sound ricocheted off the old cellar walls adding another wave of sonic obliteration to the mix. Liam would step up to the mic and with that rasping yet melodic voice and deliver each new song that Noel had played on his acoustic a few days before.

The Boardwalk rehearsal room footage of Oasis by Bobby Langley filmed in June 1992 is the perfect and earliest capture of the band and the first sign of the wall-of-sound Oasis, with the vocal melodies cutting through in a perfect primeval soup of sound.

The filmmaker knew Noel from Man City awaydays.

'When I was young, it was football, trainers and clothes. Estate couture,' says Bobby. 'In 1982 I met Noel at the match and we'd all knock about. In the late eighties in the Haçienda we'd all be in that first alcove dancing around with our joint love of ecstasy, dance music and looking at each other's clothes and nicking each other's girlfriends.

'I grew up with the Inspiral Carpets and I DJ'd with them some-times. When Noel became their roadie I remember someone pointing out, "You know that lad over there, he does everything. He does the keyboards, the drum tech and the mic checks." He was the all-seeing eye and he lived above us in India House so we'd always be in and out of each other's flats.'

After doing a film course, Bobby was looking for something to film. 'The college gave me this big fucking camera and Noel said, "I'm rehearsing this week, why don't you come down?" So me, Simon Halliday and Grimmy went down there.[1] We got stoned and I let the camera run and we filmed the whole night. When they did "All Around the World" I realised, fuck me, our mates have got this incredible band with Noel's songwriting and Liam's incredible voice. Liam looked great with gazelle trainers, his hair-cut, his walk . . . everything. He was just really on it but I don't think he even knew how on it.'

From the day he had met Liam, Bobby realised that he had a presence. 'I remember being sat outside Dukes 92 pub in town with Noel, Grimmy, Simon and Nigel who had owned Oi Polloi. About 1,000 yards away I could see someone coming towards me like a truck which was fucking veering off the road. I'm like, who the fuck is this lad who is bowling over. I'm like, something's gonna happen, and Noel said it's just our kid. He came in and he just came towards us and he was shouting and bawling about some-thing. It was great fucking rock 'n' roll.'

Working in A&R, John Brice would also visit the Boardwalk.

'The rehearsals in 1992 were mesmerising,' he says. 'I was speech-less. They tore through the set and it was spine-tingling. It was just the band and myself and they'd reached the point they'd been striv-ing for. It was the moment where I can safely say I was seeing history. Now I just had to convince my boss at Warner Chappell to sign them.'

On Tuesday, 14 July 1992, the band lugged their gear up the stairs and on to the small Boardwalk stage right above their practice room for their first headline show at the venue.

'It made sense to play there because it was one of the main venues in town and it was easy to carry the gear upstairs,' says Tony McCarroll. 'We knew we were on to something, but the music business was not interested because by that point they thought that the Manchester scene was exhausted.'

The Inspiral Carpets were still supportive and Graham Lambert was at the gig. 'Noel was doing gigs around us touring so we'd go and see him at the Boardwalk. I remember thinking how full and well-rehearsed they sounded. I think one of the positives Noel took from us, is that to get good you just had to spend time together playing music.'

Gigs were occasional and in one of the more curious moments of their pre-breakthrough days, the band actually filmed a TV appearance on a long-lost programme called *The Blackpool Roadshow*, but it was never shown. Filmed at the Granada TV studios in Manchester, the band performed two songs on a 24-hour charity telethon with 40 other acts including the likes of Alvin Stardust.

Filmed in June, this first TV recording came from a connection with Bonehead's brother Martin, with the pair of them doing most of the ad hoc managing and organising of the band at the time. They got themselves booked, by Shirley Jones, the owner of the programme, who remembers:

'We organised the 24-hour ITV Telethon 1992 showcase for Granada TV. I did the show with my brother Johnnie Doolan, who worked with Bonehead's brother, who asked him for a favour. His brother was in a band doing small gigs and he asked could we give them a stage spot during the event. There was a bit of adjusting to fit them in, but we did. The demo they provided was a bog-standard off-the-shelf cassette tape featuring two different mixes of 'Take

Me'. They also communicated a number of times by fax. The demo was handed to me by Liam who informed me I "should keep hold of it as we're going to be massive." They were really polite, really chuffed to be given the opportunity and Liam's complete positivity about their future fame was clear even then.'

Tony McCarroll remembers Oasis being introduced on stage as having 'just flown back to be with us from their tour,' to which the scowling Liam replied, 'We've just come from Burnage, dickhead. We ain't on fuckin' tour,' before the band, fortified by a quick trip to the fake Rovers Return pub, began to mime along to a tape of 'Take Me' to an audience made up of film crew and a handful of Granada staff, the other guests, a Salvation Army band and a school choir.

1992 remained Oasis's year in the wilderness but it was to be to their advantage that the London music biz had declared Manchester over and left them honing down their sound.

'It felt like I was going to be the last one to make it from my crowd,' ponders Noel. 'From 1991 to 1993 we were not particularly going anywhere but we still loved it. Nowadays two years without interest and you're finished but back then it was different. For us a band wasn't a career choice. It was something that you did because that was where you came from. Now bands get signed before they think of a name and you can be online superstars before you've even got it together.

'We rehearsed all the time, kept patient and recorded demos that never came to light and we were allowed to be shit for a couple of years. We were looking for our sound. The first demo had sounded quite Happy Mondays in a way and Liam sounded like Ian Brown because initially you just copy your heroes before you stumble across your thing. The next thing came out of the blue when In the City came along from nowhere. It was Tony Wilson's new music conference event and it's this festival-type thing for new bands and we got a slot on it.'

Inspired by trips to New York for its New Music Seminar music convention, Wilson brought his version of the model back to Manchester. Held over the weekend of 11–13 September at The Midland Hotel, it hosted a daytime conference that included keynotes, showcases and panels. In the evening young bands played nearby venues to get some spotlight or a deal. It wasn't the first of its kind but it was in Manchester and the London music biz were drawn up to the city by the magnetic Tony Wilson, who explained:

'Manchester was perfect for an event like this. Outside of London it was the only city with any kind of music biz infrastructure. When we launched in 1992 the city needed a boost because what I would call the "wonderful madness of Madchester" had gone. There was a Manchester backlash and it needed something positive to put life back into the scene.'

Noel knew that Oasis had to be seen at this event and managed to land a gig at one of the showcases at the long-closed Venue on Whitworth Street on Sunday, 13 September. A not so packed room that night watched a clutch of upcoming bands, including Machine Gun Feedback who would become Space Monkeys and sign to Factory Too; Skywalker, fronted by the charismatic late Eilidh Bradley, who would morph into Solar Race and whose powerful post-Hole grunge should have made a bigger splash; and the glam stomp of Jealous, whose singer Jason recalls:

'Gary Davies from Radio 1 was managing my band and got a few people to come and check the bands out like Feargal Sharkey and Muff Winwood. Oasis were sort of indie terrace culture. They sounded good and didn't seem to care that there was not many people in for them.'

It didn't get Oasis a deal. It didn't get them very much at all, remembers Noel.

'Not that anything came of In the City for us because nothing ever did at the time. We didn't get any record deals or anything like that but we knew that it was only a matter of time. Pete Shelley was in the crowd. He came up to me afterwards and said, "I really like the song with the wah-wah pedal" and I didn't know what to say because he's from Buzzcocks, man! They started the whole thing! Never mind the Clash, it was Buzzcocks or the Pistols for me.'

Liam Walsh remembers the gig, 'The gig that sticks out for me was at The Venue on Whitworth St. Gary Davies from BBC Radio 1 was in the audience, and I thought he'd not like them. By now, Liam stood out as a confident frontman, the opposite of the shy young man I'd serve at the Boardwalk bar.'

John Brice was also there: 'It showed the total cluelessness of the whole music industry. They were all in Manchester and hardly any of them were at the gig. They were either watching some shite gig or drinking and networking in the Midland Hotel, a stone's throw from the venue where the future of rock 'n' roll was playing. There was about 50 people there and it was mostly their mates. I don't think any of the big songs had been written yet but I remember being transfixed. Liam was looking into the middle distance, almost disinterested, but in a cool way, very compelling to watch. This, of course, became his thing: the Liam we all know and love. It was that effortless Manchester cool and dress sense that money can't buy. A few months later I remember Noel ringing me, telling me he was on a roll with the songs, he'd written four in a matter of days and three made the debut album. "Bring It On Down", "Shakermaker" and "Rock 'n' Roll Star".'

A few weeks after In the City, on a cold Wednesday, 14 October night, there was a Burnage takeover of the Boardwalk, with Oasis hauling their gear back up the stairs again and into the venue that Pulp had played the night before to play with their fellow Burnage droogs Molly Half Head. Headlining were Northwich band the Cherrys, whose brand of energetic post-Red Hot Chili Peppers funk rock had seen them signed to Steve Harrison's Dead Dead Good label.

'Noel had phoned me up before the gig and said, "We'd like you to manage us,"' remembers Steve. 'I went, "Have you got time and space to do this because you are working with the Inspiral Carpets?" and he goes, "Yeah." The really good thing with Noel, and I think this is testament to him and why I've got so much respect for him, was before the call he had said to Mark Collins from the Charlatans, if it was OK to speak to me about managing Oasis, which was really respectful to the Charlatans who I managed.'

Despite it being Molly Half Head's gig the tension between the other two bands would eventually spill over. 'I didn't end up managing Oasis in the end because of two things,' Steve continues. 'First Liam kicked off that night and there was nearly a fight on the stage in the soundcheck between him and the Cherrys. It was surreal and we were watching all this carnage. Somehow it got resolved. And then Noel being Noel just comes straight up afterwards and says, "What do you think? Are you gonna manage us!" and I said, "I need a bit of time to think about it!"

'The main reason for not doing it, though, was that they were too close in sound to the Charlatans at the time who were always understandably very precious and needed to be top dog. It was early days and Oasis were not there yet and I didn't know if there was enough space for them, but I thought that Liam Gallagher was a star in the making in the way that Shaun Ryder and Ian Brown were but he transcended all that.'

People talk a lot about the X factor – not the hoaky TV series with its pretend stars but that natural thing that very few people have. It's that innate energy and magnetism and a young Liam Gallagher already oozed the stuff and everyone who remembers him from his youth recalls a combination of fearlessness and a kind of aura that can only end up being channelled on stage.

The X factor cannot be learned and it cannot be imposed. It's that thing that when someone walks into a room, all eyes are on them whether they know it or not. It can cause fights as lesser mortals try and punch it out of the way or it can cause riots as the energy in the room soars.

Liam Gallagher spent his youth running around Manchester, waiting for the spotlight. It's this charisma that was a big part of the Oasis story. From day one when he played on stages to disinterested empty rooms, people noted that the singer had something as he stared out at the crowd, frustrated that they hadn't realised that they were in the presence of a Manchester Elvis fronting a local band third on the bill on a wet Tuesday night. This self-belief was not arrogance. It was just knowing the truth. The classic early Liam hanging from the mic perfecting his 'stillism' was the prototype to a new kind of cool – like Johnny Rotten in the Pistols, this was not about 'pleasing the audience'; the audience had to come to him.

'He developed his stage thing or as he calls it "stillism",' smiles Noel. 'I remember this interviewer asking a few years later, "They call you a cross between Lennon and Rotten but what's your stage persona man?" and he says, "Stillism" and this guy was writing it down dead seriously and we are laughing, cracking up. It would wind American frontmen up so much. He was talking to Ryan Adams about it saying about how on stage, "I'm letting it happen to me and I'm not making it happen to them, I'm just there."

'If, at the first gig, he had started behaving like Brett Anderson we would have stopped the song and said, "Woah what on earth are you doing!" The only progression on stillism was sit-ism!'

Even this early Oasis had the right balance in a curious but perfect chemistry: Liam the stillism star and Noel hunched over his guitar with a serious look on his face but owning his space, while the rest of the band were the grafters.

It takes years to be an overnight success and in 1992 Oasis were just another local band. At the time, they were not even on the list of upcoming bands in the city, like That Uncertain Feeling, Molly Half Head, Sugar Merchants or Puressence.

The Boardwalk/New Mount Street/India House/Inspirals roadie life had been a cushty number, but maybe it needed a drastic shift to change their fortunes. The first break in the pattern was when the Inspiral Carpets moved their office to a new location.

'We moved out of New Mount Street in September to a new place across town,' remembers Graham Lambert. 'So we paid Bonehead, Guigsy, Noel and Tony to help us move all our stuff overnight and the move got slower and slower as the night went on, if you know what I'm saying!'

It wasn't just the move from New Mount Street – things were changing a lot in the Inspiral Carpets' world. The band were downsizing after the Madchester glory years and into a more uncertain future.

'By December '92 that was it with Noel and us after a European tour,' says Graham. 'Noel wasn't happy roadying. He wanted to be on the stage playing, which was fair enough because he was writing lots of songs. It wasn't about the money because we paid him pretty well. I just loved how they got massive and he wrote some absolutely groundbreaking songs for people of our generation. A lot of people say their band is going to be massive, but Oasis did it! As a fellow songwriter, you can only dream about coming up with some of those tunes. He was never going to be a roadie forever, was he!'

Initially shocked and hurt by the change Noel was much more sanguine about it years later. 'The Inspirals, bless them, didn't actually sack me. They said, "We're going to South America but you're not coming." They said we can't afford to take roadies and then you would get the phone call saying, "It's not me, it's the other four!"

'Then I found out that someone else was going, but it didn't matter then. At that point the roadie thing wasn't the end of the line and this was the beginning of this new thing. So it didn't really bug me to be honest.[2] I felt that even if I had been needed for South America for two weeks I had a gig at the Boardwalk which I would have done instead. Oasis was more important now. I was addicted to it all – the sound, the lifestyle and even going for a drink after rehearsals.[3]

'I'd grown up in Manchester mythologising bands like the Smiths and the Stone Roses. We didn't think we were that fucking great then but I knew we had something because even to be a shit Manchester band is better than to be a band from somewhere else!'

Noel had been close to the Inspirals, and for a few months, they were a target of his scathing sarcasm before time healed the wounds. He also had a lot more time on his hands now.

There were also a few loose ends left over from the Inspiral Carpets period that were going to have a profound effect on Oasis, like a budding friendship with the Liverpool band the Real People who had been the support band on the recent autumn Inspiral Carpets tour.

13

GETTING REAL

Liverpool looms large in the early Oasis story, and it was here that they found an early audience with the Real People taking them under their wing. The Liverpool band got them their debut 1 March 1993 Liverpool show at Le Bateau with a band called Small who were fronted by Digsy, the charismatic former frontman of John Peel faves Cook Da Books.[1]

Local writer Kev McManus was there. 'Digsy turned up with his cousins Chris and Tony [Griffiths] from the Real People. I knew the Realies well as they were fellow Bootle boys and so when Chris asked me if these Manc lads who were hanging out with them could do a short set using Small's gear I said yes. I didn't actually have the authority to sanction this and I annoyed a few people because it meant extra work but I was so glad I'd agreed. On a tiny makeshift stage with borrowed gear they delivered a storming 20-minute set that I remember featuring early versions of the likes of "Rock 'n' Roll Star" and "Cigarettes & Alcohol". That was the first time I got to meet Noel and Liam. Liam was hilarious and clearly already thought he was a star and I spent a fair bit of time with them after that because they were always in Liverpool.'

Back in Manc Noel Gallagher was in a creative rush, writing songs that would come to define the band, like the punk rock 'Bring It On Down', and then the first true classic, 'Live Forever', which was presented to the band in the Boardwalk.

'Fuck off, you've not just written that,' Bonehead burst out as 'Live Forever' shimmied around the room, adding, 'There's no way you've just written that song!'

It must have been mind-blowing.

A few weeks later on 1 April Oasis were back in Liverpool playing the Krazy House which was like a ribald party, and at the end of the set the Real People jumped up on the stage in a ragged state to join in a long and loose jam, cementing another crucial relationship in the band's career.

By then Oasis had been recording with the Real People and Liverpool had become their Beatles in Hamburg moment as the band transformed, spending three months going backwards and forwards to the city to make several demos, with the Realies' studio experience, songwriting nous and outsider perspective having a key influence on them. They helped to draw out the talent and shape Oasis's artistic identity, pointing out a path they could follow.

Also built around two brothers, the street gruffness of the Real People's Chris and Tony would melt effortlessly into angelic harmonies in songs of vocal elixir. They were part of a scene of groups from the city, like the La's, that combined frantic guitars with effortless and brilliant melodies. To this day the Real People are still touring and delivering those sublime melodies and great songwriting, caught in a cult hinterland when their classic guitar pop should be huge.

That spring, on a fast learning curve, Oasis recorded about 20 songs over various sessions that were way above the sonic level of what they had been doing back in Manchester. Referencing Slade and Buzzcocks to get the sound right, they were already looking at that raucous melodic rush that became their early trademark.

It was at Exeter University on the first date of that tour on 25 October that Noel and the Real People bonded.

'In many ways, the Oasis story begins in Liverpool. People really started getting into it there and they really took us to their hearts. On the Inspiral Carpets '92 tour the Real People were the support band and they used to watch me and Coyley soundcheck the backline playing some of my tunes and they would say, "What tune is that, it's really boss,"' remembers Noel.

'Coyley and Noel were our sort of people and we started hanging around with them and they were fans of our band,' says singer Chris Griffiths. 'There was catering on the tour but I was still a kid then and a fussy eater. So I used to take me own Pot Noodles. Noel was the same. So while everyone else was having a really nice three-course meal, Noel would go and play guitar on his own on the stage and I bonded with him over that and over our mutual love of a chicken and mushroom Pot Noodle.'

Chris's brother Tony remembers Liam being around: 'We spotted Liam on the Inspirals tour, and we said to Noel, "Who's He? he's like a fucking star" and Noel said, "That's our kid and he's in the band with me." He already had the swagger and the attitude.'

Post tour they all kept in touch, as Noel Gallagher remembers: 'They came to see us live at the Boardwalk in November and thought it was fucking brilliant, then we went over to Liverpool to do these demos in their studio in Bootle which amounted to a tape recorder and a microphone in a warehouse and that was it, man!'

For a few months it was a perfect creative curve.

Tony Griffiths: 'We only ever heard the very early stuff that they had demoed after we had started working with them and it was fucking shit, but there were other unrecorded songs and Noel had also recorded "Married With Children" and "D'Yer Wanna Be a Spaceman?" in Coyley's bedroom [which] sounded amazing. We said, "Don't touch them. They sound really good."'

Mark Coyle's home studio on Mauldeth Road West in Manchester saw many songs and ideas recorded, with some songs from that time appearing on later releases like the November 1992 Liam-sung version of 'Sad Song' finally released on the 2024 *Definitely Maybe* reissue or 'D'Yer Wanna Be A Spaceman?' on the B-side of the 'Shakermaker' single, and 'Married with Children' released on *Definitely Maybe* proper. There was a very early acoustic demo of 'Hello', 'Rockin' Chair' and 'She's Electric', released on the 2014 *(What's the Story) Morning Glory?* reissue and many other bits and pieces.

During that period, the bands were close, as Chris reminisces: 'Me and Noel really got on like when you got a new mate. He'd phone me up in the evenings for hours and me bird was sitting there saying, "You talking to that Noel lad from Manchester again?" He was a Manc and I was a scouser and I never had a Manc mate before and we were just getting on like a house on fire.'

Inevitably this had led to working together.

'That's when I suggested to him coming down to our Porter Street place and using our Tascam 8-track. We tried to get free studio time from Hambi at the Pink Museum studio or at Parr Street to make it sound more presentable so we could try and go to companies and get them a deal, but they all passed. We were just trying to project manage really, give them a hand, as people in Liverpool do. That's why we are called the Real People. We were too soft for our own good.'

The Real People were in the unique position of seeing the band in a formative stage.

'They were rehearsing a lot in the Boardwalk and we went over,' remembers Tony Griffiths. 'They were lovely lads. All stoners. Bonehead was dead, dead funny and the best musician out of all of them. Originally it was his band and he still had a lot to do with everything. Guigsy was the most stoned and dead quiet and

Tony McCarroll was not as much of a stoner but was also quiet and a lovely fella.'

Oasis would drive over with Mark Coyle who worked the Real People's mixing desk as the Realies added their ideas and inspiration, which Tony McCarroll appreciated:

'The Real People had lost their deal and didn't want to step out of the game. They were thinking, "What's our next stage? Produce bands?" They had a great set-up and they dragged a lot out of us. They helped structure the songs. They would say stuff like, "You played that intro too long" and it made us think a bit more about it.'

Tony Griffiths agrees: 'We wanted to get into writing and producing up-and-coming bands, and Oasis was the learning curve for us to get to the other side, to being behind the camera. It was about taking all the stuff that we'd learned from people who had produced us like Jimmy Miller and Steven Street and implementing that and they were the guinea pigs.'

In many ways it was much more altruistic than that, as the Real People's Chris recalls:

'We were just doing it as a favour to some friends from Manchester who couldn't get any studio time. We didn't know how good they were until we were working with them and we thought these are really good. Then when we played the songs to the La's, saying listen to these, and everyone was saying that's actually really good.'

Still fresh to the studio the young band were finding their way.

'A lot of things have been said in previous interviews about how Liam was initially uncomfortable wearing headphones,' says Chris. 'To help I'd put the main vocal melody down as a guide so he could sing over the guide. I guess that's why sometimes people say that Liam's got a bit of a scouse phrasing! He wasn't as confident when he first started but I thought his voice was great and he was learning fast.'

Having an outside perspective gave the Real People a unique take on the songs.

'One of the main things that we did was shorten the songs down because people don't realise that to get plays on the radio you can't have a fucking six-minute-long song,' Chris continues. 'We managed to get it down to two guitar solos and shorten the songs. When you first start you are naturally more self-indulgent because you've got no grasp of how the structure of a song has got to work. Long songs are not going to get played on the radio, even if you are Pink Floyd. It's got to grab the ears. If the good bit doesn't come in early then people lose interest. The Beatles sometimes even started with the chorus.'

But Chris says the band were receptive to the ideas. 'We would say just try this idea and if it works then great. It wasn't every song because sometimes the song would already sound great. "Columbia" was a seven-minute instrumental and used to open up the set. We recorded it live at our place as an instrumental with everyone upstairs and Coyley downstairs at the desk. I said, "This is too good just to be instrumental and a walk-on tune for the live gigs," so we worked on the vocals and lyrics with them.'

Working this closely with another band is very unusual. Normally, bands are very much self-contained units, and for those three months, the two bands seemed to merge into a creative whole. Extrapolating out of that situation and working out who did what and what was influenced by who is always going to end up being awkward, with Chris Griffiths eventually getting a co-writing credit for the Oasis song 'Rockin' Chair'.

That spring about a dozen songs were recorded in the sessions including 'Cloudburst', 'Strange Thing', 'Columbia', 'Bring It On Down', 'Fade Away' and 'Rock 'n' Roll Star', with the versions of 'D'Yer Wanna be a Spaceman?' and 'Married with Children' recorded at the home of co-producer Mark Coyle ending up on the new Live Demonstration demo tape.

The first proper snapshot of Oasis, the Live Demonstration demo tape is full of promise of what was to come, from the punk claustrophobia of 'Bring It On Down' to the swaggering rush of the freshly written 'Rock 'n' roll Star'. The acoustic-driven Noel-sung 'D'Yer Wanna be a Spaceman?' was an upgrade on his late eighties demos while 'Cloudburst'[2] is a hint at the future Sex Beatles with a great Liam vocal. 'Strange Thing' was one of the earliest songs that Noel brought to the band while 'Fade Away' has a whiff of the Beatles' 'Help' with its key chord change and its lyrics about your dreams fading away.

Some of the other tracks in the sessions include 'Alive', driven by its Stone Roses-style bass line and the youthful Liam vocal. Other good songs were lost in the rush of new ideas, the Noel-sung 'Lock All The Doors' demo ended up being split with the verses used for the Oasis B-side 'My Sister Lover' and the rest on the 2015 High Flying Birds album *Chasing Yesterday*. While still unreleased 'Must Be The Music' is perhaps closest to the soon to be classic Oasis sound, with a churning riff and a more baggy Liam vocal.

In the last couple of days of the sessions another song arrived, as Tony Griffiths remembers:

'"Whatever" was one of the last tunes that we did. I don't even know whether Noel just wrote it upstairs in the studio and brought it down. We never put two and two together with the Neil Innes [3] influence. It was just a really rough demo and we helped with the string part on this little Casio keyboard. After we recorded it the song was put to bed because it was a demo. I thought that song was great but it never made the album and then they released it between the albums.'

The ultimate symbiosis was when Oasis covered a Real People song, as Chris ponders:

'One of the earliest things that we recorded with them was Oasis covering one of our songs called "Heaven Knows" that was off our 1988 "Mini LP". We did have a copy of it knocking about somewhere but we have searched high and low and can't find it.

When I moved out of my dad's, he had a clear-out and he said there's a load of cassettes underneath the bed, in a bag, so he probably threw them in the bin!'

With a comprehensive eight songs readied for a new demo, Noel Gallagher knew that you have to look good as well as sound good. With an idea for what he wanted for the Live Demonstration artwork he had a word with band friend and designer Tony French.

The ripped Union Jack swirl on the front of the cassette is a perfect piece of pop art with the flag sliding away into its own sonic vortex, going down a plughole, which Liam Gallagher explained as, 'It's the greatest flag in the world, and it's going down the shitter. We're here to do something about it.'

'They had recorded the demo tape,' explains Tony French, 'and Noel said, "We need a cover for it, can you do something?" There was a Union Jack painted on the wall of the Boardwalk rehearsal room and he said can we put something like that on the cover because it's British and iconic, so I twisted it around.

'It was the very early days of the Apple Mac and when I was at work I ran the flag through a programme called QuarkXpress, creating the Union Jack swirl, and I then stuck the Oasis logo on top, which I had done with Univers Black italic.'

When Noel saw it he thought it looked like the flag was going down a plughole and asked for a plug to be added because, as he commented, 'Tony forgot to put the plughole in the middle of the flag so we always had to explain it to everyone.'

The Oasis logo, like its follow-ups, would signpost the band's career. 'Initially I put a box around the "Oasis" logo,' says Tony, 'but Noel said, "I don't like that" so I outlined it for the demo tape, and then for the T-shirts and the posters it was filled in on top of the Union Jack and that T-shirt was a huge seller UK.'

The new artwork looked great and gave the new demo a perfect classic context, yet it would not be long before another pop art designer joined the gang.

Noel Gallagher had met Brian Cannon a few months before at New Mount Street, where they had both been running around its industrious tight-knit hive of activity.

'I'd seen Noel before, walking around and we had passed each other in the corridor,' remembers Brian. 'I thought, "Who is this guy?" But we were too cool for school to let on. One day we were both in the lift. Someone was going to have to blink first and Noel asked me about my trainers. I explained that I got them in Italy when I took mother there on a recent trip to celebrate her 60th. We went to Rome and took a day trip to Florence to the Uffizi gallery, and I bought this pair of Adidas Indoor Supers in a small backstreet store. Noel then asked what I did and I said I designed record sleeves and he said, "People want to be footballers or rock stars and you want to design sleeves!" I had done two sleeves for the the Verve and he really liked them and he said, "I'm getting a band together and you can do the sleeves when and not if we get signed." Even then he knew what he wanted and how to get it. A bit later he gave me their Live Demonstration demo and I loved the Union Jack inlay.'

The aspiring songwriter invited Brian along to one of the inter-mittent local Oasis shows.

'Noel had been mithering me to go and watch his band for ages, and I kept putting it off because I liked Noel, and we got on, and I thought they have got to be shite because your mate's band is always rubbish, but I said I would go along to their June 1993 gig at the Hop and Grape[4] in Manchester when they were supporting Dodgy.'

14

BRITPOP

In April 1993 *Select* magazine had a bold front cover feature written by Stuart Maconie about a sylph-like new London scene defying the monolithic American showbiz machine with a manifesto of Britishness that somehow each band represented in their own ways. It was placed under the umbrella of 'Britpop' – a term that we had been percolating around the music press for a few years but now found a new usage.[1]

The famous front cover photo was of Suede's svelte singer Brett Anderson with a Union Jack in the background under the provocative headline 'Yanks go home!' Suede were the current music press faves and their debut singles in 1992 had created a stir with their audacious indie glam anthems that saw their recent eponymous March 1993 album becoming one of the fastest selling debuts that year. The erudite band, with their charismatic singer and their leather and lace songs of bedsit sex and androgyne nightlife, made them the Oxfam exotic pin-ups of the new scene's suburban art pop. An art pop that turned up the style with a sassy sexiness and a link back to the wam-bam-thank-you-glam of Bowie and Bolan, the darker hues of goth, the Smiths' Smithsonian cool and the British love of dressing up.

The Union Jack had been wrestled back from the far right, and it felt cool to be British again.

Ironically, for very different reasons the Britpop cover saw no mention of either of the eventual 'Battle of Britpop' bands, Oasis or Blur, while embracing Saint Etienne, Pulp, Denim and the Auteurs as the new Brit broom that was here to sweep away the grunge scene.

While Oasis were under the radar making demos with the Real People in Liverpool and yet to play in London, Blur were not a new band. It had been two years since they had released their debut top 10 *Leisure* album in 1991, which had crammed their quirky art pop into Madchester baggy with a sound that a younger Noel Gallagher had acknowledged at the time as being a 'breath of fresh air'.

Still trying to find their own way, 1993 Blur were part of 'the Scene That Celebrates Itself', an ad hoc collection of bands, producers, managers, writers, PRs and indie faces that congregated in the Syndrome club on Wednesday nights on London's Oxford Street.[2] It was also the key hangout for the so-called shoegaze bands on the London scene – so named because they had their heads down while looking at their effects pedals. The bands created walls of treated guitar sound and were an artful, ambient take on My Bloody Valentine with groups like Slowdive, Lush, Moose and Ride, and with Creation Records being the key label. A new skinny, indie aesthetic driven by speed and good times and with linear music to match was also appearing in places like Blow Up at the Laurel Tree pub or hanging out in the Good Mixer pub in Camden Town, championed by the London music media.[3]

Britpop was a knowing retro/modern picture postcard Brit culture. It was not so much Village Green but Indie Club Preservation Society.

In a slice of convergent musical evolution, Blur's 1993 second album, Modern Life Is Rubbish, also celebrated British pop culture. It was inspired after the band's 1992 flop tour of the USA that saw them embrace the Kinks, XTC and music hall vaudeville in a more angular British sounding album.

It felt like the whole scene was getting run out of the music PR offices of Savage & Best in Camden, and any visit to their vibrant space was always fun and full of salacious gossip and a genuine connection to great music. The company run by Jane Savidge and John Best were game-changers; they did press for all the main bands in the scene whether it was with the new breed like Suede or those old lags like Pulp, the Sheffield band who had been reshaped with their own innate pop nous suddenly fitting into Britpop now. Savage & Best spotted the talent and ambition in Jarvis and some-how helped to turn him from geeky outsider to unlikely sex symbol and cool icon. They also did PR for the suited and booted Elastica who were at the core of the London scene with a tougher, punkier sound in a mix of the Stranglers' grinding basslines, Wire's short sharp shock song aesthetic and Adam Ant's sex music.

The first battle for the heart and soul of Britpop was Blur v Suede and was driven by the fact that Elastica's super cool singer Justine Frischmann had once gone out with Brett and was now partners with Blur's Damon Albarn.

Britpop was the press rage and Manchester was seen as dead despite World of Twist being perfect for the savvy new scene – even being supported by Pulp and Saint Etienne before the battle lines were redrawn. Somehow, the Inspiral Carpets curiously managed to carry on from one scene to the next and scored some of their biggest hits into the new era without the skinny, warm leatherette cool of the new bands but with their knack for writing great songs.

Hand in hand with this cultural shift was the rise of lad culture with its own bible, *Loaded* magazine, edited brilliantly by former fanzine editor James Brown. It was a cheeky mix of cartoon *Viz*-style comedy, serious culture articles and old-school pin-ups.

No one was looking up north as Britpop really meant London-based pop, leaving Oasis grafting in isolation. Despite the band's self-belief and the clutch of great new songs there was no sign of a record deal. Was there still such a thing as a maverick record-label boss driven by an innate instinctive desire to sign a band?

15

AN ACT OF CREATION

On the afternoon of 31 May 1993 Oasis were sat in a splitter van chugging up the M6 towards Glasgow to gatecrash a gig that their rehearsal room buddies Sister Lovers had invited them to without telling the promoter. Debbie Turner explains:

'One of the cool things about the Boardwalk was that you could go to the gigs upstairs for free after rehearsing. One night the Afghan Whigs were on, with Boyfriend supporting, [1 October 1992] who we asked if we could support Boyfriend in Glasgow and they said "yes".

'The next day after rehearsing we were swapping over with Oasis and I said, pretty cocky like, "We've got our first gig and it's in Glasgow." Noel looked up, and my knee jerk reaction was, why don't you do it as well? They already had connections with Boyfriend, because Coyley was doing monitors for Teenage Fan Club and all those Scottish bands. So I think because of that, Noel was able to go to Coyley and maybe sort it out behind the scenes.'

In Glasgow that night to see his sister for a few drinks to celebrate his birthday, Alan McGee, the head of Creation Records, ended up at the gig at King Tut's.

'I had no idea that Alan would be there,' Debbie points out, 'even though I was very good friends with him. He told someone, I'll go and stand in front of Debbie while she does her first gig and freak her out because that's Alan's sense of humour. Before the gig we were all really nervous and I remember Alan coming in early and there is a Polaroid of us stood at the bar chatting.'

Oasis arrived in a two-van convoy with 17 Mancs chipping in for a big Glasgow night out and nothing was going to stop them according to Noel. 'We drove all the way up to Glasgow for the gig but no one had told the promoter that we were playing and he said he didn't have a licence to put on four bands, but we ended up blagging on to play four songs as the doors opened.'

'I remember Oasis and their entourage arriving in the gold Mercedes splitter that they'd hired,' explains Debbie. 'I just remember us saying to Boyfriend if they can't play then we're not doing it. Alan was saying to the venue owner just let them play because it's not worth the hassle.'

The promoter driven was more than a bit surprised that a fourth band had turned up all the way from Manchester for a three-band bill. There was a discussion but no threat to trash the venue as the myth goes.

Alan McGee laughs: 'I got there early to see Debbie's band because she is one of the coolest people I've ever met in music. I walked into the venue and the night is running late and it's not even open yet and there was this band that Debbie has brought up from Manchester hanging about.

'I looked over and saw this amazing looking kid with a white tracksuit on. I thought he must be the drug dealer because bands at that time always had a cool-looking drug dealer with them. I then went upstairs to have a drink with my sister.'

As the doors opened the band took to the stage in front of their mates. Tony French sets the scene: 'We were sat on the benches at the back of the venue when Oasis played. It was pretty empty with people rolling in because they were on early yet it was the best performance I'd seen them do.'

'I was in the bar chatting with Gerry Love from Teenage Fan Club,' remembers Alan McGee. 'Somebody shouted, "That band's coming on, McGee", I went into the room and the cool guy in the white tracksuit was the singer so good start! The first song they played was "Rock 'n' Roll Star" and it was great and I was thinking, who the fuck is this? I bet the next song will be rubbish but it was "Bring It On Down", and that was great as well. They then played "Up in the Sky" and I was thinking I'm gonna sign these but I was quite drunk and maybe that's making them sound better than they are! Then the singer goes, "This one is 'I Am the Walrus'" and I thought this will be where it goes wrong as who can cover that? But it was a brilliant version. Now I'm thinking these are genius. I must sign them. I might have been late to the party but I got there at the right moment and I totally saw it even if there was no one else in the room.'

Blown away, Alan McGee looked at the sound guy. 'It was Mark Coyle who I knew from doing the sound for Teenage Fan Club, so I asked him who's the leader of the band and he went to find Noel who comes trotting down the stairs.'

Noel Gallagher laughs: 'Now people still try and pick over this story but this is what actually happened. I came off stage, McGee came up to me and said, "I really like your band what are you called?" and I said, "Oasis" and then he said, "Do you know who am I am?" and I went, "No!" He then said, "Do you want a record deal?" and I said, "Who with?" and he said, "I run Creation Records" and I said, "Oh right, it's Alan McGee!" He wrote down his number and I said, "I'll give you a ring" and then he said, "Have you got a manager?" and I said, "No, it's just us."

'I went out of King Tut's and got the demo with the swirly Union Jack on the cover from the van. He asked, "Is it any good?" and I said, "Yeah, it's all right!" He said, "Are there any of the songs on it that you played tonight?" and I said, "I don't think so." So he said "I don't want to hear it in case it's shit," but I gave it him anyway.'

Sonically that night the Sex Beatles juggernaut had arrived and the band had never sounded as good and as if to prove there is a rock 'n' roll god the only person who would have got it was in the room off his head and still in touch with his instincts.

'If he had seen us in January when it was not quite there he wouldn't have signed us,' nods Noel. 'But that was the night when everything clicked. We did four songs, and they were all brilliant. I love the way it all happened like a shrug of the shoulders.'

Noel and Alan had briefly crossed paths before.

'I knew about Creation Records and Primal Scream and had seen Alan in the Haçienda. There was a big cardboard cutout of him in Eastern Bloc record shop in Manchester City centre in the late eighties and I remember him being interviewed on *The Other Side of Midnight* by Tony Wilson when he claimed he had moved to Manchester in 1988 because it had better drugs.'

'As soon as I met Noel that night I liked him straight away,' explains Alan. 'This was his moment. And it was mine. I had briefly met him at Reading Festival in 1989 when he was roadying and was with someone who worked for Creation called Hannah and she introduced us. I had no idea who he was but he would have known who I was because she had told him all the mad stories about Creation. I also remember being in Debbie's rehearsal room before a Sugar gig at the Boardwalk in 1992 and we had a crafty wee spliff. I looked around the room and saw the Union Jack painted on the wall and she told me Oasis had painted it.'

Tony McCarroll saw something was going on: 'Alan must have approached Noel separately and Noel came back upstairs to the dressing room and said, "We just got offered a record deal and Alan is coming up so act cool." Nobody was interested in us and then, lo and behold, Alan McGee saw us. It was pure luck that he didn't get that train home that night and got us straight away.'

Tony French watched the whole thing unfold: 'After the gig, Liam came down for a chat and Noel went off upstairs with Alan McGee. Half an hour later he came down smirking and told everyone that the band had been signed. Creation was the right label. Primal Scream was on there. They would get it. To be honest, back then I thought it would never happen because it's so surreal sitting in the basement, listening to your mates every night and going to the pub, and then suddenly it happens.'

Ironically Debbie Turner missed the famous moment: 'After Oasis played I missed what was going on as we were setting up to play. When Alan said he was going to sign them it was no surprise because it was Alan, and he does that kind of thing!

'He obviously saw a lot more in them than Factory or other labels. Alan liked the fact that it was a Manchester band and he always liked the Happy Mondays and the Stone Roses and that whole movement but I don't think for a moment he thought they were going to be as big as they were.'

The first person to love the band, Alan McGee, was running on pure instinct. 'Factory had turned them down,' says Alan. 'Tony had the chance and said no. The band was great and Noel was a real character and he had something nobody else had. I could just feel it. He was already a star roadie. A genuine character with lots of talent and a vision, and Liam also had that star thing. Oasis seemed so perfect that I thought there must be a catch.'

That night McGee rang Creation PR Johnny Hopkins.

'It was midnight on 31 May and I'm in bed and the phone rang over and over,' remembers Johnny. 'It was Alan saying, "I've seen this amazing group. They've got real attitude and great songs and I want you to do the press." Half an hour later it was Alan again:

"They're like the Sex Pistols and the Beatles" and he called every half an hour throughout the night totally excited.'

Returning from Glasgow with a potential record deal Noel Gallagher got busy.

'The only person that I knew with any business acumen in Manchester was Anthony Boggiano who was the Inspirals' manager,' says Noel. 'I hadn't seen him for ages since I got the boot but I phoned him for advice. I said I had met Alan McGee last night and he offered us a record deal – is he liable to be taking the piss or is he serious? Anthony said, "I'll find out for you." I don't know who he called but he rang back and said McGee is deadly serious and he said, "Do you need a manager?" and I said, "I'll get back to you on that!"

'It was absolutely meant to happen. It was like he was saying I'm giving you a car now, do what you want with it but don't fucking crash it! The Creation people were like, what do you want to do? What a brilliant question to ask because it's not like they were telling you what to do.

'It was a marriage made in heaven. I love Alan. He's a believer, and once he's into you, nothing will sway him. Other music biz people said to him, "Where are they from?" and he would say, "Manchester" and they were not having it.'

Creation was the perfect label for the band and the band were everything McGee had been working towards with his vision of sixties pop art crossed with the incendiary rush of punk.

A few days later, on 3 June, Noel, Liam and Bonehead went to London to meet the label.

'Then the famous meeting takes place when we go down to London to the Creation office in Hackney,' Noel recalls. 'Me, Liam and Bonehead drove there. I was doing the Andrew Loog Oldham thing, saying leave all the talking to me. I was expecting something like Factory Records but when we arrived in this run-down street we were pretty underwhelmed. We knocked on the door and there was this sweatshop inside with what looked like illegal immigrants on sewing machines. This guy comes out and says, "What do you want?" We said we are looking for Creation Records and he said it's upstairs. Liam was freaking out, going we should have signed to EMI – what kind of office is this. I was saying this must be where they do their merch! We went upstairs and walked in and it's like a cottage industry. They seemed to know who we were straight away and the first person I see is Andy Bell who is photocopying some Ride reviews.'

'I happened to be at the Creation office one afternoon when they all turned up for their first visit,' remembers Andy. 'I was just in there for some reason and they all arrived, [these] Mancs suddenly filled the room, a change from the mostly Glaswegian accents I was used to at Creation! They had great vibes, very friendly, they were saying hello to everyone and then disappeared downstairs to the bunker with McGee, a vibey little gang looking around.'

Andy heard the demo: 'I first heard them in LA on a tape in a car with Alan McGee. I was out there with Mark Gardener working on some songs with George Drakoulias at Rick Rubin's house. Primal Scream and McGee arrived in town and because they were staying at the Chateau Marmont and we were just a few minutes away we all ended up hanging out together for a few days. Alan had this demo tape which I think he had got from Johnny Marr, the one with the Union Jack. I heard it in his hire car, it had quite a few songs on including, "Married with Children" and "Bring It On Down", if I remember right. We listened to it in the bright LA sunshine, driving up to someone's party. It was so perfect for Creation. I thought it sounded like the Jesus and Mary Chain mixed with the early Stones or something.'

Creation PR Johnny Hopkins also had a meeting with them on that first day in London: 'There was a screech of brakes and they got out of the car looking totally Manc. They came in and you could feel the excitement in the room. The meeting was like a crazy collision between the Sex Pistols and all those early Beatles interviews in America. Really funny, really cheeky, taking the piss but in a really intelligent way. The camaraderie between the three of them was just brilliant and beautiful in those early days.'

Noel Gallagher: 'In the corner someone had sprayed in black like the Jam logo on the wood chip "northern ignorance" and at that point I thought this is going to be fucking great!'

The new MD of Creation at the time was Tim Abbot. His younger brother Chris recalls, 'My brother had written "northern ignorance" on the ceiling a few nights before at one of the infamous Creation parties. Noel then came up from McGee's office, the bunker, and we just started chatting and instantly got on. He was aware of all sorts of music like the dance music I was releasing on my Infonet label. Creation bands weren't necessarily always my cup of tea, but I instantly liked this new lot.'

In the weeks that followed, Alan and Noel would go out to London clubs like Andy Weatherall's Sabresonic and the more McGee found out, the more impressed he became.

'Noel is perhaps the smartest person I've ever met in a band. He knew exactly what he was doing. His choice of the record label was correct. His eventual choice of manager was correct and that's really hard. He got a lot of it right and it really fucking worked.'

16

TAKING CARE OF BUSINESS

The stakes had now been raised. With a deal on the table things were now serious and Noel Gallagher knew that he needed a manager. He spoke to World of Twist's manager Caroline Ellary and other faces around town.

Alison Bell remembers: 'Rhys Hughes was my lodger and we would all go out together and Noel asked Rhys if he could manage Oasis but he was really busy with BBC Radio. He also asked Bindi Binning who ran In the City with Tony.'

Bindi Binning: 'Noel had sent me a tape for In the City 1992 and it was awful, but he persuaded me to put them on at the grave-yard slot at the Venue. There was about seven people watching and they were not very good. A year later he then sent me the new demo with the Union Jack on it and he wanted me and Anthony Boggiano to manage them, but Anthony didn't want to so I ended up with the demo and I have never heard anything I was so sure was going to be huge. I loved it so much I recorded it for every-body and I put them on again at In the City 1993. Over the summer I had a few meetings with Noel and Liam and we were about to sort it out then Noel said Johnny Marr had told him to go with Marcus Russell who did an amazing job.'

Running round town, Noel had made a new connection.

'What happened next was that there was always this guy at the Haçienda,' Noel says. 'I never knew his name and he always used to go on about his brother being in a band saying, "Our kid has just done a gig." One day I had a HMV bag and I just bought Dusk[1] by The The and this guy was asking about the band and I said I've been offered a deal by Creation and he said, "That's pretty cool, what record is in that bag?" and I said, "It's the new album by The The." And he said, "Our kid's really chuffed with it" and I said, "Who is your fucking brother?" and he said Johnny Marr and I said, "Wow, he's your brother! Why didn't you say!" and he said, "You never asked!" I said, "Wow, man, I love the Smiths," so we went back to mine and I gave him one of the new Oasis demos with my phone number on it.'

When Ian Marr played the demo to Johnny he liked what he heard.

'Within two days Johnny had given me a call saying, "This is Johnny Marr" and I'm going, "Wow! this is the guy from the fucking Smiths and he's called me and really likes the demo." We met up and he said, "I really like your stuff, what guitars are you using?" and I said, "I go to this vintage guitar place in Doncaster called Music Ground." He had never heard of it as he got his guitars in London, so the next day, he picks me up in a car and we go to Doncaster. Johnny gives me some advice about having to eat before guitar shopping because "you might be some time!" And then he went and bought this mad-looking Strat.

'On the trip I said, "I'm looking for a manager" and he said, "I've got a great manager called Marcus Russell" and he then passed our stuff on to Marcus and I thought if Marcus is good enough for Johnny Marr then he's fucking good enough for me.'

Sharing a musical, sartorial and stylistic sense of pop classic and even a Man City thing, the Mancunian guitarists now also potentially shared a manager. They met up again a few days later to see the Verve play Manchester Hop and Grape and then arranged for Marcus to come and see Oasis play at the same venue on 18 June where they were supporting Dodgy.

Marcus Russell had good form. He left Ebbw Vale in 1975 and studied education at Middlesex Polytechnic, where he promoted punk gigs, including a show by the Sex Pistols on 19 November 1976. After college he settled in Essex where he took up a teaching job. When his marriage ended, and disillusioned with teaching, he drifted into management with eighties hopefuls Latin Quarter. Following the Smiths' split in 1987, he managed Johnny Marr and then Electronic.

Johnny Marr's enthusiasm about this new band had got him intrigued enough to go the gig at the top of three flights of stairs at the Hop and Grape.

Touring their debut Ian Broudie-produced album, headliner Dodgy's crafted guitar indie was building them a good following that would soon see them in the Britpop slipstream. On stage at 7pm, Oasis played to a handful of people, impressing Dodgy drummer Mathew Priest:

'I remember thinking what a great wall of fucking noise. What was so clever about it was to have that voice loud and central in the mix. They were also menacing and I got it. I remember backstage the Real People were with them and there was some pretty explicit drug taking. We were more discreet in case your nan walks in! They were blatant and on all surfaces.'

After the gig, noticing Noel didn't have enough guitars, Johnny Marr gave him the Les Paul he had used in the Smiths that Pete Townshend had given him. Noel promptly took it home and wrote 'Slide Away'.

Also at the gig was Brian Cannon who Noel had invited to come and see them a couple of months before at New Mount Street.:

'I was a bit worried. I mean how often do you come across a good band? There's only one every 10 years. So what's the odds of this guy, who I met in the lift of being any good? I got there late, and I missed the start of the set. There was hardly anyone at the gig and they blew my fucking head off. I couldn't believe what I was seeing. I'm not exaggerating either. I was literally, "Jesus Christ!" It was like a juggernaut had come through the wall. I was genuinely speechless, taken aback.'

One of the early handful of people who got it, Brian had seen a future and in the next few days threw his lot in with the band. While the Creation deal was getting sorted out Noel asked Brian for a new logo that was more versatile than the Tony French one and would work across different medias, including black-and-white press ads.

'Noel was already steeped in pop art ideas,' says Brian. 'Liam was much younger but he had a good barometer and he knew what was cool and what wasn't. He's never gonna look shit and he knows instinctively what's right.'

The iconic Oasis logo was inspired by *The Rolling Stones No. 2* second album cover artwork where the band's manager – the legendary architect of the Stones' bad boy image and much of sixties pop culture, Andrew Loog Oldham – had demanded the band's name was not on the cover, just the scowling David Bailey photo, leaving only the Decca logo in the corner in its neat box. Brian took this logo and crafted and tweaked it into the the now iconic Oasis logo.

The day after the pivotal gig Noel had also phoned Marcus: 'Noel was very charismatic. He said, "Manage us." I said, "Woah, that's a big conversation." Noel replied, "Well, I'm up for a big conversation. You get my train fare and I'll be with you in two hours." I said OK and then he's sitting in a cafe in Marylebone. We got on really well and he gave me the demo.'

Having a proper manager put everything in place for Noel:

'As soon as Marcus got involved he went to see Alan McGee. When Marcus had left the office Alan called me at home and said I just met your manager and it's like, we're AC Milan and he's George Best and we're going to smash the world.

'Marcus, being a manager, was trying to get a better deal and I was saying, "I don't care, the money is not important to me, it's the people that matter." The weeks went on but you just know when you have met the right people. I knew about Creation and McGee from the *NME* and how Primal Scream were allowed to do virtually what they wanted. I remember saying to Marcus I'm not bothered about the deal, I'd rather be at a firm like this than someone telling us what to do.

'Alan then paid two grand for us to go to Loco Studios in Wales in September to demo some new songs, "Live Forever", "Up in the Sky" and "Digsy's Dinner" and we sent him the demos and he said he could only listen to them once, because if he didn't sign us it would have upset him too much. He thought "Live Forever" was the greatest thing he'd ever heard and I said I'm telling you my word is my fucking bond.'

It's easy to see how the Loco Studios version of 'Live Forever' had got McGee so worked up – with a lighter touch and an almost folk rock feel that leans closer to Neil Young, it's a magnificently moving slice of music.

'Alan used to do things like phone you up on a Wednesday and say what you doing?' remembers Noel. 'And I would say it's pissing it down here and he would say I've left two tickets for you and your brother at Piccadilly station, pick them up and come down. We are having a party at the Creation office.

'I thought fucking brilliant and we would go down and get to know all the people that were working there and they were really fucking brilliant and they loved us and they loved the tunes. We hadn't even done any gigs in London at this point so they were not basing it on anything, just our personalities and our music.'

Creation already felt like home and with this new family of noise gathering round him Noel had the tunes, the band, the team, the label . . . and the ambition.

The band's sixth and final appearance at the Boardwalk that July mapped out their gradual ascent, with the Ya Yas now supporting them and Small coming over from Liverpool to complete the bill. Each Boardwalk gig had signposted a sonic and career jump forward, with this gig finally getting them their first music press review in the *NME*, as noted by Noel Gallagher:

'We then do a gig at the Boardwalk and this time noticeably music business types like journalists turn up and there is a little review in the *NME* and it's a great review saying that Manchester has started to reflower.'

The then 17-year-old reviewer Emma Morgan had heard the Oasis demo getting played on the Craig Cash show on Signal. She went to see what the fuss was about and her review was a great early snapshot of the band.

'Shout to the rooftops and dance in the streets – Creation have not gone mad! Oasis are a genuinely fine guitar propelled pop band and they stomp out terrifyingly memorable tunes.'

The crucial first positive review in the press was a big break. They would have had national press even earlier if *Sounds*, the music paper I was writing for and covering, among other things, the Manchester scene, hadn't been closed down on 6 April 1991. If *Sounds* had kept going, Oasis would have already had a review and a feature by 1993.

On 11 August they recorded their first radio session, for BBC 5 Live's *Hit the North* show, recorded live at the then BBC studio on

Manchester Oxford Road. The show normally hosted by Mark Radcliffe and Marc Riley, saw Peter Hook joining Marc as guest presenter that night.

The band rattled through their five songs delivering wall-of-sound versions of 'Bring It On Down', 'I Will Believe', 'Digsy's Dinner', 'Cigarettes & Alcohol' and 'Rock 'n' Roll Star' that all sounded fully formed. It's a great capture of Oasis at their bovver glam best, music wise and attitude wise, as they indulge in banter with Marc Riley and Hooky, as Noel remembers:

'Mark Radcliffe would never have us on because he thought we were shit but he was on holiday so Peter Hook was guest DJing. We did "Cigarettes & Alcohol" with one of our mates playing bongos but he was just some fucking pothead who was into rap music.

'[Hooky] was saying that sounds like fucking T. Rex and we said, "Look at your leather trousers you long-haired freak!" and he said, "By the way you're barred from the Haçienda," and I said, "I already got barred three years ago!" Which I did as I had got my membership card taken off me from when they started doing body searches on people! I got found with loads of drugs that I didn't even remember having on me and I was thinking, "Bastard! I was looking for them before!"

'That was also the night we did "Cigarettes & Alcohol" and on the sunshine bit Liam sings "shieeeeen" like Johnny Rotten and that's where that thing came from, you could see a lightbulb come on in his head thinking, "That's it!"'

On 14 September Oasis played their second In the City at a Creation Records night at the Canal Cafe Bar, sharing a bill with 18 Wheeler and new Creation signing and fellow Boardwalk rehearsal room band, Medalark Eleven, whose crafted indie minimalism built around ex-Bodines singer Mick Ryan was getting noticed but never achieved the expected breakthrough.

A few delegates from In the City plus myself and a smattering of people who paid three quid to get in were at the Canal Cafe bar next door to the Venue on Whitworth Street where they had played last year's In the City and a five-minute walk from Noel's flat. Standing at the side of the venue near the stage I remember the echoing emptiness of the room and the band's invigorating tsunami of sound.

Paul Mathur from the *Melody Maker* gave them their second piece of the national press with an enthralled live review, calling them 'the best new band in Britain', adding, 'Let's get the signposts out of the way first. The Stone Roses, Happy Mondays, the Faces, the Beatles, the Sex Pistols – and, oh, about a million others – have all played their part in creating the joy that is Oasis, but it's the way they pull their influences together and invest them with an exuberant, menacing freshness that makes them so important.'

The set kicked off with brand new song, 'Shakermaker', written 48 hours before and ended with the monolithic noise and confusion of their cover of 'I Am the Walrus', and as the band ground their way to its nihilistic climax, Liam and Noel wandered into the sparse crowd and watched the rest of the band lost in its totemic groove.

There were other key connections getting made that night. Andrew 'McD' McDermid was the manager of fast rising Greenock band Whiteout, whose blue denim country rock combined with a UK indie suss was getting noticed. McD had a great indie radar and he was on the case.

'The first time I heard of Oasis was because Paul the bass player of Whiteout was dating Debbie Turner from Sister Lovers and she told him about them very early on,' says McD. 'After we finished our set at In the City we tried to go and see Oasis play but as we got there they had gone, but Sushil from the BMX Bandits had seen them and he said, "You must see them, they are totally brilliant" and he was the first person to say they're going to be huge.

'Intastella were playing at UMIST with Shaun Ryder singing on the track "Can You Fly Like You Mean It?" So, we went over there and bumped into Debbie who said, "That's Oasis over there", pointing at a couple of guys. So I went up to Liam and said,

"I manage Whiteout and we have a record deal." And he said, "Well, we're going to sign to Creation soon." And we decided to do a tour together and he wrote his name in my phone book and I sent him a Whiteout demo. A month later, Russell Warby, who was now their booking agent, rang up and we sorted out a co-headline tour for March '94.'

A few weeks later, in October, Oasis finally signed the deal with Creation. Now they hit the accelerator.

Noel was getting the full Alan McGee treatment – the genuine blow dryer of enthusiasm from the label boss. Once McGee locks into a band his phone calls to them became a key part of the process. Noel would send demos of new songs to him, and he would reciprocate with vibed-up calls. For McGee, pop culture is about the songs and the characters; and with Oasis, he had struck gold.

'I would sign the person before the music,' Alan says. 'In the case of Oasis they had both and if you have the characters with a unique vision and the music then you have dynamite.'

Also on board was local gig promoter Simon Moran who picked the band up for SJM. He put them on as support on an unlikely bill with American feminist singer-songwriter Liz Phair on 24 September at Manchester University – on the same day as Paul Mathur's perceptive rave *Melody Maker* review was printed. It would be fair to say that there was a culture clash backstage, with the dressing room shenanigans seeing the local band drink the rider, sparking a war of words between the two groups, ending up in a stand-off with what the headline band remember as 'about 20 Mancunian hard lads' and some unfortunate laddish banter.

A few weeks later, the band were back at the same venue for a show originally booked for 6 October but switched to 14 October, where they and the Real People (who didn't show for the gig) opened for the Colne band Milltown Brothers and their cloth-capped Dylan-tinged Waterboys-drenched big indie rock.

Finally they signed to Creation with one last hurdle to clear. 'There was trouble with the name,' explains Noel, 'as there was some band already called Oasis, and Creation was saying you might have to change it. We had a few options like Sons of the Stage from the World of Twist song or the Sex Beatles but it was OK in the end.'

Name sorted, the band were sent out on their first UK tour on a short Creation label package supporting BMX Bandits and, again, 18 Wheeler. Fronted by the angular pop eccentric Duglas T. Stewart, the Glasgow thrift store indie pop eccentrics BMX Bandits were one of Kurt Cobain's favourite all-time bands with their underground hit 'Serious Drugs'. They were pals of Teenage Fan Club and their loveably quirky take on sixties songwriter craft created a wonderfully whimsical mix of indie pop perfection that somehow embraced bubble-gum and the Beach Boys in a confection of dayglo indie.

Label mates they may have been but it was an unlikely combination of bands, yet Duglas hit it off with the Gallaghers, particularly Liam.

'The one I felt most connected with was, definitely, Liam,' recalls Duglas. 'He reminded me of certain guys who were in my class at school. I went to a kind of average, regular primary school in Bellshill, an industrial town in the west of Scotland. There would be a guy in your class who would be funny. He'd say something cheeky, and he'd get sent down the front of the class, where he'd say something funny, and then he'd get sent down to the headmaster's. When he'd get down there, he'd say something even more outrageous. Next thing, he'd be walking through the playground swinging his arms in the air, and you'd sort of be laughing, and he reminded me of those characters!'[2]

In October the band returned to Out of the Blue in Manchester for their second session at the Blossom Street studios to record more demos for Creation.

The session ended up with the demo of a new song, 'Shakermaker', that would become the eventual chassis for the single version after going through a long and winding road of mixes and edits.

Another older song, 'Columbia', first played live on 15 January 1992 at the band's second Boardwalk gig, and recorded at the Porter Street sessions with the Real People, was remixed and would get a limited edition release that December as the 'White Label Demo', while the third song from the session was 'Married with Children'.

It was also the first photo session the band did with photographer Michael Spencer Jones and the shots he took have become iconic over the years and saw the start of his five-year photographic journey with the band.

'I had moved up to Manchester after college and I was freelancing when the whole Manchester and Roses thing was going off in 1989,' says Michael. 'It seemed totally natural at the time, and it's only when you look back you realise how special it was. Noel had seen the photos I had done for the Verve's "All in the Mind" single and asked if I could do some with Oasis and I went to Out of the Blue where they were demoing "Shakermaker".'

When Michael arrived at the studio it was the first time he had met the band and he was immediately struck by the creative dynamic between the Gallagher brothers, with Noel directing Liam on how to play a shaker to the track. The first photo he took of Oasis was an unposed, candid shot that revealed the intimate relationship between the two brothers within the band at the time – Noel the creative driving force and Liam the genuine X factor rock 'n' roll star. He was also impressed by their boldness and confidence like how they just lifted the 'I'd like to buy the world a Coke' melody from the ad for the song without any thought to the consequences.

The series of photos caught a young band in their working environment and are great shots. When he showed the band the results they were impressed and, along with Brian Cannon and Noel, Spencer Jones became part of the creative pool who came up with or executed the concepts for the iconic sleeve art for the first three albums and attendant singles.

The next session the photographer would do with the band would be shooting the 'Supersonic' sleeve at Monnow Valley Studios a few weeks later in January 1994.

Oasis were now in fast forward.

17

NOW HERE WE ARE . . .

In late November 1993 Creation sent out 510 white label copies of 'Columbia' as the 'White Label Demo' to the music media to start building up the buzz on the band. The track instantly made an impact with its visceral power and nagging melody that sounded both unique and familiar with its sense of high-decibel longing.

Named after the notorious rock 'n' roll hotel in London where Noel and Mark Coyle stayed on roadie duties with the Inspiral Carpets and a place where, since 1975, bands have raised hell, it was initially an instrumental that after the Real People sessions had turned into a song. The lengthy opening salvo in Oasis's career had started its journey from the rehearsal jams, studio sessions and Liam's vocal before being chiselled by Noel into a mesmerising 5-minute 24-second calling card of brooding tension, dirty guitars and that killer defining vocal that went from falsetto to drawl.

'Columbia' came complete with its long coda as an early indicator of the band's extended mantra-type songs, with a mesmerising layering of guitars as a nod to the long, aching lead lines and guitar skree of Neil Young.

The song's hook, with the brothers in vocal harmony, defined the mood of uplifting dislocation at the heart of all great rock. Providing no answers in its wall-of-sound and sonic dancefloor oblivion, it hypnotises with its perfect pop/noise and cut-up Tony Benn speech loop quoting the biblical phrase 'Take away for me the noise of your song' before the of song finally dissolves into the Hare Krishna chanting sample, perhaps as a cosmic nod to Beatle George.

The White Label Demo sparked interest in a band still yet to play in London with more press and national radio play. For Liam and Noel this was only going one way and Alan McGee was more than happy to facilitate.

'It really started to happen when we released the White Label,' the Creation boss says. 'The press and radio caught fire and everything came at us and we were playing catch-up. Normally it takes time to build up a band through the music press, evening radio and then maybe a TV with programmes at the time like *The Word*.

'This time felt different in that we knew the band was genius and that Noel was totally sussed and Liam was a total rock star. Being a small cult band wasn't in their masterplan. We would have meetings in the pub with people from my label and the Creation speed dealer and Noel would say, "We are going to be the biggest band in the world!" And then it happened!'

Ride's Andy Bell caught a secret showcase gig the band played in London at the end of the year.

'Alan knew I liked them,' remembers Andy, 'so he would always pass on their demos, and when they did a secret showcase gig at the Powerhaus, he brought me with him. The set – to a pretty much empty room was fantastic, all the record company heads were standing at the back because they were petrified, so I ended up in the front row. It was in essence the same thing they took all the way to Maine Road, just a shorter set. Everything else was in place, finishing with "I Am the Walrus". Liam was off stage wandering through the room at that point. After the gig Alan introduced me to Noel and Liam, we chatted for a few minutes and I said I'd loved the gig.'

A couple of early December shows in Glasgow and Birmingham supporting Saint Etienne saw a great review from Calvin Bush in the *Melody Maker*, stating 'They are frankly, incredible.' In contrast, *NME* reviewer Johnny Cigarettes branded them 'refugees from 1989 Manc scally.'

The media battle lines were already being drawn.

Hitting the road Oasis, like all the greatest rock 'n' roll bands, created a harmony out of chaos that can just as easily flip the other way round. There was the occasional bust-up but then no great band like the Beatles, Stones, Sex Pistols, Kinks and the Who has ever existed without threatening to implode. It's this danger quotient that gives a band its edge. It may be a nightmare to deal with but any group without this is clocking in and that's boring.

Whatever tension and cracks that appeared would be sorted out and on 8 December they joined the Verve in Wolverhampton for six dates that would forge the enduring relationship between the two northern bands that would survive decades.

The Verve's melancholic, introspective and atmospheric style may have contrasted with Oasis's ostensibly more raucous Sex Beatles wall of sound but they shared an attitude and an ambition to break away from the stifling indie underground. Richard Ashcroft explained this to me in a 1992 interview on an interesting afternoon in West Didsbury where he was staying for a few months, and where we bumped into Liam Gallagher walking down the street. It was interesting to see the mutual respect between the two singers at the time with the Verve frontman a cult hero and Liam a potential new force.

'I don't really care how well we do, we could pack up tomorrow and we'd know that we'd done all this in style,' Richard told me. 'What's the point in being this special and only selling 3,000 records, we want to be as successful as possible. It's not that indie thing for me; why not believe that you can sell to a million people? It's not a sin to think big.'

The tour worked its way round mid-sized venues and were the biggest shows Oasis had played so far. Slightly ahead of the curve, some nights they were playing to fairly empty rooms but encouraged by the headliners whose singer could often be spotted in the audience, arms aloft, as they played the anthemic 'Live Forever'.

High jinks, high expectations and higher than kites, the tour ended in Bradford on 14 December. Two days later Oasis were supporting the Real People in Liverpool at the Krazy House and then a day or so after that they were booked into the studio in the same city to record a debut single.

18

YOU CAN HAVE IT ALL

Back in Liverpool Oasis delivered a gig full of musical attitude as the up-and-coming studio session engineer David Scott remembers:

'They all had their coats on, all zipped up, and I was like, What the fuck is this? They're all just standing like statues bashing out this four/four stompy thing but it sounded great. I remember I went to the dressing room afterwards. I hadn't recognised them when they were on the stage playing, but then I remembered Bonehead and the rest from the Rain demo. The Real People were a bit put out that I already knew the band because this was their baby, you know.'

A couple of days later the band went to Liverpool's Pink Museum studio to record their debut single and some demos. Whatever the plan was, it all changed during the session. Still figuring out how to get their studio sound right, Noel had brought Mark Coyle to the session as a sort of executive producer.

'The Real People were also producing as well. They were partying at first, and it wasn't until halfway that they made contributions,' remembers David Scott adding, 'I felt that I was kind of the lynchpin. I had

to stay in control of it all because I was surrounded by fucking lunatics, albeit talented lunatics! I got the session because a few weeks
before I went up to the Real People's Dock Road studio one night
just after Oasis had been in there. I played the Real People this thing
I'd been working on with Liverpool band the Stairs,[1] called "Skin
Up for Me Baby". Coyley was still there and he really liked its sound
and mentioned it to Noel and it was decided to record some Oasis
songs at the studio I was working in, Pink Museum.'

Alan McGee was keen for Oasis to record 'Bring It On Down' as
their statement debut single. He figured a Pistolian wall-of-sound
punk rock anthem seething with claustrophobia, nihilism and barely
repressed anger would be a V-sign statement of intent. According to
David Scott, though, the session started with another track.

'The story is that we were trying to record, "Bring It On Down"
for a single, but we weren't and for some reason we were mainly
trying to record a track called, "I Will Believe", but I'm the only
person in the world who seems to remember this. As a song, it just
wasn't solid enough and a bit shoegazey and the band didn't seem
to have their heart in it. I was sitting there with Coyley for hours
trying to make it sound right.'

Noel Gallagher: 'Alan had heard more tunes I had sent him and
he said demo them so I can play them to people and also record an
A-side and we ended up recording "Supersonic" by accident. He
originally wanted "Bring It On Down" for the first single and we
were in the studio trying to do that and for some reason it wasn't
fucking happening.'

It was time to take a break . . .

'It had all been getting a bit fraught,' remembers David Scott.
'They had done take after take, and in the time out, Noel banged
out this acoustic song, "Take Me Away", on his Epiphone acoustic
guitar and it sounded great. He put a slide guitar on it, played it
with a pint glass, and Coyley put it through this Roland Space
Echo and pushed the faders up and it was mixed in five minutes.'[2]

It was a million miles away from the other song in terms of quality and performance and I was like, "Wow, okay, this is good!"'

With one good track recorded it was time to get in control of the session. On the last day, 'Supersonic' would appear virtually out of nowhere remembers Dave:

'There were lots of people hanging out in the studio like the guys from Small and the Real People, so I kicked most of them out of the control room. Tony Griffiths[3] came in and I said to him, "This is not the band I saw supporting you, where's the rock 'n' roll? Where's the attitude? Where's the power? Why don't we just do something completely new?"

'I said, "The jam that Oasis had just done when I was sound-checking them sounded great. Why don't we work on that, Coyley? This is your baby, why don't you put that to them?" They were now ready for anything because they did not want to go back to that other song, so Noel got on the case and worked out the chords properly and put a vocal melody on it and they just went in and pretty much played the song in one take.'

Seizing the moment, Noel had created a slice of pop magic.

'Then the idea comes for us to write another song,' recalls Noel. 'My reaction to that was "Who's we?!" So I said you lot go and take loads of drugs and watch the telly and I'll go in the back room and try and write a song, so come back in a bit.'

The songwriter worked the chords and jotted down some rough lyrics and lo and behold 'Supersonic', a slice of pop/noise guitar perfection. Noel was on a roll:

'It's the kind of moment you look back on and wish in a kind of way that you had taken more notice of what was going on but in a way you're glad you didn't. In those days, I could go around the back and write the song in a minute, whereas today, I would be thinking of 15 reasons why it would be shit, but it came out of nowhere and we recorded it that fucking night.'

All the best rock 'n' roll comes out of a vaccum, as David Scott witnessed: 'Noel was shouting the chords out and Bonehead was showing them on his guitar neck to Guigsy so that he could get the bass line. Then the drums just started that bomb, ba, boom, boom, bah thing and Noel says, "Hang on! make that the intro" and it all fell together.'

Tony McCarroll: 'I was making this very simple beat, more playing with the splash of the hi-hats and next thing, Noel kicks the door open and says, "Keep that going!" He must have had something in his head and lo and behold we had "Supersonic". It took minutes to record and that was the perfect introduction to Oasis for the world. It just really sets the stage, doesn't it? And I'm dead proud to be the first member of Oasis that most people heard when the single came out.

'I was inspired by that brilliant lazy swing that Reni from the Stone Roses had and I always thought that keeping it simple is the key and do what the song needs. We filled each other's gaps because we knew each other so well and it just flowed.'

The magic of Oasis was that when they were switched on they were unbeatable. Off the cuff in a loose studio session they made magic even on borrowed time and borrowed gear.

Noel then overdubbed a great guitar line reminiscent in its aching spirituality to George Harrison's god-embracing spiritual masterpiece 'My Sweet Lord' – a lead line that was given its swirling movement by being stuck through a phaser like Kurt Cobain used, as David Scott explains:

'I was paranoid about anything being too rock and I thought we need to make the solo sound a bit more naive and add a texture to it so I got him [Noel] to double track the solo and that worked really well. They then took a little break while we did the vocal which at first was basically Noel la, la, la ing the tune he wanted while writing the words.'

With a bit of lubrication the words came.

'Noel needed a drink before writing the words,' says Dave. 'He didn't want whisky because it gave him a headache. I mentioned I recently had a gin and tonic and it hit me like a Class A and I was buzzing my head off. He said "I'm having that! Get me some gin and tonic!" So they went out to the offy and that's where the lyric came from.'

The gin and tonic also loosened up Noel's lyrical side of the brain and created a Shaun Ryder-style stream of unconscious nonsense with other surrounding influences.

David Scott: 'My dog, Elsa, was sitting on the white studio couch next to Bonehead. There was a coffee stain on the settee and Elsa was farting nonstop and the guys found this hilarious, because you could actually hear it! She's lying there, and she farts a massive one next to this coffee stain, and Bonehead just goes, "Your dog's followed through on the settee, mate" and that's where that Elsa line came from! The BMW in the lyrics belonged to manager Marcus Russell.'

A tumbling list of non sequiturs grabbed out of thin air from the surrounding chaos painted a surreal picture just like Marc Bolan's brilliant poetic palaver. Of course, most great lyrics make little sense. They hold the melody and create a rush of images in your head. A pop song doesn't have to be a manifesto or an academic exercise and the tumble of phrases and in-jokes in 'Supersonic' made their own sense.

Noel jotted down the lyrics and gave them to Liam, singing the melody line before the younger brother stepped up to the mic and remarkably delivered the melody perfectly with every nuance and phrasing in place.

'Noel was very regimented about it because he knew what he wanted,' remembers Tony McCarroll. 'In rehearsals, he would sometimes come in and play the song on an acoustic and the next week there would be words to it and I would be thinking, "Ah, that's where he was going." I don't know how Liam ever got the

melody of the songs so quickly! Did they meet up in secret and he'd
say, "This is how you sing this?"'

When it came to the singing Liam was an instinctive perfectionist.
Like Elvis he made sense of whatever lyrics were handed to him and
he defined them by giving everything. Every ounce of his being went
into the vocal, adding a level of intensity without losing any of the
melody that defined his style. Part of the art of writing great songs is
grabbing them out of thin air, but a great vocalist brings them to life
and turns them into something else – this was the art of Liam.

A couple of hours later and with an excellent Beatles-style
harmony added by Tony from the Real People in the breakdown
sections, they had a song exploding from the speakers. Noel knew
this had to be the single:

'We did a rough mix of it and I thought it was the best thing I'd
ever fucking heard and we sent it to McGee. Alan had been so
adamant about "Bring It On Down" being the first single with its
lyrics of being about the underclass and being an outcast. Now I was
adamant that "Supersonic" should be the first single because of the
nonsense Happy Mondays-type lyrics. So Alan went, "I think you're
wrong but it's your call . . . " For him to let us do that was great and I
have so much respect for Alan for letting me call the shots that early.'

They knew that they had the song. It must have been spine-tingling.

A couple of days after the recording of 'Supersonic' on 22
December the band were in London to record a session for BBC
Radio 1's *The Evening Session*. The new show was hosted by Steve
Lamacq and Jo Whiley, who had just been paired together by Radio
1 in the recent shake-up as the switched-on evening radio DJs that
were going to be the portal for indie.

It was all very right place at the right time.

The session's electric raucous superyob council-estate glam thrills
cut across the airwaves with a brash unstoppable confidence and
brimful of attitude vocals that demanded attention.

Attention that was going to come like an avalanche in 1994.

19

MONNOW VALLEY

Now signed and with their debut single ready for release, Oasis started 1994 as outsiders peering in on a music scene that was on the edge of a cultural shift. UK pop culture always has an insatiable need for change – it's what drives the hothouse of creativity, sometimes to its detriment, as great bands go in and out of fashion or interesting ideas are dashed in the relentless surge for the new.

It also creates a fast forward of creativity that is partially pushed by the industry and partially driven from the street where youth create their own culture and ideas with sharp dress codes and their own idiosyncratic soundtracks.

The year 1994 would be an epic one for music of all shapes and styles. Nirvana's increasingly fraught endgame had taken a dark turn with their recently released *In Utero* album which was a worldwide number one with its crepuscular self-loathing songs and pounding Steve Albini sonic mix. That February, Elastica scored a top 20 hit with their sharp and angular sardonic 'Line Up'. It was joined in the charts by Suede's anthemic ballad 'Stay Together' that nodded to Bowie while still indebted to the Smiths in an almost opposite way to Oasis, preferring the androgynous shape-shifting glam indie aspect of the band to Noel's love of Johnny Marr's pop classic melodic nous, guitar collection and gunslinger cool.

There had been a culture shift going on since the *Select* magazine Britpop cover and its embrace of Britishness. Suede's busy 1993 had seen their eponymous debut album hit number one while Pulp's upcoming spring album *His 'n' Hers* was creating a pre-release buzz with many predicting big things for the band that had spent 14 years in the wilderness. Blur's stylistic changes saw their 'Girls & Boys' single catch the new mood with a slice of great pop that heralded their spring number one *Parklife* album, which would be one of the year's defining albums and a big seller.

On the fringes, the debut album sessions for Oasis had started in January 1994 when the newly signed band relocated to Monnow Valley studio just up the road from the legendary Rockfield Studios near Monmouth in South Wales to start recording.

Initially opening its doors in 1977, the 600-year-old mill house had been a residential rehearsal space for Rockfield before becoming a studio in the eighties. It had been used by many bands including Black Sabbath, Robert Plant and Simple Minds and was owned by Charles Ward, the brother of Kingsley Ward, who owned the neighbouring Rockfield.

The whole concept of the residential studio had started with Rockfield and bands and labels loved the idea of getting it together in the country away from the distractions of city life. Of course, it didn't always end up this way and the madness would often morph into a different version.

For the sessions Oasis were joined by producer Dave Batchelor to try and capture the incendiary power of their live sound and the melodies in a tightrope walk of recording. The Scottish producer had been doing live sound for the Inspiral Carpets where he met Noel and had a great CV, producing bands like the Sensational Alex Harvey Band,[1] Nazareth, Dr. Feelgood and the Skids.

Hedging their bets, the band also had their 'sixth member', Mark Coyle, with them and initially had brought David Scott as well. It was a loose coalition of producers which when you added Noel to the mix was a case of a lot of cooks for a lot of broth. And despite the best intentions of pooling the best ears into a dream team it was always going to cause problems, as David Scott remembers:

'I went to meet the band and Dave Batchelor in their rehearsal room and I just couldn't connect with him, maybe there was a clash of roles. When we went to Monnow Valley, Coyley was also with us and he didn't know quite what his role was either. I was there to mainly be the engineer but I needed to understand what we were doing so I could make the engineering decisions. It got really confusing but I figured that everyone has got their talents to bring to the table so let's bash it out.'

Monnow Valley had a big live room where the band set up for a potentially great live sound. Their raw power could be picked up on ambient mics adding layers of primordial high-decibel electricity and noise to their wall of sound for Liam's vocals to cut through and hold the tune. This was the core to their sound yet somehow the sessions didn't quite click. Recording music is one of the great indefinables. You have everything in place – great songs, a tight band, great studio, producer and engineers, yet the environment can be overwhelming for some musicians, especially a band that has only played about 20 gigs. In different ways it can break that alchemical magic that makes all great bands – that weird energy flow between people in a room as they play. The instinctive way they just know the push and pull of each song.

Dave Batchelor favoured sound baffles between band members to avoid mic spill, which is a fairly normal procedure but broke the band's flow and their eye lines.

Tony McCarroll: 'This would be the first serious kind of recording in a proper big studio that we had done and we couldn't see each other, unlike the Boardwalk rehearsal room or the other studios we had been in so far which were pretty small places where it was a nod and a wink if the song was coming to the end.

'I was behind the big doors in Monnow Valley with a ton of mics around me and I was thinking if I hit one with a drum stick by mistake then we would have to start the take again! I think we were all quite nervous and you can hear that in those recordings. They're not as punishing sound-wise and a bit more reserved.'

The mystical 'vibe' that musicians talk about is where the magic lies. Equally important to getting a good sound is to get a good feel, as David Scott remembers:

'These little niggles start getting in the way but where it really went wrong was when we were doing "Slide Away". Dave Batchelor was down with this sort of slow-ish stompy vibe that the band had but if you listen to their stuff, they don't actually play slow tempos – they have this slow feel to them which is different.

'He was trying to get them to play slow, and I'm sitting there saying to myself, they can't play like that. We had a little drum machine set up for the tempo and we were doing take after take and it wasn't feeling any good. It wasn't right for Tony as there's an ideal tempo at which he can work. That's what the band had grown up with and what they had got used to. After hours and hours of this, everyone's getting a bit pissed off and I just said, "Do you mind if I make a suggestion? Can I play you a tempo that I think this song is going to work at?" So I just hit play on the drum machine and Coyley and Liam jumped up and went, "That's it!" Dave Batchelor was not happy and he said, "This is going to sound shit" and the next day, I was fired. Marcus Russell called me up and said, "Don't take it personally. It's Dave Batchelor's call and it's not working between the two of you. Take the money and run."'

The sessions continued as the band ground out the album, which as the recent release of the sessions shows did actually sound pretty good but lacked the band's swing and the wall of sound that would be their early trademark. Ironically, just up the road another Manchester band were also struggling to get their album finished: the Stone Roses were back in Rockfield working on *Second Coming*.

The biggest band in the country had become an enigma beyond the gaze of the music media when, in fact, they were in Rockfield trying to create their second album. Their silence added to their already quasi mystical legend of enigmatic wizards recording in the Welsh hills.

Inevitably the bands met, as the Stone Roses' Ian Brown recalls: 'I met Oasis when they were doing *Definitely Maybe*. It was the first time I had met Noel although I'd seen him around in town and I recognised his face. I thought they were good lads. I had heard a lot about them from Steve Adge.[2] He had seen them at the Boardwalk and said they were going to be massive and that they loved the Roses. I met them when Liam came down to the studio with Bonehead and Tony McCarroll the drummer and then on the street in Rockfield outside WHSmiths.'

The first meeting had happened when one night Liam, Bonehead and Tony had apparently 'borrowed' a combine harvester and drove it a mile down the road to Rockfield. Chugging along the country lanes in the middle of the night they arrived at the studio where they walked into the control room and found a stoned guru-like Ian Brown on his own doing the mystic talk. Uncharacteristically Liam was silent in his presence as they got slowly stoned with the chief.

Tony French had joined them on the combine harvester trip: 'When we got on it I heard shotgun sounds and legged it, it was probably the engine, but I was off my tits on acid at the time,' he laughs.

Nick Brine was the engineer in Rockfield working on the Roses album and he remembers the meeting: 'I was in the accommodation when I saw these lights and it was Liam and Tony. They had a cassette and said, "Can you give this to Ian? And tell him that we're Oasis." They came back a few days later and asked if he had listened to it and he hadn't yet. In the end Ian listened to the demo, and it went down very well.'

Ian Brown was cheering them on.

'I was buzzing for them,' he says. 'I remember when we were all watching the chart show on a Saturday morning in the studio and Oasis came on doing "Shakermaker" and I was saying I think they are great and they are from Manchester and it says on that little clip on the TV underneath them that they love the Roses.

'When they made it I thought it was really funny that we were supposed to be the masters and that the kids who loved us had grafted it and robbed us when we were asleep, and that's great. the Smiths and then us had made the independent scene bigger and showed that bands that wrote their own songs and dressed themselves and styled themselves could make it.

'How could we knock anyone else, especially when in Liam's first ever interview he said his favourite living people were his mum and Ian Brown. At least they acknowledged us, unlike Blur or Suede who had the baggy pants on and the bowl haircuts. Plus you always support lads from your own city and the North West in general, don't you?'

While the Roses continued to spend months trying to get their album right, the recordings of the potential Oasis debut album were not sounding right either, as Dave Batchelor admitted years later.

'In hindsight, some of those early recordings may well have fallen short in delivering the full potential of the band. And in retrospect perhaps I was not quite suited to the project. Certainly, coming out of those sessions, I could not have seen where they arrived at with *Definitely Maybe*!'[3]

Taking the mixes back to London, the band and Creation had a meeting and brought in some fresh ears to make some big decisions but first the band had their debut London show proper.

20

ARRIVAL

'The stage had been set, and the lights had gone down, and people thought Blur or Suede would be it,' says Noel, 'but against everyone's permission, the masses decided that it was going to be us. Everyone was waiting for someone to walk on and have it.'

Driven by their own willpower and innate self-confidence, and backed up by their own talent and vision, Oasis were arriving – and the gig at the Water Rats announced that arrival.

On 27 January 1994 Oasis arrived in London for their debut gig in the city at the 200-capacity old pub near Kings Cross. The reviews were glorious and the photo by Roger Sargent[1] of Liam Gallagher hanging on the mic, staring into the middle distance, was arresting and soon to be iconic. Liam's face projected a blank generation emptiness and the surly attitude of a band that didn't need your permission – a snapshot of rock 'n' roll in its perfect essence.

'The interesting thing about Liam is that he's very precise,' explains music journalist Jon Savage, 'so when he's singing those songs, he sings them perfectly. He might not act precisely but the singing is quite precise. He hits those notes and he gets all the lyrics right.

There's another side to Liam and it's always the same with fame, people get typified by the mass media, as this or that, and obviously, people are much more complex. Of course there is a kind of yobbish element as well, which people find attractive – it's like what Tony Wilson said that people want rock stars to act out what they can't in their actual normal everyday lives. Liam is the wild card and that's what keeps things interesting for everyone. It's like when I saw Nirvana in 1993 and Kurt was the wild card, and nobody quite knew what he was going to do. And that's very exciting.'

Noel Gallagher was ready: 'Water Rats was mobbed and the review had that famous shot of Liam hanging on the mic. Then the buzz really started going round and out comes "Supersonic" and that was the perfect moment to me. It's a moment that only lasts for two or three years when you are the same age as your audience and you wear the same clothes and you're financially in the same place and you've not gone off to be pop stars yet. Everyone is in the same place and it's magic and it's like, "Wow, this is it!"'

The packed venue was full of the music business, with labels, agents, reviewers, dealers and wheeler dealers, game-changers and random heads and friends of a friend on the guest list. Everyone was there to see what the new noise was about. There was something intriguing about this band standing stock-still delivering this huge sound with a standoffish attitude that made the audience go to them, all carried by their melodic rollercoaster songs. The tunes didn't go for the obvious wam-bam of speed to create excitement and instead hung in the air at medium pace while holding the tension, making the listener enter their vortex of noise, as Jon Savage notes:

'They weren't thrashing. Like the Pistols they had that slower tension and release that was more of a kind of mid-seventies rock band than a punk band because the Pistols had formed before the first Ramones LP, which is the one that had all the huge impact and made so many people speed up like the Clash and the Damned, who became speed demons. Oasis had that Sex Pistols sound but with the Beatles in there as well. I always thought of them as the Sex Beatles. Also, there was the Anglo-Irishness thing which gave them an edge in that they see the country in a slightly different way. They're not part of the English establishment and they're a bit critical and there's a line you can draw from "Bring It On Down" to "The Queen is Dead", and "God Save the Queen".

'If your parents came over from Ireland, and you're actually first generation Irish and English born in this country, then that's going to mean something, because if your parents have moved from a different country for a better life it's difficult being an immigrant and it gives you a perspective. It's really tough, and some of that toughness goes into the kids.'

Noel Gallagher watched his masterplan unfold . . .

'Being a music fan, I was already so sure that the band was going to be enormous,' he says. 'I would say to Alan McGee and the label while surrounded by everybody on drugs in the dressing room that we were going to be the biggest band in the world. I used to think I was the only person who believed this but it was unshakeable with me. I knew it. I already had the plan. I knew the songs that were going to be on the album and I knew the songs that were going to be on the next album because I already had them. It was a cakewalk. I was dead relaxed about it because I had those songs. We also had the right people behind us now and a brilliant manager who looked after everything. I guess I could have done it myself because I'd been around the Inspiral Carpets office when I was on a retainer answering their phone and being there when meetings took place, which meant that even if I was not sitting there taking notes I knew how it all worked.'

Oasis were perfectly aligned with their moment. Like the Sex Pistols in 1976 they cut across the narrative and they had the songs to back it up. They felt the same claustrophobic going nowhere suffocation of growing up on the 'wrong side' of the tracks, they had the same hopes and aspirations. They talked the talk and they certainly walked the walk and now they sang the songs, as Noel points out:

'Those formative years of the band where it grows and grows and you're the same as your audience is the perfect moment. Ultimately what separates you from your audience is the distance at the gigs. In a physical sense you are fucking miles away and then you start taking the big drugs and wearing the fur coats and wearing four pairs of sunglasses and those years are great as well. Those years are fucking insanity and they are the rock star living bit, but just before is the magic time where you never knew what was going to happen but you knew it was going to be great. Every song and every interview we would give would be hailed as a classic. If someone asked a question, I would give them an answer and all of a sudden I'm a PR genius. I didn't read the interviews as they were just a lot of swearing and ranting! Coming from up here, we would pull no punches. If you asked me what I thought of Suede, I would say they were shit because that's what I thought then. Growing up outside the music business on the streets, that was how we spoke.'

Maybe every few years British pop culture likes to recalibrate itself and get back to what it does best – that equation of clothes, music and attitude, and short sharp shock songs are a core essence. Britpop was an attempt to do this but Oasis with Liam Gallagher's sartorial street perfection and his brother's armoury of classic songs were the living embodiment of the moment and it struck a raw nerve.

'You've got to make it look easy to inspire people,' says Noel. 'Damon Albarn is up there as one of the great British songwriters but as I used to say to his guitarist, it's not about whose got the cleverest chords, it's about connecting with people. I don't know how I did it but later on when I looked out at 125,000 people in the audience at Knebworth, in an arrogant sense I might think it was because I'm a brilliant songwriter but it's not because of that, it's because there's a bald guy in the band and there are lots of bald people in the crowd thinking if he can do it I can do it as well.

'A lot of it was because of the cool of Liam or because Paul McGuigan wasn't cut out to be a rock star but there he is on that massive stage.

'You can't put your finger on it because if you could bottle it some major label would sell it and it would be worthless. It's commonly known as magic. If it's there then thank your lucky stars and hang on to its coat tails, and luckily for us it was there.'

Part and parcel of all great British rock bands is the tabloid rage. That hypocritical tut-tutting at the shenanigans of groups escaping the drudgery of the everyday grind and celebrating their momentary freedom. Oasis were about to become a headline machine.

A couple of weeks after Water Rats the band had their first foreign jaunt with a 18 February gig in Amsterdam supporting the Verve. What should have been a routine trip across the sea for a one-off show in the fabled city of good times got out of hand before they had even landed on the continent.

Perhaps the last of the great post-war rock 'n' roll bands, Oasis were always followed around by that weird term 'bad boy reputation'. It's a curious notion that bands are any worse behaved than any other group of people having a good time on Saturday-night breaks from the grind, but then of course, that's the whole point of bands. They don't just create the soundtrack – they live your life vicariously and without filter and fear.

Of course, the band knew all about rock myth. Being a natural storyteller Noel would creatively embellish a band mythology. Mixing a zero-filter honesty with merry tales and strong opinions on other bands often told with that twinkle in his eye. The endless anecdotes were both amusing and perfect at adding layers of myth to the mundane.

Add to this a loose cannon younger brother who was a magnet for trouble, running around the staid corridors of showbiz, and the raucous rock 'n' roll side of Oasis was about to become tabloid.

On the ferry to Holland a 'mad for it' Liam was on his first rock 'n' roll trip outside the UK, which always amplifies the excitement and trouble-causing potential for any young high-decibel reveller, especially one fronting one of the hottest up-and-coming bands in the country.

The band had stayed up drinking in the all-night cheesy car ferry disco that soundtracked the eight-hour trip. Someone had paid for drinks – a volatile mixture of Champagne and Jack Daniel's – with a fake 50 quid note. The bar staff pointed out Guigsy and Bonehead and the security stepped in to confront the aggrieved and tipsy band who, sparked by Liam running around the casino throwing chips in the air and some scuffling, saw them bundled into the ship's brig.

'As the fight broke out all I remember was it was a bit Benny Hill,' explained Liam Gallagher in the *Supersonic* film. 'It was fucking mayhem, man, I loved it. It was punk rock, man.'

On arriving in Holland they were all instantly deported back to the UK, getting escorted off the ferry apart from Noel Gallagher who had been in his cabin all night, underlining his different attitude to band life. He rang the Creation office:

'I spoke to Alan and I said, "Sit down, I got to tell you everyone has been arrested." He didn't say, "You will never work again", he said, "Fucking brilliant . . . is it true? Normally we have to make stories like that up every day." They sent us off to do our thing but our thing happens to be getting into trouble fighting and arguing or the roadies shoplifting at service stations. Every day there would be more stories about Oasis. It was a dream come true.'

Yet despite the rock and the roll, Noel was driven more by the music, as he told Ann Scanlon for *Vox* in 1995: 'I get pissed off, because I've written all these great songs and all anyone ever wants to talk about is Bonehead trashing rooms and me and our kid fighting. The first couple of times it was all right because, well, for a start it's true, but it's becoming a bit of a joke.'

Yet the antics also connected them with their huge audience, fed up with the smoke and mirrors polish of showbiz. They were lads and proud of it, as Liam explained to Ann Scanlon in the same interview:

'Being a lad is what I'm about. I don't define anything. I'm just me and I know I'm a lad. I can tell you who isn't a lad – anyone from fuckin' Blur, anyone from Inspiral Carpets, any band at all today. There are no lads in bands. Johnny Marr's a lad. The Stone Roses are lads. Bez and Ryder were lads, although they were a bit too laddy. Lee Mavers, he's a lad – geezer.'

Oasis were one band, but two versions! For Liam, it was about being yourself, even if that is getting drunk and fighting as well as the music, while for Noel, it was about the songs but on your own terms.

In Oasis's case, they were both right. And that was the problem.

Nine weeks after Water Rats, Kurt Cobain committed suicide. Grunge as a meaningful pop culture movement was over now its totemic talisman was gone.

Rock music was reeling, and like the Beatles cheering up America after the assassination of Kennedy in November 1963, Oasis were about to arrive . . .

21

SAWMILLS

The Monnow Valley recordings still didn't sound quite right. It's not unusual to come back from the studio feeling tired and deflated but something was lacking. The band and label kicked the mixes around trying to decide what to do, with Creation asking producer/engineer Anjali Dutt to have a listen.

At the time working as an engineer on several Creation Records projects like the Boo Radleys' acclaimed *Giant Steps* album, Dutt had worked on My Bloody Valentine's ground-breaking hard to record sonic masterpiece *Loveless* and had also grown up on punk before embracing the Byrds, Love and sixties soul. She had the talent and the ears for a second opinion and went to Olympic Studios in Barnes in London to listen to a play-back of the album.

Listening with the freshest of ears to a band then unknown to her, she found the album flat sounding and agreed that it may have to be re-recorded and was then handed the job as engineer with Mark Coyle and Noel as producers.

'They were slightly under pressure to get it done. They were also not entirely sure why the album wasn't sounding good. Was it them? Was it the recording? Nobody actually knew. And there was a tour imminent so it had to be done within a certain time.'[1]

Sitting in on the meeting, Alan McGee nodded in agreement: 'Often we would leave bands to it but if things were not working we would step in and make big decisions, and the production wasn't right and it didn't have the big sound they had live.'

They would need a rethink and a re-record and another attempt to capture their sound.

It was a measure of the ambition around Oasis that they were now sent to Sawmills studio in Cornwall where they arrived in late February 1994, hot off the back of the ill-fated Amsterdam gig.

Opened in 1974 and the first residential recording studios in the UK, Sawmills famously can be reached by a boat over the River Fowey. It had already hosted the likes of the Stone Roses, recording 'Fools Gold', Verve's *A Storm in Heaven*, Robert Plant, and XTC's brilliant psychedelic side project the Dukes Of Stratosphear.

This time the band decided to record the songs live and celebrate the spill between the instruments, adding to their wall of sound. Mark Coyle taped Oasis as if they were playing a gig, with the band members closer together in one room and with minimal sound-proofing between the amps. With the tracks in the can Noel then overdubbed numerous guitars.

'That was Noel's favourite trick: get the drums, bass and rhythm guitar down, and then he'd cane it. "Less is more" didn't really work then,' Bonehead told John Harris.[2]

Often music works by stripping layers away but some bands suit the patchwork of overdubs – famously Steve Jones spent the summer of 1977 in the studio layering up the Sex Pistols debut *Never Mind the Bollocks* album and proved that if it was done right then 'over the top' was the only way to go.

'Bonehead and Guigsy were very consistent,' Anjali Dutt told Richard Bowes, 'they were very good. There wasn't much scope for messing up. We recorded every single thing they played because we couldn't keep them together in one place for long enough. Noel did love putting layer after layer of guitar on, and Bonehead's guitar got lost sometimes.'[3]

Starting from scratch they re-recorded all the tracks with only 'Slide Away' not benefiting from the change in studio and technique.

'There was actually lots of trouble with "Slide Away",' Anjali revealed. 'It had a very slight, sort of Neil Young feel about it, and it was never quite coming together. It was done over and over and over. It dragged on a bit. It always gave trouble. In the end, we went back to the Monnow Valley version.'[4]

As ever, the singer was impatient and ready to deliver. Not interested in the endless takes and the conventional recording method of singing the vocals line by line and then dropping in words and phrases to build up a patchwork vocal, Liam could nail a song in one or two takes, as Anjali remembered:

'You couldn't get many takes out of Liam and they weren't desperately necessary either. He always sang in tune. I just remember he just sang it, usually in one take. Sometimes you'd ask for a second or third take. He wasn't keen on singing for very long. He was actually also an unusually good tambourine player.'[5]

The re-recorded songs now had that wall of sound but they couldn't get the mixes right, which at the time were just beyond Mark Coyle and Noel.

Still frustrated that their vision was not being realised Noel Gallagher knew exactly what he wanted and it was just a case of how to get there. They were now closer but would have to find someone who could come in and mix the tracks.

Enter Owen Morris.

22

ENTER THE WELSH DRAGON

Trying to capture that huge energy and attitude of rock 'n' roll at its rarefied best is like chasing an elusive elixir of greatness and the album still just didn't explode with the sonic swagger of the band.

In desperation, band manager Marcus Russell applied one of his own management maxims – 'you're in the middle and you've got to find solutions to problems' – and came to the rescue, bringing in one of his former clients, Owen Morris, who was then working with Johnny Marr and Electronic.

Born in Caernarfon in Wales in 1968, Owen Morris had started work as a sound engineer when he moved to Cambridge's Spaceward Studio at the age of 16. It was here that he started to build up a big portfolio as an engineer, with his CV already including engineering for the Stranglers.

He then worked with bands like Manic Street Preachers, Billy Bragg, the Pet Shop Boys and The The, before moving to Manchester where he worked for Johnny Marr and Bernard Sumner for five years as a studio engineer on their Electronic project on tracks like 'Getting Away With It' and then on New Order's *Republic* album.

He had the technical skills and had helped to build Johnny Marr's Clear Studios for him in Bowden in Cheshire. Manchester also had other temptations and he was running around on the local scene from gigs to the Haçienda.

'I lived in India House before Noel did and I seemed to have a reputation for being a maverick and that was good. I was at the Haçienda every weekend taking ecstasy and getting to understand everything.'

It was through his friendship at this time with Johnny Marr's brother Ian that he became aware of a new band and went to see one of their early shows at the Boardwalk.

'Ian was really into his music,' says Owen, 'and I remember him coming in and telling Johnny at breakfast that there is this ticket-tout hustler type called Noel Gallagher and he's got this band who are great. His brother is the singer and thinks he sounds like John Lennon or John Lydon. Ian would come around to mine and get fucked up and we'd talk about music and one day he said, "Here's a demo of this kid's band and they are called Oasis." We went to a very early gig at the Boardwalk but they were not ready then. Later on, I also went on that trip with Johnny and Noel to Doncaster. I remember thinking, who's this guy in the car with Johnny? Eight months later, they were recording their album and Johnny was like, "Shit, I should be producing it!" If I was still getting managed by Marcus I may well have been involved with Oasis right from the start but I had just moved on! But they were struggling to get it right and it sounded unfocused and Marcus said, "Can you try a couple of tracks?"'[1]

There could have been no more perfect combination between band and producer/engineer who was about to bring his mixing skills and chance to indulge in his Tony Visconti and Phil Spector fantasies to create a glam rock wall-of-sound production hybrid and a far different, noisier sound than his CV suggested.

In the early spring of 1994 Owen Morris was handed an instrumental take of 'Rock 'n' Roll Star' and of 'Columbia'.

'This was my trial!' says Owen. '"Columbia" needed mixing and "Rock 'n' Roll Star" needed the vocals recording because they couldn't get them right. This was a test to see if I could get the mix and arrangement right and also if I could work with Liam.'

Bringing the tapes up to Johnny Marr's Clear studio, Owen Morris set to work on them to see if he could salvage the tracks. Working quickly he threw out the rule book and almost as a reaction to the cleaner sounds of the groups he had recently been working with, cranked the life-affirming noise and within hours had found the soul of the songs. Somehow the larger-than-life Owen Morris swiftly dredged out the potential that was hidden inside the Sawmills sessions.

'Me, Marcus, Noel and Liam then went down to Loco Studios in Caerleon in South Wales for a weekend and we worked fast,' he remembers. 'That first afternoon we had recorded the lead vocals and also Noel's backing vocals on "Rock 'n' Roll Star". Marcus was listening to the mix and he kept saying turn the fucking guitars up! Which I was happy to do! I told Liam he sounded like John Lennon, which made him happy, and then told him to leave me in peace to mix because he wouldn't stop talking [laughs]. A few minutes later Noel came into the control room and asked me if I had told his brother to fuck off so that I could work in peace and when I said that I had he joked that he very much liked that.

'Then the next day, I mixed "Columbia" really quickly in about four hours and then it was a case of tidying up the tracks which, with Bonehead's rhythm guitar and Tony's simple and powerful punk drums, were a big part of their sound. They had all these guitar overdubs on them which had so many melodic ideas but they were not arranged. I tidied them up so there was no re-recording of guitars needed and those two tracks are the two best things I ever did for Oasis.'

Having passed his 'audition', the whole album was then handed over to Owen Morris to mix. Left to his own devices and getting great results, the maverick was in his element.

'When those two tracks were approved by Noel, Marcus said, "You're doing everything now." First we redid Liam's vocal on the third verse on "Shakermaker" – the Mr. Sifter verse – because they gotta change the Coca-Cola words. Liam came in and did it in one take on the instrumental track that I had. Easy peasy. I said we better redo all the vocals on the album because they have been recorded shit. So we booked Windings studio near Wrexham and Bonehead drove Liam down and we did five vocals, "Live Forever", "Cigarettes & Alcohol", "Bring It On Down" and "Up in the Sky".

'Liam's delivery was great. He's an exceptional talent. Extraordinary. Every vocal he was instantly on it and I understood how to tune them right. I'm the only fucker who could record those kind of vocals! I knew the motherfucker could sing but he was even better than I thought. He's got an amazing voice and he just blasted them out.

'Liam only did four takes on each track and I compiled them. Noel checked that Liam sang everything correctly and then left us to it. Then they went on tour with Whiteout and I was left to mix the album with Marcus for company and to check I didn't miss anything important on the tracks because he knew the songs better than I did. He would sit there and say, "Turn that fucker up!" He was good like that! Then we did one or two backing vocals – one of which was me and Marcus doing the high bit on "Live Forever". I was young and I had complete fucking control and it was easy.'

It was the beginning of a beautiful, if high-decibel, working relationship. 'I fitted in well with Noel, certainly for the first two records,' says Owen, 'because I filled in the gaps of his knowledge of how to make records, like how to record Liam and make a fucking lead vocal and I could arrange his guitars before he knew about arranging guitars. Oasis were never fucking difficult in the studio.

They were professional with me. The band was good. This is the thing that people don't think about them. Next, I went to London to Matrix Studios in Fulham. I was in my element. After years of cleaner music I was unleashed to make a big noisy record!'

The album was finally mixed and readied at Johnny Marr's studio by April 1994.

'I also mastered it there. There was no A&R from the record company. Marcus ran nearly everything. So I said to Marcus I want to master it myself, which is unusual because you normally need different ears.

'A year before, we'd remastered the first Electronic album, and there was a new box, the Apogee box A/D, where you could shove it up loud adding another 60db to the mix before distortion. We got the Oasis tapes in and I just did it really loud and really good. I remember Johnny was almost offended at how loud it was, saying to me, "You can't be that loud!"'

23

SUPERSONIC

In the pre-internet days the music media was dominated by the music press and radio, which for a normal 'indie' band was a balancing act between being underground enough for John Peel, who would only play Oasis's 'Do You Wanna Be a Spaceman?' a couple of times before losing interest, or daytime radio which was notoriously hard for guitar bands to get played on.

Yet again the gods were smiling when in 1993 the new controller of Radio 1, Matthew Bannister, gave the station its biggest shake-up for years and culled the dead wood Smashy and Nicey DJs that had clogged up the station for decades. It felt vital again and played many of the bands that would be mainstays of Britpop, creating a platform for Oasis that would not have existed even the year before with the old-school DJs who only liked the sound of their own voices.

The biggest pop TV programme by a long way was still *Top of the Pops* but you actually needed to have a hit to get on that. This left the best opportunity available to the band being *The Word*, which was the Friday night show presented by Mancunian ally Terry Christian.

The programme thrived on shock tactics and daft japes but also had genuine great music content, which had included Nirvana, L7 and Huggy Bear. Terry Christian already knew about Oasis and had written about them in the *Manchester Evening News* and seen them play. He pitched heavily to get the band on the show and even if the current series would end before the debut single, the forceful presenter got his way and Oasis made their TV debut playing 'Supersonic' on 18 March 1994.

It's one of those perfect pop TV moments, cutting through the false dancers and garish stage set with a dose of reality. The band sound great and the song, driven by Tony McCarroll's drums, really swings, while the mix favours Noel Gallagher's picked-out guitar notes; these add to the thrilling, raw excitement as Liam saunters, waves a cine camera around and hunches over the mic. He sings perfectly with a raw power and beauty with his hand on the mic in the period before he perfected his stillism hand-behind-back, nose-on-mic technique. He exits at the end of the song with the smirk of someone who knows a triumph when he sees one.

A couple of weeks later on 11 April the debut single was released. Two weeks before Blur released their *Parklife* album and a few days after Kurt Cobain had committed suicide, 'Supersonic' was the debut single from a band at the edge of the music narrative and a band in a hurry.

The debut single also kicked off the band's remarkable tradition of high-quality B-sides with the plaintive acoustic introspection of 'Take Me Away' that had appeared out of thin air in the studio session. It was the first of many acoustic Noel-sung flipsides that were in direct contrast to the A-side anthems like a parallel solo career that had started with his late eighties demos and continued through the Oasis singles.

Noel: '"Take Me Away" is as plaintive as you get and that's what made it. When we were growing up listening to records, it was important what's on the other side, and you would play both sides over and over again. I got it from the Smiths and Johnny Marr got it from the Kinks.'

'I Will Believe' came from the same sessions and was a more typical guitar rush with a cool hook and vocal in its impatient youthful rush; the four tracks were complete with a demo of 'Columbia'.

The debut single saw the first Oasis Microdot artwork. It was the beginning of a very special relationship that would help to define the band. Rarely do groups use the same artists on each record, and rarely does the art mirror and match and entwine with the music like this. Noel Gallagher, Microdot boss Brian Cannon and photographer Michael Spencer Jones were then very much on the same artful page, with a mutual love of the works of Hipgnosis whose Aubrey Powell and Storm Thorgerson had met in Cambridge in the late sixties. Hipgnosis sleeve art often created visual metaphors of song lyrics and titles driven by photography with complex staged photos using models and props that were then manipulated, enhanced, airbrushed and cut and paste like a proto Photoshop. Mixing surrealism with bold striking ideas and a quirky humour, it was a perfect complement to the post-acid fried sixties and seventies, creating powerful visual artworks, metaphors and logos. A wide range of bands like Pink Floyd, Led Zeppelin, 10cc, XTC and countless others used their artwork, which was bold and quirky and stood out.

Filtering that fantasia through a gritty northern realism and a post-punk aesthetic, Microdot had already built a reputation with the brilliant series of sleeves for the Verve. Sleeves like Richard Ashcroft in a Leeds backstreet holding a sandwich board for the band's 'This is Music' single looked magical and yet local in a brilliant hyper-reality of a new neo-psychedelic north. They would apply this in a different way to Oasis.

The artwork for 'Supersonic' was the first collaboration between them, and Brian Cannon was already immersed in the band like he had been with the Verve – often sitting in on studio sessions with the group, becoming a virtual member of the gang. Getting the vibe. The feel.

Michael Spencer Jones was bringing his visual skills into play and between them they were a perfect ping-pong of ideas that resulted in one of the great runs of band artwork.

'Supersonic' was striking in its simplicity. The thinking was that being a debut single it needed a strong visual statement of the band that explained everything about the group.

They went to Monnow Valley in January where Oasis were recording the first version of the debut album and took a series of shots with the 21-year-old Liam Gallagher out front oozing attitude and charisma, Noel sat on the keys with his guitars, and the band surrounding them. Clambering to the top of a high set of step ladders in the cluttered live room with the band in front of the famous large spherical studio door, Michael Spencer Jones caught them in their surly stand-off cool inside the studio strewn with expensive guitars, amps and cables. The camera lights were also in the shot recording a moment of a work in progress.

Capturing the young band placed perfectly in the studio with their tools in trade, you could almost see their music in a freeze-frame moment in time. It placed Oasis in their working environment and underlined their style and attitude, which was all encompassed by their singer who stared back at the camera ready to take on the world. The photographer then cross-processed the film to give the shot its blue tint, adding that Hipgnosis twist on reality, as Brian Cannon explains:

'From the start Noel was dead easy to work with. He had his own ideas and was also happy to run with whatever we thought best. From then on it would always work by the same process. I would basically be told by Creation that there was a record coming out and some artwork was required. We would have a creative meeting and we would go from there. For "Supersonic", it was pretty straightforward – the band is in the studio recording, and it made sense to shoot it there and capture the moment.'

Michael Spencer Jones had already done a trial run of a studio shot: 'I had photographed them demoing "Shakermaker" in October '93 and I got some great shots and they were impressed with the results and that led to doing the shoot for "Supersonic". Noel then said that the Beatles had a single every three months and we want to do the same, which was a great idea, especially if I was doing the photography!'

The single sleeve also saw the debut of the classic new Oasis logo. Designed by Brian Cannon it was based on the Decca Records logo on the cover of *The Rolling Stones No. 2* album, as he explains:

'Now on Creation they needed a clearer logo that would look good printed. It was inspired by the Decca logo on the Rolling Stones' second album cover which I saw in a book. The original logo idea was to try and do a version of the band name in the Adidas font – but we binned it because the font didn't suit the word "Oasis" and it made the "A" in "Oasis" look just like an "o" with a line on the side and it just looked wrong.'

Adidas would have made sense culturally but the new logo was perfect and has become a design classic.

'Supersonic' is one of the great debut singles. Defiantly raw and fully formed with its simmering tension and loping groove, it was a perfect calling card and a perfect kickback to the far too polished music that the radio played. Its punkish edge was thrilling to listen to as it cut through the airwaves in the spring of 1994.

Red Alert's Alison Bell remembers Noel playing her the track before release: 'Noel popped in the office with a cassette and he said, "Please just stop everything, just listen to this." We just sat there and went, Oh my God! As their pluggers we would drive them to radio shows everywhere and they would never turn anything down. Also people like Craig Cash and Caroline Aherne used to come into our office, have a cup of tea and we got them into Oasis too.'

Liam Walsh from Red Alert was key. 'We worked with Oasis from day one. Their record contract came through the Red Alert fax machine. I remember folding it, putting it in an envelope, and ringing Noel to collect it. We were thrilled for them and loved being part of their rise to fame.

'At this time, Red Alert was already working on radio promotions for many hugely successful bands, including bands on Creation Records, so it made sense for us to promote our friend's band, Oasis.

'Some people may think getting Oasis on the radio was easy, but they were not universally liked around the UK. It was not until they had a few hits that radio producers felt safe supporting them.'

This resulted in Craig Cash interviewing Noel on his show on 15 April. 'This was his first radio interview,' remembers the then DJ, who eventually used the Oasis song 'Half the World Away' for his and Caroline Aherne's iconic hit TV show, *The Royle Family*. 'He came in not long after and played a few songs like "Slide Away" for the first time as he'd only just written it.'

With its stark black-and-white performance video directed by Mark Szaszy shot on a Kings Cross roof, 'Supersonic' grabbed lots of great reviews. Oasis may have been late to a party that they had no interest in going to but they had certainly announced their arrival.

Music writer Jon Savage was watching:

'Oasis pretty quickly became part of a sort of national phenomenon, and were tuned in to talking about the nation. They had the Union Jack on their demo tape, so they were interested in an idea of Britishness for British youth that was different and positive in general. And I really liked that. They would use the Union Jack as a symbol. And it wasn't just Cool Britannia retro, although they probably thought it looked cool as well. The stereotype was of

Oasis as kind of thick northerners, but they're not. Noel in particular, had intention. He knew exactly what he was doing.

'I think one of the reasons everybody was going so crazy for them, apart from the fact they're fans and they really liked the stuff, is that Oasis were really the last time that a pop group became a national obsession, and people like the fact that rock groups had that power – a bit like the Sex Pistols, obviously had, and a bit like the Beatles or the Stones also had. It doesn't happen very often that the pop group becomes tied into the life of the nation. And Oasis would manage it in a way that Blur never did.'

In early 1994 Noel Gallagher looked out at the music scene and observed: 'Things were changing. It was like a year zero big bang or whatever you want to call it. The Conservative era was ending and things had gone from grunge nihilism to an optimism and it was all geared towards England. A lot of people were at the right age for fucking heroes and a lot of people didn't understand the lace shirts of the bands the music press were pushing, and a lot of people found Blur too clever and people wanted people like themselves.'

Oasis had arrived on their terms. There was no fancy team of stylists and advisors and record company people moulding and shaping them. The band were their own vision and a distillation of all the great music they were in thrall of, reinvented by themselves. All the greatest bands have always been their own narrative untainted by the naff cynicism of the market-driven industry.

It was in this cultural flux that Oasis began to get attention, and they were about to seize the moment.

24

MAD FOR IT

And then it starts.

The single opened the floodgates, and Oasis were at level one – that space where every TV and radio and press opportunity comes at you in a blur, and every move you make is freeze-framed in the media forever.

The band were whisked around long-lost TV shows like *The Beat* or *Naked City* before hot footing it to evening radio sessions and music paper interviews, where their mix of raw energy, a frisson of danger, no-holds-barred opinions and an unexpected charm – with an added dose of hilarity – made them great copy.

While Owen Morris was on his salvage job the band went out on a UK tour with Whiteout. Instead of seeing the Scottish band as rivals for the long-suffering and very patient Stone Roses audience waiting for the return of the messiahs, Oasis bonded with them and, off the back of the buzz on the TV for the upcoming 'Supersonic' debut single, were ready.

A few days after their TV appearance the tour started in Bedford at the Thirst Club where Oasis were paid a hundred quid with Pot Noodles on the rider. Even the TV appearance didn't sell out the venue which was half full with about 100 people. Whiteout were tipped for big things and both bands were seen as pretty much equals, with the Scottish band having the big tour bus and Oasis in a van driven by Bonehead – both band's fortunes and transport were going to change within weeks.

'The first time we played with Oasis was Bedford,' remembers Whiteout manager Andrew 'McD' McDermid. 'They didn't have a tour manager, just a mate helping out. They were great. They played "Rock 'n' Roll Star" and all the songs had that kind of working-class life of signing on, getting out of it and where they came from thing. Liam, obviously, already just looked like a proper frontman. He was walking around the stage like a panther, pure alpha male, like this is it, this is my chance.'

The next night the bands shared the stage at the legendary 100 Club in London. John Brice was there:

'London hadn't quite got wise to them yet, even after Water Rats. I went into the tiny dressing room at the 100 Club and Noel was still keen to sign publishing with me at Warner Chappell but my boss's favourite band were the Scorpions so it wasn't looking good. He said, "We'll probably get sued by whoever publishes T. Rex for that song that sounds like 'Get it On' and apart from the singer they don't look great and he just stands there."

'"That's the whole point!" I said. So they signed to Sony instead and a year later my boss claimed he'd tried to sign Oasis. What could I do but laugh!'

A few days later 50 people turned up at the Tunbridge Wells Forum, a small venue in a converted toilet. After the gig, Noel tried to buy a gin and tonic at the bar, but it was closed, leaving the guitar player to joke, 'When I'm rich and famous, I'm going to buy this place, and I'm going to sack you.'

By the time they had reached the Jug of Ale in Birmingham, the tour was selling out the smaller venues, as Paul Slattery, the photographer who took so many of their iconic shots, recalls: 'The dressing room at the Jug of Ale in Moseley was actually a toilet. It was one of the first group photos I took of the band. The upstairs room was packed for the gig, with most people sitting on the floor like a bunch of hippies in a cloud of marijuana smoke amazed at the electric performance.'[1]

On 5 April Oasis reached Scotland and played Lucifer's Mill in Dundee where they were now supported by 18 Wheeler as Whiteout had their own Scottish dates. That night the gig sold 17 advance tickets and 74 people eventually turned up. Three days later the band played the Tramway in Glasgow and after the gig the *NME's* John Harris met them at the Forte Crest Hotel for the famous 'Wibbling Rivalry' interview, featuring a sweary argument between Noel and Liam that set the brothers' media image in stone.

Towards the end of the tour the shock news of Kurt Cobain's suicide filtered through in one of those sobering moments. According to McD, Liam gave a really articulate, erudite speech about Kurt Cobain at the gig 'and the crowd really reacted to it.'

The tour ended with Oasis as the headliners and on 13 April in Liverpool, a few short months after they had played in the city where so much had begun to change for them, the band returned to a packed Lomax on Cumberland Street with an all-star audience including Richard Ashcroft, Cast and many local bands catching that great moment when a band goes from cult to breakthrough.

A week later 'Supersonic' entered the charts at number 31, where it peaked. It was now official: Oasis were breaking through.

On 11 June they headlined their first festival proper at the Heineken music festival in a big top at Avenham Park in Preston. Headliners were fellow Creation band the Boo Radleys who had recently scored their own top 20 album, *Giant Steps*, that placed them between their initial noisenik American underground influence and an embrace of the Beatles.

Being a free event, the big top was packed with a mix of music fans and piss-heads, resulting in a bottle being thrown and a drunken loon climbing on to the top of the tent and Liam shouting, 'Elvis get down'. Oasis had been booked by Emma Bridger from local Preston indie band Formula One who had been a music buddy with Noel Gallagher for some time. She recalls:

'I was backstage at a 1992 Ya Ya's gig at the Band on the Wall in Manchester. There were these two guys having an argument about whether Take That were the new Beatles. So I walked in and I went, "Are they fuck?" And this guy said, "See, she knows what she's talking about" and that was Noel, and Liam was like, "Does she fuck know!"

'So we got chatting and I really bonded with Noel over music. I was really big into my sixties psych stuff like the 13th Floor Elevators and Love and he was really curious and open to checking things out. We would stay up late in dive bars in Manchester or chat on the phone about music, and when they played the Preston Mill in December 1993 with the Verve we went down and saw them and were blown away. There was hardly anyone there but they were buzzing about getting signed and Noel gave me a cassette with some demos on it, and we just played it over and over again.

'Him and Liam were both full of energy, enthusiastic, charming and they hadn't got that cynicism. I think they were really good with people. A lot of people in bands are often quite introverted or a bit awkward and they didn't have any of that and the minute you walked into a room you noticed them.'

Emma saw first-hand the powerful dynamic at the core of the band: 'They're both really bright working-class lads, really quick and really on it. Both are really funny and had a really good energy to be around. Noel was a bit more serious about the music and the kind of the integrity of that which really mattered to him. For Liam it was more about living the dream of being a rock star. Liam was younger as well and he wanted to party and chat to girls and was a really charismatic person with a real charm and energy about him.'

The initial press for the band quickly reduced them to 2D stereotypes and nothing like the brothers that Emma knew. Their music had far more nous and depth than they were credited for.

'I like the simplicity of "Cigarettes & Alcohol" and "Supersonic",' says Emma. 'It's hard to work out why it's amazing. It's so simple, yet mind-blowing. It spoke to me, captivated me. They were confident enough to make it really simple or just stand there live and do nothing and it doesn't matter, it's all about the music.'

The same week they played their first hometown show for six months at the Academy 2, which was a 950-ticket sell-out. Ironically, the night they finally became a big band in their home city was the night that sparked Noel to leave Manchester. The gig was a triumph but also marked with a sadness for Noel Gallagher as this was the night that, after six years, he had split from his girlfriend Louise Jones. It sparked the inevitable move to London.

'We had to go where the action was,' says Noel. 'There was not much left here anymore. The thing that had been great had gone and people were getting shot and mugged. Nights out had become like a military operation and it was harder to be free and easy. If we hadn't had 1988/89, then 1993 wouldn't have felt so bad, but the dream had gone tits up. Alan McGee was drawing us towards London and we went and everyone loved us and it felt like home.

'I eventually moved to Camden and it was like being in the centre of things. Britpop was just starting to happen. Our record label was in London, our manager was there and I got sick of getting trains that were delayed forever or waking up on the train and someone had robbed my bag.'

Once in London, Noel lived temporarily in a flat owned by Johnny Marr and in places in Chiswick and Camden before buying his own place. He would return back up north of course – there was the fortnightly pilgrimage to Manchester City home games and the remnants of his own social life in the city. Oasis's centre of gravity now was shifting and, like the Beatles before them, they were becoming a London band with very strong northern roots. Manchester was where they had grafted the band, London was where they would celebrate it, and while Manchester birthed and framed them, London was where they would flower.

25

SHAKE ALONG WITH THEM

On 20 June 1994 Oasis released their second single 'Shakermaker', which like many songs in their early years, had a complex gestation.

Initially recorded in October 1993 as a demo at Out of the Blue Studios, with its third verse was written off the cuff by Noel in the taxi on the way to the studio as they drove past Sifters in Burnage – hence the reference to the legendary shop in the lyrics. It may have been a piece of wild inspiration or a desperate last-minute jot but it gives the song a real sense of time and place.

'Shakermaker' would be revisited the following year in a two-day session at the same studio before Owen Morris remixed the song at Matrix Studios on 2 May, readying it for mastering at Abbey Road two days later before he mastered the rest of the debut album at Johnny Marr's Clear studio. Talk about going to the wire!

Sonically the song's picked 'Ticket to Ride' arpeggio intro holds the tension before the wall of sound oozes and collapses in after the drum roll. It's a glorious swamp of lysergic attitude with a great vocal from Liam that makes the surreal and playful, playdough lyrics sound like they mean everything in the world.

The amusing nick of the New Seekers' 1971 'I'd Like to Teach the World to Sing' single, originally the new age soundtrack for a Coca-Cola advert, got them into trouble, with the ubiquitous song, imprinted on a generation's DNA, somehow making total sense in the middle of the single. Naughty, of course, but so deliciously tempting. It didn't go unnoticed and they were sued by Coca-Cola. 'We drink Pepsi now,' quipped Noel after the court case.

Over the years there have been some outrageous steals in Oasis songs but in the post hip-hop pop world where whole tracks were built out of samples, this kind of musical bricolage made total sense. Surely one of the great things about classic pop is its reference points and nods to other songs and ideas.

The song's lyrics were like a bizarre shopping list of cultural references that created a trippy tumble of non sequiturs about escape. The title itself was a briefly popular seventies Christmas toy for kids, and the lyrics detail *Mr. Men* books with an added Mr. Clean from the Jam song. Mr. Soft was a nod to the tripped-out 1987 Trebor Soft Mints ad which was soundtracked by the classic Cockney Rebel hit single of the same name. Mr. Benn was the off-the-wall kids' cartoon character, and the final addition of Mr. Sifter is a perfect nod to the Fog Lane record shop, turning it into an instant Oasis shrine for generations to come. 'Shakermaker' was now less of the gooey seventies toy than a more dayglo wonked-out take on the mundane reality of the streets and ginnels of south Manchester; one of many influences turning the local streets into some kind of neo-psychedelic playground to run amok in.

Released in late June, the single came with its B-sides including the cheeky acoustic workout of the Noel-sung kitchen sink drama 'D'Yer Wanna be a Spaceman?'; 'Alive' the rough and ready demo of an early rocker; and 'Bring It On Down', from the 15 September BBC Radio 5 session.

The single came in a new Microdot sleeve that played with the song title, imagery and sheer sound to create a striking visual of melted pop culture artefacts in a dayglo room. The image was the first of the Oasis sleeves with the twisted northern psychedelia and a jump into the wonk world of upcoming brilliant sleeves. Its trippy take on reality so perfectly matches the song, while the melted items look like they ooze with the music. It was created in Michael Spencer Jones' flat, as he explains:

'The photo was done in my apartment on Clyde Road in West Didsbury. At the time, Liam lived six doors down from me with his then girlfriend, and Bonehead was around the corner on Stratford Avenue. The concept was that if you put an Oasis song on your sound system and turn the volume up, suddenly everything in the room melts!

'I painted the wall of the studio green and then took the first photo of the inanimate objects before melting them all with this massive flamethrower for the front cover.'

Brian Cannon also recalls the creation of the sleeve:

'"Shakermaker" was meant to look like a wibbly wobbly Mr. Soft world. At that time there was a TV advert for Trebor mints where the ad was like this trippy soft gooey world and that's where the sleeve partly came from. The idea was this room is full of inanimate objects. There's no music on, and everything was just as it is and that was back sleeve. And then you can see my hand pressing play on the tape and the cassette plays Oasis and everything in the room melts, with this incredible sonic vibration coming out the speakers and just melts everything in the room. I was immersed in the band, I got them. And they got me. They trusted me. They knew I wasn't going to come up with something rubbish.'

The accompanying video snapshots the band in the Manchester they were now leaving behind. It's like a red-brick urban update of the Beatles' classic 'Rain' video replacing the regency gardens of mid-sixties London with the damp back alleys of mid-nineties Manchester.

The band stand stock-still and look impeccably cool, while Liam swaggers in his stillism with Noel just behind, looking deadpan and in control in a perfectly Mancunian red-brick backdrop of ginnels and parks. There's then a trip to Sifters with Brian Cannon as Mr. Soft, driving the car, and Liam holding up Paul McCartney's *Red Rose Speedway* album in the shop.

'The dynamic within the band itself was Noel in control, with flash points with Liam,' remembers Brian, 'which I'm guessing would have been going on since they were kids and that just carried on into the band and tabloid headlines. On the whole, though, everybody was happy to let Noel run the show because he wrote all these incredible songs and had an idea of what he was doing.'

Not that this ever seemed to stop the rock 'n' roll, as Mathew Priest from Dodgy remembers after bumping into them on a TV appearance: 'They were doing a TV show hosted by Johnny Vaughan and Caitlin Moran, and we were with them in the big green room area which had a big massive glass table in it. Everyone was milling around being polite and Oasis tuned up and cleared the table and began racking out lines. I thought, "C'mon lads you'll get thrown out!"

'Liam then came into our dressing room for a chat. They were about to go stratospheric but he was still really humble and asking us questions and not full of arrogance. He was like a pussy cat, gentle and lovely, and then the door opened and someone asked, "Liam are you in there?" and he changed and put on the swagger and went and did the TV. You could tell it was going to be massive and it helps to have someone that good looking with a voice like that!'

Primed and ready for their first big hit, the band made their first *Top of the Pops* appearance on 30 June. It was a few days after their

appearance on the second stage at Glastonbury where they dominated in front of a huge crowd, sending the single flying up the
charts. That evening after the show they listened to the chart count-
down and heard that 'Shakermaker' had gone in at number 11.

The poppermost was now within their grasp.

By the early nineties, UK music was at its lowest ebb for decades in
the USA. The sixties and seventies had seen British bands effortlessly rule the roost, from the obvious ones like the Beatles, Led
Zeppelin and Pink Floyd to the bizarre undercard of bands that got
huge like Herman's Hermits and the Dave Clark Five. It seemed
that all you needed was a cheeky grin and a British accent and to
look and sound slightly like the Beatles, and the USA would be
yours. For a long time that seemed like the natural order of things.

A decade later, Bowie broke the USA, but there had been many
misses like Roxy Music or Paul Weller or even the Sex Pistols, who had
to wait 30 years until their debut album went gold across the pond.

By the time Oasis flew out to the USA for their 21 July debut
show at the 400-capacity Wetlands Preserve in Tribeca, Manhattan,
the genuine special relationship of the transatlantic ping-pong of
pop culture from the USA to the UK and back again had dwindled
to only a handful of British bands.

The one-off teaser gig was part of the annual New Music Seminar
– the annual music biz convention showcase that Tony Wilson had
used as the template for In the City. It was the biggest event of its
kind in the world at the time and the city was teeming with venues
full of hopeful bands playing to a mixture of curious punters and
the attending music biz and media.

When Oasis stepped on to the Wetlands stage it was a totally
different ball game than the 1964 Beatles invasion. Post-grunge,
Oasis's wall of sound may have had a chance of connecting with
the more guitar orientated American scene but the culture gap was

now a gulf between the two nations, separated by more than a common language.

The debut Oasis gig, though, was packed and the reaction was good – it showed there was a possibility that they could make sense to the Americans. But they would have to tour, work hard and press a lot of flesh to make the connection and this was not a given.

The next day the band filmed a video directed by Carlos Grasso for their upcoming third single 'Live Forever', due in a couple of weeks. The video saw the band burying Tony McCarroll in a slightly sinister fashion in a grave in a New York garden. This was cut with them running around Central Park's Naumburg Bandshell, where John Lennon had filmed a chunk of his 1974 video for his 'Mind Games' single, and the steps to the south of Bethesda Fountain, with Liam sitting in an art piece chair stuck halfway up a wall.

The next day they flew back to the UK for a clutch of key shows and their crucial upcoming debut album release.

In the USA Oasis might have initially been a curio, the latest fuss from a declining British pop empire, but in the UK they were now a big noise. That summer, the gigs got bigger and wilder and the band were on the road almost permanently. As the crowds increased, there was inevitably a more unruly element turning up. This sometimes resulted in violence, like at the Newcastle Riverside live on radio gig on 9 August; after the Manchester City v Newcastle United banter someone got on stage and punched Noel. This saw the guitarist swing his legendary Les Paul, given to him by Johnny Marr, and catch himself in the face, which resulted in a trip to hospital for stitches. The band stormed off stage with singer Liam returning, brandishing a microphone stand, and snarling 'no one hits our kid' as the crowd chanted back. The result was the band's security was stepped up with an ex-army friend of Marcus Russell,

Ian Roberston, brought in. It underlined how this was moving beyond being a normal band.

By 1994 festival culture was becoming the key in the UK. At one time they had been a muddy side show to the main business of the long circuit tours that built up from clubs to colleges to the old-school 3,000-capacity venues like the Apollo – a time-honoured system set in stone. But in the last days of pre-internet pop culture things were changing fast and what had once been a clutch of key festivals like Glastonbury and Reading was beginning to flower into a festival circuit.

The post-rave scene saw a surge in festival culture, and indie bands had to adopt the new culture or die. A band like Oasis were built for the big stages – they had a big sound, big ambition and a singer whose vibe could fill the fields. The festival circuit was there for the taking, like at T in the Park in Scotland, co-promoted by Geoff Ellis, the manager of King Tut's from the night of the famous Oasis gig from a year before.

The journey up to Scotland to play the new festival had its own curveballs, with road crew member, Manchester face, and Sister Lovers drummer, Al Smith, putting unleaded petrol in the tank, causing it to break and leaving the band, roadie Phil Smith and Mark Coyle to get stoned and play frisbee across the motorway lanes as the van got fixed. Somehow they still got there for the gig and when they walked out on the stage, the packed tent of 6,000 went crazy, cementing a special relationship with the Scottish audience.

There has always been an affinity between Glasgow and Manchester when it comes to bands. The Stone Roses were like a religion in the city and their 1990 gig at Glasgow Green was, for many, the peak of the Stone Roses experience with the atmosphere in the 7,000-capacity big top off the scale and the band on peak form. That was four long years ago, and a new generation was coming into the gig world. They needed their own fix, and

SHAKE ALONG WITH THEM

here were Oasis, perfect for the moment on every level, and the crowd sang along with every song – the first time that this had happened to the band.

Glasgow, like Manchester, likes its art as arty as you want as long as it's served up with no pretension; both cities love their music with a swagger and a working-class communal rush. There is a wildness at this type of gig and Oasis not so much took the Stone Roses throne as shared in the unique Glasgow vibe.

Oasis spent 1994 on the festival circuit, sharing stages with the likes of the Disposable Heroes of Hiphoprisy, House of Pain and the Lemonheads, whose singer Evan Dando seemed ubiquitous that year, turning up everywhere, hanging out with the band and even co-writing a song with Noel called 'Purple Parallelogram' that was never released.

26

HOW YOUR GARDEN GROWS

If there is one song that encapsulated being young and British in the nineties then the third Oasis single, the yearning anthemic 'Live Forever', launched on 8 August 1994, was it.

An instant classic, the same song that had astonished Noel's bandmates when he had introduced it at the Boardwalk rehearsal room a couple of years before was now a bona fide anthem. Liam Gallagher's favourite Oasis song and the song that Alan McGee claimed was probably 'the single greatest moment I've ever experienced with them' was proof that this was no mere flash in the pan.

Initially inspired by the Rolling Stones song written about the late Brian Jones, 'Shine a Light', from their 1972 *Exile on Main St.* album, 'Live Forever' had moved a long way from that inspiration point and was a different mood than the first two singles; early evidence that Oasis had many more strings to their bow.

With another loping drum groove intro and its Neil Young-style chords and long guitar notes in the solo, the song had all of the Canadian's raw power and emotional nous. Owen Morris had cut a second section of Noel's guitar solo because it sounded 'a bit like fucking Slash from Guns N' Roses' and then he cut out the acoustic guitar intro and spliced in Tony McCarroll's drums. He then cranked the mixes, creating a seductive wall of sound for the emotional landslide of the song. Oasis had already proved that they could play loud and that they could feel the noise but there was a sensitivity to 'Live Forever' that made it one of those drop-dead classics.

The finished song has been interpreted as partly being about Noel and Liam's mother Peggy and her love of her garden as her place to escape, while capturing the band's eternal themes like their own escape from the drudgery of life and the grey sky everyday of no hope Manchester youth. There is also something about its sound and title that perfectly captures the indestructible eternity of being teenage – that live forever rush of the heady days of freedom when you discover everything in a hurry and live life to the full with no consequences. The song soundtracks that feeling making it a perfect anthem for most of the audience and a generational marker.

The core of the song is its positivity, written maybe in reaction to Nirvana's 'I Hate Myself and I Want to Die'. Despite being fans of Kurt Cobain's 'Beatles through a fuzz box' melodies and the two bands being mirror images of each other with their walls of sound and rasping, compelling singers, their differing attitudes to life were larger than the huge transatlantic gulf.

For Noel Gallagher life was for living even if you were dealt a bad hand – the opposite of the American slacker mindset of that period, with the apathetic vibe documented in the underground DIY culture spiralling out from Nirvana.

Capturing the sense of music as escape, the sleeve art was a reflective Michael Spencer Jones photograph of the house on 251 Menlove Avenue in Liverpool where John Lennon had grown up and the porch where he practised his guitar because of its acoustics. Ironically there were often more Beatles references embedded in the art than in the actual songs! The striking photograph saw the house framed by a moody sky and a colour tint that looked ghostly, as Brian Cannon explains:

'Often the idea came together very last minute and in this case because initially we couldn't think of anything! I went round to Michael Spencer Jones' house and he had that picture he had taken as another project and then added the infra-red film to get that effect.'

As Michael Spencer Jones points out, the photo was a perfect piece of framing:

'I had that picture of John Lennon's house. It was a perfect fit with the lyrics and the band loved the John Lennon reference. With the sleeves, we were very conscious of changing from one to the next colour-wise, from blue then green and now to black and white.

'The Lennon house photo was a great nod but the thing about Oasis was I don't think they ever sounded like the Beatles at all! The only reason the Beatles reference is there in the photo is because it's clever and it puts them in that frame of being the biggest band while Noel and Liam were just referencing their heroes. I wasn't suggesting there's any similarity between the two apart from in terms of being a phenomenon and in the mid-nineties they were becoming just as big.'

27

DEFINITELY MAYBE

Sometimes a band just comes along and seizes the moment and by the summer of 1994 Oasis were an unstoppable force. The potent brew they had cooked up in the bowels of the Boardwalk rehearsal rooms was seizing the moment with a genuine groundswell, as Creation's Chris Abbot points out:

'This was the most important thing about Oasis, they were the last band to make it word of mouth before the internet. If you saw them you told your mates, who then told their mates, who then came, and these gigs just embryonically grew and grew.'

Britpop had made a space, Radio 1 was playing guitar bands, and the death of Kurt Cobain had left a very big hole for a band with that level of intensity but which promised more than a nihilism.

According to Noel's three album masterplan, the debut album was originally to be called 'Datura Dream Deferred' after a chat with Johnny Marr where the guitar legend told him about a condition on giving up smoking weed that helped him dream again.

On its release on 29 August, and now called *Definitely Maybe*, the album saw Oasis take their own place in the canon of rock classics and albums that they had immersed themselves in for years. The last great British rock 'n' roll band? Maybe . . . definitely?

Keith Cameron summed it up perfectly in the *NME*: 'It's like opening your bedroom curtains one morning and discovering that some fucker's built the Taj Mahal in your back garden and then filled it with your favourite flavour of Angel Delight.'[1]

The basic formula of Noel writing them and Liam singing them created a high-decibel raucous romp and a bittersweet symphony of songs that somehow hit a perfect spot between crafted songwriting and a crafted swagger. This was an album of songs of love and escape, brimming with a poignancy and a melancholy, that saw Liam reinterpret them as attitude bombs. When the two brothers were in harmony they hit the sweetest of sweet spots and created something both volatile and thrilling.

It was that different kind of tension between the Gallaghers that created the unique energy in the band. Noel's melancholic, introspective, cynical and sometimes playful songs were turned upside down and inside out by his younger brother and yet never lost their meaning. Filtered by the band behind the two brothers it was cranked into a tsunami of high-decibel splendour – an abrasive wall of sound that you could get lost in, with great potent melodies that caught the opposing, and very British, moods of dour pessimism and euphoric optimism. It soundtracked the national psyche with a collection of great songs that dared to stomp and were also not afraid of Slade while clutching a poster of Burt Bacharach.

Gatecrashing Britpop, Oasis were about to become the biggest band in the country and their debut album was their accidental manifesto and a generational defining statement that everything aligns with – and that there was no escape from.

In 1976 the Sex Pistols had felt like the shock of the new and in 1994 Oasis, in some ways, were the shock of the old – a final reaffirmation of the power of British rock when it was in the right hands.

Noel explains: 'I used to get embarrassed going to America and the "I thought you guys were meant to sound like the Beatles?" question which preceded us, and I would say, "I've never said we sounded like the Beatles. We sound more like Slade y'know!" because they are a seriously underrated band, maybe because of "Merry Xmas Everybody" and Dave Hill's outfits. I met Noddy [Holder] a few times and he's a real gent and he loves Oasis. He's a great singer and you don't hear his voice enough. When I try and describe what we sound like I say it's rock 'n' roll pop music like "20th Century Boy" and "Cum on Feel The Noize" – they are both loud and euphoric. They are great, man.

'That music was part of my youth along with David Bowie. I used to have a glam rock compilation tape that I played in the Inspiral Carpets tour bus and they would say, "What do you listen to that for?" and I would say, "This is it!"'

Of course, early Oasis were far more than a glam rock compilation tape but they certainly captured the superyob rush of primetime glam, while also adding moments of introspection, such as on the classic 'Slide Away' or the defining 'Live Forever' with its yearning melody and aching arpeggios. Of course" there was also the sixties classics in the mix, dancing on the bones of the Beatles and the Stones. There was also a hint of psychedelia that they would explore further down the line and Johnny Marr's northern cool and the Stone Roses communal chiming euphoria, and of course, the attitude and glorious guitar wall of sound of the Sex Pistols.

Years immersed in pop culture went into the album and Noel Gallagher had soaked it all in from mad nights out in town, endless gigs, classic albums, late nights at mates' flats and the music obsessed 'weirdos' in town – and then reimagined it all with an innate genius that even he always sounds surprised to discover.

Despite its arduous gestation, the resulting album remarkably didn't sound patched together but consistently fresh and raw.

Exploding out of the speakers, it was a life-affirming rush of sound and must be one of the most thrillingly noisy records to hit the top of the charts.

'When we started, we got tangled up with that Britpop thing but we were essentially a punk band who did it for ourselves,' explains Noel. 'There was no fashion thing. It was loud and there were songs about drinking and shagging and it doesn't get any better than that!'

Every great album kicks off with a statement track and 'Rock 'n' Roll Star' explodes into action. A perfectly titled song – it deals with those eternal themes at the heart and soul of all great music as a salvation and escape. Music as a glimpse of the magic stuff that is beyond the drudgery of life. The song is a powerful glam swagger pop/noise escape that is so often at the core of classic Oasis. It empowers the listener to feel like a rock 'n' roll star on that wam-bam-thank-you-glam Saturday night out running amok down the catwalk of the British high street. Those great nights out when you feel like a rock 'n' roll star when there is no plan and you drift into town and return on a Thursday with no idea where you have been. The song is the very British binge of good times compressed into your best clothes and booze, and a sonic gauntlet thrown down to the listener.

'I wrote the song in my flat on Whitworth Street before going out and having it,' explains Noel. 'It's that kind of song. I remember being at a gig by Suede at Manchester Academy [6 April 1993] and I bumped into you and you said, "Have you really got songs called 'Rock 'n' Roll Star' and 'Cigarettes & Alcohol'? They are fucking great titles" and I was "Wow!" I always said to people then that John Robb came up to me and said have you really got those song titles!'

'Shakermaker' was one of the four singles on the album, loading it with the hits and creating the track list ebb and flow – from the riot of the opening track to the wonk groove of the recent hit single

– drawing you in and setting up 'Live Forever', perhaps the first real timeless classic that Noel had written.

'When I wrote "Live Forever" I knew enough about music to know that's not indie and is as good as the classics,' he recalls.

Again a song yearning for escape, perhaps from his own troubled youthful years, the lyrics have a profound mixture of sadness and hope that is at the heart of the best pop songs, as Noel explains:

'There is always the person who knows too much and is trying to say it cleverer than anyone else and then there will be someone like me who doesn't know what he's saying but somehow when the song is finished it says it all.'

Much has been made of the Oasis lyrics and how often they don't seem to mean very much, often by Noel himself in that very Mancunian distrust of poetry and pretension. The city, with its pragmatic soul forged in its mills and industry, also always had an added poetic Irish heart of immigrant songs that temepered the Industrial Revolution brutality. Ironically for a place that had disdain for poets, it was actually full of them – like Buzzcocks' lovelorn songs on the complexities of lust and love, Ian Curtis's dark shadows and Morrissey's bookworm vignettes. Then there was Mark E Smith's stark mysticism, John Cooper Clarke – the true poet laureate – and Shaun Ryder, who Tony Wilson had once memorably claimed was better than WB Yeats, with his brilliant stream of unconscious word play. Pop culture gave these flamboyant figures not only a space but a soap box.

Noel Gallagher once said that he 'didn't have to impress anyone with the lyrics' and while he wasn't writing for the academics, he was unwittingly compressing his and his listener's lives into song. He may have once declared fiction is 'a fucking waste of time' but he could spin a yarn or lyric as good as anyone. Perhaps it was the perceived elitism of the book world that rankled with him, yet his lyrics were dotted with poetic references and ideas. His education came from pop culture and his analytical mind was not just soaking up the chord changes and the song structures, but the words as well.

'Now that we live in a time where we must have all the information does no one believe in magic anymore?' he once said. 'A journalist was saying to me the other day, these songs must be about something and I said, "Can you not just accept that I made them all up?" Obviously they are not just random words that don't mean anything, but the word is the journalists' trade and they get really protective if it's just about the tune.'

The words could be perfectly nonsensical like a council estate Alice in northern-land aided and abetted by psychedelics and hours spent in Sifters on a crash for the ravers, sifting through the battered old vinyl and immersed in the great songs with their often brilliantly nursery rhyme lyrics. The post mid-sixties psychedelic British pop has always been one of its golden seams and both Bowie and Bolan didn't shy away from their love of Pink Floyd's Syd Barrett and his songs about gnomes and random bikes. Far from trashing this, punk continued in this vein and so did post-punk. If the sixties was two people having a party and everyone else trying to find it, the nineties was everyone having that party and two people trying to remember how to write about it filtered through council estate culture and a new psychedelic street sensibility.

But then of course the art of pop is somehow saying everything and nothing at the same time. The perfect pop poetry can be nonsensical but profound – just like Marc Bolan when he sang about a Rolls-Royce being good for his voice. It all at once sounded mysterious, intriguing and ridiculous and somehow you knew exactly what he meant. Written down, the words had their own quicksilver logic but the difference between poetry and lyrics is the sound of the voice, and both Noel and Liam have voices that use the lyrics as a vehicle for a claustrophobic rage or an emotional intelligence and sensitivity, more than either of them would ever care to admit.

'Live Forever' was the same, a song that captures the eternal optimism of youth – that one time in your life when you are free to do crazy stuff and get away with it before real life and responsibilities come and slam the door on you. Just like 'Anarchy in the UK' was less a song about Bakunin and anarchist theory, than a song perhaps about the brief anarchist years of late teenage when you are old enough to go wild and the end of your life seems like an abstract concept that only happens to other people.

The words could be the hod carrier for the melody, like when George Harrison was looking for lyrics for his classic new song, 'Something' and John Lennon tells him to sing 'pomegranate or anything' to hold the tune. Noel would have maybe kept the pomegranate line in and it would have still made sense, and you can imagine Liam sneering that fruity word and rolling the 'rrrrr's' and making it sound like it meant everything.

There was a poetry to their songs of love and fury, like dealing with the underclass psychodrama of 'Bring It On Down' with its punk lyrics sung with a perfectly vicious sneer by Liam, whose vocals bring whole other feelings and emotions into the songs as he explains:

'The madness and aggression is always there under the surface. The day that goes then God help us all! I need a bit of that, and that's still there. You don't give it a call, it's in me.'

Noel preferred to let the songs do the talking, correctly pointing out that pop doesn't need to be explained. Just felt.

'I could try and convince everybody that I was the greatest lyricist in the world when an album comes out and explain all the songs,' he says. 'That's where the press get all their soundbites from, but I don't want to dissect every line because you spoil the song for the fans.

'I don't want to know who the 20th Century Boy was!

'You see that guy in John Lennon's garden in the *Imagine* film and he is looking for meaning and Lennon says, "I wrote that on the bog!" and he goes, "No!" And he looks totally shocked!'

The songs were a curious mixture of homespun wisdom, lyrical cul-de-sacs, off-the-cuff observations or words that were stuffed in last minute to finish the song that felt and sounded good. Yet they made you feel something, like on 'Up in the Sky' which was a raucous psychedelic groove dripping with Beatles *Revolver* period fun and games. The song is like a cross between 'Rain' and its cyclic bass and the eternal drone of 'Tomorrow Never Knows', yet cranked through a punkish aggression and a near falsetto from Liam at the end of the vocal lines.

With added tape delay on Tony McCarroll's drums doubling up the swing, the Owen Morris remix of 'Columbia' has an added energy to it from the White Label version while the album version of 'Supersonic' was the same as the single. Sometimes the simplest phrases can make the biggest statements, like on Saturday-night jukebox riot classic, 'Cigarettes & Alcohol', celebrating the cheap mainstays of good times on the never-never and the futility of grinding out life in the so-called underclass. It instantly painted a picture of every pub in Manchester and beyond as much as any L.S. Lowry painting. The song was a darkly funny nihilistic social commentary anthem without the solutions, which made it more powerful as Liam cranked up the rolling 'rrrr's' in perhaps his most defining vocal over the song's riff, half-inched from the T. Rex classic 'Get it On', which had already been stolen from Chuck Berry's 'Little Queenie' in the never-ending pop merry-go-round.

It's the moments of homespun wisdom that sum up the 'get up and go before it's got up and gone' attitude. Like all the best British lyrics 'Cigarettes & Alcohol' captured the magic of the mundane. Twisted through the acrid fug of marijuana or the wobble of magic mushrooms, this was always going to create a tripped-out hyper-reality, a slightly exaggerated take on the day to day of psychedelic estates, trippy parks and boisterous nights out with mates. This street psychedelia, a twisted take on reality, was part and parcel of pop culture, from Strawberry Fields to Bolan's unicorn poetry, allied with that great British sense of the absurd from Lewis Carroll to Monty Python to Lennon.

Sometimes it's those most simple phrases that can hit the mark and some of those in 'Supersonic' are lyrical perfection – a moment of bliss in the middle of the mad scramble of life. All given that life by Liam's delivery as he memorised the song in two takes and put his own psychodrama and heart and soul into them. Surely the genius of pop is just this. It could be one crazy word sung brilliantly that made you feel something or it could be random words that you could dance to.

Liam Gallagher understood this: 'I'm good at making sense out of nonsense when I sing. There's a time and place for writing THE lyric, sometimes you just want to be free and let it roll out, if it's kind of alright, let it go.'

Noel Gallagher also understood this: 'That's the difference between the working classes and the middle classes. I'm not trying to be challenged by anybody. I don't need Brian Eno walking around with a big placard in the studio with his oblique strategies written on it. Pop music is Ob-La-Di, Ob-La fucking Da – what does that mean? It's what it means to you and that's all that matters. That really annoys those people because they couldn't define our success when it came. All the great bands that ever existed didn't have to explain themselves. I don't remember Johnny Rotten having to sit down and explain what every single song was about. It's either obvious to you or you're not a fan.'

Oasis never shied away from a joyful romp. In the middle of their melancholia or punky dramas there could be amusing snapshots of plain whimsy with a northern filter, like 'Digsy's Dinner' with its 'lasaaaaagnyah' hook line in a song that referenced one of their Liverpool mates, the irrepressible Digsy from the band Smaller – a genuine character. It bounces along and gives the album a jaunty rush of energy. One of the great things about the Beatles was their versatility, how they dared to write novelty songs – novelty songs that often came with a certain poignancy. If you understand a song like 'Yellow Submarine' then you understand the Beatles.

The Fabs' 1966 number one was, on one level, a children's song that also had its own profound depth.

At 6 minutes 32 seconds the longest track on the album, 'Slide Away' is perhaps the gem of the record. The song was written by Noel in a bedroom on the Les Paul guitar Jonny Marr had used to record *The Queen is Dead* that he had given to Noel in 1993.[2] When he played on the hallowed neck of the Smiths guitar for the first time, he found some mesmerising chords, and humming the melody grafted the lyrics. The only surviving track from the Monnow Valley sessions, it manages to combine the band's wall of sound with an aching lead line cascading over the arpeggios and the sevenths and minor chords into a glorious descending melody. A melody that underlines the sensitivity in a song about a love affair inevitably coming to the end with music to match, before being put into the Sex Pistols' sonic meat grinder. With its searing guitar sound and a 'tequila' vocal from Liam, it deals with the dreams of youth and first love dashed by the realities of life. There was also a poignancy and a sensitivity to its lyrical brawl that took the band somewhere else. For many northerners emotional stuff can only be articulated in music and not always directly – 'don't make a song or dance about it' as your parents would say. Ironically many did, creating some of the most stunning post-war pop culture.

Liam interpreted and made sense of his brother's lyrics that would range from introspective to expressive:

'I'm made up of all sorts, me. I'm not just an angry little lunatic. I got a lot of feelings – that's what it's about, man, but you don't want to go on stage like Cliff Richard. Standing up and singing at tennis matches – that's not a good look!'

For those critics who like to go on about the lack of subtlety in Oasis and how one-dimensional their songs are, 'Married with Children', which was recorded in 1992 at Mark Coyle's house on his 8-track, is a perfect example of a song written with an empathy and emotional depth. Sitting at the end of the album like an unexpected coda, the song is written perhaps from the point of view of Noel's then partner. It's somehow funny and poignant at the same time and sung with a sensitivity by Liam who takes his brother's lyrics and breathes his own soul into them, underlining its nuances and subtleties.

One of the most audacious sides of Oasis was their sometimes outrageous nicks from other songs, often with Noel Gallagher only too happy to point out where they came from in a scrapbook of musical moments from his youth almost sentimentally stitched into his own songs. It's been well documented that they got sued for lifting a part of 'I'd Like to Teach the World to Sing' for 'Shakermaker' and then there was the riff from T. Rex's '20th Century Boy' lurking in 'Cigarettes & Alcohol'.

The nicks were so outrageous and were barely disguised and perfect examples of the postmodern post-sampling cannibal culture era, when pop really did start to eat itself. Hip-hop was built on samples, and guitar bands had always nicked riffs and melodies – even the Beatles did it. Pop music only sounds original the first time you hear it.

A great example is the Verve and 'Bittersweet Symphony', which saw the band coughing up royalties for sampling the Andrew Oldham Orchestra cover of the Rolling Stones' 1965 number one 'The Last Time', which in turn was 'heavily influenced' by the Staple Singers' 'This May Be the Last Time'. Radiohead constructed 'Creep' from the Hollies' 1974 hit 'The Air That I Breathe', written by Albert Hammond, the father of the Strokes guitarist.

It's all part of the pop toolbox. Every song ever written is a version of another song with a twist. Standing on the shoulders of giants. Slight return.

Oasis were no different and Noel Gallagher was from a new generation of musicians who were sifting through secondhand shops and getting immersed in what were now considered antique classics like Neil Young, the Beatles, the Stones, Pink Floyd and many bands that were by now venerated for being the untouchable greats. He was listening and analysing and looking for the keys and cues in their music and taking parts as inspiration points to create his own songs from the wreckage.

As the last big band before the internet, Oasis were plundering the treasures of pop's past and reinventing them and making them their own.

The album came bagged in perhaps the most iconic of all the Oasis artwork which in turn has joined the iconography of great album covers like *Sgt. Pepper's*, *Dark Side of the Moon*, *Ziggy Stardust* and *others*.

It was another Microdot classic from Brian Cannon with Michael Spencer Jones creating an album cover that was a striking image of the band. The sleeve presented the group not in full V-sign punk rock ramalama but in a tasteful slice of northern bohemian sophistication surrounded by artefacts and reference points as art and music combined. The photograph was taken in the front room of Bonehead's then home on Stratford Road just off Burton Road in West Didsbury.

Initially the idea that came from Noel Gallagher was to do an informal shot like the June 1966 Robert Whitaker[3] Beatles photo from the Tokyo Hilton hotel on the back of *A Collection of Beatles Oldies* album. That candid yet playful shot of the band members confined into the bubble of stardom captured the Fabs informally but also at a peak cool, with perfect shades and hair freeze-framed in the moment when they ruled the pop world.

The idea was to create something similar with Oasis, the fast-rising band snapped at Bonehead's dining room table, as Brian Cannon explains:

'Like "Supersonic" it was to be a band shot but this time like the Beatles chilling out band shot. The other inspiration was the Dutch painter Jan van Eyck's Arnolfini Portrait from the later stages of Flemish Renaissance art where the images are full of visual metaphors. A lot of my stuff mixes pop art with nods to Flemish Renaissance paintings of the fourteenth and fifteenth centuries . . .

'The idea was to bring it all back home and have an anti-band shot, because they are not posing but sat around watching Clint Eastwood's *The Good, the Bad and the Ugly* on the telly rather than posing. The photography had to look fly on the wall, just like the Beatles shot was an informal image of the biggest band you've ever seen.'

Scouting out Bonehead's tastefully done-up house at the heart of bohemian West Didsbury, Michael Spencer Jones looked at the photo options but sensed the shot might not work in its initial framing:

'They had a band meeting and decided it was going to be at Bonehead's house. He lived quite close to me so I could walk round and have a recce. The idea was to sit around a wooden table at the back of the room but that didn't look right framed by a rectangular window with bad light, but when I turned around there's the lounge and that great bay window and it just had more aesthetics and much better light.'

The room presented more possibilities but came with its own problems, as Michael explains:

'The room was tiny. When we went back for the 10th anniversary shoot it was like when you go back to your primary school and see the tiny little chairs. So in order to get the whole band in I had to use a wide angle lens but that created another problem with those floorboards which have lines and they just dictate where your eye goes. Plus there was the domestic vibe of the whole situation, so I decided to cross-process the colour film, to get the yellows and the blues to get more of an aesthetic away from that domestic feel of the room.'

Brian Cannon: 'We literally did the test shots the week before the shoot with me lying on the floor and Bonehead's wife in the other places around the room. The reason why Liam is on the floor, is that initially all you can see are the floorboards and when Liam is there he becomes the single most striking part of the whole image. It was unconventional and to have the singer lying on the floor it showed that we weren't prepared to play the game but Liam was cool with this. He knew there was a certain level of we've got to do this to get to where we want to be.'

How do you explain to the singer of a rock 'n' roll band that he's got to lie down on the floor for the whole day? According to the photographer, the idea for Liam lying on the floor to break the floorboards' eye line came from an exhibition of mummies from the Egyptian section of Manchester Museum.

'I also thought Liam should lie on the ground because on the "Supersonic" sleeve he had been standing up,' remembers Michael, 'and I didn't want to repeat that. The only alternative was to have a him sat down and that would be like a calendar photo! So I thought getting him to lie on the floor and in this sort of transcendental meditative state would be cool. It's kind of not sleeping, but like this sort of slightly cosmic state. I didn't have to sort of direct him. He was on some sort of astral plane and that's how it comes through in the pictures. Liam totally got it. He could quite easily have said, "No way", and we would have been fucked as there was no Plan B, but Liam is a thinker. He's kind of a really clever guy and I've taken a lot of the pictures of him where he is really in a deep state of thought.'

Brian Cannon was art directing: 'We really researched the shoot. We went into all of the issues with massive research and preparation. The reason why the preparation has to be so stringent was because you have no idea what you are going to get on the day, so we had to overcompensate and make sure we had everything tested, and there was very little room for deviating from what we set out to do.'

Despite the intense planning there was a margin of error.

'All the elements like the bay window, the colours of film I was going to use, Liam lying on the floor and the band being asked to bring in various items to the shoot had been sorted before the shoot,' remembers Michael, 'but I wondered if that was enough for an album cover so I was pretty nervous about how it was going to turn out.'

On the day of the shoot when the photographer turned up, the small living room was like a party zone full of people getting stoned and drinking vodka and cans of Red Stripe. He told the non-band people to leave and clear up their cans and there was a Mexican standoff.

'I wanted the cans out and they wanted them in! So I said the larger cans are rectangular in a two-dimensional photograph and it's distracting and every single can has "Red Stripe" written on it, so you might as well call the album Red Stripe, and at that point they agreed to their removal.'

The band still wanted some kind of alcohol in the shot though, so the glass of wine was placed in the shot but filled with Ribena because it photographed better. The poster of Burt Bacharach was brought by band crew member Phil Smith as a reference to one of Noel's favourite songwriters. Phil also brought the inflatable globe, which was a neat nod to the globe that Ian Brown had walked on stage with at Spike Island. Its positioning in the shot was a hint at Pink Floyd's Hipgnosis-designed *Ummagumma* sleeve.

Being the only Manchester United fan in the band, Bonehead had brought a small photo of club legend George Best and placed it in the window which was balanced by the Rodney Marsh photo on the floor. Tony McCarroll is watching Noel's favourite film, *The Good, the Bad and the Ugly* on the TV. And just by the settee there was the ashtray near the glass of wine as a nod to 'Cigarettes & Alcohol', and a plastic pink flamingo on the mantelpiece.

'I brought the mirror from my flat to create some movement, remembers Michael Spencer Jones, 'at first the inflatable globe first was static and made the room look like a geography teacher's house! I thought it's got to move and that's when I came up with the idea of putting it up there on the ceiling with this invisible nylon thread that was in my bag, and spinning it round. Another trick I used in the shot is that the exposures are three seconds long because as I was cross-processing the film I thought, let's take advantage of that and anything that moves is blurred, so the globe looked like it was a celestial body orbiting. Finally we now had everyone and everything in position apart from Guigsy, who was the least comfortable in photographs. Then in a break between shots he just happened to lean against the window frame and cross his legs and that was the moment when we got the cover.'

The framing and the energy of the photo was now perfect, with this triangle of the spinning globe, Liam on the floor and the band placed around the room.

Michael Spencer Jones: 'Your eye is naturally guided and photographs rely on balance and the whole notion of aesthetics. Which, when you get down to a sort of deep existential level, an emotional level, it works, like when you see a beautiful sunset or anything in nature. Now we had it and I'm looking down the lens super excited that this was it.'

The definitive image was snapped and was completed with the Brian Cannon designed Oasis logo added and the album title written in Brian's handwriting at the top. They now had one of the great album covers with the right balance between down-to-earth northern red-brick terrace, a mystique and a capture of the band cool. Of all the early period artwork, perhaps this was the moment and the one that merged the music and the imagery perfectly, as Michael Spencer Jones recalls:

'It was a difficult shoot but everyone was on board and looking at the test shots saying, "This looks amazing." We had fun as well –

halfway through the shoot there's a knock at the door, and it's this guy from the Hornet Scooters who supplied a red and white Lambretta for Liam, which was a laugh plus another great photo. When the album came out we had a bit of a scare when, Bert Bacharach's people phoned up, saying, what's Bert doing on that cover? And the management said, Noel is a big fan, which led to a meeting between Bert Bacharach and Noel, and Bert now liking Noel's songs and getting the cover approved.'

Released on 29 August by Creation Records, *Definitely Maybe* went to number one in a blur of great reviews and stats, with huge sales of 100,000 copies in four days, making it the fastest-selling debut album in British history. It even broke the American top 75.

The album thrilled a generation of music fans and disenfranchised youth like Jon McClure, who was then growing up in Sheffield and would go on to form Reverend and the Makers.

'I really identified with the album as a kid,' Jon says. 'The songs spoke to me like he's one of my own and he don't want to live where he lives and he wants to fuck it all off and escape. There was also Liam's alpha bravado which was exciting, but there was also a vulnerability. All that drew me in when I were a kid. I were like, whoever writes these words, they're talking about me especially them early songs, they are beautiful, man.

'Liam doesn't lose the meaning of the songs the way he sings them and Noel could tap into people's emotions, and Liam was able to communicate that, which I think is their magic, their superpower, and their songs have become sort of woven into the fabric of the nation, haven't they? Like it's if you wanted to explain to an alien what life in northern England were like as a young lad you would play them this album.'

Noel was ready: 'I knew the record was good and it took a while to get it finished but I was like, bring it on! I was a bit concerned for Liam at the time with the band taking off. I think it was lucky he had his brother in the band as he's a bit insecure at the best of times. He was a good-looking boy and all that shit and if he wore a binbag on his head it would have looked cool. I knew he was going to be some kind of style icon, and I thought I'm with him so it's going to be cool.'

To this day the album remains one of the classics. A collection of great songs that were a snapshot of their generation. If the band had stopped here they would have still been on hallowed ground, but they not only carried on, they developed into the multi-million selling outsiders from the other UK.

28

ROCKIN'

The album out, the band continued on their seemingly nonstop tour. In the same week of release they somehow managed to play a gig in Buckley, North Wales where they were filmed for a TV show called *With,* which I presented, then Sweden and then Ireland where their hectic schedule took them to Belfast on 4 September, before flying back for a gig in Manchester at the Haçienda the following day.

The legendary Haçienda, where Noel had spent many nights five years ago in its acid house peak, was packed with indie kids and football lads in a sweaty celebration of the latest band to burst out of the city. What had been the hallowed dancefloor for the Haçienda classics was now a surging pit of trainered youth lost in the avalanche of guitars coming from the stage as Oasis arrived in their home city that they were already leaving behind. That night Andy Bell played with the support band:

'The week *Definitely Maybe* came out I was with them in Manchester at the Haçienda because they had the Creation supporting them, and because Eddie Phillips couldn't do it, I was on guitar. So for that gig I played through Noel's Orange Amps.

That night I remember telling Tony McCarroll what a great drummer he was – I still think the drumming of *Definitely Maybe* is iconic. Liam and me chatted about *World of Twist* – and the Creation song "How Does it Feel to Feel", which apparently Oasis had tried a cover of in the very early days. Ride had just put out a version of it. I remember Noel had his copy of the Bee Gees' *Best Of* with him for some reason. Just a couple of random memories.'

A few days later, they were on the other side of the world for their debut Japanese tour which, according to Tony McCarroll, was the high point of the band's early career. The Japanese are often pop culture Anglophiles, and Oasis's potent forces of great melodies and rawness was fresh and intoxicating.

The tour was a whirr of packed clubs, intense fan worship and the high life. It was all they had ever dreamt of, 'like Beatlemania', remembers Tony McCarroll before it all came down with a bump when they landed in the USA at the end of September for a one-month small club tour.

American tours have often been the graveyard for British bands. For every sky-high expectation since the Beatles conquered the USA there are the long drives, the culture clash and confused reactions that burn bands out.

Although many British bands had broken the USA over the years, success was not a given. The Beatles had opened the States up in the sixties, sparking the first British invasion, but for every British success there had been near misses and failures for the likes of Roxy Music and T. Rex and all of Oasis's contemporaries like the Britpop bands who hardly made a dent there. The bands were often too arch, too art school and too ironic for American mass appeal, yet Oasis, as the Americans liked to say, 'rocked', and a cultural divide could be bridged.

Arriving on high expectations and heralded with headlines from *Today* with its front cover story claiming them to be the 'first great band to come out of England in a long time', the exhausted group played the first few gigs down the west coast.

With Portland and Seattle out of the way, what must have been a frazzled and tired band headed south to California to play the Bottom of the Hill club in San Francisco, for their first Bay Area show with locals, the notorious, mercurial and brilliant Brian Jonestown Massacre, in support. The gig was watched by Blur and Pulp who had both played the local Fillmore venue the night before, and at the gig Liam dedicated 'Digsy's Dinner' to the watching Brit bands a year before the 'Battle of Britpop'.

Oasis that night sounded both razor-tight from touring and dangerous from exhaustion in that unique balance that makes for the intoxicating theatre of rock 'n' roll. In the city that the Sex Pistols had played both their biggest and last ever gig in 1978, they created their own dangerous wall of sound and the tightrope of tension that makes gigs enticing.

A couple of days later the band arrived in LA and the culture clash kicked in that saw them chucked off the KROQ radio station for swearing on air, followed by a kick-off with bouncers at the legendary Viper Room and a run-in with the notorious LAPD at 6am because Bonehead refused to stop playing 'Supersonic' on his guitar at full volume as the band partied in his brother Martin's flat.

Then there were the drugs. The support band had been asked for supplies. Brian Jonestown Massacre singer Anton Newcombe recalls: 'Noel Gallagher had watched us play and standing there as we're doing 15-minute songs, and then I told him that Oasis sounded like Guns N' Roses. Joel Gion, the Massacre's tambourine player, gave them some crazy speed and they were up for the next three days.[1]

And in an interview with *Clash*, he elaborated '. . . They asked him, "Can you get any sniffs?" and Joel's like, "I got some." And he gave him the tiniest little grain on the table and they're like,

"Fuck off, mate!" Joel's like, "You don't wanna mess with this" . . . They did a whole gram of, like, pure crystal meth because they thought it was just cheap 5% coke from London.

'It fucked their show and we just came on and tore it up and the next night they tried to recover in Sacramento and we showed up . . . and they were just like, "Fuck you. Get outta here."'[2]

The resulting 29 September show at the Whisky a Go Go has gone down in history as the 'Meth gig' after the night before's shenanigans. A worn-out, dislocated group turned up at the classic venue where the Doors had famously played many of the early shows – probably in far worse condition than the Manchester band. The gig sounds ragged but hardly car crash, with a couple of false starts and two attempts at the opening 'Rock 'n' Roll Star'. At one point Noel starts playing a different song to the rest of the band and his backing vocal is uncharacteristically off point. A tired Liam sits down and there is some to and fro on stage between the brothers, with Liam smacking Noel on the head with a tambourine before the singer runs out into the street. Yet they play most of the songs in some shape or form and the ragged intensity adds a dangerous excitement to the gig.

Post gig, though, Noel stormed off stage and quit the band, collecting his passport and $700 from the band's stressed-out tour manager, Maggie Mouzakitis (a key player in holding Oasis together, Maggie was a rarity in that time by being a woman tour manager), before pushing a note under her hotel room door saying he had quit.

One month after their triumphant debut album, it looked like Oasis was over.

Travelling back up to San Francisco, he spent the next few days hanging out with band fan Melissa Lim, who was the only person he knew and had met a few nights before at San Francisco's Bottom of the Hill gig.

'He was very upset so I took him in, fed him and tried to calm him down,' says Melissa. 'He wanted to break up the band. We went to Huntington Park to clear his mind. We listened to music. We went record shopping. San Francisco has a reputation of being a place where bands come to die, like The Band and the Sex Pistols. I wasn't going to let it happen on my watch. I told him, "You can't leave the band – you're on the verge of something big."'[3]

New Creation Records MD Tim Abbot finally tracked Noel down and took him on a trip to Las Vegas, where the persuasive Brummie talked him into continuing with the band and reconciled him with Liam.

In the few days mulling over his future, Noel had written 'Talk Tonight', an unusually diary-like and open song where he pondered on his life and future. The period of uncertainty and the few days hanging out were captured in a perfect snapshot of a song sung by him which was recorded a few days later with Owen Morris, who was flown out last-minute to the Congress House Studio in Austin, Texas on 8 October.

'Out of the blue, Marcus called and said we're flying out to Austin, Texas,' remembers Owen. 'It's for three days and three songs in the studio. I arrived at the airport in Austin and there's Noel Gallagher with Tim Abbot at the taxi rank, and I think, they've come to meet me, that's nice! But it turns out Noel had left for a week after the gig at the Whisky in LA. You hear these stories, they'd been up too long, and they fucked it and Noel was not happy and they couldn't find him until Tim Abbot had tracked him down. That's when he wrote "Talk Tonight". That's a fucking hell of a great session. It was exciting as fuck. Oasis were right on the edge and Noel was shouting at the band and this great stuff was coming out. He played the song to them once and expected them to know it straight away and then in two takes it's done because the band are that good, man! Then Liam says, "I'll fucking sing it now" and there it is. Then we finish it, with Noel and his angry guitars and we're out by six o'clock.'

It seems incredible that a band could produce anything under such stress and duress.

Owen Morris: 'The sessions were a different vibe. It was not a good vibe with Tony, especially on "(It's Good) To be Free" which he couldn't get right. The next morning Noel comes in and does "Talk Tonight" on his own and it sounds brilliant and then we finished off with "Half the World Away", which Noel wouldn't let Tony play the drums on. In the end it all sounded brilliant. The next day I flew back to the UK and started work on the Verve's *A Northern Soul* album.'

In the middle of the chaos, on 10 October, 'Cigarettes & Alcohol', the band's fourth and final single from the debut album, was released. The raw-edged song was a thrilling anthem of escape, making it instantly relatable to the growing army of fans that sent it to number seven in the charts.

A great swaggering rock 'n' roll tune partially constructed on the T. Rex 'Get it On' riff, borrowed by Noel like the boiled chicken he had shoplifted as a callow youth, it was cranked to the max by Owen Morris's brick wall sound capturing the band's live rush.

Noel Gallagher explained the song to *Beat Generator* magazine in Scotland:

'Who wants to waste their time working when there are better things to do? I mean, we've had jobs, shit jobs but I've better things I want to do with my life. If you have a job and love it then that's fine. I know guys who are bricklayers and they get something out of it. Same with me, I used to have this job I liked making fish tanks, I'd see fish swimming and think "I made your fucking home!"'[4]

Still maintaining their run of great B-sides there was the live version of their behemoth cover of the Beatles classic 'I Am the Walrus' oozing its psychedelic menace finally getting a release. Kicking off with the drum groove, 'Listen Up' sat somewhere between 'Live Forever' and 'Supersonic' with a great chord change in the bridge and was one of those cool songs that the band seemed to toss away on B-sides, while 'Fade Away' was Oasis at their Sex Beatles best with a song about the dashed dreams of youth.

The artwork caught the band at peak rock 'n' roll, with its semi-staged snapshot of hotel room carnage. It looked like a typical scene from their months on the road. The photo was taken in the Halcyon hotel in London after the band had been thrown out of Sweden on 14 August after the Hultsfred festival. The band, with the Verve and Primal Scream, had got drunk at the hotel bar and caused a reported £1,000 worth of damage. The Swedish incident, of course, fed neatly into the iconography of the artwork.

The rock 'n' roll carnage is a big part of the story, and turning the chaos into art was a neat trick. After all, it didn't do the Sex Pistols any harm, as Brian Cannon explains:

'We decided to have a straight up rock 'n' roll hotel room shot. I got two nights in the hotel because somehow I convinced Alan McGee that we needed a practice party the night before! Liam had been in hospital after jumping off the tour bus in Sweden and busted his ankle and that's why he's sat on the floor for the whole session.'

Meeting the band at the hotel, Michael Spencer Jones spent the night taking 600 photos of them and the scene unfolding in the hotel room.

'"Cigarettes & Alcohol" was initially a bit of a challenge,' Michael says. 'The idea was a party scene where people were drinking and smoking and going crazy. They had just got back home after being deported so were ready to recreate the mayhem of touring with some mates like Tim Abbot from Creation. I also asked some people to join in like Jane Fisher who was the Creation accountant, and Emma Morris who worked at Underworld merchandise. After being booted out of Sweden the energy levels were initially high, but it was becoming a super difficult shoot because everyone was knackered and Liam was off his face in this deep state of thought, but then there's a knock on the door and

Bonehead walks in. The party guy had arrived and the mood switched! Bonehead was the beating heart of Oasis but even more important – he was the vibes master. Now the mood was good and I got them to do a pillow fight just to loosen things up and took hundreds of shots. The composition of the final shot is great with three of them in their own spaces. It really works.'

Running out of film the photographer popped out to get some more: 'Noel said, "Can you give us a lift back to my place because I need to pick up my guitar", because if he is ever without his guitar he gets agitated. This was a major excursion, so I looked for some tunes to play in the car and I had all these unreleased recordings from the Verve but Noel picked a cassette out from his pocket and whacked it in the cassette player. It was a new song he had just written a few days before, provisionally called "Look Back in Anger". At the time he thought that the title was too long. It sounded great and I must have been one of the first people to hear it. When we got back to the hotel, he then decided to give an impromptu performance at about three in the morning. Everyone's caned and Noel is playing "Live Forever", "Supersonic", "Cigarettes & Alcohol" and "Digsy's Dinner" to about five of us. It was just, like, stunning.'

That off-the-cuff energy is what oozes out of the photo and is a perfect capture of the chaos of a band riding the helter-skelter.

After Noel had put the blocks on a fifth track being lifted from the number one album and with a Christmas single release needed, the guitarist dug into the archives and decided to revisit 'Whatever', a song that had been around since the sessions in Liverpool with the Real People but not recorded for the debut album as it needed an orchestra, which was out of the band budget at the time.

The track was finally recorded at Maison Rouge in June, as Owen Morris remembers:

'The first full session I recorded with Oasis was "Whatever", the Christmas single, in May/June 1994 at Maison Rouge Studios next to Chelsea football ground. "Whatever" took about three days, then we spent a couple of days on "Listen Up" and then did a live quick version of the B-side "Fade Away", which we should have spent more time on. We also did a demo of a new song that Noel had just written called "Some Might Say" which, typically of Noel, he introduced out of nowhere. The band were always good in the studio. They were professional about getting it done. It was easy. Tony McCarroll was still drumming then and a great drummer by the way. It was all two takes and easy.'

Released on 18 December, 'Whatever' went to number three on the UK charts and sold over 540,000 copies. The song, with its conspicuous nod to Neil Innes, borrowed a melody from his 'How Sweet to Be an Idiot', which resulted in a plagiarism lawsuit that ended with the former Rutle receiving a songwriting credit.

The song itself saw a shift in mood from their more raucous style, with added strings arranged by Noel which were recorded by the London Session Orchestra and violinist Wilfred Gibson, who had played with the Electric Light Orchestra and early King Crimson. 'Whatever' was a turning point that allowed Oasis an escape route and introduced an orchestral dexterity that they could expand on and was a musical bridge between the first two albums.

The single's artwork was a shot of the moors in Derbyshire not far from photographer Michael Spencer Jones' home city of Sheffield. The original idea was a touch more glamorous, Michael remembers: 'We were meant to be doing the shoot with the band in the Arizona desert during the American tour but when it all kicked off, that got cancelled so I had to find an open space like a desert but nearer home.'

Brian Cannon concurs: 'It was a bit of moorland near Sheffield. It was meant to be Monument Valley in Arizona and we had flown a 10,000-mile round trip to see the band split up in LA after that Whisky a Go Go gig. The plan I then had was to do a Verve-style shot with the band on the moors and we took some test shots and they looked brilliant as they were.'

As ever, the B-sides were great songs in their own right. 'Half the World Away' sounded so perfect a few years later as the theme music to the breaking wave of Manchester comedians Caroline Aherne and Craig Cash's huge hit TV series, *The Royle Family*, with the song soundtracking the same northern working-class world as the comedy. 'Fade Away' was a full-on foot-to-pedal glorious wall of sound and 'Slide Away' was culled from the album.

Out of the studio, the band's boisterous nature saw them become virtually the first group to get banned from the Columbia Hotel where they were staying for the recording sessions. The notorious hotel in Lancaster Gate, West London, where touring bands had been staying since 1975, had the famous all-night bar that had seen many shenanigans and a blind eye was mostly turned . . . until Oasis rolled in.

'Me and Bonehead and a few others had a long night in the bar and there were some drugs and some trouble,' recalls Owen Morris. 'It was after the third day of recording and we'd finished "Whatever". By six in the morning there's only us left in the bar and furniture starts getting thrown out of the window, which didn't seem to be a problem until it started landing on a Mercedes which belonged to the Columbia Hotel manager, so we all get banned. Ignition didn't bat an eyelid. They just put us in the Hilton next door, which was a much better hotel anyway.'[5]

Smashing hotels for the sake of it and not because of frustration was maybe not Liam's thing, as he joked in an interview with Ann Scanlon: 'Rock 'n' roll can be done without all the crap that's meant to go with it, and that's why I'm not into trashing hotels. People go: "Ooh, it's really rock 'n' roll, throwing your gear out the window." Bollocks! I'm in bed when all that's going on, reading the *Independent* with a glass of orange juice.'

While November had been spent touring Europe where the band was breaking out, December saw Oasis step up another level in the UK with gigs in big venues like Glasgow Barrowlands, the Brighton Centre and the Hammersmith Palais.

Somehow they ended the year intact. There had been many triumphs and many bust-ups and it was all in the red hot glare of the public eye. Oasis had no concept of hiding behind a façade; what you saw was what you got and it came with a great soundtrack.

1994 had seen them go from outsiders to the middle of British pop culture. The album was number one and 'Whatever' was number three. The maybes had turned into definites . . .

Just what would the next year bring?

29

ROLLING WITH IT

1995 defined the nineties with a diverse and compelling home-grown soundtrack from the Britpop big hitters to the electronic, and dance music underground. Documenting the disunited king-dom, Pulp's *Different Class* was released a few weeks after Blur's *The Great Escape* and Oasis's *(What's the Story) Morning Glory?*, while the rest of the year was soundtracked by an extraordinary list of great releases from diverse genres. There was Elastica's self-titled album, Black Grape's *It's Great When You're Straight . . . Yeah,* which saw life in the old Mancs. There was also the likes of Radiohead's *The Bends* bending art rock into new shapes, PJ Harvey and her stark confessional *To Bring You My Love,* while Tricky's *Maxinquaye* and Massive Attack were twisting hip-hop and post-punk out of shape. There was even classic indie guitar from Teenage Fan Club's *Grand Prix.* The cross-pollination of dance culture into hybrid new pop shapes saw the Chemical Brothers with their *Exit Planet Dust,* Leftfield's *Leftism,* Goldie's *Timeless,* David Holmes' *This Film's Crap Let's Slash the Seats* and Aphex Twin's *. . . I Care Because You Do* reinventing beats and electronic music, as well as brilliant live shows from the Prodigy, whose groundbreaking musical alchemy saw them rewrite all genre rules.

It was into this high-water mark of genre-busting music that Oasis started the year, touring the USA and Japan before returning to the studio to work on their follow-up album. By this time they had become tabloid fodder and the most famous pop stars in the country, entangled into the Britpop narrative they had studiously tried to avoid.

In April they released their debut number one single, 'Some Might Say'. The first song to be written by Noel when he moved to the capital city, it was originally demoed by the guitarist before being taught to the band in Maison Rouge during the recording session for 'Whatever' in the summer of 1994, as Owen Morris remembers: 'On that day Noel was like, "I got this new song." It's gonna be the first number one, right? Liam wasn't there so Noel was playing it to the band. Originally it was slower like the Stones or the Faces and cool as fuck and I'm thinking, "Okay, that's Noel's next big single."'

Recorded with Liam's vocal and released as a single on 24 April, partly 'Some Might Say' was a perfect, almost glam rock confection influenced by American post-grunge neo-Americana folk band Grant Lee Buffalo. It had a verse that was as melodic as the chorus while it managed to be both wistful and hopeful. The lyrics mix Lennon walrus gumboot nonsense imagery with a deeper take about the struggle of life with a first-generation Irish melancholy and that magical mix of euphoria and sadness at how you can't always get what you want – and if you do then it's never enough. Noel explains:

'Someone said to me you've got these really empowering chords and melodies, but when you sing the songs, there is a real melancholy and yet a kind of hope in them but there's also not a lot of triumphalism. "Some Might Say" is the best example of that. It's an

Irish thing – a punching-the-air type of song about how one day things will get better but at the moment it's shit. Great Oasis songs are defiant in the face of poverty and adversity and about making the best of what you got.'

With a band this volatile there was inevitably going to be casualties. The small fault lines get bigger and something gives. And the tension between Tony McCarroll and Noel Gallagher had stretched to breaking point.

Owen Morris: '"Some Might Say" and "Acquiesce" were Tony's last recordings with the band. Tony was great, man but he wouldn't have been able to play "Champagne Supernova" or "Wonderwall" and those type of songs that were coming next. Tony was more of a boom bash kind of drummer and was brilliant at that but the songs were progressing.'

Tony looks back wistfully: 'We'd hit stadiums by then and my final gig was at the Sheffield Arena in April at the last show of the Definitely Maybe tour.[1] I looked out into the stadium and it was like, wow. It was only a couple of years on from three people watching us. And then it was over.

'I was in one day, out the next. I am not a complicated character in any capacity but I am the sort of guy that will stick up for myself. Things had been said and it kind of built this tension up.

'The band were big noisy characters and there was a lot of frustration and them two [Noel and Liam] really argued sometimes. Looking back in hindsight I guess he [Noel] wanted to change things and make a new band with a different approach and sound. I think we should have stuck with what we had and see where it went and developed with each other. It was a brilliant thing to be part of but it got to be stressful. I loved playing the drums on "Live Forever", "Slide Away" and all them beautiful songs, and also those punky kind of tunes like "Headshrinker" and "Bring It

On Down". After I left I thought *What's the Story . . .?* was an excellent album. I do think they lost their way for a couple of albums after that but towards the end they gained that original sound back, that original energy.'

Tony McCarroll's last performance with the band was on *Top of the Pops* for 'Some Might Say'. The following week new drummer Alan White made his debut on the same show the day after he joined them.

It was Paul Weller who had recommended the new drummer to Noel. The former Jam man knew the talented younger brother of his own drummer, Steve, and gave Noel the nod. Alan White would go on to drum for Oasis for nearly 10 years and for four albums, making him one of the longest lasting members of the band.

Born in 1972 and influenced by his brother and classic drummers like Keith Moon, Ringo Starr, John Bonham and Mick Avory, Alan White had been drumming in his own band Starclub and playing sessions for the singer-songwriter Dr Robert. He first met Noel when playing with Creation signing Idha who, at the time, was married to future Oasis bassist Andy Bell. In 1988 he had also auditioned for future Oasis guitar player Gem Archer's band at the time, Whirlpool. The audition went well but with the drummer being only 15 he was too young to be on the road in a touring band.

Having a new drummer saw a shift in the band's sound towards a more shuffle snare beat belying Alan White's jazz background and a profound shift away from Tony McCarroll's highly effective simple yet powerful style. Both drummers were perfect for their own periods in the band, and as Noel started to shift to a more sophisticated sound it required a different style. On the new songs he would work with the new drummer, getting more complex rhythms into the songs. Alan White also had another key role in the group's dynamic, becoming Liam's best mate in the band, drinking buddy and partner in crime.

The single came with perhaps the strongest of all the classic B-sides, 'Acquiesce', which quickly became a fan favourite while generally being acknowledged to have been strong enough to be an A-side in its own right.

'I was the only one living in London at the time,' explains Noel told the *NME*, 'I was on the train travelling up to meet the rest of the band at Loco Studios in Wales and the song came to me. The train stopped in the Severn Tunnel. I had my guitar with me and started strumming away. It was pretty late at night and I was progressively getting louder and by the time we'd been sitting in this tunnel for about 40 minutes people were starting to go: "Tut! Do you mind?! We're getting bored here, can you stop playing?"'[2]

With Liam singing the verse and Noel singing the chorus line, 'Acquiesce' has often been misinterpreted as a song about the brothers' own volatile relationship, though according to Noel, it's about friendship. On hearing 'Acquiesce', Alan McGee felt it should be an A-side or at least on the upcoming album, but the guitarist knew he already had a number one in the bag with 'Some Might Say', although years later he conceded that the record label may have had a point.

Owen Morris remembers the recording session:

'We did "Acquiesce" in Loco Studios in two takes and then we get to work on "Some Might Say" which we had demoed in Maison Rouge about six months before during the "Whatever" sessions. We spend the day on it and we get a bunch of great takes which were slightly faster than the demo. I take the best bits and edit together for the backing track. It sounded a bit Bowie and good. Me and Noel were there at nine o'clock at night, having a glass and a smoke, and we suddenly go, "It's too fast, listen to the demo!" So Noel gets the band up again and we do it another time and it's fucking brilliant, but it's even faster, as it turns out, but for me and Noel, it's perfect, right?

'Next day, Liam is like, "I'm fucking singing this now." It's half 10 in the morning and we got hangovers but . . . here we go! We get it in three takes. Outrageous. Liam Gallagher is something else. Marcus turns up and goes, "That's the best singing I've ever fucking heard." Then Noel goes, "I'll put my guitars on it" and it's done within four hours. Finished. The backing track is all over the shop on that version, it speeds up yet it's actually one of my favourite Oasis recordings because it's a bit fucked and because of Liam's singing and attitude. They then all fuck off and we got two great songs. Then me and Marcus go to Orinoco studios in Elephant and Castle to mix it and Marcus is saying, "This is the fucking greatest mix ever, right? Let's not bother doing a recall" and we're done and down the pub. Then Noel popped in and said, "The guitars aren't fucking loud enough" and we have to do a lot of messing around to fix it! It's a shambles! But it's good and we get it sorted.'

The striking artwork came after an Oasis show in Southampton on 30 November 1994 when Noel had handed the melancholic and surreal lyrics to Brian Cannon.

'The brief was that he wanted every lyric in the artwork,' says Brian. 'We came up with a disused railway station, the idea being if you were waiting for a train there, then you needed educating to the fact there was no train coming!'

Michael Spencer Jones: 'The original idea from Noel was for this visual interpretation of his lyrics to be taken at Manchester Piccadilly station because it looked busy. I thought it would add to the atmosphere if we did it at a station that was not in use, with a set of characters waiting for a train that would never arrive, with the platform as a stage. After a couple of weeks I found the perfect location – Cromford Station in Derbyshire.'

The sleeve is a feast of visual references with Brian Cannon's own father at the front of the shot with a wheelbarrow full of fish and Brian's mother with a mop to echo the lyrics. Brian's local barmaid in Wigan, Carla Knox, guested in the shot with silverware on her umbrella. Liam waves from the bridge, while the figure with the watering can on the platform is Noel. Brian's PA Matthew Sankey also features as a tramp holding up the piece of cardboard with 'in need of education' written on it.

The typical attention to the detail also sees the windows of the station house replaced with blown-up images of Noel's guitar machine heads and volume controls – a detail that no one ever notices. The striking sleeve is another perfect synthesis between artwork, band and photographer, and is Brian Cannon's own favourite.

Less than 18 months after they had played the 200-capacity Water Rats in London, Oasis were triumphant Friday night headliners on Glastonbury's famous Pyramid stage, the day before the Stone Roses famously didn't make it because of John Squire's bike accident and Pulp stepped in for their big moment.

On 22 July, they were special guests for R.E.M.'s big Irish show at Slane Castle. About 100,000 people watched both bands at the top of their game – unaware that the bands had fallen out, underlining a cultural drift between British and American music culture which had once been so entwined. Fewer British bands were crossing over in the USA, and the tectonic plates of culture were already shifting. Artful British sarcasm and irony had always fallen flat with the Americans, and American brash confidence often made Brits cringe. The post-Nirvana American groups were in a different headspace to their UK counterparts. Kurt Cobain's thrillingly visceral anthems were the scream of a tortured artist while the UK scene moved towards Britpop and a lad culture that was driven by a boisterous positivity and banter and embrace of the good times despite everything.

Before the gig there had been no sign of the fallout that would occur at Slane but there was a tension perhaps sparked by interview comments from Noel Gallagher about Kurt Cobain, where he contrasted 'Live Forever' with Nirvana's 'I Hate Myself and Want to Die'. 'As much as I like Nirvana,' he said, 'I can't have people like that coming over here, on smack, fucking saying that they hate themselves and they wanna die. That's fucking rubbish. Kids don't need to be hearing that nonsense. It seems to me that here was a guy who had everything and was miserable about it. And we had fuck all, and I still thought that getting up in the morning was the greatest fuckin' thing ever, 'cause you didn't know where you'd end up at night. And we didn't have a pot to piss in, but it was fucking great, man.'[3]

Nirvana and Oasis were actually really similar in lots of ways. Noel noted this himself when saying he wished he had met Kurt Cobain and always felt an affinity with him, adding 'we are both left-handed, blue-eyed, Geminis and loved the Beatles'. The Sex Beatles through a fuzz box template had served both bands gloriously as had their blue collar talent that had hauled its way out despite the odds with both Kurt and Noel executing their masterplans. Both at heart were acoustic, introspective singer-songwriters who found a way to crank their songs into huge pop/noise anthems. Both were also fascinated by music made from all sources, whether it was the Beatles or obscure underground gems. Nirvana, though, turned their intensity inwards while the Gallaghers were more inclusive.

Michael Stipe was very close to the former Nirvana frontman and the pain for him of losing a close compadre was visceral and perhaps that was the spark point at Slane. The British and Oasis way of dealing with emotional stuff is in the music – you can sense the sensitivity in Oasis and you can feel the emotional undercurrents, but for them the music was seeking an escape. It was certainly not the heart on the sleeve drama culminating in suicide. It was about survival.

Before Slane there had been a mutual respect between Oasis and R.E.M. but something obviously broke backstage. Was this the moment the transatlantic culture ping-pong and special relationship ended?

The recriminations came later in song with R.E.M.'s 'The Wake-Up Bomb' allegedly referencing Oasis with lines that seemed to echo themes present in Noel's songs and even his age. But R.E.M. bassist Mike Mills claimed the song was not about the Mancunian renegades, so who knows?

Released on 14 August 1995, 'Roll with It' was the second single from the upcoming album. Quickly, it went from a new single to a national event, swept up into an extraordinary moment by the Battle of Britpop with Blur, turning the band's seventh single into a moment of pop history with a high-profile chart battle.

Initially, the single that Noel himself has described as 'shit' had reviewers dubbing it 'Quoasis' and comparing it to Status Quo as if that was a bad thing!

Deceptively simple ramalama rock 'n' roll can be highly effective and the Quo reference is hardly an insult: the seventies Quo were arguably a British Ramones with a magnificent run of boogie singles from 1972's 'Paper Plane' to 1979's 'Whatever You Want' boiling rock 'n' roll down to a fundamental take on the chugging riff from the Doors' 'Roadhouse Blues'.

Just like the Quo, Oasis understood the power of a two-guitar boogie with a big chorus.

Recorded in the new album sessions at Rockfield studios in May/June, the track has many plus points in its ruckus delivery, rush of noise and guitar crank. Classic gear creates a classic sound and Bonehead's Marshall amp and trusty Epiphone Riviera guitar combined with Noel's battery of Vox AC30, Marshall Combo and WEM combo and his trusty Orange Vintage Overdrive OR120 Head; with his Les Pauls and Epiphone Casinos all helping to create that familiar wall of sound in a song about being true to yourself.

In the great tradition of Oasis B-sides being equal, if not superior, to their A-sides, the much loved 'Rockin' Chair' was a song of lost love and crumbling relationships that displayed a sensitivity in its lyrics as it shimmered with a haunting wistfulness and is exquisitely sung by Liam.

With a nod to the Real People, the song's creation had its own controversy that resulted in the Liverpool band's Chris Griffiths getting a co-writing credit on the track. The other B-side, 'It's Better People', is another wistful piece, again contrasting with the stomping A-side; sung by Noel it's an acoustic workout harking back to his solo songs in a contrast to the 'riot music' on the A-sides.

The band's now hectic schedule meant that the artwork had to be done in small windows of opportunity – this forced the creative hand. With the group on the way to Glastonbury to headline the Pyramid stage, they needed a photo location somewhere in the South West. After scouting around, it was decided that a day trip to the tatty seaside town of Weston-super-Mare and its quintessentially English resort vibe of beach, pier and deckchairs would work. In the blazing hot mid-summer heat, the band sat in matching duffle coats on a row of deckchairs, each watching their own personal TV set.

It was yet another perfectly British scene from Microdot twisted through the artful lens of Michael Spencer Jones that snapped an overdressed British cool, sweltering on a rare hot day on the beach.

As British as Oasis themselves, a seaside town is pop art incarnate and like some aspects of the band a musical kiss-me-quick, a saucy smile and a bit of rough, and never above itself. If this classic run of Oasis sleeves had not included a seaside town shot, it would have been disappointing. Brian Cannon recalls the trip:

'It was Alan White's first sleeve as he had just joined and it was an absolutely red hot day and the band were sat around in their duffle coats. People were looking on puzzled by their attire. I like the back sleeve – you can see what they are looking at on the TVs.

Liam has got Alex Higgins, Bonehead has Peter Sellers in the film *The Party*, Alan White has Keith Moon and Guigsy has Ian Botham, while Noel has got himself on the telly.'

It was all good fun. But the Oasis story was about to go from seaside postcard to front-page news . . .

30

THE BATTLE OF BRITPOP

The 1995 Battle of Britpop has become one of those key mytholo-gised moments in British pop culture – like when the Beatles split up, David Bowie did 'Starman' on *Top of the Pops* or the Sex Pistols swore on Bill Grundy – times when music captured the moment, the spotlight and the zeitgeist and also the very heart and soul of the UK itself.

The 1995 Battle of Britpop was fantastic pop theatre and a bril-liant piece of ad hoc marketing and posturing that beautifully got out of control. It was the high-water point of the pop culture nine-ties and the whole narrative of the decade was played out in the full glare of the mainstream media. It somehow hit a raw nerve that opened up all the fault lines, from Blur v Oasis, north v south, middle v working class, art school/university v council estate, indie v major, Manchester v London, upstart northern city defying the London music biz. Whether either band fitted exactly into these clearly defined new fault lines it didn't matter – this was a snapshot of mid-nineties UK.

Added to this was a cordite whiff of politics, with the youthful new leader of the Labour party Tony Blair aligning himself with music culture and his own upcoming Brit pop-politics scrap with an eye on the youth vote to help ignite his future election campaign. And it all came together in one of those moments when pop, politics, class and culture aligned into a glorious and messy whole.

It was not just a chart battle for the number one, it was a chart battle for the soul of British culture. Now that Oasis were seriously on a trajectory to be the number one band in the UK, Blur and their label was up for some fun and games, not realising how serious Oasis were.

All pop careers are a series of great set pieces, some by accident and some by design. Oasis had seen their fast rise signposted with key releases as well as rock 'n' roll incidents that kept them in the spotlight. To make that step to the front pages and the mainstream, they needed something else and it was handed to them on a plate by their rivals Blur and the Battle of Britpop.

The debut album was still flying high and 'Some Might Say' had been their first number one a couple of months earlier and the upcoming second album was much anticipated, but when an inter-band rivalry turned into genuine animosity then an alpha-male bun fight for the spotlight it became a perfect pop moment.

Ironically, neither band had even been considered Britpop. That was all Suede, Pulp, Saint Etienne and the Auteurs' business. Also, Oasis had not seen Blur as rivals and even had a passing interest in the then much bigger band back in 1991 when Liam said he liked a Blur single, possibly their Stone Roses pastiche 'There's No Other Way'. At the same time, Noel had liked a 12 October 1991 Blur gig at Manchester Academy, agreeing that 'they are a great band with a good frontman'. In 1994, both bands had been hanging out after Oasis's debut San Francisco show.

There had been a skirmish at the February 1994 Brit awards where Oasis had won the best newcomer and Blur the best band awards, with Liam heckling Blur all the way through the ceremony. In May, Alan McGee had a party in Covent Garden to celebrate 'Some Might Say' being Oasis's first number one; Blur had gone along and something went on between Liam and Damon, upping the ante.

What the rival camps came up with was poptastic genius. Spotting Oasis's new single 'Roll with It' was due out on 14 August, Blur shifted the release date of their next single, the jaunty Kinks-infused 'Country House', to come out the same day in a deliberate fight for the number one slot. It was ironic that what some consider the band's weakest early single would have such an intense spotlight shone on it when the media mania exploded. As Noel Gallagher pointed out years later it would have been better to go head-to-head with Blur with 'Cigarettes & Alcohol' versus 'Girls & Boys'.

Initially Creation barely noticed.

'The Blur camp were much more competitive about it all. I wasn't that interested in a chart battle at first,' remembers Alan McGee. 'For us it was just a laugh, but Oasis management Ignition were really up for it.'

Blur had always been driven by frontman Damon Albarn's copious talent and competitive ambition. Born in London but growing up in Colchester, he had a theatrical bohemian background, with his late father once managing sixties underground band Soft Machine before moving to Colchester to become the head of the art college.

Inevitably, Damon moved back to London, drifting through acting college and working in a recording studio before enrolling at Goldsmiths college, where he formed a band with fellow Colchester emigres, the guitarist Graham Coxon and drummer Dave Rowntree. Bassist Alex James, originally from Bournemouth, was a fellow student at Goldsmiths and joined later. Inspired by the J.D. Salinger book, the band then called Circus, became Seymour in December 1988, before signing to Food Records in 1990 and having their name changed for them by their label.

Blur's debut single in October 1990, 'She's So High', hit the top 50, and its April 1991 'There's No Other Way' follow-up was a sprightly slice of indie rock melded to a Roses wah guitar shuffle beat and hit the top 10.

Their 1991 debut *Leisure* album somehow found the common ground between Syd Barrett and Madchester and was a top 10 hit and 1993's follow-up, *Modern Life is Rubbish*, saw a further embracing of a very British art pop as a reaction to a disastrous debut American tour. The band's now more modish, almost two-tone style indie embraced a certain Britishness. The album slipped in and out of the charts at number 15 and Blur were now being overshadowed in the first battle of Britpop by the new London scene cool of rivals Suede, whose indie glam and fluidity seemed to capture the moment.

If Suede had won the first unofficial Battle of Britpop then round two was going to be for higher stakes. Sensing an opportunity to create a great story, Blur's label boss, the late Andy Ross, vamped up the Blur v Oasis tension between the two bands into a chart battle two years after the April 1993 *Select* magazine Britpop front cover.

It was odd, yet fitting, that the Battle of Britpop concerned two bands who both denied they were in the 'scene', as Jane Savidge from Savage & Best PR, who had already landed Suede an astonishing 17 front covers, notes:

'It's not London's fault that the greatest band in a generation – the Stone Roses – took five years to release their second album! Britpop was definitely happening but it was a very different thing before Oasis turned up. That *Select* front cover with Brett came out in April 1993. At that point in time it was just a few journalists trying to work out whether there was a connection between bands who all wore the same cheap clothes they found in junk shops and wrote songs about pebble-dashed graves and spying on your friend's sister from a wardrobe.

'And there was. Exactly a year later – 5 April 1994 – Kurt Cobain died and a week after that Oasis released their first single on to the stage that already had been set by Britpop and Kurt's death. They were good enough to bulldoze everything in front of them. And that's not meant to be a criticism, it's just that Oasis were a natural phenomenon and they pressed all the right buttons.

'When you think about it, old Britpop was quite quaint actually – "Razzmatazz", "Metal Mickey", "For Tomorrow" – but Oasis changed all that. In fact they changed it so much that – for a little while – bands like Blur and Suede actually tried to be more like them. Only for a little while, mind you.'

The carefully curated new scene of bands now had a gate crasher – a gate crasher that Jane Savidge welcomed:

'I loved Oasis – although I was jealous that they were competing for space with Savage & Best bands like Suede, Pulp, Verve and Elastica. Funnily enough, I saw all those Oasis early London shows – Water Rats, 100 Club – and I was absolutely smitten with them, though I couldn't really tell anyone as they wouldn't have believed me. I even went to their first ever US show at Wetlands in New York in 1994 and had an argument with an American fan of the band who was standing next to me at the front of the gig, and who asked me at the end of the show whether I thought Liam had enjoyed performing. I remember saying, "No, he doesn't get any pleasure playing for you guys," and he said, "But he was tapping his foot all the way through the concert." To which I replied, "No he wasn't. And he will never tap his foot on American soil. Don't you get it?" So, look, I was a defender of Oasis's indifference to everyone and everything even then – and yes, I got them.'

The gate crashers were certainly not shy retiring violets, remembers Jane:

'They were always in Camden, and living round the corner from our office by '95. In fact, I can remember walking up Parkway to get to work late summer '95 and seeing Liam walk into the Spread Eagle pub, going behind the bar and putting a cassette of *(What's the Story)* *Morning Glory?* on – even though the album wasn't out for another six weeks – and playing it really, really loud so it blasted out on to the street. Then he came and sat out on one of the chairs at the front of the pub and nodded his head for the next 45 minutes.'

Despite not seeing themselves as Britpop, Oasis were now centre stage with the Battle of Britpop and rose to the occasion. Of course, this was a chart battle that Oasis were never going to win. Blur had the machinery of EMI at their disposal, which meant a surefire hit with more formats and discounts; while Creation, despite being part of Sony, were a much smaller operation with a stretched staff making mistakes. For one thing the sleeve had the wrong barcodes, resulting in unrecorded sales, which drove Ignition mad. Working at Creation, Chris Abbot was there when the media caught fire:

'It was on the *Nine O'Clock News*. . . . Me and Liam were on the train to London the next day and stopped at Crewe and I see Robbie Williams just standing at the train station on his own, then he got on the carriage and started to do his poems, and talking about leaving Take That. That night, me, Robbie Williams and Liam Gallagher, the two most recognised people in the country, went into Soho, and the Battle of Britpop had started and it was all about to go crazy and me and my brother Tim, who was consultant at Creation, were right at the heart of it.'

The ensuing battle had cranked the tension between the two bands. It got very heated, with Noel quoted in the *Observer* saying, 'I hope the pair of them [Damon Albarn and Alex James] catch AIDS and die because I fucking hate them two.' It was an offhand, out of context remark that he deeply regretted in the same way as the Manic Street Preachers' eloquent bassist, Nicky Wire, also regretted saying he had hoped 'Michael Stipe goes the same way as Freddie Mercury' at a gig in 1993.

The Battle of Britpop now spiralled out of the music papers and into the mainstream media and was memorably featured on the

News at Ten. Pop culture was back in the headlines and it propelled both bands into the heart of the national psyche.

In week one Blur sold 274,000 copies while Oasis sold 216,000. The EMI juggernaut had got the number one single. It was the best week for singles sales for 10 years, making the music biz the ultimate winners. Britpop had become a marketing term. A brand for record stores to rack out records. HMV ordered 50,000 Oasis albums for a Britpop promotion and Marcus Russell put his foot down. Like the band, he didn't want Oasis lumped in with the scene. Oasis also pulled out of the Britpop Now TV special hosted by Damon Albarn because they saw themselves as a classic rock 'n' roll band. Not Britpop.

Blur may have won the battle but they would lose the war, as Alan McGee explains.

'When the Oasis album came out in October it went ballistic, selling 350,000 copies in the first week. The people had spoken! Oasis would go on to sell more than 20 million copies of that album worldwide, which was far more than Blur or all of Britpop put together.'

The Battle of Britpop saw Oasis go from big to supernova and into the daily papers and main TV news. It was the kind of exposure that they could only have dreamt of thanks to Blur.

In the end it was both bands that won the war. Oasis and Blur ended up defining British pop culture in the nineties. Over the decades the hostilities have ceased, with Damon Albarn later explaining, 'I value my friendship with Noel because he is one of the only people who went through what I did in the nineties.' There were also musical collaborations, with Noel playing guitar on 'We Got the Power' from the 2017 *Humanz* album for Damon's perfect dayglo pop synthesis band, Gorillaz, that struck gold in the USA in a way that Blur, being so quintessentially British, never could.

31

WHAT'S THE STORY?

Weeks after Tony McCarroll's last appearance with the band on *Top of the Pops* for 'Some Might Say', the band moved into Rockfield Studios to start work on the second album. The studio was already legendary not only for the Stone Roses' lengthy sessions that Liam Gallagher had briefly gatecrashed the year before, but for a whole host of bands stretching back into the late sixties making classic records. The residential studio in South Wales was the go-to place for classic sounding recordings and getting lost inside an album.

This time Owen Morris was in control from the start and his can-do hurricane of energy roared through the recording that saw the album only taking 15 days to record, including a two-week gap between the two sessions after the ruckus between Liam and Noel.

Despite this blip the atmosphere in the studio on both sides of the fight had been excellent and highly productive with tracks going down at the rate of one a day.

'I arrived at Rockfield Studios on May the fifth at 10am to start work on the album and Brian Cannon was already in there,' recalls

Owen Morris. 'He was on the sessions more than anyone else, apart from me and Noel! He was doing his "research" for his sleeves, which are up there with the greats. Brian had bought a white Rickenbacker bass guitar and when Noel turns up he says, "I'm starting a band" and Noel says, "You're not in a fucking band you do artwork." He didn't form his band, but he stayed and we had a great time. I could talk about Brian forever. He was good to have on the sessions. Entertaining as fuck, a cross between Kenneth Williams and Alex Higgins, and he made me, Noel and Liam laugh.'

Left to their own devices and on a golden streak, the band and producer were on a roll.

'The strange thing about *Morning Glory* was that I had total freedom,' says Owen. 'There was no record label watching over you. No A&R. Marcus was in control of getting Oasis product done easily and nicely while Alan McGee turned up at the end of the recording and said, "This is fucking genius." Noel would be there listening and say, "That's fucking great, maybe turn the guitar up!"'

There are so many roles a producer can play in making and shaping an album. What's interesting about Owen Morris was that he had cut his teeth in a more structured, more hi tech studio environment getting a precise sound, and now it was about capturing a moment.

'It was very much let's just fucking do this. Let's get the mics up and record. Noel would put a guide acoustic guitar track and guide vocal down to a click track and then we'd overdub the rest of the band. The new songs were less raw but sounded great and pretty early on it was clear that the album sounded different to *Definitely Maybe*. The initial aim was to make an album that sold as many as that had and it was on the way to half a million even then. No one had any idea of just how big this record was going to be.'

Just like all great music, these sessions went fast, as studio engineer Nick Brine remembers:

'We started with "Roll with It" which took a bit of time to set up but then we motored through 15 songs in 15 days,' says Nick. 'It was hit after hit. Just incredible songs. Owen was on fire not just with the production but also with what he was adding to it. Alan White had just joined the band virtually the week before but was on it straight away. He'd listen to the song once and in a couple of takes he'd have it. We worked at the edge. Like cutting the tape to edit it, which could sometimes be chaotic. Once we lost a bit of tape with the snare on it and there's about 500 pieces of tape hanging up on the walls and Owen said, "I don't know what I've done with it!" And then he found it stuck on the bottom of his shoe!'

The sweet spot of a great producer is to capture the moment, make sense of the chaos and not to kill the track.

Owen Morris: 'I was good at recording them quickly. Let's get the band set up and fucking record. Get on with it and be confident. I was very anti poncing around when I was recording. Rather than spend two fucking days on a fucking drum sound I got it in 20 minutes. It wasn't like you had to fuck around. All of the recording on *Morning Glory* was easy and everyone there wanted to be there and it was fun apart from the break in the middle!

'Noel had great equipment and a great fucking amp. So did Bonehead. Alan White could really play and Liam sang brilliantly. Liam Gallagher, man, what the fuck! What a singer. He sang fucking "Wonderwall" at 11 in the morning. I was barely up and he's like bouncing around saying, "I'll fucking sing it now."

'They used to freak me the fuck out doing this last-minute stuff like with the arrangement of "Wonderwall", which was pretty much written the day before Noel got the backing track down with Alan. The next day, once they decided who was going to sing it, Noel sat next to Liam and sings it to him once in the control room. Liam gets the words, the phrasing, the timing and the whole song in one go and he says, "I got it!" and goes straight in and sings it perfectly. It was freaky deaky. Liam had the whole song, and he had never fucking heard it before. Very peculiar. I've never seen that before. Liam was almost scarily in tune with his brother's songs. Noel would then listen once and check it was done OK. Then he would go, "He's got it" and leave me to do three more takes with Liam, and maybe a fourth one where he'd give it a bit more. Then Liam would be like, "I'm bored now" and go the pub. Then I would mix until I was happy and then Noel approved the mix.'

The innate understanding between the brothers despite the flashpoints is the band's core, says Owen:

'I mean, Liam – what a beautiful human being and funny as fuck, he's pointing at his chest saying, "These are my songs, they're all in here, right?" And he fucking means it. I've never seen anything like it. Some songs they had rehearsed like "She's Electric" or "Whatever" but often it was like "Wonderwall" – straight in there. The sessions were the most happy times I ever had in a studio.'

Chris Abbot, now in his role of Creation's A&R for Oasis, went to Rockfield with Liam and Brian Cannon after the bust-up, with strict instructions from Marcus Russell to try and keep them all out of trouble: 'Noel hadn't come back yet but late one night Owen was playing the mixes of "Some Might Say" over and over again and they had kind of gone into this next realm, and it sounded like greatness to me. I just thought, this album's just gonna knock it out of the park. And the whole feeling was this rise that you just witnessed in 12 months was breath-taking.'

Nick Brine remembers Noel Gallagher playing 'Wonderwall' literally sat on top of a wall:

'Rather than doing the guide in the studio he sat on the stool at the top of this wall and played the chords which we then used for the band to play along to. It got redone but you could hear all the birds singing, which we used for the start of "Hello".'

Paul Weller dropped in to play lead guitar on 'The Swamp Song', as Nick explains:

'He also did the insane harmonica playing on "The Swamp Song". It was all done in about three hours. Him and Noel had fucked off by six in the evening. He was a total gentleman and almost disgustingly good at his music. Very impressive. His playing was full of soul and humour and total commitment. Noel was like a pig in shit that day. We all were!'

Some of the songs appeared while they were in the studio, as Owen Morris remembers:

'Noel only had the riff to "Champagne Supernova" when they were going into the studio. He had never sang the song to anybody before but he got his entire arrangement while we were there and then a day or two later he says to Liam, "Here's the song! Let's record the vocals."'

With expectations through the roof – and despite splitting up briefly in the middle and with a new drummer who had been in the band seven days – Oasis caught the mood and the moment. They delivered a classic and defied the second album syndrome.

If the first album had been about escape from pre-fame life in Manchester then the band's biggest selling album has come to define them and it certainly has all the facets of Oasis – from Saturday night glamorama anthems like the opening 'Hello' to the stadium filling anthems like 'Champagne Supernova'; plus the huge arms-aloft ballads like 'Wonderwall' and 'Don't Look Back in Anger' or the pure pop eccentricity of 'She's Electric'.

It was all part of the masterplan. Future band member Andy Bell bumped into Noel at the Creation office and remembers him playing many of the songs in track order for the album months before recording.

The album may have seen a shift in the songwriting style with a clutch of epic landscape songs, anthemic choruses and introspective ballads, but the first two songs are classic Oasis barnstormers. Fittingly 'Hello' opens the album with a swagger of guitars, but then that was the masterplan from when the song was written back in 1992 when Noel had sung and recorded a demo of it at Mark Coyle's home studio. The opener is a slab of glam updated to the mid-nineties, with the stomping rush of big guitars and the surging sound of T. Rex or Slade at their far away peak, yet twisted with the Sex Beatles chord changes and wall of sound. The borrow from Gary Glitter's 'Hello Hello I'm Back Again' on the song's outro was from before the glam star had disgraced himself and a court case saw that the song's real writer and producer, Mike Leander, who died the following year, got a co-write credit.[1]

The pre-album hit single 'Roll With It' is an urgent cry for self-determination – just the kind of affirmation that Oasis always soundtracked and one that resonated with their audience. Another almost glam stomp, the song may be looked on as Oasis by numbers, but those numbers were pretty damn good and sometimes a rollicking, upbeat blowout song has its own magic.

The first big stylistic change on the album was for 'Wonderwall'. Originally titled 'Wishing Stone', the song beautifully exposes the band's sensitive side; it might be Noel's paean to friendship or a tribute to his then partner Meg Mathews. The lyrics, like the band's record sleeves, are peppered with pop culture references to the Beatles and the song's title is taken from George Harrison's 1968 solo soundtrack album for a film of the same name.[2] As ever, Liam owns the vocal as he croons the song. It shows the beauty of music itself being able to somehow say the unsaid, articulating emotional rescue and finding the words that are not always there.

'I always just thought I'm a guy with a cig in the ashtray and a guitar and a pen and a piece of paper. That's it. No more than that,' Noel told me. 'I'm just making things rhyme drinking a can of Red Stripe in the Midland hotel, thinking, Marc Bolan couldn't have written lyrics this way. He'd have had a feather boa on! Shaun Ryder is one of the absolute fucking greats of all time and he will not have it that he's a genius. You try to tell him how good he is but he will not fucking have it, right? And he's up there with Dylan, right?'

The album contains some of Liam Gallagher's great vocals – that point in time between a youthful sweetness and a raw power yet with an atom bomb intensity and Liam is one of the very few whose voice had it all.

The album also saw Noel sing some of the big songs for the first time, despite initially being unsure about his own singing: 'The reason I started singing some songs was because Liam had developed this habit of walking off stage when he couldn't be fucking arsed. So then when we did *Morning Glory*, I said to myself I'm gonna sing one of the big songs and I said to Liam, "Do you want to sing 'Don't Look Back in Anger' or 'Wonderwall'?". At first he hated "Wonderwall" then until somebody from the record label said that is going to be a worldwide hit so he decided he was going to sing it and I sang, "Don't Look Back in Anger". But I hated my singing in Oasis, up until *Don't Believe the Truth*.

'When I would write for Liam I was always thinking how to tailor the melodies to suit his attitude. So if I had to sing those songs with me "doing Liam" it wouldn't work. The more I sang my songs though, the more I wanted to do it. It's like a fucking drug. But the reason I didn't do it off the bat was I wasn't really interested.'

Rich in complexity yet simple, sparse and layered, 'Wonderwall' had so many subtleties that are really effective and allow the sentiment and the emotion to really breathe in what would become the band's signature song. It's delivered impeccably by Liam who gets inside his brother's song in the way that only he can. Further proof that despite the flare-ups, there was something telepathic about the pair of them.

Owen Morris remembers the mix:

'I had three hours to spare before we went to see the Bluetones play in Hereford and my friends brought me some nice ecstasy in so I did the mix. Wonderful. In two hours it was mixed and it's the biggest thing Oasis have ever done and it pays for all our lives.

'What a pleasure it was to fucking record Liam Gallagher. He got this vocal done in four takes. Remarkable. Even under all that pressure and being chased by the paparazzi and having to do multiple changes of cars and all this shit, he still turned up and delivered. I then wrote the cello part which was played on a Mellotron by Bonehead.'

If this album was going to be about choruses, then 'Don't Look Back in Anger' comes armed with one of those huge hooks that fills a stadium. It's an anthem with a yearning melancholy and is another big song in the band's canon with its powerful emotional hook line and lyrics about a mythical Sally looking back on her life without regret.

The chorus is huge and all-embracing but perhaps the key line in the song was in the second verse about the fecklessness of rock 'n' roll, striking a note of cynicism and honesty about the notion that music could change the world. Perhaps this lyric is the most honest appraisal of the role of Oasis: they were not here to change the world but to fill it with songs.

And yet the song's communal power went beyond pop music and its healing redemptive quality was felt in the mass singalong whether at Oasis gigs or on the terraces. The song took on a whole new meaning when its theme of defiance chimed with a Manchester that was hurting after the 2017 bombing at the Ariana Grande gig at Manchester Arena; it became an unofficial anthem for a city in pain, which added to the song's powerful emotive appeal.

It had been debuted as an acoustic solo piece with Noel singing the then untitled song without the second verse and with slight lyrical differences at Sheffield Arena on 22 April, apparently only four days after it was written in Paris where they were playing with the Verve.

It's the most Beatlesque song on the album with the 'Imagine'-style piano on the intro played by Bonehead. There was also a nod to Mott the Hoople's anthemic take on Bowie's 'All the Young Dudes', especially on the chorus, yet somehow sounding like its own thing in a yearning pop classic.

Often overlooked 'Hey Now!' is the lost gem on the album. Its repetitive structure with the verse carrying the melody, and the chorus with its tricky time change, meant that the second-longest track on the album never got played live. After the last two songs' departure from the signature sound, 'Hey Now!' is back to the Sex Beatles wall of sound with cranked melodic chords and a great youthful vocal from Liam. The song has become almost a cult classic for fans and its extended outro is a first sign of what would come in the future.

One of the album's curios and split into two parts of under a minute each, 'The Swamp Song' was constructed from Alan White's drums from its live debut as the opener for the recent Glastonbury set. The rest of the song was built on top by Noel and a visiting Paul Weller, which explains why the original title was the punning 'the Jam'.

Not recorded at Rockfield and the only track with Tony McCarroll on drums, the single version of 'Some Might Say' was the sonic bridge from the debut album.

One of the second batch of songs recorded at Rockfield Studios when the band reconvened after the fight, 'Cast No Shadow' was about the then frustrated artistic ambition of Richard Ashcroft, who had just split the Verve for the first time in 1995 after the Owen Morris-produced difficult recording sessions for their second album, *A Northern Soul,* with its title track partially about Oasis – their northern fellow travellers in the madness of the times. The Wigan band had been fellow travellers but fortunes had changed, with Oasis going supernova while the Verve were marooned with their psychedelic freakouts. Add to this hallucinogenic drugs, tour burnout, wilful creativity and interpersonal band relationships, and it was a miracle the album ever got made and reached number 13 in the charts before the band collapsed. They then reformed in 1997 to record their iconic *Urban Hymns* album where they hit the sweet spot between their sonic adventures grounded in great song-writing that may have been influenced by their close mates in Oasis.

The song came with poignant lyrics about the inadequacies at capturing what Noel wanted to say in his lyrics and also about Richard Ashcroft reaching for the stars and not quite getting there, as Noel explained to Steve Lamacq:

'I don't write songs about many people – I've written songs about him [Liam], I've written songs about me mam, I've written songs about my wife, I've written songs about Richard Ashcroft.'[3]

Like 'Wonderwall', the song was an introspective stripped-down acoustic lament with perhaps a nod to the crafted songwriting of Bert Bacharach.

Nick Brine remembers the song appearing out of the ether:

'Noel wrote a couple on the train on the way to the studio, like "Cast No Shadow". He sat there and played it to us in the control room and just hearing him with the guitar playing these songs for the first time was amazing. He put a guide track down with the guide vocal, and then we put the drums on, and we'd layer all the instruments.'

Originally written in 1992 and demoed at Mark Coyle's, 'She's Electric' dares to deal a great vaudeville romp and is similar to other jaunty songs like 'Digsy's Dinner' while creating great pop. It also has a gritty wit and creates a snapshot of northernness with its mixture of 'magic in the mundane in the pouring rain' Mancunia and a love of absurdity with a chipper, yet acidic northern wit. Yet, as ever with Noel, it has a twist of wistfulness in its make-up, especially with Liam's falsetto chorus and the guitar gently weeping its chords. There is also perhaps an unintentional slice of self-analysis in the line about not getting along with a sibling.

Constructed from the debris of two songs with the temporary titles 'Blue' and 'The Mirror & The Razorblade', 'Morning Glory' also has a nod to Neil Young's 'My My, Hey Hey (Out of the Blue)' and R.E.M.'s 'The One I Love', with the riff a good starting point before the song spirals off in its own direction. The lyrics capture the moment of pure mid-nineties hedonism – as well as its darker side.

The pinnacle, of course, was 'Champagne Supernova'. The whole album and indeed the whole of the nineties felt like it had been leading to this moment. The song builds up from a dreamy, almost ambient psychedelia as the guitar notes chime in the intro before Liam perfectly intones the lyrics. It's a generational anthem and a real 'shiver down the spine, hands in the air' moment; a sun coming up, stoned off your head, live forever moment. The lyrics ostensibly are a clutch of abstract good-sounding phrases that on the surface mean little but, as ever, mean everything, sounding like an ode to being blissed out in the forever – surely the most perfect mood for a rock song to capture. As the song builds it's one of Liam's great vocals, and he sings like the pied piper, leading a generation into a nirvana, as Nick Brine points out:

'As I watched him do that vocal it just struck me that it was a magical moment. Time stood still and I can remember what shoes I had on and what I was wearing. I remember that moment, and it's just been with me forever. Liam could just go in and turn out a vocal in one or two takes. It was just magical the way he walked in and made sense of somebody else's lyrics and their raw emotion and understand what it's about and deliver.'

Noel, to this day, claims to have no idea what the song is about. '"This writer, he was going on about the lyrics to Champagne Supernova,"' he told the *Sunday Times* in 2009, '"and he actually said to me: "You know, the one thing that's stopping it being a classic is the ridiculous lyrics." And I went: "What do you mean by that?" And he said: "Well, 'Slowly walking down the hall / Faster than a cannonball' – what's that mean?" And I went: "I don't fucking know. But are you telling me, when you've got 60,000 people singing it, they don't know what it means? It means something different to every one of them.'"[4]

Owen Morris still marvels at the song:

'The song went back some time, Noel had played me the chords during the "Some Might Say" session and told me that he wasn't sure if Tony would be able to play the drum parts. After we recorded the track, Paul Weller came in to do his overdubs when we were mixing at Orinoco Studios in Elephant and Castle. It was in the afternoon and I was crashed out on the settee, still hungover and the rest after a night of madness with Brian Cannon. As I was getting freshened up he plugged his Gibson SG into his Vox AC30 and it was his sound straight away and with Noel he played a handful of different solos. Noel plays the more distorted one and Paul Weller is the louder one. After that, he went into the vocal booth and improvised some backing vocals for the track.'

Underpinned by Bonehead's harmonium, Paul Weller's guitar solo really underlines the song's crescendo like the sonic reflection of getting high and reaching a blissed-out state. It's the sound of dawn coming up at a rave; the moment when an all-night session in a flat melts into that moment of peace at dawn before everyone connects on the chemical and astral plane; or at a gig when the power and magic of music stops time and everyone is locked in that moment.

The album artwork was full of the mystery of the champagne supernova morning after the night before, as it catches a moment with an artful Hipgnosis tension in a posed snapshot of early dawn in Soho.

It was a different kind of 'morning glory' than the one Melissa Lim, who Noel Gallagher had stayed with when the 1994 tour collapsed, had used when answering the phone, taking the title's phrase from the song 'The Telephone Hour' from the film *Bye Bye*

Birdie. Of course, we all know that 'morning glory' is American slang for an early-morning erection but there is also something morning glory about nature's own dawn rising and the album cover captures that blissful mystery when the day is reborn after an all-nighter.

It was quite a different image from the original idea Noel Gallagher had.

'Noel said that they had been recording riot music so we thought the artwork should reflect that,' recalls Brian Cannon. 'One idea was for a guy who works in the city having his breakfast with a Molotov cocktail about to be lit behind him. When we actually heard what they had recorded that changed, especially listening to tracks like "Wonderwall" and "Cast No Shadow" but one day I'm going to do the riot cover for someone.'

The image also had a mystery and danger element that doesn't resolve, with the two mystery figures walking towards each other on the empty early-morning Berwick Street in Soho. Are they on a collision course? The concept came from Brian Cannon. Initially it was meant to be Noel and Liam but neither was in a rush to get up that early for a photoshoot and the sleeve perhaps works better without them, adding to the mystery.

The cover shot, which cost £25,000, was taken by Michael Spencer Jones to the side of Select-A-Disc record shop, (which later became Sister Ray), on 23 July. Brian Cannon has his back to the camera, passing Sean Rowley, who later went on to create the Guilty Pleasures concept.[5] In a neat touch typical of the obsessive detail of the Oasis sleeves, Owen Morris stands further down the street with the only master tape of the album held over his face.

The new concept had been sparked by a conversation Brian had had with Noel.

'There was a mystique about that album and if the first album was a kecks-down full-on rock 'n' roll record, the sleeve summed that up,' says Brian. 'The mystery of the music on the second album was reflected in its sleeve. Noel used to bang on about how an answer just provokes more questions. That interested me and the idea was to have a sleeve that itself was a mystery and a question with these two guys passing in the street – you have no idea of where they are going. One of them is walking off on the back sleeve like he's saying, "What the fuck did he just say to me?" It was taken at six in the morning and the first shot we took was the one we used although we spent another two hours taking shots. Owen Morris was waving the actual master tapes of the album around, pissed out of his mind, which, thinking about it now, was not the best idea!'

The tape-waving producer recalls the session:

'We did the photo for the album cover at six in the morning and then we go back to the hotel to play the piano and eat breakfast. Brian said to me, "The cover Owen, it's like north meets south, but one of them's a ghost, right?" And I looked at him and laughed, "That's amazing Brian!"'

If Brian was 'north' then Sean Rowley was 'south', and one of the new London mates of Oasis. He had met Noel Gallagher the year before at the Sunday Social club put on by Heavenly Records at the Albany. It was here that an eclectic mix of post-acid house music was played by the likes of the Chemical Brothers. It was as rock 'n' roll as the post-acid house club scene got, with Bobby Gillespie, Paul Weller, Tim Burgess and Noel Gallagher having mad nights out to a great soundtrack.

For Sean Rowley it was a game-changer:

'It was at that club that I had had a flashpoint moment and I signed up for the rock 'n' roll circus and I jacked in my job as a producer of *The Big Breakfast* on the TV. I had already met Noel backstage at Glastonbury 1994 when Oasis had just played and my opening line to him was "Fuck me that was amazing." I was on half a pill and I came up to "I Am the Walrus"!'

Bumping into Noel around town, he would often go to his home, Supernova Heights.

'My favourite part of a night out was going back to someone's house. That was the quality time of relationships and friendships as the party continued and the music got to be a central part of the madcap nights and into the next day. From that I came up with a radio show idea which Noel was a guest for called *All Back to Mine* where the guest would talk through their favourite songs. Noel liked really eclectic stuff, from the Billy Taylor Quartet's "I Wish I Knew How it Would Feel to Be Free", which was known in the UK from being on the Barry Norman film review show, Haçienda classics, Talking Heads and obscure post-punk and we had bonded over The Lovin' Spoonful.'[7]

It was not long after this that Sean got the phone call from Noel to be on the album cover: 'He said they were having a meeting so come over to the hotel. Noel was into his artwork and he loved Hipgnosis, and Microdot created these concepts. I think the initial idea was for it to be Noel and Liam but that didn't happen; it was not that they got pissed and didn't make it because I was asked to do the photo a week before. The reason I was chosen was because Meg Matthews had suggested me to Noel. In the shot I was Noel and Brian is Liam.

'Michael was in charge of the photo session and everyone met the night before at 10pm in order for us to be ready when the light came up. There was a lot of walking up and down the street to get the shot and I didn't realise the end image would have a slightly blurred effect on it.'

Sean smiles: 'Because, brilliantly I'm on the biggest selling album cover of the decade and you can't tell it's me!'

On release the album sales were through the roof.

Gold this, platinum that . . . within four years of forming, Oasis had defied all expectations and were now the biggest band in the world and top 5 in the USA album chart. Released on 2 October 1995 *(What's the Story) Morning Glory?* went on to sell 22 million copies, making it one of the top 50 best-selling albums of all time and the best-selling British album of the decade.

The reviews were mixed and missed the point. The album's universal themes were matched with a universal music. It now exists in that ubiquitous ether reserved for bands whose music is everywhere. Even Noel is bemused by its sheer scale.

'You only become aware of how big it was 10 years after when you see 14-year-old kids at your gigs who were not even around when "Don't Look Back in Anger" was written,' says Noel. 'That little record has so much legs and the amount of fucking love for that album is incredible. I don't give a shit when people say they love that album the most and more than the others, at least we had that one.'

It was the perfect album of the moment . . . *Loaded* magazine, lads and ladettes, good times with a whiff of working-class culture was allowed into the pop culture mainstream – the mid-nineties UK was soundtracked by Oasis and everything they touched was turning into gold. The tabloids were turning the band, and the Gallaghers especially, into 2D cardboard cutouts of drugs, scraps, scrapes and outrageous quotes, creating a simplistic version of the complex characters they were in real life.

It's just the way it works in the UK – a nation fascinated by surface and bored of depth – and the tabloids obliged, distracting from the news cycle and ironically distracting from the band's own precious art but the band were a gift to the red tops, as Alan McGee observes.

'Oasis were now off the scale. Not only did they write great songs but they wrote great headlines. There was no filter with the way they spoke and the way they behaved. They were a dream for any label but perfect for Creation because they were so rock 'n' roll.'

Fame turns people into seductive, sellable 2D images. With Oasis that was drugs, kick-offs and good times, which is fun but ultimately destructive. At the time the band were happy to oblige, with Noel talking about putting cocaine on his cornflakes for breakfast – feeding the tabloids lines with his gift for storytelling, an asset in the blurred reality of fame. Liam lived it as the natural born rock star cutting across protocol because that was his birthright. He understood his destiny. Many have talked the talk but few can walk the actual walk.

And it was a distinctive walk.

'It starts with your haircut, the way you dress, the furniture in your house, the way you mow your lawn – that's the kind of thing we are into,' Liam explained. 'It's not just about the music. We're not trainspotting. We don't sit down and say we are going to make an album that sounds like the Beatles and that's it. People go on about us sounding like the Beatles but I think we sound like a British rock 'n' roll band. I don't wake up in the morning trying to sound like John Lennon or whatever, that's just the way it is. I got a guitar at my house but I'm limited to what I can do, but it's pretty amazing what comes out of it. I refuse to be taught. I have got to work it out myself. I play it now and then and then get frustrated and put it down and fucking volley it across the room and then it's in pieces!'

Pop art violence! Like Gustav Metzger teaching Pete Townshend how to smash a guitar as Auto-Destructive Art! Rock 'n' roll incarnate!

Despite the aggro, Liam had more talent than even he realised and maybe in the future would write songs.

'I'm good with melodies,' he said. 'I can think of bits to add on to songs like three different tunes to add to one song. But it's the words I find hard to write. There's a limit to where I can't go any further. I'm not about singing technique, just fuckin' aggy shit. If you like that, then I piss all over everyone put together.

'Stagecraft is beneath me. I don't do that moving around shit. John Lennon had bagism and I have stillism. As soon as the guitars are on, then I'm away. I do my thing. I sing and I don't run around. I don't stand still all day though or I wouldn't get anywhere! I don't think about it. I just go on stage and do what I do. Honestly man, I don't feel we have to prove anything. We have got to connect because we have great songs but if you don't connect with the people, then there is no point, is there?'

Chris Abbot: 'I remember when they were on *Top of the Pops* and someone like Jimmy Nail said something to Liam and he replied, "I'm only a kid, you know." I was thinking about it, and I looked and I thought he was only a kid when all this stuff was taking place and he retained that for a long time. Fame didn't go to his head. He was very much the kid next door for as long as he could be.'

Oasis were already the last great rock 'n' roll band. Everything would change in the next few years and the internet would turn the world upside down. There would still be big bands – but a band that told their own story and had arrived due to sheer talent and word of mouth, and connected with the national psyche, was going to be impossible in the internet age and its distractions.

With the album selling millions, all Oasis had to do now was ride it out, according to Noel Gallagher:

'I was completely and utterly ready for the album being massive because I'd worked with the Inspirals and had travelled the world with them. They might not have been in the same league but I knew what was going to happen but on a much larger scale. I had read enough copies of music papers and watched enough documentaries about bands to know what was going to happen. I was ready for it.

'That's what I liked about U2. It was the bigness of it. To me, in Manchester people's ambitions seemed to be to play Gmex and that was it and I was like, fuck that! We never shied away from the stadiums even if the showmanship means nothing to me. I can't run up and down a catwalk like Slash or the Edge and I'm not as adept at putting together a show. I do what I fucking do and it works.'

While Noel was ready for it, other band members were finding it hard to cope. The toppermost demands commitment and the band's relentless schedule saw burnout. Just back from Japan and about to set out on their second American tour of the year with new drummer Alan White settling in, Guigsy temporarily quit on 13 September, citing nervous exhaustion.

The band had to cancel a run of shows including Blackpool Empress Ballroom – where the Stone Roses had played the classic gig in 1989. The call went out for a bass player and Scott McLeod from the Ya Yas stepped into the breach a week later. His tenure in the band was brief, lasting just over four weeks, including appearing in the iconic 'Wonderwall' video and doing most of the American tour. He quit before a show in Pittsburgh saying that he 'missed me bird', and just before a prestigious TV appearance on the David Letterman show, which meant Bonehead stepping in on bass and the rest of the tour getting scrapped for the second time in two years.

Weeks later, he contacted Noel Gallagher claiming he felt he had made the wrong decision. Noel, as quick as ever, replied: 'I think you have too. Good luck signing on.'

Guigsy returned for the Halloween show at La Luna in Belgium and then the run of huge sold-out shows at Earl's Court a few days later where Noel introduced him to the crowd. 'Have you seen our new bass player?' he quipped.

Guigsy had returned just in time for the band to have their biggest hit. Released on 30 October as the third single from the album, 'Wonderwall' broke their sonic mould and was the band's first huge worldwide hit. 'Wonderwall' was everywhere you went, heralding their arrival and catapulting the album into becoming one of the biggest sellers of all time.

'After he heard "Wonderwall" Alan McGee called me up nine times in the middle of the night,' laughs Noel. 'He was going, this is the big song! We were all thinking it's not very rock 'n' roll but McGee was going crazy!'

'The album came at a time of a low ebb for me and for Creation,' remembers Alan McGee. 'I was out of rehab and struggling but when Noel played me a demo of "Don't Look Back In Anger", "Wonderwall" and "Morning Glory" it changed everything. It really picked me up and I knew then that the band had truly cracked it and we had the biggest album of the decade on our hands and Oasis were going to be one of the greats.'

As ever, the single came with the usual clutch of good B-sides with a new one that Noel had written at home in Camden and rushed into Maison Rouge the next day to record 'The Masterplan'. Musically, it's almost Bond film soundtrack with its broody strings and descending bass line played by Noel and a song of introspective baroque darkness that he also beautifully sang. It also features a great backwards guitar solo and some tasteful piano playing from Bonehead. In the great tradition of Slade's misspelt titles and Noel's dyslexia, 'Round Are Way' technically should be called 'Round Our Way' but sounds all the better for its northern vernacular.[8] The song is an upbeat knees-up with a rare horn section giving it a Stax brass romp over the loud guitars; it's a semi-autobiographical song about a new day dawning, with amusing throwaway lines.

'I would smoke weed and do a lot of drugs so I would not always be writing about my surroundings and songs would be more personal but without looking too far inwards,' says Noel. 'I'm not comfortable trying to find out where that place is but it has a magic. They were everyman songs that have stood the test of time through the generations . . . There is a magic of singing uplifting melodies tinged with sadness in the words. Irish rebel songs are like that.'

To make up the three-song quota of B-sides they added the full-length version of 'The Swamp Song', with both halves from the album stuck back together.

The four tracks were packaged in one of the most striking sleeves from the Microdot team, with a mysterious looking sixties-style blonde in a picture frame adding a mystique to the single. The inspiration, according to Brian Cannon, came from Belgian surrealist art and a love of placing familiar objects in unfamiliar, unexpected contexts:

'I would always refer to where the band was coming from musically and lyrically, for example for "Wonderwall" I referenced René Magritte or maybe something from the Belgian renaissance that spawned the immensely popular Baroque Flemish style. Those paintings were almost photographic in their delivery and they would tell a narrative in a single frame by having points of reference to help the story.'

Initially, though, it had been a different model on the cover when it had been decided to go up Primrose Hill near the Creation offices and take a photo of Liam through a picture frame by some trees. Brian faxed the idea to Creation but for some reason he didn't hear back and assumed that this meant it was OK to go ahead with the photo session, with Michael Spencer Jones taking the shot.

'I faxed to see if everything was all right to just crack on with it and asked if I needed to make any changes then let me know,' remembers Brian. 'I heard nothing back, which wasn't unusual, so we got on with it. What I didn't know was that the fax machine had run out of paper and they hadn't seen the sketch I sent!'

It was during the session with Liam that they realised that something was wrong, as Michael Spencer Jones remembers:

'I was on Primrose Hill and after a few shots of Liam I could hear a bloke shouting at us and jumping out of a black cab. I thought it was a fan yelling at us through the railings down at the bottom of the park so I carried on the shoot but he kept on shouting and then I realised it was Noel Gallagher.

'He was not happy at all, shouting, "'Wonderwall' is a love song!" and there is no way our kid was going to be in the artwork! So we quickly ended the session and set up again the next day, this time with Anita Heyert who worked for Creation Records and in a slightly different location on Primrose Hill. After getting a great shot I used the same black-and-white infra-red effect on this cover as I did on "Live Forever".'

The final sleeve is actually more effective than the aborted Liam shots. There is a mystery to the picture, with Anita looking like a waif-like apparition on the hill adding a bewitching mystique to the artwork. It makes it one of the band's most effective sleeves, as Brian agrees: 'It looked great in the end. It's an eerie shot.'

32

TOPPERMOST OF THE POPPERMOST

In 1996 Noel Gallagher made a typically tongue-in-cheek aside that Oasis were now 'bigger' than the Beatles. It was a quip that referenced John Lennon's quote about the Beatles being bigger than Jesus to Maureen Cleave in the *Evening Standard* in 1966 which caused a furore in the USA.

While not attracting the ire of religious types Noel's comment caused its own friction.

George Harrison may have been one of the greatest songwriters and coolest looking rock stars of the sixties, but by 1996 his proclamations on any modern music were often in grumpy old man territory. When asked about Oasis he replied, 'The music lacks depth, and the singer Liam is a pain, the rest of the band don't need him.'

Not only does this show a lack of the understanding of the dynamics of what makes a great band but also a blind spot to what makes a magnetic frontman. It was also pretty wounding to Oasis who adored the Beatles.

During mid-nineties interviews on Steve Lamacq's Radio 1 *Evening Session* and with MTV, Liam, as ever, came out fighting, full of the spirit of a true punk. 'If any of them old farts have got a problem with me, then they should leave their Zimmer frames at home and I'll hold them up with a good right hook. I still love the Beatles and I still love George Harrison as a songwriter in the Beatles, but as a person, I think he's a fucking nipple. And if I ever meet him, I'll fucking tell him!'

'We never slagged Paul McCartney off, or George Harrison or Keith Richards, until they started having a go at our Liam, really,' explained Noel. 'You've got to stick up for your little brother, haven't you?'

The rowdy new band was upsetting the apple cart and it was a measure of just how big they now were that they were trading barbs with the elite. With the band in the exclusive big league, the now aptly titled fourth single from the album, the anthemic 'Don't Look Back in Anger', was released on 19 February 1996. The second number one from the album, the much-loved song has now joined 'Wonderwall' as an evergreen busker and terrace favourite. It was also the first A-side to be sung by Noel Gallagher, who would go on to sing six more.

The B-sides included the glam stomp of 'Step Out' that had initially been intended for the album, but after Stevie Wonder's people had requested 10 per cent of the royalties after noticing that the chorus was similar to his 'Uptight (Everything's Alright)' it had been shifted to B-side duty where it fits better. Meanwhile, 'Underneath the Sky' features twisting and turning unusual chords and a cool guitar sound from Noel picking out the backbone riff. Liam delivers a defining vocal, dropping his trademark intensity for an almost angelic pleading voice. Perhaps as a crafty refute to the critics who were still putting the band down for sounding not just like Status Quo but also Slade, the band delivered a riotous cover of the black country glamsters' 'Cum On Feel the Noize'; it was a thrilling homage to the raucous pounding superyob glam of the original.

The single came with artwork that was a nod to Beatle nerds with a back story of its own. On 22 August 1968 the normally placid Ringo Starr had quit the band, fed up with the fractious studio tension and not being appreciated by his younger cohorts. Ringo went to Peter Sellers' place in Sardinia and sat in the sunshine and came up with the original idea for 'Octopus's Garden'. On his return George had covered his drum kit with red, white and blue flowers as a welcome back and the band carried on for another year or so.

This episode inspired Brian Cannon: 'We hired a studio in Wembley and the Oasis road crew brought all the band's equipment in and we set it all up. Meg Mathews ordered the 10,000 carnations. They were red and white and we had to get a work experience in to dye 3,000 flowers blue. If you look really closely you can see a dollar bill on the amp with Noel Gallagher's head on it because I like sleeves where you notice hidden stuff 10 years after.'

Another chart topped, and with no Oasis recording planned until later in the year, Noel Gallagher now satisfied his creative itch by working with the Chemical Brothers. The resulting track was his second attempt to fuse the groove of electronic dance music with rock 'n' roll since the early Oasis cover of Cartouche's 'Feel the Groove'.

Initially formed in Manchester, the Chemical Brothers had moved to London where they became the DJs at the Heavenly Sunday Social, mixing big beat electronics with guitar cuts. They had then been instrumental in taking dance music into a new era that was half band dynamic and half electronic groove with a series of great releases.

Ever the dance fan, Noel was interested in producing something for them. The Chemical Brothers, though, came back with a track called 'Mark One' for him to try a vocal on. With its droning, almost sitar like mantra pulse and speeded up 'Tomorrow Never Knows'-style drumming, it sounded like the acid Beatles blasted into the future. It was perfect for Noel to add the vocal line from an old song of his called 'Comin' on Strong'. It took a day to mix and was released later in the year in September and shot to the top of the charts.

'I remember at that point doing the record with the Chemical Brothers. Now it felt like everything I did turned to gold. I ambled in and did "Setting Sun" and it sold 250,000 copies. It was a massive single and I felt I could do anything.'

On 22 and 23 March 1996 Oasis returned to their spiritual home for two sold-out headline shows at the 8,000-capacity The Point in Dublin. What was a triumphant homecoming was ruined by the tabloid intrusion of the *News of the World*, a new low even by that paper's standards.

The now defunct Sunday tabloid paid for the Gallaghers' estranged father to fly out to Dublin and turn up unannounced at the hotel where they were staying, hoping they would either get an unlikely emotional reunion story or more likely a tense situation or even a fight.

There is not a shred of humanity in these kind of cynical, manipulative stories and gatecrashing someone else's space to create a reaction with something this emotionally painful. It's not like Oasis were a band short of their own stories.

With Tommy Gallagher ensconced in the bar of the Westbury hotel by the tabloid, it was only a matter of time before the post-concert band and crew would see him. It was Liam that spotted him first and was held back by Bonehead, ever the peacemaker, and Liam's own bodyguard, while the singer gave his father a piece of his mind. Fortunately before the situation got too out of hand Noel walked over and got Liam to go to his room and slipped upstairs himself, defusing a potentially volatile situation that must have had him seething. It was a moment of emotional turmoil and remarkable self-control that stopped the tabloid getting their story and exacerbating an already fraught situation. But it sadly put a downer on two great nights in Dublin where the band were the toast of the town.

From now on the security around the group was cranked up, starting with the big stadium gigs that were the key to their triumphant summer.

At the end of April 80,000 fans saw Oasis play two nights at Manchester City's Maine Road in the perfect synthesis between pop and football culture. The two sold-out shows were their biggest headlining gigs yet, and a dead cert sign of just how big this was getting. The old stadium that was eventually closed in 2003 was the perfect conceptual homecoming venue for the famous City fans.

That night the atmosphere was epic – the tension and release of the gig was palpable and you could feel the surge from the crowd who filled the stadium with waves of humanity. In the tight back streets and terraces that surrounded the ground the atmosphere was less joyous as the large crowd squeezed into the narrow roads on the way to the stadium and gangs of lads were getting up to all kinds of mischief.

Inside, the atmosphere was like a cup final, like back in the days of Man City's own holy trinity of Francis Lee, Mike Summerbee and Colin Bell, especially on the peaks in the set such as when they played 'Acquiesce' on the second night. The song may have been a B-side but it was greeted like a huge number one hit. Dead Dead Good's Steve Harrison was blown away by the scale of the band now:

'When they played Maine Road they were like Led Zeppelin. That size of band. The anticipation of the crowd before they came on was phenomenal. Then they played and they held the crowd in the palms of their hands. That night I tried to get the then chairman of the club, Francis Lee, to work with Oasis, but he didn't understand pop culture.'

Some of the most iconic photos of the band come from this gig. Jill Furmanovsky, who was now working closely with them, took a defining shot of Noel Gallagher standing there with his arms outstretched trying to take it all in. The whole audience is in front of him with their arms in the air in a moment of supreme communal bonding. It's when the magic of high-decibel rock 'n' roll and its totemic power transcends everything and actually does live forever in a photo that says everything about the group and their relationship with their fans.

A few days after Maine Road the guitarist flew out to the exclusive sun-drenched enclave of the Caribbean island of Mustique for a break, briefly leaving behind the high pressure mania of Oasis for what would become a working holiday.

Escaping the fevered atmosphere of being the biggest UK band for decades, he went partly to rest and partly to pile up the demos for the next album. A long way from Mark Coyle's 8-track and the Boardwalk basement, it would now be in a villa owned by Mick Jagger where Noel remembers writing and recording demos of songs that would eventually make up most of the upcoming third album.

'If I'm being honest I was dialling in,' Noel remembers. 'I hadn't got any more songs left and stuff like "All Around the World" had been written in the Boardwalk days. From 1994 to 1996 every song that I'd written for the first two albums, plus B-sides, all remain really famous songs to this day; but then you're doing loads of drugs and surrounded by loads of people saying you are God. Of course, you just think, "I'll just go and write another album on holiday. In fact, I won't even write an album in Mustique. I'll write it on the plane on the way there. I'll write it in the fucking queue at immigration – that's how good I am!" When people heard the demos, they were going fucking crazy, and I was like, "Wow, this is a piece of piss!"

'We're all geniuses with hindsight but looking back on it now somebody should have said, "Take some time out here. Just fucking get off the train. Just park it."

'Back in those days, if you announced you're making an album the frenzy never went away. There was press trying to get on to the island of Mustique. The fact that I was from Burnage flying on Concorde to Mustique, hanging out with Johnny Depp while trying to write an album was already fucking insane before I'd even started.'

The first couple of weeks had been spent partying with his partner Meg, PR guru Fran Cutler, Kate Moss and Johnny Depp, but the sun lounger and flopping out on the beach was not for him. The writer's block that had descended on him for six months after *What's The Story . . .?* began to recede, and the stockpile of songs worked out on his trusty acoustic started to build.

After two weeks he rang Owen Morris and asked him to fly out to record some demos. The producer joined him with his TASCAM 8-track recorder, a drum machine, a vocal mic and a keyboard for Noel to work out the string parts.

Recording the acoustic and an electric plus the vocals, with the drums programmed by the producer, the songs began to flow. Owen Morris thought there would be a couple of new tracks to demo and was pleasantly surprised that there were 15 in total.

'It was great,' Owen recalls. 'It was Johnny Depp, rum punch, cooks making your food and Kate Moss. I was in Mick Jagger's house and swimming in his sea! What the fuck! We did all the songs in a week, recording from midday to early evening. I had my own little chalet by the airport, which is where the aeroplane noise came from that we eventually used for the intro of "D'You Know What I Mean?" There were no drugs, by the way, just rum punch and bit of weed, and we fucking belted it out and we had all the album demoed and its running order apart from "Magic Pie".'

The sun in Mustique melted away the pressure, and the songs seemed to flow. For some fans the demos are the true heart and soul of *Be Here Now*, stripped away from the eventual mega over-the-top production but missing the Liam touch.

Already with the mega shows like April's two-night stint at Maine Road under their Elvis belts all that was left for Oasis was to trump themselves. They were on their own version of the Stone Roses' classic run of 'event gigs', from Blackpool to Ally Pally to Spike Island, but, of course, their run was on steroids.

The two shows (they could have sold out five) at Knebworth on 10 and 11 August were to be bigger than Spike Island. Far bigger.

Noel: 'I remember saying to someone before our first album came out, "What was the capacity of Spike Island? 32,000?" I then said I won't rest until I've done a gig that's 33,000, because the Roses were it for me.'

In just two years Oasis had gone from outsiders on the wrong side of pop culture to being the biggest UK band since the Beatles. Their music was now ubiquitious and the Gallaghers were the most famous people in the country. The August gigs at Knebworth, in the grounds of a stately home near Stevenage, were to be the pinnacle.

Knebworth itself was already a byword for mega gigs from hairy seventies behemoths like Pink Floyd, Genesis, the Rolling Stones, Queen, and Led Zeppelin's last ever UK show. It is the biggest single stage venue in the UK with a capacity of 125,000, which is 30,000 more than Wembley Stadium. In total, 2.5 million people applied for the £22.50 tickets to see Oasis, which was just over 4 per cent of the UK population at the time, and a record for an event that can only really be measured in photos of endless joyous heads stretching to the horizon.

Now bigger than the big league, they hadn't just touched the national psyche, Oasis were the national psyche.

This was truly the high-water mark of the band's meteoric rise, with all the attendant madness and excess. Each VIP was gifted a pair of binoculars to see the gig and with 7,000 people in the back-stage area it was opulence in the extreme, as music journalist Roy

Wilkinson remembers: 'The backstage hospitality village was at once amazing and absurd, like some nouveau riche rock answer to Henry VIII's Field of the Cloth of Gold – this time down to cocaine-victualled Mancunian villeins rather than a swan-stuffed uxoricidal monarch.'[1]

Knebworth was big, as Noel Gallagher ponders:

'It was mad . . . It was all about statistics with stuff like one in seven people with red hair wearing black shoes were going to this concert. Before the gig I went to visit the site and was driven through the grounds. I got out in this huge field and I said, "Where's the stage?" and they said "Over there" and I looked and there was this vast sea of nothingness.

'They then said, "See that tree right down there," and I looked miles into the distance and said, "Yes" and they added, "Well you see the other tree behind it? That's where the stage is gonna be." I said, "How are they going to hear us?" So they then showed me all the technical things for the sound and I thought how could this not be a great show. That summer was all big gigs like Maine Road and then the two shows at Loch Lomond[2] and a week later it was Knebworth and we were still only halfway through our second album tour cycle.'

On the day of Knebworth the band arrived by helicopter into the backstage area. As they flew over the site, the sheer scale of it became very apparent to Noel:

'I remember thinking I've seen all the documentaries about Woodstock with the endless crowd shots from a helicopter and it's now us from fucking Manchester! I remember the build-up to the gig really clearly but the weird thing is that if I close my eyes, I can't remember walking out on stage at Knebworth at all! There's a picture of me at Knebworth taken by our photographer Jill Furmanovsky playing to a sea of people. The band are miles away from each other and there is this one poxy little lead coming out of my amp playing through one delay pedal on a massive stage and that was all. These days I've got a whole NASA control fucking spaceboard for my guitar effects but then, wow! There was no stage show, it was just some shitty black-and-white backdrops and no big effects.

'It suddenly dawned on me then that when I met the people who worked in the music biz in the early days and told them how massive we were going to be that they must have thought I was bullshitting. A year after that everyone was going it's ludicrous that these guys have got this big with their songs about nothing. I was like, fucking hell, I did warn you and I did let it be known that that was what was going to happen! I always said we would never be elitists and if a million people wanted to come we would play to a million people.'

Noel's innate self-confidence was not mere braggadocio. It's natural for the English to play down their talent and pretend they were lucky, so it's almost refreshing when someone is honest about their assets. Noel Gallagher was always a curious engaging mix of imposter syndrome and an unshakeable confidence.

As a music fiend who spent hours, days and months immersed in music he knew his songs were good enough. He trusted his own instinct, and he also knew that when Liam wrapped his vocals around the songs, they caught fire, creating a once in a generation moment which was peaking at Knebworth.

That weekend they shared the huge stage with the cream of the current crop of British bands like the Manic Street Preachers and the Charlatans who were still recovering from the loss of their keyboard player Rob Collins in a car accident while recording at Rockfield Studios weeks before. The emotionally charged gig saw Duffy from Primal Scream stepping in at last minute and Liam Gallagher movingly dedicating 'Cast No Shadow' to the late Hammond player.

'We also had the Prodigy who were fucking great, they certainly do not do stillism!' laughs Noel. 'Not only that but we had big guests on stage with us like Paul Weller and John Squire. Steve

Adge, the Roses tour manager, told me that John was going to come to the gig so we said let's get him up for "Champagne Supernova", and in his John way he just kinda let it be known that he would quite like to play and up he turned.

'He had flu and stayed on the tour bus all weekend and he kind of floated on and did his thing and then floated off again. It was a beautiful moment. Everyone on stage was a Mancunian and getting him up there was our way of saying that if it wasn't for the Roses then we wouldn't have been there. It was a nod to them from us. The two biggest cultural events of the separate decades were Spike Island and Knebworth, and he was at both of them.'

Knebworth was the high point of Oasis and of a collective consciousness that went back to Noel Gallagher's late teenage years at the burgeoning late eighties raves. E melted barriers and the gonzo nights dancing in squats, clubs and fields to blaring sound systems and the communal rush of acid house were vital in framing Oasis, with their own songs of inclusivity and escape from the mundane creating a magical world of sound and vision. It was like a rave but with very loud guitars.

'I remember Travis, who were symptomatic to me of the music that followed us, saying that they would never play arenas. I was like, it can't work if it's not arenas. It's got to be in thousands and not in hundreds. We were in that phase of all are welcome to come and see us. It was as much for them as it was for us.

'A lot of that came from the big raves I went to like Joy[3] and Live the Dream in Blackburn or Sunrise[4] with all those people dancing in a field and it was beautiful. The government and the police did not understand what was going on and were saying that if there were more than four people there then it was considered a rave. They wanted to make money out of it and create super clubs but for that two years when it was illegal warehouse parties and in fields, that was the revolution! It was the kind of thing I would never say from the stage because it would be too Bono-like but Knebworth was all about the "us".

'Knebworth was the last time that we were all together with the audience and after that it went stratospheric and we were living in big houses and flying around in private jets.'

The whole notion of fame and success is intriguing and there is no rough guide, explains Noel:

'I was never afraid of success because I knew I could handle it because ultimately I knew who I was. I knew I wasn't a made man. I knew Phil Spector wasn't responsible for me or George Martin or Nigel Godrich or Steve Lillywhite. I'd done it myself. I'd picked up that guitar and learnt to play it starting on one fucking string. I signed off the dole four years before Knebworth to be the biggest thing there ever was. I was going to drink and fuck and snort my way through the whole lot but it was never going to beat me. I always knew that there was going to come a point where I would say I've done it all now. I'd been to the dark side on more than one occasion and lived to tell the tale. It was a pride thing and it was never on the agenda that it was going to beat me or our kid. It was never going to be "woe is me, the pressure of fame!"

'You have to make it look like the best job in the world. There is nothing worse than those cunts whose second album is about how difficult it is to be famous. The middle-class "experiment" with drugs, the working class just get stuck in. ' Noel laughs, 'It must be horrible being mobbed by girls, it's fucking shit getting free drugs.

'The difference between my attitude and other people's is that I'm not embarrassed by it. I don't think I'm better than anyone else. I don't think I'm more deserving of fame than anyone else, but I'm more understanding of the game and of what it's all about. The highs and the fucking lows. When you get on the fairground that is rock 'n' roll you are getting on the roller coaster and that's the most exciting ride of them all. You've just got to enjoy it so when you get off at the other end you can say that was a fucking blast! You don't go to the fairground and go to the haunted house off your head on crack surrounded by vampires. You want to be as high as a kite and if you go down, you go down fucking fast. That was my theory to it all . . . '

Knebworth itself was a totemic generational moment.

'Ultimately, I'm so glad we did Knebworth and one of those events that was like an Isle of Wight or Woodstock,' says Noel. 'I remember at the time saying everyone should go away and form a band and it became apparent when that little mini explosion of bands came out later like the Arctic Monkeys, the Libertines and the Coral. That made me feel really proud. It's really special when people say it meant so much to them, like Kasabian who would say they couldn't wait to come home from school to see what Oasis had been up to in the tabloids and it made them want to get out of bed in the morning and when they were old enough, pick up guitars. It was a bit like the Sex Pistols thing at the Free Trade Hall in Manchester sparking the Haçienda.'

The two nights were certainly euphoric and life-changing but where could they go next? Once you are at the toppermost of the poppermost was the only way down or could they just get bigger and more bombastic? For Noel, it was probably as good as it got:

'For me Knebworth was where really the story does end in a way. We knew this was the zenith and we all realised it was now too big. Alan McGee always gets melancholic about it also because he went to rehab afterwards. I don't know what I feel about it now. Maybe I wish we could have played better!'

And when you get to the top of the slide . . . where do you go next? Alan McGee says:

'Knebworth was the high point for the band and the label. Noel had a point to prove and he really proved it. Everyone could now see that Oasis were the biggest band in the country. It was national news. We should have walked away then with that being the perfect ending but how could we?'

The same thought had crossed Noel Gallagher's mind.

'The only regret I have from Knebworth is not coming off that stage and just letting *Morning Glory* go away and land and settle,' the songwriter explains. 'I was watching a documentary when James Brown, the music journalist, was talking about Oasis and he said that "For once the biggest band in the world were the best band in the world" and that was pretty cool. We should have stopped there, walked off stage and gone away for a bit but we couldn't and we carried on.'

Live fast, die young and leave a beautiful looking corpse was the old-school creed of rock 'n' roll. It's obviously a stupid way to live your life but in terms of band careers it sometimes makes sense. If Oasis had walked off the stage after Knebworth and left on the highest of supernova highs, never to be seen again, it would have been conceptually perfect, but why should a band shape its career to fit a concept?

Some bands may have ridden the wave or taken a holiday but Oasis, being Oasis, just did more of everything, which would now get even louder.

Yin and yang, hello goodbye, up and down, one step forwards and one step back . . . only Oasis could follow up a triumph like Knebworth with a near disaster not even two weeks later. The volatile nature of the band, of course, was one of their magnetic qualities for outsiders. They never faked anything and their hearts were certainly on their sleeves; it saw them often snatch defeat from the jaws of victory and then somehow thrive in the following chaos.

The biggest crime in pop culture is to be boring, and Oasis were never boring.

On 23 August they were due to film an *MTV Unplugged* appearance that would become more famous for the inherent chaos that was always bubbling up just beneath the surface. Launched in 1989, the *MTV Unplugged* sessions were a big deal at the time. Featuring a filmed acoustic live session from a band, they had often been iconic, from Neil Young delivering a stunning take of his *Harvest Moon* classic to the most famous one of them all, Nirvana whose unplugged was eventually released as an album and is arguably their finest performance, with harrowing, brilliant covers of songs such as the Vaselines' 'Jesus Wants Me for a Sunbeam', David Bowie's 'The Man Who Sold the World' and Lead Belly's 'In the Pines'.

Filmed at the Royal Festival Hall, even the rehearsals for the Oasis show were fraught with problems, with Liam complaining of having a bad throat and walking out, and Noel having to cover most of the vocals. When it came to filming time, Liam hadn't turned up. The rumour was that he had been out drinking for a few days. Almost inevitably, he had been hanging out with Owen Morris the night before, as the producer remembers:

'The night before Liam didn't do MTV, he had been in my hotel room getting wasted, and I got the fucking blame! It was the first time I had seen him for eight months so we went to the pub and drank too much Guinness. And then Liam decided he didn't want to fucking sing on that MTV thing. I didn't know he was gonna fucking go loop the fucking loop, right?'

Now that it was obvious the iconic singer was not going to do the session, MTV scrambled for a plan B. They had already taped a full rehearsal with the band and there was talk of using that footage mixed with a Noel led performance, but the cost of editing meant they elected to go with the guitarist singing the whole session.

Cameras on, Noel announced, 'Liam ain't gonna be with us tonight cause he's got a sore throat. So you're stuck with the ugly four,' and carried it off perfectly, bringing his own more plaintive takes on his lyrics compared to his younger brother's captivating vocals with a now watching Liam sat in the upstairs seats heckling, which further cranked the tension as the 'ugly four' delivered the session. Whatever was going on, it made for riveting viewing and added to the helter-skelter dynamics of the band that defied boredom and conventional careerism with moments of madness like this.

With *(What's the Story) Morning Glory?* in the top 5 of the American charts, the tour should have been a triumph. The sheer scale of Knebworth and the huge success of the album and 'Wonderwall' had put them on a supernova footing. The discipline required to get to the top, forged in those endless hours of rehearsing in the Boardwalk seemed to be dissipating though. The internecine tension between the two brothers, amped by the pressure and further cranked by the cocaine and the post-Knebworth malaise, were playing out in lots of different ways.

'The Knebworth thing was with us when we went on that plane to America,' says Noel. 'I guess subconsciously we must have felt we had done it with *Morning Glory* riding high in the American album charts and "Wonderwall" in the top five.'

The MTV filming had been a warning sign and now the band had to play their first date on the American tour with no singer, who had decided, last minute, that he needed to go house hunting with his new partner, Patsy Kensit, after moving out of the flat he had been renting. This left Noel to front the band at the first gig in Chicago and sing the whole set and songs like 'Champagne Supernova' for the first time ever, after supports from the Screaming Trees and the Manic Street Preachers.

Even the Stones at their most decadent hadn't been this unruly.

After joining the tour for the second date at the large Glass Palace venue on the edge of Detroit, Liam had the now famous confrontation with the late Mark Lanegan, the then lead singer of the Screaming Trees. The stand-off was sparked when he called Lanegan's band the 'Howling Branches' and it descended from there. On paper it may have seemed an odd bill but, like Nirvana, whose totemic frontman Noel felt an alignment with, Mark

Lanegan was close to Kurt Cobain and Oasis and they and Screaming Trees had things in common. Both had a melodic take on anthemic noise and an ability to weave introspection into the high-decibel void. Both singers were renegade Irish blood transposed into alien nations and reacting in their own ways. It's a shame they bumped into each other at the wrong time in their lives and fell out so badly as there could have been much mutual respect with Mark Lanegan being a fan of Oasis, but it wasn't to be, and the festering ill will carried on until Mark's death in 2022.

The tension carried through the next few shows before arriving in New York where Oasis were appearing on the MTV awards on 4 September. On the show, the band performed a loose version of 'Champagne Supernova' with a clearly discontented singer ad-libbing 'up your bum' into the song and spitting on the stage. It's as electric in its tension and unpredictability as prime-time Doors.

The tour staggered on for a few dates with Noel grimly grinding the shows down before it all finally imploded on 10 September, two hours before stage time in Charlotte at the Bristow Nissan Pavilion, when the guitarist pulled the tour and flew home on Concorde. The rest of the American tour and follow-up legs in Australia and New Zealand were pulled.

Oasis had imploded. It was big news.

'Liam had an argument with Bonehead about a leather jacket and we were all on fucking drugs and I was saying, "Calm down!" and we blew out four really big gigs,' explains Noel. 'At that point the band could have gone one way or another. There was mayhem when we got back to England, there was chaos at the airport. I couldn't believe the amount of press that was there. We had only cancelled a few fucking gigs. It was insane. We had to get driven from the airport to a secret hideaway and we were now in the tabloids all the time. After that, the drugs started to take over. We shouldn't have gone on that tour in the first place. What we should have done after Knebworth was just fucking disappeared.

'It was the classic thing, which we never, ever learned in Oasis, which was biting off more than you can chew, but when you're cocky little working class lads and someone says, "There's another six-week tour of America, you might be tired . . . "I would say, "Tired? What are you fucking talking about? We're fucking there, mate!" But when you get older you realise it's the adults surrounding the band that should have not let that happen.'

Noel knew the damage had been done. 'You can get away with unprofessionalism in the UK but the Americans could not understand how we could blow out gigs or be too pissed to meet that guy at the record shop who would rack the records.

'Marcus was based in England and we never had an American manager and we were left to our own devices. We were on Epic records in the USA and it doesn't get any more corporate than that. Their two biggest acts were Whitney Houston and Celine Dion and then there was us. They didn't get it for a long time, even with the album at number two in the charts. They think you are trying to trick them somehow because you're playing "Rock 'n' Roll Star" and no one is moving except for the drummer.

'Musically we could have smashed it, but they are so attuned out there to people like Chris Martin and Bono who give a lot to a crowd, but Liam is into his stillness, which was great of course but they find that offensive out there. They are into showmanship and a stage show and they couldn't believe that "you guys just stand there!" If you act like Mick Jagger they get it but they were so intimidated by the way we were on stage. They didn't know what to do if you were not performing like a ludicrous idiot. Alan McGee always said we were too Mancunian for America and "it's no surprise that none of you from that city have ever done anything there!"

'We were expected to go and repeat the staggering success of the UK – I'm sure McGee and Marcus were not thinking that but someone at Sony was. I had already been to America with the

Inspirals and I knew that New York and LA were great but the rest of it can be like a Wednesday afternoon in Bury.

'Our reputation preceded us for being somewhat tetchy, "Here, these are the guys that fight all the time." Yet we didn't fight all the time although we do like an argument, particularly in the press, but it's often tongue in cheek, but because Americans have a different sense of humour they think it's all real!'

Band PR Johnny Hopkins saw the genuine band dynamics: 'There was so much love between the brothers at first, and the atmosphere around the band in those early years was just beautiful and hilarious. Maybe it changed after Wibbling Rivalry which created an expectation.'

The cultural differences between the UK and USA baffled both sides. Noel explains: 'They said we were going through the motions because we were not as big in the USA, but I found that quite insulting. In England we call that nonchalance. I remember a girl from the label was driving us around to do press in Seattle and she asked me what Creation Records was like. She was horrified when I said they get us drugs and have their own drug dealers.'

Despite this pervading feeling of car crash, the band were actually the most successful UK band in the USA for years, and decades later, when they reformed in 2024, they sold out their biggest ever shows in minutes because, in the end, it's the songs that really matter.

Only eight weeks after the triumph of Knebworth and in a state of flux, the band returned to the UK. Noel says: 'The press started saying we were gonna break up. It was all fucking nonsense and the tabloids were out of control. It was a really negative time. So what do we fucking do? Instead of all going, "See you in a year", which is what we should have done, we go straight into the studio, which, looking back on it now, was fucking lunacy.'

On 7 October, the fractured band, driven by a blur of cocaine, entered the most famous studio in the world. Owen Morris: 'We should have recorded *Be Here Now* before Knebworth in the summer of 1996 when the mood was right and everyone was happy. They did Knebworth in August and it all fell apart in September with Liam not going on the beginning of the American tour because he went to buy a house with Patsy. After that it was all pretty fucked.'

Of course, when you finally get into Abbey Road, where the Beatles had made musical history, there is only one thing to do.

On arrival Oasis spent the first few days blasting the Beatles out of the speakers at full volume, as Nick Brine remembers:

'Where do you go once we've been to Rockfield? Abbey Road! When we got there, we played all the Beatles albums in a row. A couple of days later, Oasis were having a day off and George Martin, who had called Noel "the finest songwriter of his generation", popped in and said, "I'm George, are you with the Oasis boys? I'm showing Jim Carey around." I then got a full tour of Abbey Road! From George Martin!'

Owen Morris was ready:

'Noel had just signed the biggest fucking publishing deal ever, which Marcus had got him without anybody hearing the fucking songs, so we had to go in and record. So we're in Abbey fucking Road and I've got my new Jag and we got two drug dealers and one of them works for the *Sun* and one of them works for the *Mirror* and they are on the payroll and they hated each other. We started recording after the American tour got cancelled and there was some tension and the vibe wasn't good. They were genuinely not getting on and I'm like, "OK, here we go!" The rest of the band was just freaking and saying we'll just play when you want us to fucking play. Yet they still got through it and Liam's vocals on *Be Here Now* are amazing because the brothers fucking know each other inside out and when he went to sing he sounded great.

'Noel's also got his best mate Mark Coyle back in there for the first time in ages. Lovely man, Mark, I like Mark Coyle but suddenly there are two producers there and it's confusing. There's no rational thought going on at all from any of us but somehow we recorded a few backing tracks in the madness, "It's Gettin' Better (Man!!)", "D'You Know What I Mean?", "Magic Pie" and "The Girl in the Dirty Shirt."'

With all the headlines from the American tour fallout and the sheer size of the band post-Knebworth, the media was camped outside waiting for titbits. Instead of letting it be, it was like the dog-end days of the Fabs all over again. With too much press intrusion and their attendant pills, thrills and bellyaches – and complaints about the band being too loud from the other people at Abbey Road – the surrounding chaos was getting too much, even for Owen Morris.

'We couldn't get any peace and quiet to get on with the album,' the producer says. 'Everything was fraught and stressed. On top of that, we were getting the press sneaking in at night.'

Abbey Road was a great experience but the surrounding chaos was getting in the way, as Nick Brine explains:

'The press intrusion and that kind of circus was so difficult. You have no idea how that is unless you're in the middle of it, and how intense that was when trying to make a record. How they handled it was actually amazing. One of my jobs was to lock the tapes away every night because we had people coming in the studio trying to steal them. It was also my job to take Liam to the pub and sometimes there would then be all these people that Liam's brought back from the pub. One night it would be Richard Ashcroft and Steve Cradock [from Ocean Colour Scene] and on another night it would be Helena Christensen and Christian Slater. I found Jarvis Cocker one morning on the sofa asleep. I must have locked him up in the studio by mistake.'

The post-pub party soundtrack in the studio was often the album itself.

'Liam would play the mixes through the really loud 4K PA that we had set up, often blowing the drivers,' remembers Nick. 'He would be there with whoever had come back saying, "What do you think of this? It's the best thing ever, right?" And he'd sing along to every word. One night he didn't have anyone to bring back, so he went to the studio upstairs and said to Teenage Fan Club, "You're the second best band in the world, come and have a listen to the album!" and I remember them pinned to the back wall as he sang the whole album in their faces!'

The whole crazy scene was getting too much, even for Owen Morris: 'So after a couple of weeks, me and Mark Coyle go and see Noel and say, "I think we should just stop the album. Let's take a break. Everyone's heads have gone", but Noel said, "No we're fucking carrying on!"

'So we carry on but we move to Ridge Farm in Surrey and spend three or four months there and get most of it recorded. It's fucking insane. There's still press outside. There's police circling around. Liam needs all the fucking security just to get there because he's Liam Gallagher and he can't go anywhere without the press and paparazzi following him.'

All great rock 'n' roll comes out of some kind of madness. It's remarkable that they were even there at all since their fractious tailspin after leaving the stage at Knebworth. The inner tensions, fallouts and big cancelled tours would have ended most bands but somehow Oasis were recording despite the cranked up really high atmosphere around them. Owen Morris recalls:

'There were dealers and there were drugs. Then there were all these security motherfuckers and other people hanging about and I was sat there in the control room thinking, who are all these people? It was chaos and madness but we'd get through the day. We'd get some drums done then Liam would turn up and sing with what was now 12 takes instead of four but he was still really up for it. He's Liam Gallagher. He's like, fuck them all, I'm going to sing this.'

There is a romantic notion that bands are benevolent democracies and all decisions are cloaked in peace and love and consensus, but the reality is that every band needs a leader and every project has to have a vision. This means herding sheep and lone wolves and trying to get a sense of direction. You only have to look at the Beatles *Get Back* film to see the unenviable position Paul McCartney is in as he tries to cajole the rest of the biggest band in the world to wake up from their late sixties stupor.

This was Noel's role in Oasis – he had the songs and the sense of direction and was not awkward about pushing the band along to make things happen. It could seem pushy, as Owen Morris laughs:

'Noel, and I say this advisedly, had turned into a megalomaniac by now. He really thought he was God! Fucking hell . . . he was god! He was Noel Gallagher and he had more money than God!

'At the start I would be saying, "Can we get the band in to rehearse?" And he's like, "No! I gave them a fucking cassette so they should be able to play the songs perfectly!" Here's two words . . . "Noel" "Gallagher". There's a fucking beautiful and strange human being and the cleverest and most talented man I have ever fucking met!'

The album now took its own trajectory. The surrounding chemical madness was part of this, plus the stream of ideas from Noel, which now had space to be explored with the endless possibilities of the multi-track studio. This was now in excess because Owen Morris had worked out a way to record guitars on to 96 tracks of digital, as Nick Brine remembers:

'When he heard about that, Owen's eyes lit up. The song was now never finished until there were no tracks left. If we had used up 88 tracks then we could still have eight more guitars. It was an over-the-top production. The songs were now evolving with more and more layers and with different sounds from amps and pedals. Owen is great at working with that sort of stuff so it just kept going from there and was obviously fuelled by everything that was going on.'

The album continued throughout the autumn and into January.

Owen Morris: 'We had started in October in Abbey Road, then we went to Ridge Farm. Then in January, me and Liam went in to do some vocals in Air Studios in London. Noel had gone back to Mustique with Meg and Johnny Depp and Kate Moss and we had all these backing tracks, so I went in with Liam for a couple of weeks to do the vocals and also spend a lot of time down the pub. But we got three or four vocals done like, "Stand by Me", "My Big Mouth" and "Be Here Now", some big vocals, right?

'It was just me and Liam, because Liam was saying, "I want to fucking sing and hang out in the studio and listen to the music, right?"

'When Noel got back, though, he rang me up and he was like, "What the fuck is this?" I was in Wales and it got a bit heavy so I rang Marcus and said, "This is all a bit much right?" And Marcus said, "You're not fucking quitting."

'So Noel came in the studio and I thought he's gonna be a bit fucking tense with me. Paul Weller was there and it was all cool and Noel said, all friendly, "Let's do some guitars . . . " and we were back on it again.'

Mixed at George Martin's Air Studios, the songs started to come together with their sound cranked up to 11 out of 10 and no bottom end because of the coked-up studio vibes. There was layer upon layer of guitar overdubs and songs that broke the three-minute pop template and were stretched out with long outros, which all helped to make the album a staggering 72 minutes of sonic landslides. 'Everything louder than everything else,' as Lemmy from Motörhead had once described his own band, and the album was a suitably over-the-top capture of a peak hedonistic time and sounded all the better for it.

'It was a different vibe now,' says Owen Morris. 'Noel and Liam had decided that Brian was a bad influence and he had been banished from the studio. So it was mostly me and the Abbot brothers, Tim and Chris. I love the Abbot brothers, by the way, beautiful people.

'I banished the rest of the band, well Liam, basically, because it was too much chaos. I said, "I need to listen and concentrate, Liam." So the Abbots would turn up with a bag and we'd hang out and wait for Noel to come down.

'That was a weird, weird time, but we got it done, but it wasn't as good as before. I dunno, maybe I will listen again one day, but there was just too much of everything. I remember thinking can we get a custom version CD that goes to 100 minutes? Because then we can make the songs all longer with more fucking guitars and noise . . . that's where my head was at!'

Finally, in March 1997, they went into Miloco's Engine Room, formally known as Orinoco, to do the last mixes, finally ditching the 4K rig they took around with them to blast out the mixes, which saved their ears.

Somehow, the album was now finished.

33

BE HERE NOW

Peak drugs. Peak rock 'n' roll. Peak volume. Peak good times. In 1997 everyone was breaking into heaven . . .

On 7 July 1997 the new Oasis single, 'D'You Know What I Mean?', was released. Heralded by its blockbuster monochromatic *Apocalypse Now* video of swooping, slow motion helicopters and exploding flares, it put the bomb into bombastic and looked and sounded big and moody, expensive, dark and decadent, perfectly framing the first sighting of the band's new material.

The video was a long way from 'Supersonic'. This was a big rock band with a big budget rock video and a big song full of big sounds. The brickwall music was now matched by a brickwall video, and the moody work was all Hollywood epic for the band's new single that was a hint of the shape of things to come.

Clocking in at 7 minutes 22 seconds, 'D'You Know What I Mean?' was their longest single yet. The slow burn intro of the plane noises from Mustique, flying speaker to speaker, set the scene before the drums even kick in proper. The groove itself is built on a drum loop of a slowed down sample from N.W.A's 'Straight Outta Compton', creating the loudest drums on an Oasis release so far. The juggernaut groove was perhaps a nod to the Chemical Brothers' 'Setting Sun' track and a move away from their usual guitar-heavy chassis and a harbinger of future sounds.

The song defines magnum opus with a defiant swagger, as it churns on the loping, slowed down hip-hop groove. It then builds on an increasing tsunami of sound, with surging guitars piling on to that behemoth beat that defiantly swaggers to the end of its near eight-minute stint. Perversely, this was the only time that Oasis sounded like the Stone Roses – not the crystalline pop of 'Made of Stone' but the Second Coming's heavy Led Zep grooves.

Liam's rasping vocal and the feedback guitars add to the brooding vibe, with an added bleeping morse code inspired by 'Strawberry Fields Forever'.[1] The lyrics also manage to cram in a couple of Beatles allusions, to 'The fool on the hill' and 'I feel fine'.

Owen Morris marvels at the vocal delivery:

'He's so full-on you think he would rip his throat, yet he can still fucking sing now. He never does a warm-up. Before going in he does none of those scales and all that shit. He just steps up to the mic and delivers.'

The song is a slow builder, holding the tension for as long as it can as it stretches the fabric of their three-minute pop perfection and was the band's third number one, selling 370,000 copies in its first week on account of its naggingly anthemic chorus hook.

The B-sides featured 'Stay Young', a fan favourite deep cut, not loved by its writer Noel and originally intended as the light-hearted 'novelty' track on the album, like a 'Digsy's Dinner' or a 'She's Electric'. Its pure rush of sunshine pop had been replaced by 'Magic Pie' on the album and the track became yet another one of the band's legendary B-sides. The demo of 'Angel Child' showed that the tradition of Noel-sung introspective acoustic pieces hadn't died out, while the also Noel-sung faithful cover of David Bowie's classic 'Heroes' was a good time rumble.

Brian Cannon's sleeve concept was to have Liam – imperious behind his shades, as a young king surrounded by the band – staring at the camera while the crowd looked away, apparently reflecting the shifting political scene as Labour were about to sweep into power for the first time in almost two decades. In a return back up north, the black-and-white Michael Spencer Jones shot was taken by the Blind Steps in Wigan, so-called because they went past the blind workshop on Darlington Street in the town centre.

Number one in July and the album out in August, Oasis were back and so were New Labour as the knock-on effect of Britpop had reclaimed the pop art Union Jack. When Tony Blair won the 'Britpop' election on 1 May 1997 it felt like a cultural shift with the new broom of political 'poptimism' of the then feelgood, youthful prime minister. His pop culture nous had given Labour a new sheen before brushing away the crumbling grey Tories. Blair had been pop culture savvy enough to align himself to Britpop, bringing in Alan McGee to his Creative Industries Taskforce, which resulted in the New Deal for Musicians to provide financial support and three years of development time for unemployed musicians.

With this he caught the current pop culture moment to soundtrack a vision of a shiny new forward-facing country that he took right into 10 Downing Street. Of course politics, like pop culture, is very much an ebb and flow business and even as D:Ream's 'Things Can Only Get Better' anthem was blasting out on victory night, there were naysayers – and within months disappointment and backlash would be the norm. The same thing would happen to Oasis, burdened by huge expectations and a feeling of nothing can match the thrill of the first big hit.

The band were now living full Spinal Tap, with the volume cranked to 11, in big London houses and run-ins with paparazzi at flashbulb events were frequent. The Gallaghers were now the most famous people in the UK and had recreated the sixties heyday of mainstream pop culture in the more overheated, cynical nineties.

Every day they were in the tabloids with their subtleties and nuances reduced to V-sign flicking cartoon characters. The peak media moment that summer was when pop and politics collided in one of the most famous set-piece moments of the decade. Neatly placed a few weeks after the landslide Labour election victory and a few weeks before *Be Here Now* was released, Noel Gallagher and his then partner Meg Mathews – along with Alan McGee and his wife Kate Holmes, media and arts faces like Helen Mirren, Eddie Izzard and Lenny Henry – were invited to 10 Downing Street on 30 July by the pop culture savvy new prime minister, creating one of the most (in)famous events of the decade, the Cool Britannia party.[2]

There has always been an awkward interface between politics and pop, like Harold Wilson giving the Beatles MBEs back in 1965, or the knighthood for Mick Jagger in 2003 but not Keith Richards. One side shakes hands with the other but both eye each other suspiciously. A young Tony Blair, of course, had grown up in the pop generation and had done a very good Mick Jagger impression in some kind of Rolling Stones-style band called Ugly Rumours at St. John's College, Oxford, along with future editor of *Q*, Mark Ellen on bass. Despite this rocking pedigree from the new PM the Cool Britannia party has received criticism over the years, including Noel Gallagher himself:

'I just thought, if the Prime Minister of England wanted to see me, then, fuck me, I must be a fucking geezer. I was convinced that I was going to get a knighthood that night. You live and learn, don't you? I congratulated him on his success and he congratulated me on mine and we chatted about married life.'[3]

Noel was ultimately disappointed with New Labour:

'Nothing really changes, does it? Same shit, different day. What was it: "We're all middle class now". I find that really insulting. Being middle class is just one step closer to topping yourself, if you ask me. It's just the most boring thing I could ever imagine.'[4]

The connection had initially come about with a 1996 Brit Awards speech from Tony Blair about British music. The same night Oasis had won the Best Band award and gave Tony Blair a shout-out. Labour then rang Alan McGee and asked if the band could play the party conference in Blackpool, which showed a slight misunderstanding of the band's hectic schedule. Alan McGee went up to the event and presented Tony Blair with an Oasis gold disc, which was news all over the world.

'Labour got a dose of Britpop cool from us and we managed to align Oasis with them,' remembers Alan. 'I brought Noel Gallagher to the party. We got a lot of flak for going to the Cool Britannia event but I'm glad I went and it's funny that me and Noel were lurking around 10 Downing Street.'

The party itself was mayhem. There was a media scrum and the flashlights were popping as they arrived and two worlds collided right at the heart of the mainstream, as Alan McGee remembers:

'We all believed that Tony Blair was going to get the job done and that we really were going to have a revolution. When Tony Blair shook Noel's hand the cameras were flashing like crazy and that photo ended up everywhere, and then we went back to Noel's house and watched it on the news all night!'

Oasis were now being here. Soundtracking the madness at the top. Had they got too big too quick? If so, they were unapologetically enjoying the ride in a way not seen for a long time. *Be Here Now* was the peak of everything.

End-of-the-century pop culture had begun to fracture, and by 1997 Britpop was already a distant memory. There was no dominant scene any more as indie guitar bands and rock 'n' roll competed with hip-hop, girl and boy bands and pure pop for attention.

In 1997 the surrounding music scene was now moving on with Radiohead's May release of *OK Computer*, an acclaimed album with an emotive and yet far more complex style of indie. Blur's eponymous fifth album had been released that February and saw them swerve away from Britpop and embrace the American lo-fi art indie that was much closer to innovative guitar player Graham Coxon's terrain. The Prodigy's astonishing success with their June 1997 *The Fat of the Land* album somehow mashed together the best of punk, industrial, techno and rave culture into a thrilling new whole, powered by the massive success of the 'Breathe' and 'Firestarter' singles. It saw the band somehow cross over into the heart of the mainstream worldwide, with the late Keith Flint dancing around like a terrifying, yet loveable made-up marionette – a sci-fi update on the Johnny Rotten public enemy number one freak show. Even Oasis's close pals the Verve had moved to another space with their *Urban Hymns* album that was released that September. Gone were the psychedelic 'mad Richard' freakouts and 'in' was crafted songwriting and huge anthemic songs that saw them become huge that autumn. 1997 also saw great releases from the Charlatans, Mansun, Super Furry Animals and Primal Scream, with the latter's *Vanishing Point* album that was part of their dark trilogy that soundtracked the comedown from the hedonistic years.

Then, in August, Princess Diana was killed in the Paris accident. Her death dominated the news cycle for months and it was into this confusion that the country's biggest band would propel their new release. There was now a different national mood and a post-Britpop comedown. If the first two Oasis albums had caught the national mood, maybe *Be Here Now* missed it.

Arguably with its scale of ambition it was the sound of the end of the sixties, finally closing a door on that decade in 1997. It was the end of an era when records signposted history and the end of music being in the middle of culture. Of course, there have been big bands since then but they don't seem to hog the centre of national attention like Oasis did. The lineage that had started in the UK with the Beatles and run through Bowie, punk rock, Joy Division, the Smiths and the battle of Britpop, was coming to an end. Jon Savage argues that *Be Here Now* killed Britpop, but it could also be argued that the album also ended the period when rock music itself still mattered, just before the internet took over and changed everything.

Everything about Oasis in 1997 was about excess: from the record sales, the lifestyles, the notoriety, the interviews, the swagger, the drugs and the chocolate-brown Rolls-Royce that Alan McGee had given Noel the year before for making him a multimillionaire. The bigger you get, then the more detractors you have and everyone had an opinion on them. In the constant rush of pop culture, times were always changing.

'By 1997 Oasis were the biggest band in the UK which brought a different kind of pressure,' says Alan. 'Everything about the band was big. It was the peak of the "cocaine on cornflakes" period. They were living the rock 'n' roll lifestyle to the hilt and were totally open about it and it was going crazy.'

With its title taken from a book by Ram Dass, *Be Here Now* was to be the end of Oasis mark one.[5]

Like other maligned albums of excess, like the Rolling Stones' *Their Satanic Majesties Request* or the Stone Roses' *Second Coming*, *Be Here Now* sounded great in an altered state in the control room with everything cranked to the max. Its very ridiculous nature and its amped-up over-the-top grandiose pomposity are a soundtrack to a moment in time and perfectly capture that Garden of Eden moment when a band gatecrashes the hallowed ground. All the hoo-ha about the long songs and the gonzo production have now become so set in stone that there is an element of confirmation bias to them and a lazy go-to opinion on the album that is always worthy of a revisit.

Clocking in at one hour eleven minutes, *Be Here Now* was big in every way possible.

If the first album had been written in the skint twilight of dole and dead-end jobs and dreams of escape, and the second album was that rush of success and hedonistic thrills, then *Be Here Now* was the cocaine horizons, and a missive from the high-decibel toppermost. It was the culmination of a journey from council estate ne'er-do-wells to global superstardom and all its trappings.

'I know where we lost it,' Noel Gallagher told *Q* magazine in 1999. 'Down the drug dealer's fuckin' front room is where we lost it.'

And yet . . . Did they really lose it?

Music can be many things – it can be punk rock realism, post-punk minimalism, dancefloor hedonism or it can be over-the-top bacchanalian lunacy and a no-holds-barred self-indulgence. Sometimes bands are meant to be ridiculous and everything is meant to be louder than everything else in a celebration of the huge rush of being larger than life. *Be Here Now* was a psychedelic album made on cocaine. Noel Gallagher went into the OTT zone while tracking up endless guitars, with no one to rein him in, least of all himself, and this is what makes the album work.

From day one Noel had loved long outros. 'Live Forever', 'Columbia' and other early songs have, in varying guises, endless spiralling outros to the songs – it was one of the band's calling cards – the guitar pile on. Layers of guitar lines that build to the sonic climax like psychedelic mantras with Oasis free to go creatively berserk in the studio.

The original Mustique demos may be more stripped down but apart from 'All Around the World' their structures and lengths are the same; they were meant to be epic because who says a song has to be three minutes long?

Layers of ideas and guitar lines were defined as songs by Liam's ever-captivating drawling vocals bringing it all back home. There is an argument that the album is peak Liam, capturing his defining rock 'n' roll voice between youthful rage, range and power with a maturity that saw him approach songs in different ways without ever losing his Liam-ness.

'Liam's vocals are astonishing and the best thing on the album along with Alan's drumming,' Noel points out. 'Everything else was fucking dreadful and rushed. When you hear Liam's vocals isolated it is fucking really great, one of the great voices, an amazing voice. When we started I don't think he was aware of anything before the Stone Roses and that was what was great about him. Someone said to me he's the only frontman who never wanted to be Mick Jagger. Liam was a guy in a tracksuit and stood there and looked great. The band was 50/50 between his great singing and attitude and that lack of Mick Jaggerness, and the song going on behind him catchy as fuck and raw.'

Being there then, Oasis were on the plateau and revelling in it and the album reflects this with many people listening to this day wishing they truly could *be there now*.

The opening statement of intent is pure juggernaut Oasis, 'D'You Know What I Mean?', the already released opening salvo single that set the stall for the new steroid sound. Even if you turn the volume all the way down, second track 'My Big Mouth' still sounds loud, and it's Liam's voice that yet again cuts through on a track that harks back to the big wall-of-sound rushes of prime-time earlier Oasis. Owen Morris somehow manages to find space for all the noise and confusion and the endless overdubs and makes sense of the madness. Rock 'n' roll is meant to be larger than life and this sounds even bigger than that.

Written last for the album and referencing Tony Blair's October 1996 speech, 'Magic Pie' is one of Noel's stadium ballads that is actually enhanced by its endless mantra-like ending which builds up and up over an endless vista of guitars and even a choir of harmonies. It's a 'Hey Jude' live-in-the-TV-studio moment of building a sonic tsunami before clattering into a messy ending. With Noel now singing more, it gives the band a Beatloid balance, a switch in moods from John to Paul. Noel's sweeter voice on the song definitely works in the same sort of space as he explores the effect of drugs while trespassing in the rock 'n' roll garden of Eden and into the temple of delights.

With one of the band's great melody lines and its communal all-pervading chorus line, 'Stand by Me' is, according to Noel Gallagher, about 'brotherhood'. It was the second song lifted from the album as a single and reached number two in the UK chart.[6] Liam's plaintive vocal – one of his greatest deliveries – sees him dig out a huge well of emotion from his brother's lyrics. He sounds especially emotive on the bridge on yet another big ballad. The song is classic Oasis and the high point of the album as it hooks around a great verse and a huge chorus with its nod to Mott the Hoople's mighty cover of David Bowie's glam anthem 'All the Young Dudes'.

Behind the bombast there were subtleties, like the introspective lyrics of defiance in fan favourite 'I Hope, I Think, I Know',[7] a song that has that sort of melodic, anthemic rush of primetime Manic Street Preachers and words that resonate with anyone who tries to make something of their lives. With a nod to his then current beau, Meg Mathews, Noel's 'The Girl in the Dirty Shirt' is a love song and one of those quirky pop rock numbers that stops Oasis albums from being just out and out rockers or stadium ballads.

Of course, any album that is going to celebrate the overblown preposterousness of rock music is going to have a whiff of Led Zep's mystical high-decibel sound that the Roses had attempted on the *Second Coming* and Oasis's take is the voodoo-blues flavour of 'Fade In-Out'. More than any other UK city, Manchester seems to produce guitar players who like to get a bit Jimmy Page and the track holds the tension and then the explosive release of rock at its best with the long intro building, before the drums come for the full release and the song hits a groove with a surprisingly adept slide guitar from Johnny Depp.

'Don't Go Away' stands out because of its simplicity and heart-felt touching introspection, in a song about family. The production is stripped back to a chiming guitar and a beautifully scored horn section that hints at Noel's eclectic tastes and his appreciation of the artistry of Bert Bacharach. The song is carried by its wistful melody that allows the more melancholic and introspective side of the songwriter to be exposed in lyrics beautifully conveyed by Liam, who was apparently moved to tears and took his brother's lyrics and sentiment and ran with them.

The album's title track grooves along to Noel's beloved glam boogie guitar churn that takes the track to the peak Bolan boogie Quoasis that he had perfected in those long hours in the Boardwalk a few years before. It's a great groove that also features a kooky hook line played on Johnny Depp's toy piano.

The longest track on the album, clocking in at 9 minutes 20 seconds, 'All Around the World' has another 'Hey Jude' coda that makes time stand still with its hypnotic repeat. The closest sounding to early Oasis, 'It's Gettin' Better (Man!!)', sees the return of the Sex Beatles wall of sound and a melody that contrasts the guitar rush with an almost croon from the singer, with Liam repeating the title about 35 times, which somehow works. Then perhaps the best guitar solo on the album explodes out of the ether in a flurry of notes that combine a feral excitement with a melodic rush before the song goes into one of the long outros beloved by the band at the time.

As the track goes down in a flurry of noise and flames, 'All Around the World (Reprise)' fades back in with an instrumental orchestral take, as Oasis slip and slide back into 'Pepperland' with what feels like George Martin at the controls of the yellow submarine. As the track ends you can hear Brian Cannon's footsteps and a door slams shut, maybe on Oasis part one – there would be more albums and more touring but things were never going to be the same.

When a band is at its imperial Sgt. Pepper phase with an album as over the top as *Be Here Now*, it demands an 11 out of 10 sleeve to match and one last statement from the golden era of record sleeve art. After this, budgets would be slashed across the board, and with music moving to the internet and the slow death of 12-inch sleeves, there was no space left for such gonzoid adventure.

If the band were indulging in a banquet of sound and peak excess, then they needed a sleeve to match and one that also ended up poking fun at itself with the ultimate rock 'n' roll cliché of the Rolls-Royce in the pool as the central theme.

Microdot were given an open brief and a budget of £75,000

'It was an outrageous budget,' laughs Brian Cannon. 'It's not like you turn up at a hotel in the middle of the countryside with the biggest band in the country and stick a white 1972 Silver Shadow Rolls-Royce in a swimming pool for nowt. The initial idea was even more over the top. Because the album was called *Be Here Now* each member was to be photographed in a different "here" in a location of their choosing anywhere in the world.'

The band came back to Brian Cannon with their suggestions.

'Guigsy was going to be on a beach in the West Indies watching cricket and smoking a spliff. Noel was going to be on that flat top mountain called Devil's Tower in Wyoming USA, which is where the aliens land in *Close Encounters of the Third Kind*, and Bonehead wanted to be in a Rolls-Royce in a swimming pool as a homage to Keith Moon.[9] Then we were going to superimpose Liam over the top of them.'

There were some other versions of the proposed photo sessions that never came to pass, as Michael Spencer Jones recalls:

'The four images would feature a different band member in a different location and Liam was going to be in each shot making an appearance. I remember Noel initially wanted to be photographed up a tree with his guitar, and Alan wanted his photo to be in an East End pub. In the end we went with the Rolls-Royce shot because it was the most striking idea and we didn't have the time to fly around the world to do the shots.'

After going through several ideas for a location for the shoot, like Lord Astor's Cliveden House in Berkshire, where the Profumo scandal of the sixties had taken place, they eventually settled on the former home of Victor Lowness, the *Playboy* magnate, Stocks Hotel in Hertfordshire. It had a swimming pool in front of the large house for the Rolls-Royce and an air of the decadence of wild parties in the seventies, making it the perfect location for the 16 April shoot.

Of course, Microdot were not going to stop there, and in the tradition of some of the Oasis sleeves there would be random artefacts and objects placed in shot.

Brian Cannon: 'We knew that whatever was put on the sleeve would be dissected with the band being so big, so let's play with that and get them all at it. So we took Liam and Noel to the BBC props warehouse in White City and literally chose objects at random. And what I predicted would happen, happened.'

The sleeve is full of Easter eggs like the 1955 Zündapp Bella scooter owned by Liam, which was a neat nod to the band's partial mod roots, while the calendar at the front displays the album's release date. Originally set to 3 September it had to be photoshopped for the new release date of 21 August. Also photoshopped out was the top of a phone box[10] in the pool that was too distracting, parts of the tree in the background, and the arms of the clock next to Alan White that hints at the timeless nature of the band.

In the background on the other side of the pool Noel is looking through a telescope at the inflatable globe placed maybe as a part homage to the sleeve of *Definitely Maybe*. The globe is on top of an amp with a sky blue (of course!) Fender Jag leaning on it – an interesting choice of guitar as he was an Epiphone or Les Paul player. Guigsy was getting out of the swimming pool next to a sixties-style television which has the album cover of Pink Floyd's *Ummagumma* on it.

'That Floyd album is my favourite all time sleeve because the artwork on that cover goes on and on,' explains Brian.

The day before, a crane had lowered the Roller, hired from a scrapyard, into the swimming pool and on to its frame of scaffolding before the pool was refilled, which took all night, and the water was then tinted blue so it could be seen in the shot.

Inevitably the whole process attracted a lot of attention. The tabloids were there with a photographer posing as a guest at the hotel, which was still open, lurking in the bushes and taking photos for a spread. Of course the resulting article guessed totally wrongly the significance of each item on the sleeve, as Brian Cannon remembers:

'The *Sun* had a story about us saying that the objects we picked had all these Beatles and Stones references, which was hogwash. They were saying stuff like Noel had picked a telescope because John Lennon once had one. They made it all up. I think that the only thing they got right was the number plate reference on the Rolls-Royce.'[11]

One of the generators blew out, meaning in the end it was the daylight shots that were used instead of the more atmospheric night-time sessions which came with a party vibe described by Michael Spencer Jones as 'Alice in Wonderland meets Apocalypse Now'. It's a description which captures the resulting artwork and the Jill Furmanovsky spread of images of the band for the inside sleeve in a snapshot of a very different, crazy time.

But then what's the point of rock 'n' roll if you can't get ridiculous now and then?

34

WHERE DID IT ALL GO WRONG?

In 1973 at the peak of his notoriety, the world's then best footballer and the real fifth Beatle, George Best, was in the middle of one of his periods away from the game. Staying in a hotel, he was in bed drinking champagne with a scantily clad Miss World with £25,000 in cash scattered around the room when the porter walked in and, looking at the player, famously said, 'Tell me, George, where did it all go wrong?'

Just like the legendary player, Oasis were suspended in success. The 'coke years' had burned bright and burned fast and *Be Here Now* was the pinnacle. But then it eventually caused burnout for Noel.

'These days people see *Be Here Now* as where it all started to go wrong for Oasis,' ponders Alan McGee, 'but I still believe in that album. There was way too much coke in the studio and it affected the sound because coke makes everything top end and no bass, but its sheer scale makes it work.'

Released on a wave of expectation and excitement, the album was a blur of steroid statistics. At the end of day one in the UK it had sold over 424,000 and by the Saturday this was up to 663,389, making the album the fastest selling in British history. In the USA it went in at number two on 152,000 sales and was only 771 copies short of being a straight-in number one. In the years since, the album has racked up 9 million sales, defying the notion that it was some sort of flop. To this day it remains a fan favourite in defiance of the reviews and even some of the key players behind its creation.

Ironically released to the best reviews of their career, hindsight now claims that this was where Oasis 'fucked it up'. For some it's a big and bloated album fired by the tidal wave of coked-up excess that the band had surfed, yet what makes the record is that it is a snapshot of the madness and draws you into its over-the-top *Apocalypse Now* vibe. Maybe it was a measure of how dour rock music had become in the mid-nineties, how sensible its ambitions were, that a record as ridiculous and dayglo and bombastic as *Be Here Now* was judged a failure.

Initially, though, the reviewers had been tripping over themselves to praise the record, reacting to the negative press that *(What's the Story) Morning Glory?* had received and then watching as that album caught the moment and sold 22 million copies. It felt like everyone was willing the new album to be a classic before they had even listened to it. Then there was a collective change of heart and *Be Here Now* was judged a failure and a bloated coke-inspired rock folly. The critical consensus was reflected by writers like the late Dan Lucas on Under the Radar website who summed up the new zeitgeist: '*Be Here Now* is more than a bit shit. It is nothing new to say that it is an overblown mess: over-produced, with too much of everything, coked-up and excessive in every regard.'

A year after its release Owen Morris was still bemused: 'I said to Marcus, *Be Here Now* a disaster? And he said it sold 9 fucking million copies . . . that's not a fucking disaster.'

Few records have invoked so many extremes so quickly. Extremes in ideas, ambition, sound, recording and in chaos and execution, and then, on release, in reaction. It was all too much, as someone once sang, for some fans and reviewers who still wanted the shorter sharp songs of the debut album and not the longer OTT mantra-type songs of the new Oasis. Since its release it's become the most divisive album of the nineties. It's the album that Jon Savage claimed 'killed Britpop' or the *NME* called 'one of the daftest records ever made'. It was called 'a monster that cannot and will not be contained' in a perceptive review by the late and great Dele Fadele in *Vox*, while *Rolling Stone*, despite embracing the melodies, thought that it was 'music built for impact, not explanation'.

The last big album before the internet took over saw a level of security for the review copies that annoyed critics; who were given preview copies on cassettes after they had signed contracts and promised that no one else could listen to them, which, as Alan McGee points out, really pissed people off:

'The press now had it in for the band. It was particularly difficult for Oasis, who were seen as a people's band, like your mates in the pub to have this corporate type of campaign which didn't suit them.'

Noel Gallagher agrees: 'Everything that you could write about Oasis had been written, so the only thing that was interesting to say was to start slagging us off. *Be Here Now* actually got good reviews at first because as this editor told me, everybody had slagged off *Morning Glory* and it made the press look like dick-heads, because then the people spoke and it sold millions. So they weren't going to get caught out the second time . . . '

These days it's even sniffed at by its prime creator, who sees *Be Here Now* as where the band 'lost it'.

Noel: 'If I had taken a year off I might have written songs like "Little by Little" and "Go Let It Out" and that would have made all the difference to that album. I've come round to it over the years and I get why people like it, I love "D'You Know What I Mean?" I love "My Big Mouth". I've recently started playing "Stand by Me" and Liam sounds great on it and people fucking love that song.

It's probably the best song on the album but we blew the chance to be really super stratospheric because there was nobody telling us what to do and that was our Achilles heel. We signed to Creation for that freedom but there were times we could have fucking done with someone saying 'take a step back, nine minutes is too long for a song!'

Years later, Owen Morris describes the final album mix as 'terrible', and Noel Gallagher agrees: 'It is shocking. All the things you shouldn't do when you're mixing a record, we did tenfold. We really should have given it to somebody with a fresh perspective to mix. Coyley and Phil, my pals from Manchester, summed this album up best, saying, "It was just meant to be played once, on that day, high as a kite, preferably in the park, pissed – then never listened to again,"' he laughs.[1]

The lazy clichéd dismissal of it as the 'coke album' though, overlooks a great sprawling psychedelic work that mirrors the cranked-up mid-nineties when the UK came out of its shell. The mystical toppermost that so few get to see turned out to be a plush studio deep in the night with the music pouring out of the speakers full-blast, with band members and producers tranced out by the volume and the drugs. 'Full of cocaine, bottles of Fanta and fried chicken,' as Noel quipped, cranking everything up, piling on ideas and untouchable in the rarified atmosphere of the runaway success of a band in their imperial phase with no outside influence in a gated studio where time stands still. A place where you feel like you live forever and the world melts away and everything is done to excess.

Make it louder! Longer! More of everything! It's the rock 'n' roll dream!

For many fans, though, *Be Here Now* is the ultimate Oasis album – it's layer upon layer of Oasis at the peak of their creative madness. Maybe for those caught in the crossfire of its creation it must be exhausting, but with headphones on it's a real trip and a psychedelic masterpiece.

These days Owen Morris treasures that crazy period of those first three Oasis albums:

'Working with that band, how much can you fuck that up. Seriously? It sounded amazing because of Liam's fucking singing and Noel's fucking songs. *Be Here Now* was pretty fucking chaotic to make but it got made and mastered and came out with Brian Cannon's very astute, yet again, fucked-up cocaine artwork. Then I did a few more B-sides and after that Marcus said to me, "I think you should step back from Oasis." I said, "I'll wait until I don't get asked", and I didn't get asked again. I had got away with it but then Noel gave up coke and Brian was gone, and they didn't want me back. They wanted to move on. It broke my heart!

'But I had a really good time for fucking two and a bit years, and it pays for my fucking wonderful life. When I consider how many drugs we were on and how mad everything was, it's amazing people didn't kill each other!'

To this day the producer still can't listen to the album. And yet, maybe Oasis didn't stall with *Be Here Now* . . . It copped the back-lash for a scene that the band had never really been part of from people who still hadn't forgiven them for gatecrashing it. For them the band were asking for it and had got too high too soon.

Like Tony Blair's New Labour, they had coasted in on a wave of optimism and excitement and then crashed and burned, and yet the band's confused legacy survived much better than the government.

The album may be full of coke confidence and Manc swagger cranked to 10 but already the paranoia that comes as the downside to the white line was kicking in, and there are already streaks of unprecedented self-doubt in the grooves.

Over the years Noel Gallagher has looked on the album with disdain, calling it his 'coke record'. He has often stated that he would like to one day remix the album and remove the excess guitars and the sonic bluster, shave the long endings and find the songs inside the tsunami of sound. It would be an interesting exercise, like Paul McCartney's remixes of *Let It Be* where he removed his hated Phil Spector layers of gunk from the original songs. But while it would be great to hear the songs breathe, there is something quite addictive about *Be Here Now*'s ridiculousness and its ludicrous over-the-top rush of ideas and guitars.

A month after its release, the second single from the album, 'Stand by Me', was released on 22 September and reached number two in the charts. The anthemic song was part inspired by a phone call Noel Gallagher had with his mother, who like all mothers was worried if he was eating properly, referring to the guitarist's endless diet of Pot Noodles. Taking his mother's advice, he cooked up a Sunday roast which inspired the song's opening line before the song picks up on its varied themes and riffs around love.

It was released with the rocking Oasis rush of '(I Got) The Fever' hooking around a big Liam vocal and a twisting and turning lead line. Sung by Noel, 'Going Nowhere' was peak Bacharach and orchestrated, while the standout 'My Sister Lover' was lost as a B-side, with its big chorus and lyrics of spiritual self-doubt and its title perhaps nodding back to the Boardwalk days of Debbie Turner's band.

'I don't think it's about my band,' she ponders. 'I don't even know what the words are, to be honest. Noel just likes words and phrases and starts with that. It'd be nice if it was a tribute to us, but I don't think it is. Maybe he was listening to Big Star at the time whose song we took our name from.'

The single's striking artwork is of a middle-aged couple snapped in the seventies looking into each other's eyes and caught the theme of the song in a homespun way that resonated. The photo looked like the sort of faded photograph on every mantelpiece up and down the country and was chosen by Brian Cannon.

'With the single called "Stand by Me", the artwork made me think that it needed a shot of a couple in love celebrating the sanctity of marriage looking at each other,' recalls Brian. 'The couple were my ex-girlfriend's grandparents and the picture was taken in the late seventies in Bethnal Green in their house, and it looked amazing which is why I chose it. Her father, who took that photo, also took pics for the Loch Lomond and Knebworth brochures. The mass wedding shot on the back was a different kind of love and came from a photo library. It's a scene from the Unification Church joint wedding held at Jamsil Main Stadium in 1992 and all the people who had got married only met each other that morning, which I thought was an interesting twist but it's still the theme of stand by me . . . '

Like the album the single was an OTT portal to a time when rock 'n' roll really mattered.

Be. Here. Now.

Despite everything, Oasis were now just about the biggest band on the planet.

35

ALL AROUND THE WORLD

The band were still on tour when the third and final single from the album and also their last single on Creation was released on 12 January 1998. 'All Around the World' was one of the oldest songs written by Noel Gallagher going back to the Boardwalk days, and the lengthy track, which ran to almost nine and a half minutes, remains the longest song to get to number one in the UK.

'With "Supersonic", I had worried I was never going to write another song after that 'cos I thought it sounds that good,' remembers Noel. 'Two days later I superseded it by about 50 fuckin' times. The reason we didn't record that song then is because there wasn't enough money in Creation Records' bank balance to pay for the production.'

The video was a perfect match and cast the band back into 'Pepperland' in their own yellow submarine. Directed by Jonathan Dayton and Valerie Faris it was as detailed and lavish as the album and took months, and a big team of animators, to complete.

The B-sides were made up of the classic Oasis stomp of the Noel-sung 'The Fame', left over from the Mustique sessions, which sees him looking at the wreckage of the hotel room of fame itself. Almost like a precursor to his post-Oasis solo work, 'Flashbax' slips from seventies rock to a trippy bridge with its whistling solo. The final cut is a cover of the Rolling Stones' 'Street Fighting Man'.

The artwork was inspired by a photograph now known as 'Writing in the Sand, Miami Beach, February 1964', taken by Paul McCartney out of the hotel window on the Beatles' first American tour, that snapped the band's names written in the sand, while they were recording their second appearance on *The Ed Sullivan Show*. The Oasis sleeve is a striking update taken by Brian Cannon on Bournemouth beach because the avid Wigan Athletic fan was there for an awayday and needed the shot. He had to borrow Dorset Fire Brigade's extendable ladder to get the correct perspective and created a simple but highly effective image and another cool pop culture nod.

While the single hit number one in the UK the band were out on a world tour. This time the wheels stayed on. Despite most of the American interviews and reviews seeming to expect them to implode at any moment, they managed to complete an American tour which Noel has great memories of:

'When we went on the Be Here Now tour it was fucking brilliant. We had such a laugh. It was just that we truly didn't give a fuck, and people loved us for it.'

They were still genuinely dangerous rock 'n' roll stars in a field of jobsworths, or as Noel explained to the *Melody Maker* in March 1998, 'You're a rock star for crying out loud. Rock stars aren't supposed to be well behaved.'

The support on the American tour was an interesting choice. Cornershop, the Anglo-Indian indie crossover band whose compelling mix of scratchy Velvet Underground chords, sitar drone and almost mantra-like Indian vocals collided with catchy indie tunes, noise and psychedelia, making them an enticing prospect.[1]

On paper, the bands would seem poles apart but Oasis's willingness to mess with the formulae was often overlooked. Cornershop were captivating sonic adventurers who were about to score a much-loved number one hit that February with the Norman Cook remix of their 'Brimful of Asha'. Noel got in touch and invited Cornershop out on their upcoming American tour, which bemused the band initially.

The band's singer-songwriter Tjinder Singh told the Oasis Podcast, 'Liam was in a hotel room and he heard a song ['6am Jullandar Shere'] on MTV. . . [and] their manager Marcus Russell had seen us in New York . . . He described us to them as "The Velvet Underground with sitars" and that was it sold.'[2]

Early in 1998 the two bands set off on the American leg of the Be Here Now tour.

'It was big-scale and it was wonderful. Everyone really got on and we had a good laugh with them.'

On the tour Noel Gallagher would perform on stage with Cornershop playing bass on '6am Jullandar Shere' before recording 'Spectral Mornings' with the band, adding cool guitar textures and riffs to the track that somehow collides the Velvets to Trad India in a perfect groove. Coolly, the 14-minute track also ended up being planned as the world's longest remix – a staggering 24 hours long! Tjinder Singh still enthuses about Noel Gallagher's work on the song:

'He didn't just do a couple of guitar lines . . . He must have done about 15 takes of different types of guitars.'[3]

The bands reconvened a few years later when Cornershop played one of the three nights Oasis headlined at Finsbury Park in 2002.

'For us, it was great,' says Tjinder. 'We weren't bottled off. We did the gig, and there were certainly a lot of bottles of piss going around, but that's just how it goes when you've got a crowd like that.'

In the stopgap between albums proper, November 1998's *The Masterplan* was the greatest hits album that only consisted of B-sides. The reverse of their singles had always been a fascinating undercard that showcased the other side to Oasis. Often introspective acoustic songs that contrasted with the A-side anthems, sometimes interspersed with rockers that also underlined the fact that the band were the last great B-side band. This justified a compilation of their flipsides and it would go on to sell 3 million copies.

The sixties and the seventies were the golden age of the B-side, with seven-inch singles released as two song missives. Pocket money saved up, you already were in love with the A-side but the great bands always had a classic B-side. The Beatles had pretty well invented the concept with songs like 'Rain', 'I Am the Walrus', 'Revolution' and 'Strawberry Fields Forever'. In the seventies Marc Bolan continued the tradition along with Bowie and in punk the Sex Pistols' B-sides were all killer, while in the eighties Johnny Marr, being a pop culture classicist, made sure the Smiths also delivered great B-sides. But it was Oasis who venerated the form and maybe, arguably, ended up being the greatest B-side band of them all.

'As much as it was good have those great B-sides, I wish I'd have saved some of them for *Morning Glory*, or *Be Here* Now and then that would have made the album,' ponders Noel. 'Then a part of me thinks it's way cooler opening a stadium show with three B-sides. Nobody else can do it.'

The ability to almost hide classics was a sign of just how strong that original creative rush was for Noel Gallagher, and when they were collected together on *The Masterplan* it seemed far less a stopgap to fill in between albums than a necessary statement and a celebration of the B-side culture, almost a stand-up new album in its own right.

The title track 'The Masterplan' came with a fantastic L.S. Lowry pastiche cartoon video that had Liam and the band as matchstick men swaggering around the terraced streets of Manchester, paying homage to their northern roots with nods to Blackpool and the Johnny Roadhouse guitar shop, before they all slope off into different doors on a terraced street just like the Beatles in the *Help* film.

Any album that opens with 'Acquiesce' is off to a great start and the Sex Beatles rocker is Oasis at their very best and a firm fan favourite. 'Underneath The Sky', originally the B-side of 'Don't Look Back in Anger', is a warm and convivial romp that is like one of Slade's less raucous mid-seventies works. The other B-side of 'Some Might Say', 'Talk Tonight' is one of Noel's plaintive acoustic workouts and one of the most popular songs on the album.

The B-side of 'Stand by Me', 'Going Nowhere' sees Noel play out his Bert Bacharach fixation with an orchestrated slice of magic which makes you yearn for a whole album of this stuff maybe in the future? Going back deep in the archives 'Fade Away' was a slice of wall-of-sound early Oasis, with Bonehead's searing guitar a constituent part of its snarling appeal when it was on the B-side of 'Cigarettes & Alcohol'. Dwarfed by 'Wonderwall', 'The Swamp Song' always felt more like an incidental album cut than a B-side. With two minutes shaved from it, the live version of 'I Am the Walrus' is quintessential Oasis – one of those covers that owns the song. Also from 'Cigarettes & Alcohol', 'Listen Up' could easily have slipped on the debut album like a mix between 'Live Forever' and 'Supersonic' but with its own wonderful, twisting, turning melody. The B-side of 'Roll with It', 'Rockin' Chair' is one of the great early Oasis songs, with its yearning vocal and heart-melting melody. 'Half the World Away' already seemed permanently entrenched in popular culture.

As a stark contrast the other B-sides from the same single '(It's Good) To Be Free' is churning, drawled, cranked guitar Oasis with a touch of Neil Young to its big guitar hooks. The B-side of the more recent 'D'You Know What I Mean?', and an older song that was once mooted to be on *(What's the Story) Morning Glory?*, 'Stay Young' walks the tightrope between being melancholic and raucous with an almost pleading chorus – yet again, it could have easily sat on *Be Here Now*.

Perhaps their peak B-side single was 'Some Might Say', which provides 'Headshrinker', a glam rock stomp with a slapback vocal and a big boogie riffola, while the final track on the compilation is the title track sung by Noel with an orchestral backing. It's a song of baroque pop reflection with some great backwards guitars on it – the B-side of 'Wonderwall', it is a genuine fan favourite and had taken on a life of its own.

The conceptual artwork also saw the first change in the band's logo, as Brian Cannon explains:

'The packaging concept was Noel's idea. The front cover is a photo by James Burns of a young kid who is meant to be Noel Gallagher teaching his elders sitting in the classroom about music. It's like a comment on the world trying to figure out how the band did it. On the blackboard there is the musical notation for the song "The Masterplan", which we had had to get a musicologist to write as, like most musicians, Noel can't read or write music. Building on that concept the whole album packaging looks like a school report, so to fit in with that we changed the Oasis logo to look like a school crest.'

Tidying up the past and not planned at the time, *The Masterplan* was the last album Oasis would release on Creation Records. Moving forwards, Noel was already back in the studio that autumn demoing new songs for the mooted fourth Oasis album.

Over the next 18 months they would drastically change nearly every part of their operation and a new Oasis would emerge like a phoenix from the ashes.

36

OASIS 2.0

After a half-time team talk from the wily player manager, Oasis took to the pitch for the second half with a reshaped team that, despite a change of shirt and logo, was still recognisable as the overwhelming force that had swamped the opposition in the first half. The star striker was still there, full of swagger as the new look squad switched from their high-decibel style to a more stripped-down, sophisticated modern system where a subtle, patient build-up was utilised. It took the fans some time to get used to it, but as the years have rolled past the shift from frantic kick-and-rush to tippy-tappy shapeshifting music has revealed many hidden gems...

There was simply nowhere to go after *Be Here Now* – it was physically impossible to get louder. Oasis had maxed-out on everything. A smart operator would move somewhere new, and within a couple of years a very different Oasis would emerge from the glorious wreckage. There would be a profound shift in and around the band that saw them carry on in much-changed form. Part of this was down to Noel Gallagher's change of lifestyle.

'I wanted some time out if only to write some songs, but the party just carried on round at my house and I was fucking out my mind all the time' he recalls. 'Then at one party an actress said, "I love this house do you want to sell? I'll give you three million quid for it." She phoned her dad and got a banker's draft and I sold my house at a party. I then bought a place in the country, because I thought, that's what you do. The only thing was it was just on the edge London where you could get the fucking tube so the party just moved out there and people were staying for fucking three days.

'If the biopic ever gets made I'd be getting up and it stinks of fags and booze and I open the fridge and there's a stranger in there asleep.

'I thought "this has got to stop", but other people were not having it. Everyone else carried on so I had to get rid of all these people and some of them were my mates. It was a big sea change and difficult times. For a lot of people cocaine was not a drug and they would say, "I get it, all right, you've stopped drinking but you will still have a line of cocaine, won't you?" So I had to move on.'

Noel also had panic attacks, which are far from a trivial affliction, with the heart suddenly pounding, shortness of breath and palpitations that feels like a heart attack. He'd checked into hospital in Detroit on tour and a few other times feared for the worst, later quipping: 'I wouldn't have made a good dead rock star. I'm not handsome enough.'

'I had panic attacks for only a few weeks, but they stopped after I got some sleeping tablets and started drinking water. Once I had a month off the booze and the drugs it turned into two months and I was like, "I prefer this now."'

For their own survival Oasis also streamlined and changed – soon there would be a new line-up, a new producer, new art director and even a new logo and a new sound – as they stepped back from the brink and reconvened without the pressure of being a generational behemoth. Burned out from the pressure of having to write up to 20 songs a year, Noel opened up the songwriting, starting with Liam's contribution to the upcoming album, 'Little James'.

The band was beginning to shift gears. There were some big changes coming.

In November 1999 the most iconic label of nineties indie was gone when Alan McGee closed down Creation.

'It had got too corporate and not what I got into rock 'n' roll for,' says Alan. 'It was not punk rock anymore. I decided to end the label on a high and the last release was going to be the upcoming Oasis album that they were working on, but Sony pulled the plug on Creation when they heard I was leaving.'

'I stepped back,' explains Noel, 'all my friends from the nineties had moved on and I was happy in my little bubble . . . and that went on for ages. It was not a conscious decision but it felt natural. After Creation we didn't want to sign a major deal and somehow we convinced Sony to give us our catalogue back and start our own label.'

The birth of Noel's first child, daughter Anaïs, in January 2000 had also focused his mind. A profound change in life, it meant the end of the extended teenage phase of loose living and led him to see the world in clearer terms. Without the mood-enhancing drugs, and as a reaction to the *Be Here Now* behemoth, things were changing fast. A new team would soon be in place with a new producer and not Owen Morris. Also, there would be no more Brian Cannon.

'For five years I had been in the eye of that hurricane and saw it all and it was remarkable how down to earth and sane they were with what was going on', says Microdot's founder. 'It all went a bit Pete Tong after that, the band left Creation and they stopped working with Owen. There was no animosity, it just had to change just like when the Beatles didn't work with Robert Freeman anymore. It's all to do with the progression.'[1]

The drugs, the music, the lifestyle was insane and life was good at the top of the holy mountain, but like any smart operator they had to change. Drugs and alcohol were discouraged in the studio, which would bring different problems, as Noel explains:

'I felt we needed to change it up. We couldn't carry on doing that forever. I didn't know what it was we were going to change into. Instead of taking five years out, which is what mysterious rock stars do, Liam kept asking, "What are we doing? Where are we going?" and the band being a responsibility meant I wrote my way through it with the next album.'

At the end of the year Noel Gallagher had started demoing the songs for what would be the band's upcoming fourth album, *Standing on the Shoulder of Giants*. As ever, the prep was meticulous.

The new songs were initially recorded at his home studio set-up and then he took them to Wheeler End Studios in Buckinghamshire at Huckenden Farm to finish them off.[2] It was close friend Paul Weller who had introduced Noel to the residential studio after he had worked there a lot himself.

The studio was set up by the blues guitarist Alvin Lee in 1980 and since then the studios had also been used by George Harrison, Robbie Williams and many others. Between 1998 and early 1999 the new songs were demoed with the assistance of Mark Coyle and Paul Stacey,[3] creating a mini band within the band with Paul becoming more and more important to the creative process over the next few years. The engineer had originally joined the band as an additional keyboard player to play the string parts on the Be Here Now tour. Noting his musical prowess, Noel then brought him along for the sessions to record 'Teotihuacan' for the *X-Files* soundtrack and then the new album demos. He also played bass and keyboards as well as lead guitar on new songs like 'Fuckin' in the Bushes' and the guitar solo in 'Roll it Over', backwards guitar to 'Who Feels Love?' and acoustic guitar to 'Where Did It All Go Wrong?' Paul Stacey continued to work with the band on all their other albums, co-producing with Mark 'Spike' Stent the band's first live album/video, *Familiar to Millions*, in 2000, and to this day still works with Noel on his solo albums.

All the new demos were sung by Noel sketching out the lyrics and melodies apart from the first song that Liam had written for the band since Noel joined, called 'Little James'. With the luxury of time Noel prepped the songs' arrangements and sounds from song sketches on his Walkman using the studio to demo the songs perfectly. More pre-planning. More control. Keep it tight.

The demos saw a different Oasis beginning to emerge from the wreckage. Maybe as a reaction to the bombast and chaos of the last album and a reaction to the post-Knebworth come-down.

Album written, the band met in London early in 1999 to rehearse. Then in April/May they moved their operation to the south of France for the recording sessions at the Château de La Colle Noire, a stone castle up in the hills near Montauroux, not far from Cannes. Draped in vines and once owned by Christian Dior, the castle had a studio. Like an updated take on the Rolling Stones's famous early seventies jaunt to the south of France to Villa Nellcôte on the Cote D'Azur to record their *Exile on Main St.* double album, they turned the castle into their studio and it was here that during the summer Oasis began to record their fourth studio album.

'We fucked off to the south of France for three months and grew sideboards and we ended up looking like a cross between the Wurzels or if we had just got out of the Maze prison in the seventies,' laughs Noel.

In a deliberate move to break habits and to push the sonic envelope, Noel had ditched his backline and invested in new gear. This was a roots and branches musical reconfiguration which saw him buy different old guitars, weird pedals, amps and, aided with the luxury of no immediate deadline, saw him take the chance to experiment and find new sonic textures.

This time there was also no Owen Morris. Getting away from the juggernaut sounds and lifestyles of their *Be Here Now* period was part of the new regime and Oasis brought in Mike 'Spike' Stent to co-produce the album with Noel.[4] The producer was seasoned in this out of the box way of working and had carved away much of the soundscape of modern pop, deconstructing and then constructing new musical landscapes.

Spike Stent had made a name for creating very of-the-moment mixes and his career seems to encapsulate all corners of modern pop culture. From his mixing on the fly with KLF in the late eighties that sealed his reputation in creating captivating 12-inch singles remixes, he went on to work with the likes of Massive Attack, Björk, Neneh Cherry, Madonna, Mansun, Beth Orton, Depeche Mode and Spice Girls and his mixing on U2's *Pop* changed their sound drastically.

With his armoury of new pedals and a willingness to fuck with the Oasis sound, Noel had found a keen collaborator. The producer's love of guitar effects pedals was across the board, even putting the beats, vocals and keyboards through a sonic manipulation. Looking for new sounds without tipping over into avant-garde noise he kept everything frameworked within the song. Nudging the band away from their partial sixties framing it allowed their psychedelia to be upgraded and updated with loops, and studio trickery was added to coax their songs into darker, sparser, almost industrial and yet pop soundscapes that was very much of the end of the millennium.

It was during the recording that the final and most visible change to the band occurred when first Bonehead and then a couple of weeks later Guigsy both left the band. The guitarist left the group to officially 'concentrate on other things', later adding that he quit because being in the band was no longer fun with the post *Be Here Now* regime and he wanted to spend more time with his children.

Two weeks later, days before the album was meant to be completed, Guigsy felt the time was 'opportune' for him to leave before the nine-month tour planned for the following year. Noel Gallagher saw it coming:

'I found it a really uninspiring time to be in the band because unbeknown to us at the time Guigsy and Bonehead were angling to leave. McGee was winding down Creation and there was this strange and not very uplifting atmosphere.

'Success had hit Guigsy the hardest. He was not ready for it all. When we all started we were on the same level musically but then I got at the turbocharger and I was writing all the songs and when they were orchestral things the rest of them thought, "Where am I going to fit in with all this orchestral shit?" and I don't blame them for that.

'I used to feel sorry for them but Guigsy would be constantly stoned and he would either not say a word for two days or be very nervous about doing gigs. It was a relief for him when he decided to call it a day. Not that I've ever spoken to him about it but I knew he was going to be alright sitting in the garden, watching cricket and smoking weed without having me and Liam arguing about who was the greatest Rolling Stone or having a proper barney over what was the greatest Christmas single of all time. So I guess it was kind of a relief for Guigsy to be away from all that!'

The core of the band, which was now multi-instrumentalist Noel, Liam and Alan White, continued with a bit of help from Paul Stacey who Noel described as having 'an incredible ear for guitar sounds'. They replaced the recorded bass and guitar parts from the recently vacated members, with Mark Coyle adding electric sitar and some other parts.

'I didn't find the music around me very inspiring,' says Noel. 'I'd had my big bang moment when everything that I had learned as a teenager I'd put into practice and made those earlier albums. It was now a case of what happens next? I'd be a liar if I said I enjoyed the chaos. Two members had left but of course we're going to carry on and get other people. I think people got bored of the chaos of Oasis particularly our American record company who hated us. Some of the people in the office used to look at us with real disgust because we wouldn't do anything and not meet anyone we had to.'

At an August press conference Noel and Liam confirmed the pair had left the band, announcing:

'They've both got kids and I suppose it's a natural thing that they don't want to leave their families. We've got to respect that. It's no use kicking in Bonehead's door and going, "You've got to come on tour". We could see it coming, but we didn't expect to be sat here today saying this. It's a bit of a bummer, but like I say, the show's got to go on. We were a bit shocked at first but we've just got to get on with it. We've got a record to finish off today and we've got to go and tour it.'

When asked about who would be joining, Liam quipped: 'They've got to be a tad taller than me, have a nice taste in shoes, have a decent haircut – and not be a Man U fan.' His brother added: 'There might not be a stampede to join the band anyway, we've got a bit of a bad reputation.'

The recording then reconvened to London at Olympic Studios where Spike Stent had learned his trade as an engineer to do the overdubs and finish re-recording the former members' parts.

The band then sourced two new members who would join the band after the album was recorded: Andy Bell, the guitarist from Ride and Hurricane #1, who switched to bass, and after Johnny Marr said he could step in while they were looking, Gem Archer, the singer/guitarist from Heavy Stereo joined to entwine his guitar with Noel's – with both switching lead parts instead of Bonehead playing barre chords and Noel taking the lead.

In many ways both new members were already part of the family, both having been in Creation bands, and they all knew each other from various gigs, festivals and parties. There had been a time in

1989 when Ride were Alan McGee's favourite new band in the world. Their youthful, gliding neo-shoegaze melting into blissed-out songs broke through on their debut October 1990 *Nowhere* album which was a critical and commercial success. From County Durham and initially in the Edge, then Whirlpool, Gem Archer was the guitarist and singer in Heavy Stereo, whose glam-fused indie stompers had also seen them become a core Creation band. They had supported Oasis and were on the Gallagher radar.

Andy Bell: 'I had moved to Sweden at the start of 1999 soon after my first kid was born, and was living a very quiet life after putting an end to Hurricane #1. A friend of mine called Cliff Jones, who had been a journalist for a guitar magazine and interviewed me in the early nineties, had put a band together called Gay Dad, and I went to see him when they came to Stockholm, and then a few weeks later he called me to see if I could take over last minute for their guitarist who was ill or something. It was for a week of gigs in Germany I think. I said yeah, and then Cliff ended up telling the music press I was joining Gay Dad. This wasn't true but anyway it never happened because either Paul or Liam Gallagher saw the article and apparently said let's get Andy for Oasis. So I get this call inviting me to come and audition and I flew over the next day.

'I blagged it on the bass, I didn't really know what I was doing but I managed to do enough to get the gig. The four strings of a bass are the same as the first four strings of a guitar, and I knew the songs on guitar, so I just played the root notes. The next part of the audition was us all going to the pub. I didn't disgrace myself or ask any stupid questions so at some point Marcus Russell appeared and said, "Andy, the boys want you to join!"

'Back in Sweden I found a bass somewhere and spent a few hours a day for about a month teaching myself all of the bass lines inside out. At the end of 1999 we went on tour in the USA, and that was the start of 10 years of incredible highs, mad times, noise and confusion!'

The first missive from the new look Oasis was 'Go Let It Out' released on 7 February 2000, which wasted no time going to number one and selling just under half a million copies. Noel talked of the track sounding like a modern-day Beatles, not so much in xeroxing the classic sound but more in the attitude of mixing an artful approach to the cutting-edge tech and ideas of the time that Spike Stent was bringing to the proceedings.

Much anticipated, 'Go Let It Out' was a sneak preview of the new Oasis. Gone was the wall-of-sound guitars, gone was the root note bass lines, gone was the brickwall sound. The drums were loud, crisp and clear with Alan White playing against a Johnny Jenkins's 'I Walk on Guilded Splinters' drum loop that entwines with the compressed drums. The song smoulders with its cyclical bass line building up momentum layer on top of layer, holding the tension as the guitars paint their own urgent picture against the fluttering Mellotron played by Noel. Liam's voice was the only real remaining constant from the past, bringing his classic rasping vocal to the track. It added an urgency to its loping grooves as he drawled through Noel's poetic lyrics.

The accompanying video to the track directed by Nick Egan was also the first glimpse of a new line-up who were temporarily a four-piece, with Gem Archer, who like Andy Bell didn't play on the album, making his first appearance as the band mimed the song with Noel on bass. The video has Liam giving it full icon stillism in its first half, oozing his classic cool on the open platform of an old-school double-decker bus, winding its way to the band in the barn with the singer joining the temporary four-piece band with an acoustic guitar.

It may have been all change but one tradition that seemed to be standing firm in the new regime was the great B-sides. With its minor to major, almost John Barry film score shuffle, 'Let's All Make Believe', is a pretty song drenched in melancholy and a sense of loss which is beautifully delivered by Liam. Not only a great title that someone like Nick Cave at his most dark lord would have been proud of, the Noel-sung '(As Long as They've Got) Cigarettes in Hell' is another subtler piece that is built around introspective Mellotron parps with Noel singing a perfectly measured, resigned vocal over the top; it amusingly ends with a smoker's cough over a myriad of backward guitars.

Initially it was a shock not to see the Microdot/Spencer Jones creative axis artwork but the new sleeve underlined the new regime. The new art director was Simon Halfon who combined a mod's eye for the sharp and angular with the eternal cool of jazz. His CV contained covers he had worked on like the Who's *The Singles*, George Michael's *Listen Without Prejudice Vol. 1* and the Style Council's *Café Bleu*.

The striking Andrew MacPherson image was inspired by photographer René Burri's classic shot of a rooftop with tiny mysterious figures on it in São Paulo, Brazil, in 1960, with the sleeve photo taken from the rooftop of 452 Fifth Avenue of five lads playing football. Initially the image was meant to be the band but that changed when two of them had left.

Released on 28 February 2000, *Standing on the Shoulder of Giants* was the introspective hangover after *Be Here Now* and all the better for it, despite being the worst performing Oasis album so far and confounding some fans who were expecting the Oasis of old.

Curious for a band that often gets criticised for not changing, they had turned their sound upside down and inside out with drum loops, dark lyrics, introspective soundscapes and atmospheres, and a sparser yet more psychedelic sound that was quite a different proposition.

Even the album title seemed humble, perhaps giving a nod to those classics that Noel Gallagher was never embarrassed about talking about. Pissed in a pub he had taken the phrase most famously associated with Isaac Newton from the edge of the British

£2 coin and written it down on a fag packet but missed the 's' off shoulders and amusingly had also written 'bum title' instead of 'album title' next to it.[5]

Post-release, Noel has often dismissed the album, stating he made it for the sake of making an album and 'had no reason or desire to make music at the time' but this does the record a disservice.[6] It was hardly throwaway and came from a period of flux when the song-writer was digging deep into his soul and trying to make sense of his situation with, perhaps, the most personal lyrics from his career. It was not a place he was always comfortable with and later records would see him veer away again from the obviously self-confessional.

'I like the lyrics on *Standing on the Shoulder of Giants* because I was writing from a position of truth,' he says. 'That was the album where the words were not making it up as they went along. I was coming off the gear but not going into rehab and I was then slowly getting addicted to prescription drugs, which was worse and just substituting one drug for another.'

You can feel the comedown drugs in the new music.

'It was a bit of a hangover and some of the songs weren't great and original members had left. I really like the words on "Gas Panic!", "Go Let It Out" and "Where Did It All Go Wrong?" If I could have married the lyrics on that album to the tunes on *Be Here Now* that would have been great. I would give them to Liam and we would have a quick run-through and he would just do them not questioning anything and they sounded great. The lyrics are, and I won't use the word "dark", but they are quite personal to me like on "Gas Panic!", which is about drug comedown and all that shit. I was getting divorced as well so that's in there. It was all the price to pay for years of fucking partying for me because I'd been on it since 1986. Everything had been great, Madchester, the Haçienda, acid house then Oasis . . . But then there was the kind of bit where it comes to a full stop and you realise "I've got to get my finger out here" and it didn't come naturally. You're getting older and you got kids. Then after the album came out Gem and Andy joined and from that moment it was kind of steady and the next album *Heathen Chemistry* was alright and the one after, *Don't Believe the Truth,* was great.'

For some, like Richard Bowes from the excellent Oasis podcast, the album was a necessary bridge between the two halves of the band's trajectory.

'*Standing on the Shoulder of Giants* was the album Oasis needed to make, if only for themselves. It's arguably their most important, as the departure of Bonehead and Guigsy and the subsequent recruitment of Gem Archer and Andy Bell breathed new life into the band, laying the foundations for their twenty-first-century output. Aided by Mark "Spike" Stent, the wall of sound is replaced by more textured and diverse sonics, and it includes three certified classics in "Fuckin' in the Bushes", "Go Let It Out" and "Gas Panic!" as well as Liam Gallagher's first composition, "Little James", which has its detractors, but it paved the way for the likes of "Songbird".[7] The album's importance to the Oasis story should not be underestimated.

'Despite the public perception, the twenty-first-century iteration of Oasis was a far cry from the preceding years. While the singles were – broadly – representative of what the people thought they wanted, the albums showcased their sonic evolution. *Standing on the Shoulder of Giants* is the sound of two brothers and a drummer just about holding it together while everything else (record labels, relationships, even the band itself) fell apart around them, but pushing forward because they know they must.'

With the new broom in the room, Noel Gallagher was unzipping and stripping the Oasis sound and putting it back together again in a different order while creating an album of modern psychedelia. He was now moving away from the guitar, bass and drums of the Britpop era and, perhaps inspired partially by his collaboration with the Chemical Brothers a couple of years before, moving into a partial melange of electronica and guitars which had always been a big part of his musical interest. There was an ambition to do something quite different but moving a behemoth band with big audience expectations like Oasis is not that simple.

Like the Beatles in 1966/67 – this was about seeing how far you can push your music within its own framework but in modern terms. It embraced the hallmarks of the band's sound while still rolling up for a mystery tour which Noel, their most on-point critic, explains:

'When you're an oik from Longsight and you write a song called "Rock 'n' Roll Star" people think it's amazing, but if you are a slightly overweight 31-year-old with a cocaine habit and write "Rock 'n' Roll Star" in a chalet in the south of France people think you're a cunt! I wrote the first two albums in the shadows and then once the spotlight was there I kind of froze in the headlights and started to second guess myself. I think it was the pressure of the expectation of what we should be doing after *Morning Glory* when we were a huge stadium rock band, so let's make everything rock. I couldn't keep the level of songwriting up and if I could have done then I'd be in the same fucking room as Bowie and Lennon. I didn't have enough great songs and there's a couple of howlers on the album.'

The opening track 'Fuckin' in the Bushes' comes in with super compressed drums creating an industrial dance groove for the blues guitar riff to dance over. The instrumental is then cut with samples from Murray Lerner's *Message to Love* documentary about the 1970 Isle of Wight Festival that was headlined by Jimi Hendrix and the Doors; with the title of the song provided by a local resident disproving of the hippie invasion of the island, telling the film crew that there were 'Kids running around naked, fucking in the bushes . . .' The rant at the beginning of the song is the festival promoter Ricky Farr shouting at the many gatecrashers turning up for the biggest rock festival audience of all time. And to provide a neat balance to all the chaos, another older island resident is sampled on the song coda embracing the hippies, 'I love it! Room for everybody here. Yes, all are welcome . . . !'

Coming in with a loping drum groove, the album's lead-off single 'Go Let It Out' was a smouldering Oasis anthem, while a twenty-first-century psychedelia is played out in 'Who Feels Love?', which would be the second single from the album and is its most tripped-out moment. The billowing ballad delivered by Liam is a lysergic smorgasbord with all manner of reversed effects and guitar sounds shimmering and moving across the mix. That mix of electronica and head fuck sound sees the influence of the dance crossover bands like the Chemical Brothers, and even a nod to their new pals Cornershop's more mantra moments which marry the new tech of the dancefloor to the sixties psychedelia, creating a modern tech trip. Released as a single in April, it may have been their first single not to reach the top three since 1994 but was a worthwhile experiment.

Proving that there were still rockers in the new regime, the album picks up the pace with the barnstorming 'Put Yer Money Where Yer Mouth Is', which sees a classic Liam vocal that references the Doors' 'LA Woman' in parts as it rasps perfectly over a stomping track. In this period, Noel wrote few rockers like this and the prevailing mood was more introspective and downbeat, with detail and texture taking precedence.

Liam's songwriting debut, 'Little James', is a surprise as the public image of the wild rock 'n' roller is peeled back to reveal a playful piece about Liam's then partner Patsy Kensit's son, James, from her previous relationship with Jim Kerr from Simple Minds. The song celebrates that eternal Peter Pan teenage world that the best rock stars exist in.

For many people, Oasis never moved beyond the wam-bam-thank-you-glam stomping wall-of-sound anthems but there were countless examples of the band stretching out, like the massive attack of 'Gas Panic!' The song dealt with the comedown and burn-out of drug abuse and is one of the great examples of just how good Liam's vocal interpretations of his brother's lyrical inner psyche are – taking Noel's trip into the dark side of his burned-out soul and making sense of it.

With its churning Neil Young-style riff and big solo, the Noel-sung 'Where Did It All Go Wrong?' also has a whiff of Paul Weller to Noel's vocal delivery as the song title references the infamous George Best hotel room story. It's a wistful song about the rich and famous people that used to party at his house with their self-destructive problems.

With its soul-searching resignation, 'Sunday Morning Call' is another one of Noel's epic widescreen ballads and a song that he has gone on record as hating over the years. An all too detailed evocation of 'People who used to always turn up on my fucking doorstep, but at ungodly hours of the morning – and these are proper, well-off, rich, famous people, quite young. And they'd be running you through their drug and booze hell,' and the hungover emptiness of the morning after the night before.[8] It was also a metaphor for the comedown after the early years of Oasis and the Britpop hangover. Released as the third single from the album with its attendant B-sides 'Carry us All' and 'Full On', the song is hated by Noel so much that it's not listed on their *Time Flies . . . 1994–2009* compilation album.

Picking up the pace, 'I Can See a Liar' is one of the few big rock riffs on the album. Liam brings the ruckus with yet another great ribald vocal, enhanced by the tight Lennon slapback on the vocals reading the riot act. Harking back to the big sound of *Be Here Now*, 'Roll it Over' is the kind of ambitious anthem that drips the melancholic melody that Oasis always nailed. Liam's fantastic vocal gives the song a transcendental and moving power – never has he managed to sound so intense and yet so vulnerable. The song also has an epic fade-out complete with choirs and a soul-searching Dave Gilmour-type guitar picking out the notes.

Simon Halfon's sleeve design was the first Oasis album to have the title on the cover and was part two in the pretty cool concept that was played out over the album and its three accompanying single sleeves. If the 'Go Let It Out' artwork had zoomed in on the five lads having a kickabout on a roof (representing the band), then the front cover of the album was the whole New York skyline image. The 'Who Feels Love?' single had the skyline reflected in a woman's glasses and the 'Sunday Morning Call' single sleeve featured a scene from inside one of the buildings pictured on the album cover.

While losing the idiosyncratic homespun charm of the older sleeves, the new sophisticated image from photographer Andrew MacPherson of the New York skyline fading from day into night and capturing the passage of time across the sleeve, was effectively classy and underlined the stylistic musical change on the album. It was also emblazoned with the new band logo designed by Gem Archer from a suggestion by Noel who had liked the font on a guitar pedal.

Made up of a complex combination of 30 images, the resulting front cover artwork was only made possible by the recent release of Photoshop 5 and was the first known use of what is now called the 'Day to Night' technique. To get the effect Andrew MacPherson's initial raw images were taken over a 36-hour period from the top floor of 500 5th Avenue in New York as the remnants of Hurricane Charley passed by off-shore.

On release, the musical and visual gamble paid off. While never realistically in with a chance of matching the dramatic heights of their earlier albums, the release scored 600,000 UK sales and a hit album that saw Oasis settling down, almost deliberately, as a big band and not the freak show phenomenon they had become with the last record. In the USA, though, it only hit number 24 in the charts unlike the number two of *Be Here Now*. A Walmart ban for 'Fuckin' in the Bushes', cancelled tours, not grafting the US festival circuit, and music beyond the simplistic formulas of American radio was all getting in the way for the time being.

Rather than 'Where Did It All Go Wrong?', it was now a case of where would they go next?

The reconstructed band went on a world tour with their two new recruits. Andy Bell was ready:

'Even as a guitarist I initially didn't really have any idea of how to play a bass. I just knew the strings were the same notes. If the song goes A, D, G, I know where those notes are on a bass. I can busk along. I managed to do enough in the audition and then I went away and absolutely became a bass player in about two months. I did not want to mess this up. I took a massive amount of pride in nailing it to a level where a force-10 gale could be playing and I'd still be playing those basslines and playing them right. A big element of that was Alan White, who was extremely patient with me. He'd come in early and we'd practise together. A lot of the songs have got similar tempos but different basslines. "Supersonic" does not feel like "Columbia", they've all got something about them. Whatever that thing is, it's really well built.

'My whole ethos as a bass player was to get in with the kick drum and just try and be that heartbeat for the band. You've just got to be in there as a rhythm section. To stand so close to Whitey on stage, I went deaf in one ear because of the cymbals. But it was all about getting to the heart of that sound and keeping that heart pumping.'[9]

Somehow they managed to get through long legs in Japan and even tour the USA unscathed, but when they got to Europe it all fell apart. On 24 May Noel quit the tour in Barcelona after another bust-up with Liam. He then flew back to the UK, quitting overseas touring and only playing the final eight sold-out dates in Britain in

July and August, which included two shows at Wembley and the Reading and Leeds festivals.

For the European shows Noel replaced himself with Matt Deighton from Mother Earth and Paul Weller's band, who, fortunately, or because someone had a great deal of foresight, had learned the set.

The reconvened band with a returned Noel fell apart on the disastrous second night at Wembley that was planned to be recorded for the *Familiar to Millions* live album. A chaotic and heavily drinking Liam, reeling from the break-up of his relationship with Patsy Kensit, resulted in a poor show and the live recording substituted his vocals from the recent concerts in Yokohama.

Yet when the band reconvened on 15 July for the first of two nights at Bolton, the fragile line-up sounded seamless with a set of greatest hits, some recent album cuts and a killer cover of Neil Young's powerfully moving 'Hey Hey, My My (Into the Black)' in the encore.

May and June 2001 saw the wheels put back on the Oasis charabanc with the band spending a few months on the road in America on the amusingly titled 'The Tour of Brotherly Love'.

The triple-headed tour saw them share the bill with the Black Crowes with the American band's bluesey, Stonesy rock 'n' roll, and Spacehog the UK band who were big in the USA while unknown in the UK. The sucker punch of the tour name was that each band contained warring brothers. Maybe they spent the tour swapping familial tips. Now a decade old they marked this anniversary with the autumn 2001 '10 Years of Noise and Confusion Tour', which celebrated the 10 years since they were formed by playing in what were, for them, smaller venues like Manchester's 3,500 capacity Apollo, where they played two nights.

There was also a pile of new songs to attend to . . .

37

THE SOCIETY OF SPECTACLE

Pop culture in 2002 was a mix-up of the endless parade of talent show chancers who had their brief moment of glory before being quickly returned to the 'real world' while the 'judges' gloated and pumped up their own egos while throwing cabbages at the performing 'peasants'. It was also a garage rock revival bookended by the Strokes and the White Stripes, sparking a rush of energy into the scene. Meanwhile Oasis, like the Stereophonics and Coldplay, were often labelled 'dad rock' because of their loyalty to the holy trinity of guitar, bass and drums as the tools of their trade. The barbs bounced off their parkas as they still retained the mystical power of melody and connected with an audience that existed beyond the critique.

Even pop itself was no longer the centre of attention, becoming a soundtrack to the Society of the Spectacle. Everything in modern life was living in a never-ending present with pop culture, politicians and technology existing all at once. If in the sixties every Beatles single had been a cultural landmark moment, in the early noughties, it was the iPhone that was the freeze frame 'do you remember where you were?' moment in time . . .

From 2002 onwards no musical artist would stretch all the way to the cultural horizon – the best they could expect was to be, literally, an oasis in the madness.

Away from the numbers and in the time off after their Standing on the Shoulder of Giants tour, Oasis self-produced their upcoming album in Wheeler End and mixed it at Olympic. They now had an open lease on Wheeler End and a creative isolation to indulge their muse. The new album saw their next stylistic transformation, which would be less drastic than the big change after *Be Here Now* and a return to the band dynamic with the new full five-piece line-up.

'We didn't have to pretend to be something that we were not,' remembers Noel. 'We were middle-aged fellas playing guitars. It was really enjoyable and calm and we were all in the same boat and roughly the same age and we all had kids. It felt like a real band for the first time since the early days. We had our own little studio out in Wycombe doing our thing. Liam became a lot calmer because he was writing songs.

'I insisted the others write because I was struggling with writing 20 songs every two or three years and then touring. It's difficult to explain to other people who don't do it because you're the golden goose that's laid the egg a few times and they just think you must write them in your sleep.

'I remember the first get-together we had with Andy and Gem and I was like, "Have you got any songs? Let's hear them because you're not just along for the ride!" And I enjoyed that period of Oasis when everybody was contributing. Liam never said he wanted to write but he had songs. I thought "Little James" had a great childlike simplicity to it and then he came up with "Songbird" which is fucking amazing. I love that song. It's really beautiful.

'I really enjoyed being in the studio doing someone else's song. I would be waiting to be asked to play on it and just put the guitar part down. I had never had the chance just to sit there and observe it happening before and I enjoyed working on the other guys' tunes. Initially they tried to write Oasis-type songs but I said, "Just write a fucking song, and if it's good enough, we'll use it." Now all I had to do was write five songs and concentrate on the singles and make them mega, so that's why all the singles are mine, bar one or two, because the pressure was off.'

The first of these Noel written singles was 'The Hindu Times'. Released on 15 April, the song was a barnstorming statement of intent and a return to the good-time art of creating the great rock 'n' roll of their early years. If the original demo had been a slower grunge ooze, the final version is improved by its picked-up pace with a mosh-pit chorus and naggingly hooky guitar line.

While many think the song is about drugs or people on drugs, the songwriter insists it's about nothing at all as it builds up to its big chorus. The incendiary ending of the intoxicating guitar lick sounds like a heavy metal sitar, which carries on into the Simon Halfon designed cover art using the image, 'snapshot of India' by Barry Dawson from the photographer's *Arts and Crafts of India* photo book.

With wall to wall great reviews the single became the band's sixth number one in the UK. It also saw a revival of the introspective B-sides of quality songs buried just out of view. Left over from the *Standing on the Shoulder of Giants* sessions was 'Just Getting Older', a contemplative Noel-sung song of disillusionment with a way of life that he had now mostly discarded. A plaintive honest resignation note to the all-nighters of the rock 'n' roll life, it was coming to terms with, well, getting older. The second B-side, 'Idler's Dream', is an emotive love song and the only Oasis song with no guitars and drums on it, with Noel singing to a delicate and melodic piano line.

The stark black-and-white performance video was directed by the legendary British film-maker W.I.Z. whose shadowy, beautifully lit videos for the likes of Massive Attack ('Inertia Creeps'), Ian Brown ('My Star'), Marilyn Manson ('The Fight Song') and the classic mini film 'Weekender' for Flowered Up had set the standard for groundbreaking videos. Filmed at Abbey Road instead of the original idea of in the multi-coloured sensual explosion of New Delhi, the monochromatic cool of the video actually works better, especially with the iconic end shot of the two brothers sharing the mic.

Maybe it was having the time to stretch out at Wheeler End or an increased sophistication but the next Oasis single from the upcoming album, 'Stop Crying Your Heart Out', released on 17 June 2002, was a big stirring ballad perfect for pub closing time with the jukebox cranked and arms-in-the-air heartfelt rush. With a maturity and complexity to the songwriting you would expect from a 36-year-old songwriter, it underlined that Oasis had moved on from their noisier roots and were able to tap into different emotional terrain.

Liam's croon wraps itself around the song and its pulsating orchestration and the full five-minute captivating melody was an update of 'Slide Away' meets 'Don't Look Back in Anger' – the kind of yearning songs that mixed the acoustic introspection of one side of Noel's songwriting with the stadium nous of the other.

The art of darkness video, again directed by W.I.Z., was of a young woman walking through the city streets of maybe LA deep in thought, seeking her own 'stop', and ends with a twist of darkness that is edited from the TV version where she is sat on a jerrycan of petrol hinting at an act of self-immolation. It's pretty dark stuff, but the song's lament and inherent sadness touched a lot of fans. The theme of finality is further hinted at on the sleeve art with its bold 'stop' sign painted on the road somewhere in the outback of the USA in a photo taken by Andrew MacPherson for the Noel Gallagher and Simon Halfon design.

These two big hits signposted the return of Oasis and on 1 July 2002 their fifth album, *Heathen Chemistry*, was released. Named after a T-shirt Noel had bought in Ibiza with 'The Society of Heathen Chemists' written on the front of it[1] and recorded with the new line-up, it was recorded as a band. That sense of camaraderie and swagger of the group dynamic marked a move away from the introspection, dark shadows and loops of the last album while also showcasing a couple of the band's most loved anthemic ballads. For many fans, though, *Heathen Chemistry* remains a mixed bag, as Richard Bowes from the Oasis podcast explains:

'Within certain corners of fandom, *Heathen Chemistry* is regarded as the weakest Oasis album, yet not only does it contain two anthems in "Stop Crying Your Heart Out" and "Little By Little", but the entire album also pervades a sense of joy missing for some years. With the new line-up firmly established and a new democracy to songwriting introduced with Noel writing only six of the 11 tracks, not including hidden track "The Cage", the band approached it as a debut album, self-producing with Mike "Spike" Stent mixing and sounding suitably galvanised with a renewed sense of purpose. Treated as a whole, it's a perfect distillation of what made Oasis.'

Now with Andy Bell and Gem Archer on board they could create a tension and release and the heathen chemistry of a full electric rock 'n' roll band again, especially on opening track 'The Hindu Times', which is quintessential rock 'n' roll Oasis. The swaggering 'Boys Are Back in Town' anthem is built around that great searing, iridescent guitar hook cutting over the chugging boogie riff that harks back to the Quoasis of yore, building the foundations for the shuddering chord changes over the chorus. The result is a euphoric song with a chorus that soars even higher. 'The Hindu Times' was proof that the sonics that typified the first two albums were still well within the band's reach and it's one of their best rockers, and when it switches keys towards the end, it creates a genuine tingling rush.

Originally written for a film starring Jude Law called *Love, Honor, and Obey*, 'Force of Nature' is an angsty stomp rocker that throws out the lyrics over a chugging, almost glitter glam beat and attendant chords. The song was Noel's choice for the lead-off single from the album but fortunately, in commercial terms, he was persuaded to go with 'The Hindu Times'.

Gem's debut for the band, 'Hung in a Bad Place', rides rough-shod over a slashing chord that cuts over the wall-of-sound riff that surges like the Sex Pistols' cover of the Stooges' 'No Fun' and is given the full caustic Liam treatment with a great vocal. It's in total contrast to the big song off the album which remains the band's third most streamed song, the second single, 'Stop Crying Your Heart Out'. A plaintive piano ballad with a deceptively simple melody it was cranked through a big, almost, *Be Here Now* production into an epic scale which has been reciprocated by its popularity. For a band who made their name with big bolshy noisy songs, Oasis also knew how to tug the heart strings. It's sung impeccably by Liam who digs deep to bring a necessary sensitivity, which somehow transcends the song's influences to create a genuine moving and dramatic piece.

Described as 'a perfect song, I wish I'd written it as I fucking love it,' by Noel, Liam's own 'Songbird' has the same sort of upbeat innocence as his 'Little James' as he sings a love song to his then fiancée Nicole Appleton. The song digs deep into an open hearted-ness and a dropping your guard for your art that Lennon displayed on his most famous songs. At this point of time Liam was in his peak Lennon period and would often be photographed looking like various versions of the Beatle legend; one Liam myth even claims that he said he was a reincarnation of the much missed Beatle and he even named his 1999 born son with Patsy Kensit, Lennon Gallagher.

'John Lennon means everything to me,' Liam told the *NME*. 'I wouldn't say he's a better songwriter than McCartney . . . But I like Lennon's stuff more because it's a bit more beautiful, and it's more mad . . . His voice is the main thing I love . . . Political voice? Don't give a shit, couldn't care less about politics. But everything else – his singing voice, his songs and his words – means the world to me. You get bored of Lennon and you get bored of yourself, don't you? And I ain't getting bored of me.'[2]

The other big song of the album, 'Little by Little' sings of the world that the Gallaghers had come from as it builds towards the huge terrace anthem chorus that has all the hallmarks of a 'Don't Look Back in Anger' part two with a killer chord change for the bridge.

'That was one of the good ones on the album but there just wasn't enough of them,' explains Noel. 'I was coming back. The ghosts of the nineties were well and truly gone. I was happy again and looking to the future and not the drugs world of my old friends. Oasis weren't the fucking hot shit now and that was good for me, because I could write in the shadows again. I was starting a new lease of life. I got divorced from Meg and I had met Sara.[3] I was in love again and writing songs like this and "She is Love", "Stop Crying Your Heart Out."'

The band's new bassist Andy Bell made his songwriting debut for the band with 'A Quick Peep' – a deliberately inconsequential instrumental with a twist of band favourite, Peter Green's brilliant black magic blues of the early Fleetwood Mac. The song serves as a jaunty break between the previous big ballad and the psychedelic vibes of the drone trip '(Probably) All In My Mind', which revisits the drawling lysergic moments of the last album complete with one of those cyclical Macca bass lines that made the Beatles 'Rain' such a classic. The song envelops with its acid rock sprawl and yearns back to the simpler world of 1966, and sieves it through the Stone Roses 'Waterfall' with its churning guitar-laden raga drones.

As the trip fades, the next track is a perfect switch in mood to the almost Incredible String Band acoustic acid folk of 'She is Love'. The brisk and captivating tune was a love song written and sung by Noel about his new partner Sarah MacDonald. Its poetic musing on love was inspired by the Lebanese-American Kahlil Gibrans best-selling book, *The Prophet*, proving that despite amusing quips in interviews about having never read any books the songwriter was a closet reader. Gibran himself was a big influence on pop culture, with Elvis Presley being a fan and John Lennon borrowing his poetic line 'Half of what I say is meaningless' from his 1926 collection *Sand and Foam* for his song 'Julia'. David Bowie had given him a nod in his song 'The Width of a Circle' and even President Kennedy borrowed 'Ask not what your country can do for you—ask what you can do for your country,' from one of the poet's letters. The track itself was also released as a double A-side with 'Little by Little' – the only time the band ever attempted a double A-side single.

Proving that he was now the creative dark horse in the band, Liam's other song, 'Born on a Different Cloud', is another big anthemic yet introspective warm gun of a song. The sombre tune sees the singer giving it the full Lennon mind games, complete with that trademark slapback on a song he had written in the south of France while playing basic chords on a piano and finishing a melody that would have done his brother proud. Not only did he sing it like Lennon, he was inspired by Frederick Seaman's *Living on Borrowed Time* book about the iconic Beatle and his last years when he seemed to sink into a torpor in New York before his assassination. It must have been a head fuck for Liam to read about the working-class hero whose pain and energy had created the Beatles, and in turn the sixties, who was just 10 years later trapped into a feeble half-life that makes you want to reach through the pages and shake him from his sleep walking. Far from 'we all shine on' – the last years of his life were like a dimmed bulb.

The song, though, is a musical love letter from one Anglo-Irish working-class hero to another that hopefully learning a lesson from him.

The album ends with another Liam song, 'Better Man', which has the sparse stomp of John Lennon's early solo career and his post-Beatle peak of searing confessional songs played out over jagged blues riffs and sparse slapback pulsating drums. Liam gives it his peak Lennon, summons up the ghost of the sabre-toothed Beatle, singing like a confessional shaman he digs deep into his own soul looking to be a 'better man'. It's a great track and maybe one of the most underrated in the band's catalogue.

Typical of someone who was a record fiend and had obsessed over vinyl and run out grooves, it was only a matter of time before Noel put a hidden track on the end of an album and after a 30-minute wait we get the album's final song, 'The Cage', which is an oddly haunting Peter Green rolling blues.

The album artwork concept of the moody monochrome band shot came from Noel, with Simon Halfon realising his vision with the motion blur photo which has the brooding atmosphere of the classic Joy Division photograph by Anton Corbijn at Lancaster Gate Underground station in November 1979. The Oasis shot was taken by Andrew MacPherson at Paris Gare de Lyon station, but as Simon Halfon explained to *GQ*, it didn't go entirely according to plan:

'It was February, not the best month weather-wise to spend a week outdoors. After checking in to our hotel, Liam commented that there was a very "dark vibe" in the air . . . We were then told the hotel had been commandeered by the Gestapo during the war. The mood didn't lift that whole week, as Noel and Liam were not on great speaking terms. . . . The album image came about almost by accident as we waited for the Métro.'[4]

Despite being number one, the album was almost a sideshow in the band's own trajectory and remains full of deep cuts and lost gems and Noel felt trapped by his own success.

'The new albums came out and I believed in them but we would go on tour and no one was really interested in new songs,' the guitarist laments. 'They just wanted to hear *Morning Glory* and *Definitely Maybe* and we fell into the thing of just doing the same 12 songs from the first two albums and then some new ones that no one was bothered about. The powers that be weren't that bothered about us having hits but by the same rule, I just didn't want to become a touring band and just play the same fucking songs for the next 50 years. We didn't play "Wonderwall" for years and we did the stupid thing of when we went off we'd play it over the PA and the crowd would stay behind and sing it.

'I was kind of stood at a crossroads, and didn't know which way to go. That period it's pretty fucking hit and miss but the songs that were good were good. I'm a product of my record collection and once I'd exhausted the Beatles, the Stones, the Kinks, the Who, the Small Faces and the Sex Pistols and all that, I was left waiting for something to happen; then these new bands came along like the Strokes and the White Stripes and there was new music that was great and it was energetic and it was up.'

In September 'Little by Little' was released from the album as a double A-side with 'She is Love' and reached number two in the charts. The track was originally meant to be sung by Liam but in a rare moment, he just couldn't get the vocal and it was handed back to Noel to complete.

The cover art was a homage to the American pop artist Robert Indiana and his iconic *Love* artwork series that proliferated over cards, posters and the famous *Love* statue in downtown New York City. The promo video by Max & Dania was filmed on 'Heathen Street' and has Noel Gallagher sat in the doorway as a busker – maybe as one of the thousands of buskers playing Oasis songs at any given moment in the UK – and features *Trainspotting* star Robert Carlyle miming to the song as a disconcerting figure only a few inches high, before growing to giant size like a modern-day pop culture *Gulliver's Travels*.

'Songbird', the last single to be pulled from the album, was the first single to be written by Liam and he defied his tabloid image by showing that his best songs displayed a tender side with a beautifully simple and direct acoustic-driven song. Most people seemed to expect Liam to write barnstorming psychodramas about fighting so the song was a bit of a shock.

Released in February 2003, the song was the band's fourth top-three single from the album. The recorded version retained the demo's brisk acoustic tenderness but moved it away from its more Beatlish inflections by dropping the original 'I Should Have Known Better' harmonica from the demo and making it sound like a standout creation in its own right. The video, directed by Dick Carruthers, who had directed the *Familiar to Millions* documentary as well as *Standing on the Edge of the Noise*, was like a UK take on John Lennon running around parks in New York for *Mind Games* in 1973. Liam sits under a tree with his acoustic in Hyde Park, performing the song and walking through the park, brushing past his current partner Nicole Appleton from the band All Saints, who the song was written about, before chasing and then getting chased by his dog!

38

DON'T BELIEVE THE TRUTH

Eleven years since their debut Oasis were no longer the outrageous outsiders who had stormed the palace gates and were now rock 'n' roll veterans. Ironically, the most volatile and incendiary of the bands that had broken through in the Britpop era were just about the only band still going.

'It's difficult to be going for that long and have that level of success and still be there or thereabouts doing stadiums and being number one,' says Noel. 'Working with a family member is not always easy, yet if the greatest strength is your greatest weakness then having one of your family means that no matter what happens someone's got your back at all times. You can push each other's box pretty quickly but that was rare and we were all growing up and growing older.'

2005 was a good year to come back with a rock 'n' roll record. American garage indie bands like the Strokes and the White Stripes were still setting the agenda, Kasabian combined Oasis swagger with beats, and the Kaiser Chiefs' indie populism was like a

Boomtown Rats to Oasis's Sex Pistols;[1] the rebels and the renegades were represented by the Libertines' crack cocaine headlines yet poetic albums. Damon Albarn's reinvention as Gorillaz was hitting paydirt with his huge selling *Demon Days* album and in Sheffield, a young band called Arctic Monkeys were buzzing on the local scene and on Myspace and would soon be the leading UK band of a new generation. These were the last years of the old model of UK pop culture – the music press/radio/*Top of the Pops* route for bands was already crumbling and about to collapse completely into the online world of social media and yet Oasis still mattered.

As ever the new album recording had been a long and winding road. The search for new ways to say the same fundamental things had started in December 2003 and concluded in January 2005 and the album had been through the usual demo stages.

To give things a twist they brought in cutting-edge remixers and electronic music group built around Richard Fearless and Tim Holmes from Death in Vegas. Interestingly, it was Liam who was the original contact after recording a great lead vocal for a track by the duo, which was a psychedelic groove complete with backward guitars called 'Scorpio Rising',[2] and liked what he heard.

Hired to produce the album in December 2003, work proper began in Sawmills studio. Between them they recorded 10 songs over three weeks including 'The Meaning of Soul, 'A Bell Will Ring', 'Turn Up the Sun, 'Mucky Fingers', as well as 'Eyeball Tickler'.

Initially things seemed to be going well. Noel told interviewers that the new album would be out in September and that he had already chosen a single to be released in July, saying it would be 'a psychedelic Rock 'n' roll Record' while praising Liam's new songs.

Then drummer Alan White was fired four days before Xmas 2003 after not turning up for a rare band meeting.

After a short break and a rethink, the band reconvened at Wheeler End with Noel now producing. These sessions saw a new direction with Zak Starkey, the son of Ringo, brought in to replace Alan, resulting in songs like 'Part of the Queue', 'Let There Be Love' and 'Lyla'.

'Oasis were the least traumatic and most fun of any band I've ever been in. There was none of the brother shit when I was there because we were so good no one wanted to ruin it. It was great to be part of and they were the greatest band of their generation.

I knew them from 1995 when my band the Face rehearsed at John Henry's and I said to Liam, "the greatest rock n roll singer in the world has met the greatest drummer in the world!" In February, after Alan left, Marcus rang me and I went to Wheeler End. The first thing I did with them was Layla,' remembers Zak.

The drummer came armed with a great reputation. As a youth he had been taught to play drums by Keith Moon and was a talented firebrand whose way of playing married the styles of the two best drummers of the sixties – his father and the Who legend – but with a modern twist. His Beatle credentials made him a great fit and a cool nod to the Fab Four, and although he was never a full member in the now Oasis Four, his presence would be all over the album. Oasis decided to start mostly from scratch and only four of the already recorded songs would make the final album in various forms [3] and the other six 'were not good enough to even be B-sides', according to Noel. Death in Vegas were out of the picture by March not because of their production but because Noel felt that the band's own songs were not good enough.

With the album going nowhere sonically the band had a listen to a pile of contemporary records and were struck by the sound on the Jet and Dandy Warhols records. They were both produced by Dave Sardy who was a former member of American alt-rock band Barkmarket and whose sister Marcia had once played keyboards for the Fall. He had initially cut his producer teeth with heavier post-grunge bands like Helmet, Orange 9mm and Cop Shoot Cop before he caught Oasis's beady eye. 'The recording at Wheeler End wasn't working out so Liam instigated the whole Dave Sardy thing,' explains Zak Starkey.

The producer remembers it was Liam who was the first person from the band who got in touch and a track was sent over for him to do a test mix on, followed shortly after by three more songs. Listening to the tracks, the band liked what they heard and told the producer that they wished they had started with him from scratch, while deciding to scrap the album and start all over again.

'Whether anyone wants to admit it,' explained Dave Sardy, 'Noel was kind of the co-manager of the band. He's a very smart guy, as is the manager, Marcus Russell. The two have an amazing partnership.'[4]

The producer was booked and flew in to the UK to oversee brand new recording sessions at London's Olympic Studios before persuading the band to come to LA to work in studios he was more familiar with. Zak Starkey explains: 'Dave said "let's record in LA," and we couldn't argue with that. We had a great time in the city, recording and getting meditation lessons from Bungalow Bill (as in the Beatles song). We did all Liam's tunes first because Noel was delayed getting in because of some legals. Me and Noel then recorded some songs together and the band would be added after.'

Like *Definitely Maybe*, it was to be third time lucky for the album after operations shifted to LA that October. Here they spent nine weeks recording at Capitol Studios which had a history that was like a roll call of pop culture, from Frank Sinatra to Bob Dylan to Paul McCartney. They also worked at Olympic Studios in London and overdubbed at Village Recording Studios in LA – another studio with a big-name history. For some reason, sunny extrovert LA had always loved Manchester's grey-sky bands with their cynical souls and the vibe was reciprocated. By the end of November, the album was finally in the can but not before an unlikely adventure.

With Dave Sardy having worked with Marilyn Manson a couple of years before, an unlikely friendship was struck up between the two bands at the time. Ostensibly coming from different ends of the musical spectrum, it was Manson's bass player Twiggy who was the huge Oasis fan to the point of even having a tattoo of the band. Somehow he had got the singer interested, who now declared his love for what he called the 'cocaine album' of *Be Here Now*. With the Dave Sardy connection, the Gallaghers went to the Marilyn Manson LA show where the freakshow singer dedicated a song to them as Noel told the *NME*: 'He comes on stage and shouts, "I wanna dedicate this song to the two biggest fuck-ups in England." Me and our kid are looking at him, and then looking at each other going, "He means you, 'cos Lord knows he don't mean me."'[5]

Released in early May 2005 and trailing the long awaited album by a few weeks, the first new song from Oasis for nearly three years was the churning street fighting man rocker, 'Lyla'. The track became the band's seventh number one and saw the band back on *Top of the Pops*. It was Liam's last appearance on the decades old much-loved show that would soon be a casualty of the now fast-changing landscape of pop culture. By daring to release a slice of rock 'n' roll in 2005, 'Lyla' embraced the retro and made it sound modern. It had been some time since a vocal that intense had been heard in the mainstream and the song's tension cut across the airwaves. A stadium-stomper driven by Zak Starkey's four-on-the-floor kick drum pumped the heartbeat with a pounding primal energy. Designed as a riot song, this was classic noisy Oasis sounding like the Faces at their tumultuous best and a reminder of their calling-card rousing anthems, with Liam's searing power vocal reaching for the stars. It was an instant radio smash with its pounding rush of guitars building the tension and exploding with a cool gonzo guitar freakout – with the fluttering piano at the end sounding like the ghost of the late and great Nicky Hopkins giving the coda a flavour of the Stones classic, 'She's a Rainbow'.

The flipside featured Gem Archer's 'Eyeball Tickler', a rush of neo-punk rock and an impatient song that sprints along with its own intensity, while 'Won't Let You Down' is an acoustic-driven workout.

The single was bagged up in a bleak black-and-white shot of the band in a very austere and post-punk moody silhouette. It was the first sighting of the new monochromatic artwork for the upcoming album and singles campaign. The stark shot was the work of art director Simon Halfon who took Noel's initial idea and Lawrence Watson's fish-eye photo and filtered it. The video from Tim Qualtrough matches this Twin Peaks darkness and was set in a claustrophobic flat full of tension, powders and a muscle dog, with a woman getting hassled by two men. It then explodes into colour when she escapes to an Oasis gig in a surreal club that gets more twisted as the drugs kick in with that dislocation that the chemicals bring.

Finally released on 30 May 2005 by Big Brother Recordings, the band's new acoustic guitar-driven classic British retro album *Don't Believe the Truth*[6] was a welcome return to the rock 'n' roll. The glorious wall-of-sound epic jugger-noise of the Owen Morris era was now long gone and the return to a more guitar/bass/drums-based sound was this time driven by acoustic guitars, leaving more space and urgency. Even Noel was pleased with the results:

'I fucking love this record. We made a really good album that actually could stand up against the early ones. We all knew what everybody was capable of and it was the first record that Zak had played on. "Lyla" was great. It's the one concession to a big stadium anthem kind of thing and "The Importance of Being Idle" was brilliant.'

It was also embraced by the still huge fanbase, with Richard Bowes among them:

'Their most British-sounding album, *Don't Believe the Truth* was the zenith of Oasis in the twenty-first century. The two number one singles, "Lyla" and "The Importance of Being Idle", sit comfortably alongside their best work as Noel, freed from the burden of writing stadium anthems, produced songs that were sonically and structurally breaking away from his usual template. Indeed, the most Oasis sounding songs came from Andy Bell and Gem Archer. It may have had a troubled gestation, but once Dave Sardy took control of production duties, he unearthed a band rediscovering a winning formula while adding fresh ingredients.'[7]

Dave Sardy's tight and concise production makes the band pack a punch with big songs that typified the sixties but cranked with a powerful propulsive industrial hi-tech new millennium sound. Noel explained that the album is his favourite of Oasis Mark 2, mainly because all the band members contributed to the songwriting making him the magnanimous chief!

'It's a great record,' Noel enthuses. 'We were on it and we'd found a producer, Dave Sardy, who got on with everybody and was really good. It's the one album where everybody stopped writing Oasis-type songs and just started writing songs. Liam's tunes were really good, like "Guess God Thinks I'm Abel", I fucking love that song. It's amazing and I loved playing and recording it. Andy's song, "Turn Up the Sun", is also fucking great. The singles were good and I was concentrating on writing them as I didn't have to write everything. I know a single when I hear it and I always picked the singles. Initially the radio plugger said there was no singles on the album and then "Lyla" and "The Importance of Being Idle" were both number one and "Let There Be Love" was a big hit.

'We had a great time mixing it. We were away for months and months. It was the peak of Oasis Mark 2. We looked good. We felt good and we sounded good. The album was great and the gigs were great and we were back doing big fuck-off stadiums all over the world. Even the videos were great and I'd come through my curmudgeon phase where I was normally like, "Videos, fuck off!"'

The album opened with Andy Bell's 'Turn Up the Sun', which is perhaps his finest moment in Oasis with its haunting, sixties TV theme-style intro before crashing into a classic Oasis primal guitar ooze. It also features a great rasping vocal from Liam who carries the song's madness. It was the first album opener not written by Noel and ends on a hypnotic arpeggio that is more reminiscent of Ride's baroque shoegaze, as Andy explained to Richard Bowes:

'At first it was really downbeat, very lo-fi, quiet and hushed like the La's B-side "Who Knows". I gave it to the guys and then one day I turned up at rehearsal and they were already playing it with this huge rock 'n' roll makeover, and it just blew my head off. They made it what it became. On the demo, the first line was: "I carry a sadness", which fits the early version of the song. In rehearsal that got changed to: "I carry a madness", which works so much better when you have Liam singing it, and I loved it. That was the effect they had on the song, it makes it Oasis.'[8]

Noel remembers the song being brought in: 'Andy played it to me and I was like, that's fucking great with the intricate guitar part and then he started singing, "I carry the sadness everywhere I go . . . " And I was like, "Let me stop you right there! Liam won't sing that" and we changed it to madness.

'Sometimes I'd write a song for Liam to sing and I'd look at it and go, "OK that's not about him, that's about me and my missus" and he'd be very quick to spot that. So I used to not wholly rewrite them but changed it from "me" to "us" or "I" to "them". So he couldn't say, "Who's that about? Your missus?" And I could say, "No, it's about everyone's missus." There were a lot of songs that I'd write from a place of truth and then filter it and take the edges off a little bit so he could sing them and he was great at that.'

'Mucky Fingers' is a powerful affirmation and proof that they could still kick out the jams. It twists the Velvet Underground classic I'm 'Waiting for the Man' into new shapes with the hypnotic pounding monotone piano driving the incessant guitar chords.

Initially, Noel had planned for the track to be the lead-off single from the album, perhaps with a Liam vocal, but the instant number one 'Lyla' was a perfect first missive and helped power the album to the top of the charts.

With three songs on the album, Liam Gallagher was hitting a songwriting stride with a clutch of tunes that also saw the first inter-band co-write to appear on an Oasis album, with Gem Archer. 'Love Like a Bomb' is their ambitious piece that breaks out of the verse/chorus structure to switch effortlessly between sections. Starting with a strident string-breaking frantic acoustic guitar attack locked in tight with Zak Starkey's metronomic military beat and an intensely claustrophobic vocal from the singer, it then explodes into the mid-sixties regency mod 1967 meltdown.

The short sharp shocks of the acoustic on the previous track link in neatly to the same kind of sound that punctuated the intro of the album's other big hit single, 'The Importance of Being Idle'. The song updates the Kinks' kitchen sink noir vignette observations on British life into the now. It kicks off with abrupt La's-style acoustic strumming before entering the classic sixties music hall of the primetime Kinks of 'Sunny Afternoon' and 'Dead End Street' – those Ray Davies, snapshots of British life that still resonate – making the song an art rock outlier in the endless rush of the surrounding singles chart quick-fix hits.

With its witty lyrics crooned by a falsetto from Noel, the song was an autobiographical paean to loafing, with an added vaudeville romp. It was a wheels-on-fire creation and a slice of perfect pop with amusing lyrics celebrating laziness. The song was inspired by Stephen Robins' piss-take self-help book, *The Importance of Being Idle: A Little Book of Lazy Inspiration* that Noel had found in a mound of stuff while cleaning out a garage – and was perhaps a nod to his own halcyon days of skiving at work.

A song in a rush, 'The Meaning of Soul' is a short sharp shock of barely two minutes. It's perhaps the band's fastest song as it rushes at breakneck speed like something off punk legends the Damned's first album played on an acoustic, or sixties freak beat played fast and dangerous and sounding like it could fall apart at any moment. The track almost crashes into the next Liam song, the cleverly titled 'Guess God Thinks I'm Abel', which is a brisk acoustic workout that taps into the singer's dreamy optimism and breezy melodic prowess. It also pinpointed an introspective depth that was yet again beyond the 2D public image with its soul-searching mystical lyrics and off-kilter melody.

Breaking their own mould yet again, 'Part of the Queue' is a brisk workout that takes jazz chords and makes them work in a moody pop context like the Stranglers had done in 1982 with their huge hit, 'Golden Brown'. Driven by some great jazzy shuffle beats from Zak and aided by percussion from Lenny Castro, who had also worked with Stevie Wonder and Quincy Jones, the song is one of those breezy curveballs that had always dotted the band's albums and is another song about escape from the city.

Written by Andy Bell, 'Keep the Dream Alive' could be a portal in time to the summer of love San Francisco, especially with the chorus which is the song's sweet spot, and the chiming outro with its weaving guitars, as Andy Bell remembers: 'This was inspired by the David Essex film *Stardust*, and had a sample from the film on it – which I now wish we had kept in. It's the conversation between Adam Faith and David Essex which starts off with David Essex refusing to go and be interviewed, and Adam Faith trying to persuade him to.'

A deep cut, Gem Archer's 'A Bell Will Ring' revisits the 'Tomorrow Never Knows' drum riff with a crunching room ambience and cranked compression, underpinning an infinite chime of Revolver-style guitars and a smouldering Liam vocal. Dave Sardy's sharp production sees every guitar resonating and even allows the buzz of an amp humming at the end.

Like a melancholic introspective grown-up big brother to 'Acquiesce', 'Let There be Love', written by Noel, is sung by both brothers in a moment of harmony. The plaintive piano-driven song dripped the mystery and melancholy of early seventies Lennon from somewhere between the stark confessional of his debut *Plastic Ono Band* album and the lush warmth of the follow-up *Imagine* album but with a sharper production. The twin vocals work perfectly, switching the mood of the track from Liam's mix of yearning and rasping intensity in the first half to Noel's pure croon over the Mellotron that submerges beneath the gorgeous middle section of 'Space Oddity' synthetic strings.

The album's stark artwork was even more monochromatic than *Heathen Chemistry*. Almost brutalist, it came from a concept from Noel Gallagher who wanted a series of anonymous garage doors graffitied with the album title. The striking cover had a post-punk minimalism to its style and the sleeve gave no clues to the songs in a deliberately stark concept that was realised by Simon Halfon, with the album title added to the garages by Luke Dane. In his first work with the band, photographer Lawrence Watson took the picture with a fish-eye lens to give it an otherworldly look. He also shot the stark black-and-white image of the band for the inner sleeve.

'This was shot in a park in London,' explained Lawrence. 'I'm not going to mention where because I'll probably get in trouble or charged by the park. Initially, Noel had the idea of doing the shoot in front of "suicide bridge" to get the London history in the background but that sort of thing doesn't really work. It's fine for the human eye to look at it but once you put four people in front of it you don't really see much.'[9]

For many the album was an emphatic return to form and it spawned two number ones and one number two single. Outsiders to the end, the band were passed over by the 2006 Brits and snubbed the awards.

The reviews were mixed but the album was a number one in the UK with increased sales and reached number 12 in the USA. Hitting the road with a big world tour certainly helped crank up the album sales and they ended up playing to over 3 million people in 26 countries, powering the album on to worldwide sales of 7 million.

During the festivals leg of that world tour they released the second single, 'The Importance of Being Idle', from the album on 22 August. It was their eighth number one single and the second time that a Noel-sung song had been to number one. It also equalled the Beatles' record of 19 top 10 singles in a row.

The video, shot on Caradoc Street in East Greenwich, was the band's best. The black-and-white film, created by video director Dawn Shadforth,[10] starred Rhys Ifans, the Welsh actor and former Super Furry Animals singer, as a high-kicking funeral director presiding over his own funeral in a macabre dance routine as he literally danced himself to the grave. It's a tongue-in-cheek homage to the classic gritty sixties British kitchen sink dramas – where stark reality and dark humour mix for the funeral in a cobbled northern town – as well as a nod to *Billy Liar* and the Kinks' video for 'Dead End Street' which was banned by the BBC for being 'too macabre'.

The single came with Liam's rasping acoustic 'Pass Me Down the Wine' B-side that evokes a mystical late sixties film score that fits very well with the A-side in terms of atmosphere and sound and also Gem Archer's acoustic 'The Quiet Ones'. It was all bagged up in the artwork of a guitar with the song's lyrics hand-painted on it from a concept by Noel Gallagher and photographed by Lawrence Watson.

Just in time for Christmas, the third and final single from the album, 'Let There be Love', was released. The song was further proof that Oasis could do sensitive as well as anybody and scored them a number two in the charts, with its cover shot of a set of keys designed and executed by Simon Halfon again with Lawrence Watson. Perhaps a sketch put together in the studio but an effective capture of atmosphere, the haunting and melancholic introspective song flipside, 'Sittin' Here in Silence (On My Own)' was another piano-driven track with an unexpected glockenspiel solo in the middle in a song written and sung by Noel. There was also a live version of 'Rock 'n' Roll Star', which, despite being a raucous reminder of the band's calling card, was also a pointer to perhaps the lack of effortless brilliant new B-sides that used to pepper their earlier releases. The live cut was reflected in the video, which was a collage of recent shows from the summer at Hampden Park and the City of Manchester stadium. The huge surging crowds with their arms aloft stretching into eternity and rippling across the arenas are a perfect snapshot of the enduring appeal of the band and how embedded they now were in the national psyche, all captured in a multi-camera shoot directed by Dick Carruthers from the upcoming *Lord Don't Slow Me Down* Oasis rockumentary.

In 2006, while the band was taking a couple of years off, it was time to take stock and deal with the past and construct a legend before someone else did. Noel had spent his teenage years immersed in other band's stories and music and at some point a cool operator becomes a cool curator and it was inevitable that an Oasis collection was going to fill in the fallow years between albums; which meant the release of their first greatest hits compilation, *Stop the Clocks*.

Despite having said they would never release a greatest hits while they were still together, the album came about when Sony forced the band's hands by stating they would release one anyway. Noel got on board to ensure quality control for what would now be the last release for the label.

Named after a song of the same name that they had attempted to record several times but could never get quite right until it was finally recorded for Noel's post-Oasis project, High Flying Birds, the 18-track album was less of a chronological run through the band's classic singles and more of what Noel described as a perfect set list for a dream gig.

The aim was to create the ideal intro to the band for future generations – the future versions of the younger Noel and his mates in Sifters clutching their newly bought compilation albums to start their journey into the sound of a band they had discovered.

The distinctive artwork for the cover was designed by the legendary British pop artist Peter Blake, the foremost British pop artist who often played with objects and pop art symbols in his own iconic art. Translating the pop art that was coming out of fifties America into a more British version he referenced pop culture icons, objects, figures, motifs, and logos positioned across his compositions that were sometimes paintings, and in the case of his *Sgt. Pepper's* sleeve a photograph mixing 2D and 3D objects.

Blake's artwork was often a cut-up regurgitation of pop culture realigned into new and different shapes – just like Noel Gallagher was doing when he wrote songs from a bricolage of old, new, borrowed and blue.

Initially there was talk of something based around the Granny Takes a Trip[11] shop iconography, but when Noel Gallagher went to see the artist they decided to create something from the items lying around in Peter Blake's studio. The random found objects were placed in a cupboard and on a small table and photographed, as Peter Blake explained to the *NME*:

'The *Definitely Maybe* cover was in the back of my mind. What intrigued me about it was that although some of those objects meant something to the band, you couldn't possibly know what some of the others meant! It's using the mystery of *Definitely Maybe* and running with it.'[12]

Unlike Blake's cover for Paul Weller's *Stanley Road*, where the objects meant something to Weller, *Stop the Clocks* was made up of random items with Noel approving of Peter's signature Snow White and the Seven Dwarfs in various predicaments, Liam picking an Elvis piece and the pop art legend adding Dorothy from *The Wizard of Oz*. They were going to use an image of Marilyn Monroe but potential image rights violation meant a Michael Caine photo was a better bet.

Once the objects were in place, Lawrence Watson photographed them and then within a day, it was all taken apart again, existing only in that moment . . .

Phew! Pop art perfection!

Art director Simon Halfon had already worked with the iconic pop artist on the Paul Weller sleeve, as he explains:

"*Stop the Clocks* was the second project that I had worked on with Peter Blake . . . For Oasis we decided to create a still life collage, bringing together elements that we found in Peter's amazing studio that would become a piece of art for one day and one day only.

'It had been a while since Peter had done anything of this kind and it was a real joy putting the whole thing together, carefully adding items like the small Snow White figurine that had previously graced the *Sgt. Pepper* album cover, almost 50 years earlier.'[13]

A time to reassess and recalibrate. The clocks were stopped and the album was a huge success and a reminder of the potency of that back catalogue, with it becoming the seventh best-selling album of the year in the UK.

Of course, the clocks don't actually ever stop and the career curve of most rock bands is like life itself, starting with a frantic childhood and then rampaging through the pills, thrills and none of the belly-aches of the crazy teenage years. Then in an intense flurry of activity, the band builds up and explodes with a series of albums, singles and tours, and then settles down into the middle-aged spread of the album/tour trajectory before this cycle begins to slow down and they amble into the sunset of old-age classic band status. By 2007

Oasis were slowing down and a very different band now existed in place of the group that had first appeared on the scene.

In June, the band recorded a great version of the Beatles' 'Within You Without You' for the 40th anniversary of the *Sgt. Pepper's* album. In a magnanimous mood, Noel asked Liam to pick which Sgt. Pepper song they should cover, figuring his brother would choose a song like 'A Day in the Life' and a chance for both brothers to sing the John and Paul sections, but the singer insisted on covering the only George Harrison song from the iconic album, which featured the spiritual Beatle backed by Indian instruments.

It's an inspired choice and the cover version shows a different side to the younger Gallagher – he really gets inside the song and owns it with his vocal giving a glimpse into a more reflective, spiritual side. When it came to recording the song, Noel got the band to cover the version from the recent 2006 *Beatles Love* compilation – the remix album of the Beatles which had created mash-ups of Beatles songs for the Cirque du Soleil show called 'Love' produced by George Martin and his son Giles. This version tentatively mashed up 'Within You Without You' with 'Tomorrow Never Knows' – Oasis would take a sledgehammer to the idea and create something quite wonderful.

The band's only release of the year came that autumn with a one-off single, 'Lord Don't Slow Me Down'. The not quite full-on and isolated release is in many ways one of the great lost songs in the Oasis canon. The Noel-sung single was, (perhaps because it was download only), the band's first not to reach the top four since 'Cigarettes & Alcohol' back in 1994. Driven by a classic Yardbirds-type riff, it was full of late sixties switchblade thrills and allowed Zak Starkey to show off his swinging stomping drums, incorporating two lightning flash drum solos and some cool cowbell action underneath the guitar solo. The original recording had Liam singing over the same backing track and it's a different proposition altogether, yet both brothers' vocal takes on the song, while giving a different aspect, sound good and give it a very different twist.

Released as a download single and a limited edition 12-inch single in October, it promoted the recent release of the Oasis rockumentary of the same name, which followed the band around on the recent Don't Believe the Truth world tour. Hitting the cinemas in November 2006 and shown on Channel 4 in the UK, it was a document of the later period band still in its pomp in the arenas and stadiums worldwide.

The tidying up of loose ends and the end of another era. It would be a couple of years before the band re-emerged.

39

DIG OUT YOUR SOUL

A year after their world tour had ended in Mexico City, the band were back in Abbey Road in 2007 recording their new album with Dave Sardy, taking full advantage of that studio's classic set-up and legendary live room before relocating to LA from January to March 2008 to mix the album with Dave Sardy at The Village Recorder.

The first result was 'The Shock of the Lightning' single, released on 29 September. The powerhouse rush of the single heralded the upcoming album with another twist in the Oasis sonic chassis. Underlining that there was plenty of creative juice left in the band's tank with the urgent twisting neo-psychedelia, it had more than a nod to the incessant rhythms of German seventies Motorik music like Neu, with its constant 4/4 kick drum pumping the heartbeat and building the tension. The track's edginess was aided by its swift recording and its quick execution, capturing the instant karma of cutting-edge creativity of a song born in the moment – the purest and most exciting way.

Somehow combining a big anthem with art rock and a compressed anger-is-an-energy vocal from Liam; this is one of the great Oasis moments. Some say the singer's vocals had suffered over the years of rock 'n' roll, but he sounds even more urgent than ever on the song, and with Dave Sardy's exquisite compressed pumping production, the track explodes out of the speakers. In the post B-side era the other track on the single was the Chemical Brothers deconstruction and rebuilding of another album cut, 'Falling Down', into a rhythmic beat shuffle.

The new Oasis sound that was hinted at on the single was under-lined by the new art team working on the graphics. Gone was the post-punk monochromatic of the last two albums, replaced by an explosive lysergic dayglo. The single's suitably apocalyptic psyche-delic imagery was designed by Julian House and was a hint towards the sound, feel and visuals of the upcoming album.

Artist, musician and owner of Ghost Box records, Julian House specialised in hauntology – a critical theory that examines how the past haunts the present – and he had made his name designing sleeves for Primal Scream's striking *XTRMNTR* album cover, as well as sleeves for Stereolab and the Prodigy. His distinctive collage-based designs incorporated influences from Peter Saville's stark design lines, HP Lovecraft's horror to Lewis Carroll's wonderland and Saul Bass's movie graphics. This reflected the stylish neo-psy-chedelic twists and turns of the new Oasis album, creating a whole new brand identity with a style that collected images from found art like old record sleeves, comic books and pop art collaged together in new and different ways, reflecting Oasis's own creative process.

He also made 'The Shock of the Lightning' video that was '67 psychedelia cranked into the twenty-first century, with computer graphics twisting a performance video into a mind-melting trip as it embeds the graphics and images across the screen in a digital fast forward. Melting the surreal landscapes of Terry Gilliam and Polish graphic designer and cartoonist Jan Lenica, Julian House and Julian Gibbs as the INTRO design team were constantly looking for new ways to meld their art into different medias and visions, combined with the free hand that Noel Gallagher gave them, they were responsible for helping to create the striking visuals for the artwork and the video.

Times may have been a changing but there was something cool about Oasis's splendid isolation. As the world started its slide into uncertainty with the global financial crisis and the most severe economic downturn since the Great Depression, the music industry, perversely, saw a digital boom and a live upturn powering its best year for some time before its own decline and fall crept in with streaming. The golden age of guitar-driven pop culture was long gone apart from the stunning success of the Arctic Monkeys and it was into this flux that Oasis returned with their new album in October as veterans; the beats-driven *Dig Out Your Soul* was released on their own Big Brother label and would still swagger in at number one in the UK and was their first top five in the USA for over a decade.

More digging their own soul than reinventing the wheel, the album was a far darker, noisier record than you would normally find topping charts in 2008.

'When I was sequencing it I decided to front load the record,' explains Noel. 'People have said to me, and this is not my opinion, that it falls off a cliff on side two, but Liam's got a great song at the end of the album called "Soldier On" which I play the drums on. He's got another great one, a ballad, "I'm Outta Time". Most of his songs are not rockers, which is ironic as he used to say to me, "Write some fucking rock and roll songs!"'

A glimpse into his real soul?

'Of course . . .

'There's a couple of odd tunes on the album. "Bag it Up" is fucking bizarre. It's a mad song about looking back on the days picking magic mushrooms in Errwood Park. Do you know what was really soul destroying? Somebody went, "Geri Halliwell has got a song called 'Bag It Up.'" For fuck's sake!'

'The final Oasis record was a lot of recordings that were from scratch,' Dave Sardy explained. 'It was an actual producer/artist relationship, where we butted heads. Everyone in that band is a producer, everyone had an opinion, but at the end of the day it worked. It was an actual situation of seeing how much further we could push it and how much better it could get.'[1]

The album showcased a band that could still write big songs that still worked within their own parameters but also showed an unacknowledged willingness to experiment and move on. Tweaking away at the sound, adding gnarly psychedelia and motorik beats to their populist chassis, they still scored a number one album. In the new age where everything was available all at once it often seemed that their ability to move forwards was ignored, as a defiant Noel Gallagher explained:

'You get critics saying Oasis "never change their sound," correct me if I'm wrong but you're not writing in a new language. You're still writing in paragraphs and in sentences and not writing upside down or back to front! So excuse me if I write in the language that I use.'

The first side of the album sounded like a latter-day greatest hits jukebox of pounding rockers or songs that would stretch the sound out into molten, almost drum and bass rhythms. For long-term fans like Richard Bowes the album saw the band more than capable of doing great work with some killer singles. It also fed into the unique tension that gave them a dark energy of their own as it played out in their mix of anthems and dark psychedelia.

'It's an album of two halves and, in some ways, a fitting finale,' says Richard. 'Six of the first seven songs represent Oasis at their finest; "The Turning" could go on *Morning Glory*, and on "The Shock of the Lightning" they finally found the perfect fusion of the Beatles and the Sex Pistols and, as the last single to date, in "Falling Down", they displayed a demonstrable evolution from "Supersonic". The last four songs are functional but highlight Oasis's evolution into a grizzled psychedelic rock band. With hindsight, you can hear the tension in the music preceding the band dissolving, but they did so with characteristic ferocious intensity.'

The tight, punchy production from Dave Sardy creates a mystery with its cool psychedelic twists and textures and everything is cranked to the max but in its own space.

With most of the songs written by Noel Gallagher with three from Liam and one each from Gem Archer and Andy Bell, this was the most Team Oasis album yet, an album of stark modern psychedelia 'revisiting some of my trips as a younger man' as Noel quipped.

There are sonic hints here of a band about to move on, like Noel on 'Falling Down', and a diversity of styles and possibilities that was stretched to the max by the Amorphous Androgynous mix of that single – a masterpiece of space jazz dub trip in every way possible.

The opening track, 'Bag it Up' instantly makes a big sonic statement with slashing guitars and big drums power-housing the song's dark soul. The album delivered perhaps the biggest drum sounds the band used, with the pounding marriage of Zak Starkey's propulsive playing and Dave Sardy's mix often putting the drums into the centre, and it really works to create an epic widescreen sound. The steroid groove of the song holds the tension that replicates the pounding heartbeat of a drugs rush with all its nervous energy and twisted highs. Noel's paean to his youthful drug adventures creates a dark shadowy song and there is a level of intensity in Liam's vocal that is hypnotic.

The track switches from the dank claustrophobic verses to the release of a compelling and unexpected great chorus, and the outro, with its night terror Mellotron, is a cimmerian shiver of the triple bad acid of the Rolling Stones' *Their Satanic Majesties Request*.

With its moody vibes and shimmering piano line glued to the drum's shuffle groove, 'The Turning' is Oasis closer to the shimmering sci-fi drum and bass of Goldie and his rhythmic soundscapes. The moody rainswept song has a hypnotic shapeshifting feel and captures the same sort of groovy moods and rainy-day vibe as the World of Twist classic 'The Storm', complete with Liam's scorched-earth vocal on the chorus with the different edges and sounds he pushed from his throat which are still highly effective without losing their intensity.

A song about the redemptive power of love, 'Waiting for the Rapture' saw Noel singing about meeting his new partner Sara MacDonald, over a shamanic Doors-style stomp with a zig-zagging Cold Turkey guitar slash. Celebrating the soul power of settling down with a new love, the song sings of the profound things in life away from the constant fast lane of rock 'n' roll highs.

The first single released just before the album, 'The Shock of the Lightning' was a super compressed rush of pulsating German seventies underground getting to jam with the Stones. Liam is at his rasping seer best here as he delivers his brother's lyrics on the litany of love. They still sounded genuinely dangerous on these kind of songs while creating a new type of mangled punk rock with a genuine emotional heart and soul.

Liam's 'I'm Outta Time' sees him entering a John Lennon world that had been sadly vacated since the late Beatle's senseless murder. It's the album's big ballad with a guitar solo that melts time like Pink Floyd's Dave Gilmour in his early seventies pomp. The piano-driven song described by Noel as 'deceptively brilliant' was possibly about the end of Liam's marriage or, as some observers ponder, the band's own fracturing. It steps up the sophistication in songwriting as he pulls out a plaintive and unusually pensive vocal on yet another slice of melancholic introspection. It also features a John Lennon sample taken from one of his last ever interviews where the former Beatle explains why he lived in New York: 'As Churchill said, it's every Englishman's inalienable right to live where the hell he likes. I said, "What, do you think it's gonna vanish? It's not going to be there when I get back?"'

The slow loping blues groove of '(Get Off Your) High Horse Lady' kicks out its jams along to a trip-hop shuffle with a bass-heavy twisted psychedelic groove. Halfway through Zak Starkey kicks in with a pounding take on the same groove, as Noel explains: 'The oldest song on the album, originally demoed for *Heathen*

Chemistry. It wouldn't have made the album, but the bass is so heavy, it forced its way on to the final cut.'

The third and last single to be pulled from the album is also the last single to be released by Oasis so far. 'Falling Down' is more brisk psychedelia with a nagging mystery, with the 'Tomorrow Never Knows' drum shuffle given a drum and bass shimmer plus a touch of Brian Jones' Mellotron adventures with the Stones. The track has the urgent rush of drum and bass and magnetic pull of the dancefloor in an example of the band's willingness to play around with their sound that is so often overlooked.

The sitar drone that oozes over the drum loops of Gem's 'To Be Where There's Life' is another slice of classic off-kilter acid rock. Liam's powerful cosmic vocals sit well in these psychedelic adventures. The song is a stripped-down stream of consciousness built around a great cyclical bass groove given lots of space to breathe with the guitars stripped away. To be truly psychedelic in 2009 you had to embrace the new tech and twist it into new shapes like Primal Scream had done on their 'hangover' records – the dark trilogy of albums after the glow of *Screamadelica*.

One of the three Liam tracks on the album, 'Ain't Got Nothin'' is a fight song that is full of the swirling limbs and chaos of a bar-room brawl with Zak Starkey bringing his Keith Moon educated drum violence to the proceedings and creating a volatile musical concoction. The song is old-school snarling Oasis – a big punk song as the protagonist demands the truth whatever it takes – the primal demand of all great rock 'n' roll.

Andy Bell's contribution, 'The Nature of Reality', is a blues riff cutting across the kind of huge drums that Hugh Padgham recorded for primetime mid-eighties XTC, giving the song a pounding percussive stomp that sounds like a template for the future Tame Impala in a very personal song, as Andy Bell explains:

'The riff on it is great, kind of "Helter Skelter" meets T. Rex. Lyric wise, I'm kind of defining my belief system at the time, which had been derailed slightly, in the process of me going through a divorce. It was a weird time for me but to their credit the band went with it, and I appreciated them including this on the album, mad lyrics and all.'

Driven by a strident bass line and a ghostly vocal, the hypnotic Liam song 'Soldier On' has a flavour of the very early solo John Lennon in its compelling groove. The minimalistic bass and acoustic song is driven with a vocal full of aching mystery with a haunting melodica threading its way through the song's trippy dub outro.

As ever there were songs from the demos that didn't make the cut creating 'what ifs' for fans, like '(I Wanna Live In a Dream In My) Record Machine' which was attempted, but they couldn't get it right and it was later recorded for Noel Gallagher's High Flying Birds. They also ran out of time to complete 'Come on Outside', while the Liam written 'Boy With the Blues' was another piano-driven slice of melancholia. The song had been mooted as a single as far back as 2006, maybe as part of an EP, but there was no agreement on how it would be released and it ended up on a TV soundtrack – one of the great lost tracks.

For what would end up being the last album for the band it's an intriguing sign-off. Not the exhausted last gasp of a burned-out group but one that was stretching out and changing its sound and looking to the future. The fact they delivered a strong album despite their own internal dialogue is quite something, but this time the cracks were not going to get papered over forever and the clock was running down on Oasis.

The album's striking Julian House artwork resulted from a brief from Noel for a 'psychedelic, apocalyptic design'. It sparked the designer's love of a very English surrealism with the collision of apocalyptic imagery and fairy tales and what he calls 'pre-pop art', with a punk psychedelic collage riddled with references to the album and Oasis themselves that spread out across the whole marketing campaign.

As ever with Oasis, the artwork references the band with witty visual puns like the half-eaten apple on the cover maybe as a nod to the Beatles' Apple label, while the 'Come In, Come Out!' headline on the bottom left of the sleeve references 'The Shock of the Lightning' chorus, with the album's music captured in its raucous melancholic artwork and the new hand-drawn fonts for the new trippy band logo.

The album title came from the legendary cartoonist and illustrator Ralph Steadman who was originally going to do the album artwork.[2] When he asked what the album title was they told him that there wasn't one yet. The band had gone through titles like 'Bag it Up', 'The Shock of the Lightning' and 'Standing on the Edge of the Noise'.

He was given the songs and lyrics and Noel asked him to come up with a title 'as long as you don't just call it Oasis'. Looking through the lyrics Ralph Steadman took the title from the lyrics of Gem Archer's song, 'To Be Where There's Life'.

Initially, the album campaign looked good, with high charts places and initial sales – 15 years in and Oasis were proving to be both an irritant rubbing up the right people while still retaining a huge core following.

Just in time for the almost annual Oasis Christmas release, the 1 December single, the piano-driven Liam lament 'I'm Outta Time', stalled at number 12 in the chart – the first Oasis single to miss the top 10 since 1994's 'Shakermaker', and ending the band's streak of 22 consecutive top 10s. Perhaps the track was a grower – decades later it's easily the most streamed track from the album. The B-sides included 'To Be Where There's Life'; an unexpectedly tasteful remix of 'I'm Outta Time' by Marilyn Manson's shock rocker band member, Twiggy Ramirez; and a faithful Jagz Kooner remix of 'The Shock of the Lightning', that tweaked the song into a new fusion of cutting-edge dance. The rock 'n' roll song's pulsating beat was one of the two remixes Jagz did for the band, as he remembers:

'Noel sent me "The Shock of the Lightning" and "The Turning". I was on a train with no headphones on but I could already hear that "The Shock of the Lightning" was like a kraut rock kind of tune while "The Turning" was like a DJ Shadow breakbeat-esque kind of thing. Noel had always been drawn to the sounds and the people I've been associated with like David Holmes and Andrew Weatherall and with the remix he wanted to make something more space rock than techno. It shows that Noel's always been quite experimental and happy to be taken out of his comfort zone.'

The video of the single was directed, again, by W.I.Z. Filmed in black and white, it centres on Liam on a surreal journey through the moonlit English landscape of Gloucestershire's quaint Bourton-on-the-Water that has the same flickering twilight neo-nightmare feel as the Rolling Stones' 1967 video for 'Dandelion'. It ends with Liam lying down in profile in a visual reference to John Lennon's *Imagine* album cover artwork.

Although it was not planned at the time, the 9 March 2009 release of 'Falling Down' was the last Oasis single, five months before the band finally imploded. Written by Noel Gallagher and sung by the guitarist, the song, with its moody dark psychedelia over a quicksilver drum pattern, was a great mix of dance and rock that builds to the epic chorus in a track that is a bridge to his post-Oasis solo work.

Like the end days of the Beatles, these bridging tracks between the band and the post-band solo careers are always fascinating as well as being a nod to where the mothership band could have gone next. For Noel Gallagher, this was one of his favourite Oasis tracks, perhaps because it combined his twin musical loves of the dance-floor and the guitar into a seamless whole. The extra tracks included a great remix of the track by the Prodigy, which is many fans' favourite version. The video is like a mini film and stars Natasha O'Keeffe from *Peaky Blinders* as a minor royal who gets snubbed by the band at a reception in a nod to their not too sympathetic view of the monarchy.

THE FINAL CURTAIN

With seven legs and 118 shows Oasis set out on what would be their final world tour before their reformation starting in Seattle on 28 August 2008. It was planned to end at the I-Days Festival in Milan a year later.

Despite the tour selling out there were frustrations, as Noel explains: 'There was a kind of undercurrent of, "Well, they should really call it a day", from the media etc. whereas now, of course, we're seen as up there with all the greats. Oasis back in 2009 were not lauded. I felt that people had stopped listening to the new records and were coming to see us trot out the hits. It's a position I never wanted the band to be in.'

Behind the scenes there was tension. It takes a special kind of resolve and discipline to get through a major tour and to put on a brave face, or at least put on a show and work around the personality crisis inherent in most intense creative combinations.

'We did the record and that was great,' says Noel. 'Then about three weeks before the tour started Liam didn't want to do it. We both knew he would do it but it just felt like the band was coming to its logical conclusion. Liam didn't seem happy. Andy and Gem, bless them, would never take sides and Chris Sharrock had just joined [on drums] and I was done with it.

'We were mixing the album in America, and I was bored of sitting around so me and Gem went to the Guitar Center, bought a 4-track and set it up in the corridor and I recorded demos for "The Death of You and Me", which is still one of my best ever fucking songs, "(Stranded On) The Wrong Beach" and "Soldier Boys and Jesus Freaks".[1]

'I listened to them and I thought I don't hear Liam singing any of these and the more I listened to "The Death of You and Me" the more I thought how are we gonna play that in a stadium? It's like a ragtime! And it started to dawn on me that I've got to move on and I don't think I can do the loud guitar thing anymore.'

In the Oasis camp the relationship between the brothers was deteriorating. As the tour progressed they started travelling to the gigs separately, which is understandable for anyone who has to spend 24 hours a day with their work mates in high-pressure situations. Weary older musicians often describe long-term careers as like a marriage without the sex before realising that most marriages are the same!

Pre-tour there was the normal handbags banter in the press interviews. In an interview with *Q* magazine, Noel had explained: 'I don't like Liam, he's rude, arrogant, intimidating and lazy. He's the angriest man you'll ever meet. He's like a man with a fork in a world of soup.' Liam had hit back in the *NME*. 'It takes more than blood to be my brother . . . he doesn't like me and I don't like him.'

Things were off to a bad start and were going to get worse in Camp Oasis. There had been disagreements over whether Liam's new clothing line Pretty Green could have an ad in the tour programme, which Noel had put a stop to. There was a weariness and a tension and maybe an underlying feeling that there was nowhere else left to go – maybe creatively everything had been done and all that was left was the greatest hits tours? The brothers' relationship had completely deteriorated, as Noel later explained to *Esquire* in 2015.

'The last six months were fucking awful, it was excruciating. Me and Liam had a massive fist-fight three weeks before the world tour started. Fights like that in the past would always be easy to rectify but for some reason I wasn't going to let it go this time. I was just like, "Fuck this shit". And there was an atmosphere all the way around the world. By that stage I was flying separately to the rest of the band, which I have to tell you was fucking great.'[2]

With this kind of vibe at the beginning of the tour it was remarkable that the brothers almost made it to the finishing line.

Highly respected in band circles, new drummer Chris Sharrock was taking the place of Zak Starkey who was away with the Who. The Merseyside-born drummer brought his explosive powerhouse style to the tour, adding his stick-twirling flamboyance. He had started playing in 1981 for the likes of the Icicle Works, the La's (where he had drummed on the classic 'There She Goes'), World Party, the Lightning Seeds and Robbie Williams's live band.

As the tour rolled on into 2009, they played the first of three concerts at Manchester's Heaton Park on 4 June. I remember the gloriously feral atmosphere and Jon McClure from Reverend and the Makers eulogising the band's genius down my ear all the way through the gig. It felt like the band were finding a way to exist into a career middle-age, but then the wheels started to wobble again as they suffered the ignominy of the power going off in the middle of the set due to a generator failure. The packed field of 80,000 fans in the biggest municipal park in Europe stood in awkward silence as the band left the stage twice before wandering back on, stating that it was now a free concert with ticket refunds. A few years later Liam was still rightfully not happy about the fuck-ups that were out of his hands.

'Some bits of the tour were good but some of the sound problems were getting beyond a joke,' the singer says, like at Heaton

Park. We wanted that to be our Spike Island, a proper legendary Manchester gig.'

The next month the band played three huge Wembley gigs with Reverend and the Makers as support. Jon Mclure remembers great shows but lots of tension:

'Things were obviously very tense between the brothers. They had separate dressing rooms and you were either Noel's mate or Liam's mate. There were not many people who sort of went between the camps. On the last night, they had this party in the England football team home dressing room and Liam burst in. We were all absolutely flying our tits off, and Liam is right in my face and he went, "I want to ask you what's your favourite type of pea?" I said: "I like garden peas actually with a bit of gravy and mint jelly . . ." and he looks me up and down, and says, "You don't like mushy peas?"

'I thought this is like a fucking trick so I said, "I just told you, I like fucking garden peas with gravy and mint . . ." He looked me up and down and he poked me in the chest and went, "You're alright you!" Apparently, he uses little devices like that to check whether people are alright and if you know your own mind, and if you do, then you're a geezer . . .'

After Wembley the band flew out to Japan and South Korea, before returning in late August to the UK to Bridlington Spa Pavilion, readying themselves for two big headline shows at the V Festival. The first one near Stafford on 20 August went OK but a couple of nights later in Chelmsford things started to fall apart when Liam pulled out claiming he had laryngitis and they were replaced as headliners by Snow Patrol.

An angry Noel later told the press that his brother was hungover and the tension cranked up.

There were just three big festivals to play: 28 August in Paris, 29 August in Konstanz and 30 August in Milan. Could they limp over the finishing line and then take a few years out and recover?

On 27 August they flew out to Paris . . .

The tension that had been building up in the camp was now ramped by the recent shenanigans at the V Festival.

Like all the great Manchester bands, Oasis had two strong characters at their heart and soul. Two different facets of the same diamond. Just like the Smiths with Morrissey and Marr, the Stone Roses with Squire and Brown, and New Order with Hooky and Barney – the crux and the core of the band was two powerfully complex competing visions – it was the strength of all these groups and ultimately their Achilles heel.

On 28 August, nearing the end of the world tour, Oasis rocked up to play the 80,000-capacity Rock en Seine festival. The band were headlining a heavyweight bill that included Madness, Yeah Yeah Yeahs, Keane, Vampire Weekend, Amy Macdonald, Faith No More, the Offspring, the Prodigy, Bloc Party and MGMT.

As the day built up to show time there was an awkward brooding atmosphere backstage. The final bust-up between the brothers took place in the small pre-gig communal area in front of the rest of the band. They had always worn their hearts on their sleeves and now the sleeves were rolled up.

A backstage witness said: 'Liam was goading Noel constantly and then the two just snapped.'

Noel explained what happened in a press conference speaking about his new project, Noel Gallagher's High Flying Birds: 'He [Liam] was quite violent. It was a bit like WWE wrestling and he thought he was Randy Savage. Liam does the "Fuck you and fuck you and fuck you" and he kind of storms out of the dressing room. On the way out he picked up a plum and he threw it across the dressing room and it smashed against the wall. For whatever reason he went to his own dressing room and he came back with a guitar and he started wielding it like an axe – he nearly took my face off with it. It ended up on the floor and I put it out of its misery. There were people who were in the band, not saying anything. People were looking the other way and it wasn't even a big dressing room.

We were all involved in it and nobody was saying anything. So I thought, "I'm fucking out of here."[3]

Another witness remembers: 'There were proper punches and Liam smashed up one of Noel's guitars. Liam was like a man possessed. He was swearing constantly and was really angry. Medical staff were called, along with security. Noel got out as quickly as he could. This was a truly vicious fight – quite horrible.'

The situation beyond repair, Noel Gallagher exited the building.

Oasis had been here before. At the brink. They had cancelled gigs and tours but this time, minutes before stage time, was different.

It was going to the wire as Noel sat outside in the car brooding for 10 minutes. Forty thousand people were waiting for the band to arrive on stage in five minutes' time.

Decisions. Decisions. Decisions.

The tour manager looked over . . . Noel had had enough and said, 'Fuck it, I can't do it anymore . . .'

He had decided to quit.

For the second time in a week Oasis had pulled out of a headline festival slot. Madness were installed as the headliners and the audience, waiting out front, had no idea what was happening until the news was broken to them by Kele Okereke from Bloc Party who were the band on just before Oasis. Relishing the situation, after an online fallout with Oasis a few years previously, he walked on stage with his tour manager and announced: 'Oasis have cancelled. So I'd like to take this moment to say, "That's a shame, isn't it guys?" So I guess by default, we are headlining. I'd like to dedicate this next song to anyone who really wanted to see those inbred twins.'[4]

Initially the audience thought he was joking until the screens at the side of the stage confirmed the story that Oasis's performance had been cancelled due to 'an altercation within the band'.

Outside the festival bubble the news was first leaked and broken worldwide by Scottish singer Amy Macdonald who tweeted: 'Oasis cancelled again with one minute to stage time!!! Liam smashed

Noel's guitar, huuuge fight!' Followed up with: 'I'm gutted :-(feel so bad for all their fans!'

And then: 'I have never heard such loud booing!! Was terrifying.'

And then as the news filtered backstage that this was more than a temporary fallout and a cancelled gig . . . 'Noel's quit'. 'Was told by promoter about guitar smashing incident. I wasn't there before you get carried away.'

Then Noel released a statement: 'It's with some sadness and great relief to tell you that I quit Oasis tonight. People will write and say what they like, but I simply could not go on working with Liam a day longer. Apologies to all the people who bought tickets to the shows in Paris, Konstanz and Milan.'

A couple of weeks later Noel released a full statement on his occasional tour blog, 'Tales From The Middle Of Nowhere'. He added: 'The details are not important and of too great a number to list. But I feel you have the right to know that the level of verbal and violent intimidation towards me, my family, friends and comrades has become intolerable. And the lack of support and understanding from my management and band mates has left me with no other option than to get me cape and seek pastures new.'

He went on to thank fans, after his decision to leave Oasis brought an 'amazing' 18 years to an end. He went on to say the rock group's success had been a 'dream come true', adding: 'I take with me glorious memories.'

He also apologised to fans in Paris who were disappointed when Oasis cancelled following the bust-up: 'Apologies are probably not enough, I know, but I'm afraid it's all I've got,' he wrote. He also said sorry to fans who'd hoped to see them at the V Festival in Essex the previous weekend. 'Again, I can only apologise – although I don't know why, it was nothing to do with me. I was match fit and ready to be brilliant. Alas, other people in the group weren't up to it,' he said. 'Now, if you'll excuse me I have a family and a football team to indulge.'

Of course, Oasis had to go out like this in a blaze of glory. The band was too raw, too visceral, too real to 'uncouple'. There was genuine passion and emotion that welled to the surface. Six years later, Noel added an interesting hindsight on the split:

'We had two gigs left and I reckon if I'd had got to the end of that tour and I had six months off I would have just forgotten about it. But the straw that broke the camel's back was the night in Paris and that was a fight . . . fight in Paris had not happened that night, we may well have just dissipated, and I would have done a solo record, but as it happened, fate decreed that it was going to end in a blaze of guitar swings. I'm glad it ended that way and I think if you asked anyone and they were being honest, they would say it ended at the right time. I don't think I could have gone on and written another Oasis record so it just felt like the end to me . . . If I'd thought there was anything left to achieve I wouldn't have left Oasis . . . You name it, we did it all.'[5]

Shellshocked, the rest of the band briefly pondered continuing and then quit. A few years later Liam also offered his own, calmer hindsight, explaining:

'Listen, we had an argument. We always have arguments. That's the way it was. I just think that it was not about an argument though, our kid just wanted out. He had done his time with the band and that's fair play but all he had to do was talk about it and leave. It was purely about him being a dick and me being a dick, so yeah, I was disappointed but you have to move on.'

Dave Sardy reflects: 'Truthfully, I'm more surprised that they stayed together as long as they did than I am that they broke up.'

Noel looks back in wisdom (not anger):

'Despite everything the gigs were great. They were massive shows. One of the last gigs we ever did was one of the best and was at the River Plate Stadium in Argentina, but it just felt like it was coming to its logical conclusion and it did and I was cool with it. I knew my songwriting was changing and it was getting less slinging on a Les Paul and turning up the amp, and at the same time the first two albums were still growing. No one had stopped listening to them and they were selling more records than ever and you're a slave to that in a way.

'In all this journey, I've always felt, and I know it's a hippie thing to say and I'm not a hippie in the slightest, but I've always felt kind of guided and that something will happen, and the band came to its logical conclusion at exactly the right time. Then I had two years off, and I started a family with Sara.'

For Liam, the writing had been on the wall, as he explained a few years later: 'I had kind of seen it coming. Our kid had distanced himself from us anyway. There's a lot of talk about me travelling separately with different dressing rooms but that was just lies. I was always a band player. . . Noel just wanted out. It was like putting down a pet when it's in agony. You got to do the right thing and let it go.'

For Liam, though, there could be no retirement from being an icon. Elvis will always be Elvis.

'Retire? What and just sit around? I don't think so. There's lots to do. I got music in me. It's coming from somewhere. I don't think they will let me retire till my time is up. I still have that passion and the drive to get behind the mic and give it some. It's all in there. It can't get sucked out of you, man. It's good to keep my feet on the ground, do a lot of walking, otherwise I would freak out. It's your own fault if you end up in a bubble. People say it's not work being in a band but it fucking is, but it's also the best fucking job in the world.'

And then it was all over . . .

There would be more than a decade of barbed comments flying back and forth in interviews or on Twitter in a rerun of the post-Beatles antagonism. There would be solo careers – Noel put together Noel Gallagher's High Flying Birds and his crafted songwriting flew high for four albums. Liam had quickly launched Beady Eye with the remaining members of Oasis and their debut was a great slice of ramalama glam punk and their second disappeared. Then the iconic frontman did what he does best by just being an iconic frontman – all Liam had to do was walk on stage and sing and the solo number one albums seemed effortless.

He was born to do it. He had no other choice. Like Elvis. Himselvis.

Noel and Liam.

Liam and Noel.

They never did get boring. There were post-Oasis solo careers, radio silence, rumours, barbed quips on Twitter and 16 years of not seeing each other after a lifetime living in each other's pockets.

The reformation rumours never did end. Every now and then there would be rumblings . . . Every year they would go from a whisper to a scream. And then silence.

Venues would be booked and unbooked. Fans hoped and despaired.

A generation wanted its soundtrack back and one last chance to revisit the band, and also their teenage selves, and reconnect with their past to make sense of their future. Oasis were embedded that deep into the heart of culture. They meant a lot. It was emotional. Very few bands ever mean that much.

Yet it looked like a never ever never.

Then in June 2024 I went to the legendary Sifters for an interview with Noel Gallagher about the 30th anniversary edition of *Definitely Maybe* to be used by Oasis to promote the album. He was as smart, funny, cool, hip and engaging as ever, but he was also very warm about Liam . . . 'If songs were drinks – mine's half a Guinness on a Tuesday. Liam's is ten shots of tequila on a fucking Friday night. He added a menace to these almost romantic tunes and that's what made it special,' he quipped with that glint in his eyes.

Weeks later, the interview went online on the Oasis YouTube channel. Three days after that, on 27 August, the band announced they had reformed and everything went crazy.

'The guns have fallen silent. The stars have aligned. The great wait is over. Come see. It will not be televised. Oasis today end years of feverish speculation with the confirmation of a long-awaited run of UK and Ireland shows forming the domestic leg of their OASIS LIVE '25 world tour.

'Oasis will hit Cardiff, Manchester, London, Edinburgh and Dublin in the summer of 2025. Their only shows in Europe next year, this will be one of the biggest live moments and hottest tickets of the decade.'

It added: 'The Oasis live experience is unlike anything else. The roar that greets them as they step on stage. A set full of wall-to-wall classics. The spine-tingling sensation of being in a crowd singing back every word. And especially the charisma, spark and intensity that only comes when Liam and Noel Gallagher are on stage together. The brothers have flourished with their own projects since the band split in 2009, with 10 UK #1 albums between them as well as countless festival headline sets and stadium and arena shows. But Oasis is something else. There has been no great revelatory moment that has ignited the reunion – just the gradual realisation that the time is right. Yet the timing must be a subconscious influence.'

A world tour was then announced where the band were playing bigger stadiums than they had ever played before. Somehow, by splitting up and reforming 15 years later they had become the biggest band in the world again.

Noel and Liam.

Liam and Noel.

Don't look back in anger . . .

Rust never sleeps . . .

Live Forever.

NOTES

Introduction

1. Noel Gallagher to Ann Scanlon in *Vox* magazine, 1995.

Chapter 1

1. Owen Morris, 'Classic Tracks: Oasis "Wonderwall"', *Sound on Sound*, November 2012.
2. Cable biography, https://www.bandplanet.co.uk/forgottenbandplanet/cable/cablebiography.htm
3. A. D. Amorosi, 'Oasis at War: Liam and Noel Gallagher's 10 Biggest Fights', *Variety*, 27 August 2024.

Chapter 2

1. 'Council Skies' was the last solo album and single Noel Gallagher released in 2023 before Oasis reformed. The video of the single features this author. The album was named after the book of illustrations of working-class life by the artist Pete McKee.

2. Jason Holmes, 'Paul "Bonehead" Arthurs Goes Back to His Roots After Oasis', Huffington Post, 30 January 2014.

3. Soon to be renamed the Carousel Club, the Astoria was at 210 Plymouth Grove in Ardwick. It later became the International 2 – one of the key venues in eighties Manchester where Noel and Liam both saw the famous 1988 Stone Roses gig. The owner was Gareth Evans (born Ian Bromley), who also managed the Stone Roses – who would rehearse there. It was demolished in the early 1990s.

4. Tim Jonze, 'Noel Gallagher: "I liked my mum until she gave birth to Liam"', *Guardian*, 5 August 2019.

5. Krissi Murison, 'Interview: Oasis star Liam Gallagher and his children talk exclusively about fatherhood and family life', *Sunday Times*, 16 June 2019.

6. Originally broadcast 9 October 2012 on RTÉ One. https://www.youtube.com/watch?v=MRD8m52CJuw

7. Liam Gallagher to Ann Scanlon, *Vox* magazine, 1995.

8. Craig McLean, 'Liam Gallagher: "My mam hit me round the back of the head with a brush for skipping school"', *Daily Telegraph*, 10 January 2018.

9. Craig McLean, 'Liam Gallagher: "My mam hit me round the back of the head with a brush for skipping school"', *Telegraph*, 10 January 2018, https://www.telegraph.co.uk/men/thinking-man/liam-gallagher-mam-hit-round-back-head-brush-skipping-school/

10. Originally broadcast 9 October 2012 on RTÉ One. https://www.youtube.com/watch?v=MRD8m52CJuw

11. Noel Gallagher to Ann Scanlon, *Vox* magazine, 1995.

12. The Howard Stern Show, 'How a Head Injury Led Liam Gallagher Into Music' (2017), https://youtu.be/TbSQmBZBYVk?feature=shared

13. The exotic punk kid that Noel had seen that late seventies afternoon was known as Dot Dash Derek because of the black exclamation mark dyed on to the back of his head.

14. The same auntie who got Morrissey's autograph for Noel.

Chapter 3

1. The gig in July 1986 to celebrate the tenth anniversary of punk in Manchester.

2. 'The Haçienda Must Be Built', from *Formulary for a New Urbanism* by Ivan Chtcheglov.

3. Graham Massey from 808 State used to be the postman who delivered Noel's dole cheques!

4. Right next to Hulme, further south of the city centre, is Moss Side, which was notorious at the time for gangsters and gun violence. The area has changed a lot since then.

5. From the Irish word *síbín* for home-made whiskey, it came to mean an illicit bar or club where drinks were sold without a licence. In late-eighties Manchester many shebeens I went to were in the cellars of Moss Side terraces with spliff and Red Stripe and attendant sound systems.

6. Suite 16 was the Rochdale studio formerly known as Cargo Studios, then owned by Peter Hook, that was one of the key locations for post-punk. Bands like Gang of Four, the Fall, Joy Division, Dead Or Alive, Section 25, the Membranes and many others recorded there. The Stone Roses' demo was recorded there in May 1988.

7. It was a benefit concert in protest at Clause 28, which was a law in the United Kingdom that prohibited local authorities from promoting homosexuality in any way.

8. Pete Garner was one of the coolest and nicest people on the whole scene. He left the band, allowing Mani to join.

9. A fixture on the local scene, the Waltones' crafted jangle indie saw them build up a good following and release three singles in 1987, and a debut album *Deepest* in 1989, before guitarist Mark Collins joined the Charlatans in 1991.

10. At the International 1, 3 June 1988, with Mirrors Over Kiev and Hollow Sunday.

11. Sunrise 'Back to the Future' rave at Longwick, Buckinghamshire.

12. Liam Gallagher in the first edition of *NME Gold*, 26 October 2017.

Chapter 4

1. The Stone Roses' drummer, Alan 'Reni' Wren.

2. Perhaps named after the Chameleons' song?

3. Not Your Usual Page, 'Bonehead Interview', 28 July 2020, https://nyupmu-sic.wordpress.com/2020/07/28/bonehead-interview/

NOTES

Chapter 5

1. Shotton and Jobling were known as 'the Bailey Brothers'; the phrase related to their never-made film *Mad Fuckers*.
2. I went to a few of these and the site of the ravers and the families in the street in the cold night air shouting to the prisoners in madcap conversations was perhaps as perfectly Madchester as you could get.
3. A pirate station based in Stockport that had DJs like Terry Christian, Jon Ronson, Craig Cash and Caroline Aherne.

Chapter 6

1. Noel Gallagher interview, *MOJO* magazine, edition 332, July 2021.
2. The Mill makes the room sound large but there was barely enough room to fit the band in. Next to the band room, the Inspirals' keyboard player Clint Boon had another small room with his recording equipment in for making the band's demos.
3. Mark Coyle worked as a sound technician for many bands throughout the 1980s including the Stone Roses and Happy Mondays. When Oasis started, he was brought in as a sound technician, a position he held until 1995. He also produced the majority of Oasis' debut album *Definitely Maybe*, which included the demo of 'Married With Children' recorded in the bedroom of his house.

Chapter 7

1. Vickie Scullard, 'The secret behind Oasis' sound – according to the man who put Liam behind the mic', *Manchester Evening News*, 3 August 2019.
2. Jonathan Heaf, 'Liam Gallagher: "My thing was the whole cliché: the sex, the drugs, the rock'n'roll"', *GQ*, 30 July 2017.
3. Born in 1947, Brendan Shine is an Irish singer, television presenter and accordion player from Athlone with 40 chart singles including five number ones in his home country.
4. Liam Dennehy to Kyle Dale.

Chapter 8

1. The title was misspelt as 'Reminice' on the handwritten track listing on the cassette case – the handwriting looks like Liam's and the demos are recorded over other bands' demos, like the Harrisons.
2. Michael Bonner, 'Introducing Oasis: The Deluxe Ultimate Music Guide', *Uncut*, 18 June 2019.
3. Jonathan Heaf, 'Liam Gallagher: "My thing was the whole cliché: the sex, the drugs, the rock'n'roll"', *GQ*, 30 July 2017.
4. Michael Bonner, 'Introducing Oasis: The Deluxe Ultimate Music Guide', *Uncut*, 18 June 2019.
5. BBC, 'Liam Gallagher – God or Goon?', 3 December 2002.
6. Vickie Scullard, 'The secret behind Oasis' sound – according to the man who put Liam behind the mic', *Manchester Evening News*, 3 August 2019.

Chapter 9

1. Born in 1960, Greg Wilson grew up in Merseyside and became a ground-breaking DJ in 1975. His broad tastes saw him play New York electro music at the Haçienda during his short but highly influential stint there in 1983.
2. Quality Manc rap crew whose Kermit managed to carve out his own career with Shaun Ryder in Black Grape.
3. Brian Cannon to Oi Polloi, 21 December 2018.

Chapter 10

1. The demo ends with the studio version of 'Take Me' from the recent Out of the Blue studio session.
2. Known to every band as 'Sue from the Boardwalk', Sue was a key figure in the band scene.
3. Nigel Lawson who ran the shop, dealing perfectly observed 'urban rambling' styles. Adidas Nizza: originally designed for the basketball court

in the 1980s, the Nizza range boasts a rubber toe bumper and breathable canvas.

4. Tony Ogden was the singer from a band called World of Twist.

Chapter 11

1. The Ya Yas may not have broken out but their 'See No Rain' remains a great lost slice of guitar garage.
2. Where the Wedding Present and the Chameleons come from.

Chapter 12

1. Simon Halliday is now head of the 4AD record label; this Grimmy is the brother of broadcaster Nick Grimshaw.
2. The news that Noel was no longer with the Inspiral Carpets was a shock to the local scene.
3. Often round the corner from the Boardwalk at the City Road Inn on Albion Street.

Chapter 13

1. Small would soon change their name to Smaller and Digsy would later be immortalised in the song 'Digsy's Dinner'.
2. The re-recorded version is the B-side to the August 1994 'Live Forever' single.
3. Former member of Bonzo Dog Doo-Dah Band whose 'I'm an Urban Spaceman' mixed music hall with hippie and surrealist humour in a big hit. He was also the instigator of the perfect Beatles pastiche the Rutles, whose takes on Beatles songs were so brilliant that many Beatles fans, including Noel, like them as much as the Fabs.
4. The venues still exists – now called the Academy 3 at the University of Manchester.

Chapter 14

1. I had been using it since 1987.
2. A basement bar near Tottenham Court Road tube station. From 1989 until Britpop a few years later, the promoters Andy Allen and Jared Pepall hosted the club frequented by Blur, Chapterhouse, Ride, Senseless Things, 5.30 etc.
3. Perhaps another Savage & Best innovation – the beat-up boozer was round the corner from their office and they took the bands down there for meetings, sprouting a new micro-scene.

Chapter 16

1. The The's fourth album, released on 25 January 1993, was the band's final album to feature Johnny Marr.
2. Duglas Stewart to Harry Mulligan for *Louder Than War*.

Chapter 18

1. The great lost Liverpool band whose tripped-out garage rock was a favourite with Noel Gallagher and many others.
2. Noel played Epiphones because of the Beatles and because they looked and sounded good.
3. Bass and vocals for the Real People.

Chapter 19

1. Dave Batchelor had been in Tear Gas, the band that became the Sensational Alex Harvey Band.
2. Stone Roses tour manager and key player in their crew.
3. Martin Kielty, 'Oasis' First Producer Recalls Abandoned Album Sessions, Ultimate Classic Rock, 17 September 2024 https://ultimateclassicrock.com/oasis-dave-batchelor-interview-2024/

NOTES

Chapter 20

1. Roger would also work very closely with the Libertines, making their *The Libertines – There Are No Innocent Bystanders* documentary.

Chapter 21

1. Anjali Dutt to Richard Bowes in *Some Might Say: The Story Of Oasis: The Official Book Of The Oasis Podcast*, Pen and Sword, 2025
2. John Harris, *Britpop! Cool Britannia and the Spectacular Demise of English Rock*, Da Capo, 2004.
3. Ibid.
4. Ibid.
5. Ibid.

Chapter 22

1. Not the version from Glasgow Cathouse as stated.

Chapter 24

1. Paul Slattery, 'A year on the road with Oasis', *Guardian*, 14 January 2009.

Chapter 27

1. Keith Cameron, '*Definitely Maybe* review, 9/10', *NME*, 27 August 1994.
2. Not only the guitar that features on the Smiths album *The Queen Is Dead* but that was also formerly owned by the Who's Pete Townshend – the guitar would get broken later in the year when an invader got on stage at the Oasis Newcastle gig.
3. The British/Australian photographer took many of the classic mid-sixties Beatles shots including the similar informal shot on the *Revolver* album and the notorious 'butcher cover'.

Chapter 28

1. Will Hodgkinson, 'Life with the Brian Jonestown Massacre: "Each day I go into battle"', *The Times*, 9 September 2024.
2. 'In Conversation: Anton Newcombe', *Clash*, 12 October 2018.
3. Aidin Vaziri, 'Oasis reunites after 15 years: Rediscover how a San Francisco woman saved the band', *San Francisco Chronicle*, 29 August 2024.
4. Noel Gallagher to *Beat Generator* magazine.
5. Ignition were, and remain, Oasis's management.

Chapter 29

1. 22 April 1995, where they debuted 'Don't Look Back in Anger'. According to Noel, the song was written in Paris and played live for the first time at the gig a few days later.
2. Noel Gallagher to the *NME*, 31 October / 7 November 1998.
3. Noel Gallagher on the *Stop the Clocks* DVD.

Chapter 31

1. Mike Leander was also the only person to score strings on a Beatles song apart from George Martin when he worked on 'She's Leaving Home'.
2. Musically, 'Wonderwall' sounds nothing like the George album, which was a collection of songs mainly played on Indian instruments with a trippy twist and is a great off-the-wall release.
3. From the *Evening Session* with Steve Lamacq on Radio 1, October 1997.
4. Dan Cairns, 'Noel Gallagher on how Oasis got their groove back', *Sunday Times*, 8 March 2009.
5. Celebrating the kind of music that people actually liked instead of the cool stuff they pretended to like.
6. The first show was with Noel, Xmas 1997.
7. New York Greenwich Village band led by John Sebastian whose mid-sixties folk act are best known for their biggest hits 'Summer in the City' and 'Daydream'.
8. Northern for 'around our way'.

Chapter 32

1. Roy Wilkinson writing for the *Quietus*.
2. At Balloch Country park on 3 and 4 August to 40,000 people each night.
3. Joy was planned to be the biggest acid house rave in the north. Held at Stand Lees farm near Rochdale on 5/6 August 1989 and organised by the Donnellys from Manchester clothing firm Gio Goi, court injunctions put a dampener on the event that expected 30,000 people and fewer made it.
4. 30,000 people went to this on 12 August 1989, the same night the Stone Roses played their classic gig at Blackpool Empress Ballroom.

Chapter 33

1. 'Strawberry Fields Forever' is not only Noel's favourite Beatles song but his pop song of all time for 'its experimentation, words and melody.'
2. Cool Britannia was a media buzzword for the mid-nineties UK boom that was initially a 1967 Bonzo Dog Doo-Dah Band song title. It was revived for the American *Newsweek* magazine 1996 cover, celebrating the then Britpop music and culture, and peaked with the 1997 *Vanity Fair* cover of Liam Gallagher and Patsy Kensit photographed on Union Jack pillows.
3. Nick Paton Walsh, 'Noel looks back in anger at drinks party with Blair', *Guardian*, 31 October 1999.
4. Ibid.
5. Perhaps the key book from the counterculture sixties, the title of the book *Be Here Now* comes from a statement made by Bhagavan Das during Ram Dass's journeys in India. It brought a spiritualism to the moment in its texts from the Harvard professor about yoga and eastern mysticism. It was also quoted by John Lennon in one of his final interviews, December 1980. 'Some people will do anything rather than be here now.'
6. Even when Oasis didn't make number one they still got a silver disc for 200,000 sales.
7. Rumoured to be an upgrade of older Oasis song, 'The Red, the White and the Blue' – but unlikely.

8. The wild man drummer who couldn't even drive took the hand brake off a Lincoln Continental and it bumped into a wall at a hotel in Flint, Michigan in 1967 on his 21st birthday party after a huge cake fight with support band Herman's Hermits.

9. The iconic red British phone box made an appearance on the *Be Here Now* live set because the set designers based their design on the unaltered original album cover.

10. The reg plate was changed from MDH119K to SYD724F to reference the police van on the cover of the Beatles' *Abbey Road* and was also a nice unintentional nod to Syd Barrett.

Chapter 34

1. Noel Gallagher to Keith Cameron for *Rolling Stone*, 15 October 2016, https://www.rollingstone.com/music/music-news/watch-noel-gallagher-talk-missed-opportunity-be-here-now-118783/

Chapter 35

1. Both their first two singles were produced by your author, who also initially recorded the band's debut album for them.

2. Tjinder Singh to Richard Bowes in *Some Might Say: The Story Of Oasis, The Official Book of the Oasis Podcast*, Pen and Sword, 2025.

3. Ibid.

Chapter 36

1. Robert Freeman was an English photographer and graphic designer best known for his work with the Beatles.

2. Nicknamed 'Wheeler End Gentleman's Club' by Noel.

3. Recording engineer and also guitarist in the Lemon Trees and Black Crowes, Paul Stacey would go on to play and engineer future Oasis albums.

4. Spike got his nickname from Wayne Hussey of the Mission because of his then spikey hair, when he was engineering that band's album for producer John Paul Jones in 1987.
5. A few drinks plus his dyslexia combining.
6. Chuck Klosterman, 'Noel Gallagher After Oasis', *Grantland*, 20 September 2011.
7. The first Liam-penned Oasis single, from *Heathen Chemistry*.
8. Noel Gallagher to *Uncut*, March 2000.
9. Andy Bell to Richard Bowes in *Some Might Say: The Story of Oasis, The Official Book of the Oasis Podcast*, Pen and Sword, 2025.

Chapter 37

1. The title of 'The Hindu Times' was also spotted on the front of another T-shirt.
2. Tom Goodwyn, 'Liam Gallagher: "I like John Lennon more than Paul McCartney"', *NME*, 19 September 2012
3. Sara MacDonald, to whom Noel was married from 2011 until 2023.
4. Charlie Burton, 'Meet the man behind the most iconic album covers of all time', *GQ*, 3 December 2020.

Chapter 38

1. Boomtown Rats genuinely had a great run of singles in the early punk era.
2. Co-written by the video director Andrew 'W.I.Z.' Whiston.
3. 'Turn Up the Sun', 'Mucky Fingers', 'A Bell Will Ring' and 'The Meaning of Soul' which were either reworked or re-recorded.
4. Dave Sardy to Joe Bosso, Music Radar website.
5. 'Oasis' Noel Gallagher: "My night with Marilyn Manson and Kenickie"', *NME*, 4 August 2009.
6. The title came from Noel's phrase about media collusion in the rush to war in Iraq in 2002.

7. Andy Bell to Richard Bowes in *Some Might Say: The Story Of Oasis, The Official Book of the Oasis Podcast*, Pen and Sword, 2025.

8. Lawrence Watson to the Pretty Green website.

9. One of the best and most creative video makers in the UK who also made eye-catching videos for Kylie Minogue, Primal Scream and Garbage.

10. One of the key Kings Road clothes shops in the swinging sixties.

11. Peter Blake to the *NME*.

12. Jenny Brewer, 'Simon Halfon unpacks the visual references in his album artwork for Oasis, The Who and George Michael', It's Nice That, 16 November 2020.

Chapter 39

1. Jeff Slate, 'Noel Gallagher and Dave Sardy on the Making of "Noel Gallagher's High Flying Birds"', Rock Cellar, 16 February 2015.

2. The artist had pop culture form having worked with Pink Floyd for *The Wall* and also Hunter S. Thompson.

The Final Curtain

1. All High Flying Birds songs.

2. Alex Bilmes, 'Noel Gallagher is *Esquire*'s December Cover Star', *Esquire*, 1 December 2015.

3. Noel Gallagher's High Flying Birds press conference, 6 July 2011. https://www.youtube.com/watch?v=p_OBngICXRo

4. Liam called Bloc Party 'a band off of *University Challenge*', while Noel dismissed them as 'indie shit'. Okereke replied, 'I think Oasis are the most overrated and pernicious band of all time.'

5. Alex Bilmes, 'Noel Gallagher is *Esquire*'s December Cover Star', *Esquire*, 1 December 2015.

FUJI
JP-IIx
60
Extra clear sound
MANNOW VALLEY
SONY
OASIS
FN
OASIS DEMOS
CDing-II
A:
OASIS . NEW
KING TUTS
TDK
BOARDWALK 1992
dBS+90
90